THE KEY TO HEALTH AND REJUVENATION

THE KEY TO HEALTH AND REJUVENATION

BREAKTHROUGH MEDICINE FOR THE 21ST CENTURY!

YOUR LIFE IS IN YOUR HANDS

Andreas Moritz

Copyright © 1998, 2000 by Andreas Moritz
All rights reserved.
No part of this book may be reproduced, stored in a retrieval system, or transmitted by any means, electronic, mechanical, photocopying, recording, or otherwise, without written permission from the author.

ISBN 1-58500-354-9

1stBooks-rev. 4/3/00

About the Book

The Key to Health and Rejuvenation puts the responsibility of health care back where it belongs - into the hands of every person. Treating the symptoms of an illness requires great effort on behalf of the body and has little or nothing to do with restoring health. Such an approach may at best keep the symptoms of disease at bay, which by itself can become a major risk for more serious complications to arise at a later stage. In contrast, healing occurs effortlessly and naturally once the conditions for the body to return to its most natural state - perfect balance and utmost efficiency - have been met and fulfilled. The author describes in detail what these conditions are and gives the methods how to achieve this state of balance regardless of age and previous health problems. Perfect health is a basic birthright that has been claimed by only few. *The Key to Health and Rejuvenation* opens the door for everyone to lead a stress-free life and enjoy continued youth and vitality, for the rest of one's life.

In this book, Andreas Moritz reveals the laws responsible for creating health, illness and aging and gives a complete account of the four most common causes of disease regardless of whether it is a simple infection, heart disease, cancer or AIDS. The basic theme running through the book is that it is difficult to treat disease but it is easy to create health, the latter being entirely the choice and responsibility of the individual. *The Key to Health* and *Rejuvenation* includes a complete self-help program, part of which is derived from the ancient medical system of Ayurveda. The presentation is packed with useful information on all major health issues and suggests effective methods of cleansing the blood, liver and gallbladder, intestines, kidneys, blood vessels, lymphatic system and cell tissues. The resulting renewal and rejuvenation of cells and tissues throughout the body opens us to a new sense of life that can be filled with harmony, peace and excitement.

For Reasons of Legality

The author of this book does not advocate the use of any particular form of health care but believes that the facts, figures, and knowledge presented herein should be available to every person concerned with improving his or her state of health. Although the author has attempted to give a profound understanding of the topics discussed and to ensure accuracy and completeness of any information that originates from any other source than his own, he and the publisher assume no responsibility for errors, inaccuracies, omissions, or any inconsistency herein. Any slights of people or organisations are unintentional. This book is not intended to replace the advice and treatment of a physician who specialises in the treatment of diseases. Any use of the information set forth herein is entirely at the reader's discretion. The author and publisher are not responsible for any adverse effects or consequences resulting from the use of any of the preparations or procedures described in this book. Readers should use their own judgement or consult a holistic medical expert or their personal physicians for specific applications to their individual problems.

Contents

Introduction	xi
Chapter 1: The Mind/Body Mystery	1
Chapter 2: The Laws of Illness and Health	13
Chapter 3: The Four Most Common Causes or Risk Factors of Disease	21
Chapter 4: Most Diseases Start in the Digestive System	35
Chapter 5: On the Road to Good Health	49
Chapter 6: A Life of Balance	71
Chapter 7: Useful Self-help Programmes	109
Chapter 8: Man's Foremost Killer Diseases	139
Chapter 9: Rethinking AIDS	171
Chapter 10: Global Misinformation	187
Chapter 11: What's Supposed to be Good for Us	213
Chapter 12: It may be Useful to Know…	243
Conclusion	265
Useful Addresses	267
Other Books and Products by the Author	269

Introduction

Good health is the most precious and important thing one could possibly have. This is true for a baby as it is for the elderly, a mother, a doctor, the common man on the street, or the president of a country. Whenever our body becomes sick or does not perform up to what we consider normal, we may enter a state of discomfort, fear, or depression, which can only be released by restoring the body's former health and vitality. To truly feel comfortable within our surroundings and within us the body must relinquish *all* forms of "dis-ease." "The Key to Health and Rejuvenation" can help unleash the tremendous power of healing that is present within you and restore balance on all levels of body, mind, and spirit. This establishes a permanent comfort zone or continuous sense of satisfaction and provides the basis for a creative, successful, and rewarding life.

When ill health arises or when our body starts to age suddenly we tend to look for a solution that promises a quick relief. Today, there is a drug or treatment for almost every ill. It seems to be engraved in our belief system that by suppressing or eliminating the symptoms of a disease we automatically eradicate the disease. Yet nothing could be further from the truth. Each time we remove a symptom without attending its cause we further distance ourselves from regaining the balance required for continuous health and vitality. Then good health remains but a dream for us and we may resign to sayings such as "Well, that's part of life."

Regaining one's health is not about having a quick fix, it is rather a restructuring process that affects every part of one's life, i.e., job, relationships, emotions, etc. It would be too simplistic to assume that a few vitamin pills, a new wonder drug, an operation, or even natural therapy could, in the spur of a moment, undo the effects of many years of neglect, which the body had to endure because we didn't have the time or opportunity to nourish it properly or let it sleep, exercise or be relaxed enough. "The Key to Health and Rejuvenation" is about setting the preconditions for the body to do best what it knows best -- creating and maintaining balance -- regardless of age and previous health problems. The key to creating balance in every aspect of your life can be found when you start taking responsibility for your own health.

This book deals with the practical issues of health, such as lifestyle, diet, nutrition, exercise, daily routine, etc., many of which I have derived from Ayurvedic Medicine -- the most ancient and complete system of natural health care. You will learn to apply a number of highly effective and profound cleansing procedures that can have no less than miraculous effects on your physical and emotional well being. The angle of simplified scientific knowledge and understanding used in this book provides the reasoning and generates the motivation for "turning" the key to health and rejuvenation. This element also sheds light on the most common diseases and medical practices that everyone ought to be aware of today.

Concerning the improvement of personal health and well being we require a major shift in both individual and collective consciousness, away from the programmed expectations of illness and ageing towards the anticipation of continual youthfulness and vitality. The old saying that everyone has to age and die seems to be a repeatedly verified belief doctrine that most people in the world "follow" without even questioning its validity. Could it be possible, instead, that illness and old age occur *because* we believe they are inevitable and subsequently and without our conscious awareness reinforce such beliefs by adopting a harmful lifestyle, diet, etc.? Right from childhood our parents, teachers, and society have "sentenced" us to the "fact" that the body has no choice but to deteriorate and eventually die from old age or an illness. This generally accepted belief generates a distinct feeling of being out of control, of being dragged down the dark corridor of time by a mysterious power called the ageing process.

The feeling of not being in charge or control is one of the most common causes of physical and mental ill health; it is generally referred to as "stress." The recognition of being vulnerable generates fear that in turn triggers profound biochemical changes in the body. These changes become the physical "reality" of ill health and ageing. Through the intimate psycho-physiological (mind/body) connection every thought and feeling alters our experience of health and well being. A bout of depression can paralyse our immune system and falling in love can boost it.

If you are convinced that ageing is natural and cannot be avoided then this will be the reality you create for yourself. Likewise, you can also draw on a greater force than the one you have used until now and prove to yourself that growing old and being affected by disease are merely the manifested projections of ignorance about the real nature of life. Disease and ageing are *not* part of our body's genetic design. Even the so-called "death-gene," which is in charge of terminating the lives of cells in our body according to their various predetermined life spans, is the one that keeps us alive. Without this gene we would all die from cancer within weeks. In this sense, controlled destruction is the giver of life and life that has gone out of control can be the harbinger of death. There is nothing in the normal original set-up of our body that could indicate it is causing its own ageing or diseases. But there is enough evidence to show that ageing and illness originate in the combined effects of fearful, negative mental attitudes and emotions and excessive accumulation of toxins in the body.

As a human race, we are about to recognise the vanity of participating in the *hypnosis of social conditioning* that keeps our mind veiled in the cast shadows of illusion. Many of us have already let go of the fears and doubts that keep us from realising our tremendous inner powers. But to make a real difference in life we will need to employ our vast potential of energy, creativity, and intelligence for the more important issues in life and for generating waves of continual happiness. One of the keys to unleash this potential is the body itself.

The body is constantly engaged in replacing its cells, which in itself is a miraculous and extremely complex process, unmatched by anything man has ever created (*please note: whenever I use the terms 'man' or 'mankind', I am referring to both genders*). The numerous types of proteins that make our genes and constitute the cells in our body are turned over within 2-10 days. Radioisotope studies show that 98 percent of the atoms that compose your body today won't be there in a year's time. The renewal process affects all parts of the body, includes our blood, muscles, organs, fat, bones and nerves. With the continual replacement of your cells you should be able to have a new body and consequently a new lease of life, at least every new year. In this book you will learn about the body's built-in mechanisms that can stop the clock of ageing and make you younger and healthier the older you grow.

We are right in the middle of a tremendous global transformation that has already greatly influenced if not shaken up the very foundation of conventional medicine. The old division of body and mind into completely separate and independent entities is crumbling fast with the knowledge supplied by the more progressive wings of medical science such as *Psycho-Neuro-Immunology* or *Mind/Body Medicine*. Even though the artificial division of body and mind, which is based on the old and outdated paradigms of understanding human nature, has never really existed, it was nevertheless powerful enough, and still is to a certain extent, to make man believe he is essentially a physical being. Since the importance of the mind in the field of health was greatly ignored, this division had also far removed any possibility for achieving a near-perfect state of health. As it is will become apparent in this book, instead of eradicating disease from the surface of the earth, the purely symptom-oriented approach to health care has immensely limited the success of medicine in treating disease and to some extent even contributed to the occurrence of chronic diseases world-wide.

Only now are we beginning to recognise the inseparability of these two opposites (body and mind) in life. The breakthrough discoveries in the field of *Mind/Body Medicine* have already helped thousands of people regain their health. They show that mind and body never exist as separate or independent entities. A hand never writes a letter without the mind ordering it to do so. You cannot even move your eyes to read these words unless your mind has given you the definite instruction to follow their sequence. Our life is controlled by what could aptly be called "super intelligent bodymind." Without its supervising presence, the body's 60-100 trillion cells with their over one trillion biochemical reactions per second each would proportionally generate more chaos and confusion than could be created in the case of the dissolution of the universe.

You can experience this perfect relationship of mind and body when you get a stomach-ache from feeling upset, or when you faint from receiving sudden bad news. Some people have literally turned grey overnight due to a traumatic event and others blush when they feel embarrassed. Heart attacks can be triggered by a single bout of anger or intense anxiety, regardless whether the arteries congested or clear. All thoughts and feelings are readily translated into chemical compounds within the brain and within every other part of the body, thereby altering physical appearance and performance. In fact, every bit of mental activity leaves us with a specific physical sensation, known as emotion. Emotions are composites of both mental impulses and physical effects and they equate to the total of your health as a human being.

Your endocrine system, which produces hormones in response to your mental experiences, is indeed your personal drug store or inner pharmacy. It can make any drug you need and you are the pharmacist who writes the appropriate prescriptions. Depending on your emotional response or reaction to a particular event or problem, the drugs and their dose vary accordingly. They may be the stress hormones *adrenaline, cortisol* or *cholesterol*. When released into your blood stream in response to anger, fear, or rejection, the hormone secretion can save your life but in the long term it may damage the blood vessels and impair the immune system. Your happy emotions, on the other hand, manifest as *endorphins, serotonin, interleukins,* or other drugs that are related to the experience of pleasure and joy. If you produce enough of them you may even be able to arrest the ageing process. Carefully controlled studies have shown that you can reduce your biological age by 10-15 years within ten days, provided your interpretation of life goes through sudden, positive changes, but you also can put on 20 years within a single day if you enter a state of hopelessness and depression. Hormones can have extremely powerful effects, both in a positive and negative sense. Yet more powerful than hormones are the thoughts that trigger them.

Today there are numerous recorded cases of what are called "spontaneous remissions." A remission of cancer or other serious illness may occur when a person has experienced a state of sudden and unprecedented happiness. Others "fall" into the spontaneous emotion of laughter, which consequently may stop a terminal illness. Our physical set-up is capable of providing hitherto unknown and extremely powerful chemicals in response to a new perception of reality. This intrinsic ability of the human mind/body system will evolve our endocrine system to a much higher level of efficiency and bestow abilities to our body beyond our current understanding or imagination. The mind/body connection will be discussed in greater detail in the book since it is an essential tool to improve our physical and mental health.

The journey of developing a permanent state of health and vitality is not so much about treating disease, which is the main concern of conventional medicine. True healing is more about re-establishing the flawless connection that exists between body and mind. The darkness in a room disappears when we switch on the light and so does disease by improving health. Good health remains an unrealistic dream when the focus is on disease.

A basic natural law states that *energy follows thought*. If disease is your point of focus, you are going to be stuck with it because disease thrives on negative energy. Over 90% of all diseases in our Western civilisation are chronic by nature; for these there are no successful treatments available. The inadequacy of our medical system in successfully dealing with chronic disease is rooted in our collective conviction that we need to get rid of the symptoms of disease. If we focused instead on setting the preconditions that are responsible for creating and maintaining health, it would naturally return on its own. It is not disease that needs attention, it is the patient who requires love, care, nourishment, and the feeling of being complete again. The single most important experience that the unbalanced bodymind needs to heal is the experience of happiness, which results when an existing congestion in the body is removed.

A fascinating study showed that happy people are unlikely to catch colds, regardless how often you expose them to a cold virus. Also people who are in love show a higher resistance to disease. To create a positive state of health in itself can be a happiness-generating event. Happiness returns spontaneously in a person who, suffering from a cold or a disease, starts to feel better again. Only happiness is attractive for life, whereas disease is not. Unhappy people can never be truly healthy, just as unhealthy people can never be truly happy. A person, who suffers from cancer and learns to apply the methods of regaining his happiness described in this book, can be cured but if he continues hating his mother or father then even the best of therapies will fail. By focusing on disease or negativity in life one remains stuck in one's unresolved anger or conflicts. This in turn will have a powerful immune-suppressive effect and prevent healing from taking place. Focusing on the destructive characteristics of a disease can therefore not serve as an inspiration for healing and complete recovery. There is in fact nothing to be gained from the fascination with disease but everything to be gained from the fascination with health.

The human body has no built-in programme for sickness, but it has many programmes to maintain a state of perfect equilibrium or balance. It is the nature of the human being to be perfectly healthy but it is up to us to set the preconditions for these programmes to work. Healing is absent when happiness is absent. Bereaved persons whose sense of joy has virtually become non-existent demonstrate this clearly. Widows rank among the highest in the risk groups for cancer. Sadness, due to loss of a beloved, blocks a person's immune response to fight cancer cells even though his or her T-cell count may be normal. The latest studies on heart disease show that lack of happiness and job satisfaction are heading the list of risk factors for heart attacks, far more endangering to our health than animal fats, alcohol, or cigarettes.

The main purpose of life is to increase happiness. Any action that does not support this most basic principle of life is destined to fail or create problems. This is true for the field of health as it is for every other area in life. Most of the advice given in this book has an uplifting or a clarifying effect, thus providing a solid foundation for creating and maintaining good health. The *liver cleanse* described in chapter six, which can remove hundreds of gallstones from the liver and gallbladder within a few hours, can by itself trigger waves of utter wellness and eliminate deep rooted anger and frustration. The clearing of severely blocked ducts and channels of circulation in the body can have truly blissful effects and change one's priorities in life. With the continued improvement of your health you may find yourself entering a state of completeness where the pieces of the puzzle of life will be placed in their proper places.

As you read about the various ways of improving your physical health, try to remember that it is tightly linked to your mental and emotional well being. Should you suffer a particular disease like cancer, heart disease, or AIDS, apart from dealing with the physical aspect of the imbalance you will also need to attend its mental counterpart. Disease is not something that you "catch," instead it is something you create by repeatedly making the same mistakes that prevent your body and mind from regaining their natural state of balance or health.

We do not have to have permission from anyone to improve our health because this is our natural birthright. The advice given in this book is not meant for curing diseases because it is not disease that needs curing, it is the patient who needs to become whole, happy and vital again. You can never really cure a disease because disease only occurs when health is no longer being generated. But once you have allowed balance to return to your body and mind, disease will disappear by itself just as the darkness of the night disappears with the light of the day.

Most of the data and research that is mentioned in this book is based on "reliable" sources such as published papers and scientific journals. But although I have cited scientific research studies throughout the book to clarify and illuminate basic insights, it is my opinion that research in itself cannot serve as a reliable source of truth and reality. The reason for this assumption is the fact that there can never be any kind of research that will remain unaltered by the changing factors of time and space, the unaccountable subjectivity of the researchers and the researched, and the intended purpose of the research.

It is my opinion that scientific research should not be used to formulate a particular truth in life since it is very easy to use it as a means of manipulating opinions and beliefs. I suggest that you take any statement or argument you are not sure about into your heart and ask your body how it feels (there is a *body-testing* procedure in chapter one). You will receive a definite answer from your body, which will signal either weakness or strength, or any other form of discomfort or comfort; depending on the input. This book is about enhancing your intuitive and cognitive abilities rather than presenting mere book knowledge to satisfy intellectual needs. "The Key to Health and Rejuvenation" is not a foreign element we need to introduce from outside. *You* are that key and this book is there to help you use it for your own benefit as well as that of mankind.

CHAPTER 1

The Mind/Body Mystery

Mind over Matter

The united force of our body, mind and spirit continually searches for nourishment, strength, and happiness. To fulfil the purpose of this force, the body uses food, water and air to renew and sustain itself, the mind chooses a task that keeps it creative and active and the spirit seeks to give love and share happiness in order to continue growing and expanding in life. A delicious meal prepared by a loving mother can serve all three aspects alike. Enjoying one's food can be a spiritual experience as it can be a physical and a mental one. Being totally "present" while eating triggers both pleasure hormones and a sense of union between the person who eats, what he eats and the process of eating. A beautiful piece of music soothes not only the spirit but also relaxes the mind and the body.

Everything that we experience, physically or mentally, has a bearing on our entire being. Each one of our thoughts, feelings, and emotions causes profound and dramatic changes in our body, mind, and spirit. Think of the consoling and loving words of a friend when you felt low in yourself. Did you feel encouraged and uplifted afterwards? Your body, first bent over, tired, and tight, suddenly began to elongate and feel relaxed and energised. The depressed look on your face turned into a grateful smile and you said: "Thank you, I am feeling much better now." Or remember an instance in your life when you anticipated bad news of some kind. The fear you experienced may have had a paralysing effect on you. But one piece of positive information given to you just seconds later might have restored or even increased your physical strength and self-confidence. The sudden good news elevated your feelings and brought a smile to your face. A split second was enough to trigger a profound internal transformation that changed everything from within you. For a moment you have experienced a state of utmost health.

The gently spoken words and the loving care by your friend triggered profound biochemical responses in your body, which were powerful enough to alter your posture, relax your physical expression, and improve your mood. Research informs us that all our thoughts, feelings, emotions, desires, intentions, beliefs, or understanding are instantly translated into *neuropeptides* or *neurotransmitters* in the brain which in turn serve as chemical messengers of information.

Scientists have already located over a hundred different *neuropeptides* and many more are believed to exist. A nerve cell or neurone produces and uses these peptides to transmit information to another neurone. This form of transmission or "firing" occurs simultaneously in millions of neurones. Immediately after the transmission ends, the peptides are neutralised by enzymes, erasing all physical evidence of that thought or feeling. Yet we have stored the information in our memory bank. If need be, we are able to retrieve or remember it.

This simple example shows that our brain can not be the ultimate authority of our body. How do the millions of neurones know which type of neurotransmitter they need to make for each specific thought? What causes their simultaneous "firing" throughout the brain? In the more recent years scientists have discovered that these chemical messengers are not only made by brain cells but also by all the other cells in the body. This raises the question whether we think only with our brain cells or also with other cells in the body. There is indeed enough scientific evidence now to show that skin cells, liver cells, heart cells, immune cells, etc., all have the same remarkable ability to think, emote, and make decisions as brain cells.

The cells of our body are equipped with receptor sites for these peptides, which explains why every cell knows what every other cell does or think. There cannot be any secrets between cells. Every impulse somewhere is an impulse everywhere. By utilising these chemical pathways, the body can translate a strong emotion of fear into chemicals that order your adrenal glands to trigger the secretion of the stress hormone *adrenaline*. Once it is released into your blood stream in sufficient amounts, your heart will begin to pound and the blood vessels leading in your muscles will dilate. This pre-programmed defence strategy of the body makes it possible for you to run away from a perilous situation or to avoid being run over by a car. However, this effect, known as the fight or flight response, constricts other important blood vessels in the body such as the major arteries in the internal organs and also elevates the blood pressure.

If this stress response occurs on a regular basis it can cause considerable damage to the whole body. While the adrenal glands secrete *adrenaline* each cell of the body also produces this stress hormone. After the initial burst of energy and physical strength, the cells suddenly turn "jittery" and your body starts shaking. You may feel as if you have lost all your energy in the process. Without your conscious control you have actually practised "mind over matter."

Testing Your Mind/Body Response.

At this point I would like to suggest that you apply a simple muscle test derived from the healing method of *Behavioural Kinesiology*. This test will demonstrate to you that at each moment your mind exerts total control over your body. I will refer to this test throughout the book whenever it may be indicated to find out whether a particular food, medicine, beauty product, situation, environment, or even a particular desire is conducive to your health or not.

Everyone practises "mind over body" at all times. However, most of us do it unconsciously. The main purpose of this test is to bring this intimate relationship of mind and body to the surface of your awareness and truly experience it in a very concrete and conscious way. Whenever you apply the muscle test, you will instantaneously reawaken the wisdom of your body and strengthen your natural instincts and intuition.

To conduct the test, find yourself a partner. Follow these simple steps for muscle testing:

1. Both of you need to stand. Your <u>left</u> arm should hang down relaxed by your side, while your <u>right</u> arm is extended in a horizontal position, with your elbow stretched. [If you are left-handed, use your left arm for testing.]

2. Next, ask your partner to stand in front of you. Look at a neutral place, such as a door or a wall, and try not to think of anything or anyone. Ask your partner to place his/her <u>right</u> hand on your left shoulder to keep your body posture in a stable position, and his/her <u>left</u> hand on top of your right arm, just over your wrist.

3. Now, ask your partner to press down on your arm, while you try to resist the pressure. Ask your partner to press down on your arm quickly and firmly, but not in a jerky manner, and not longer than about three seconds. The idea is to maintain the pressure only as long as it takes him/her to notice your arm s strength of resistance. Pressing longer will make the muscle weak, and produce a faulty test result.

4. Your arm muscle should be testing strong in this neutral state. [Please note that a particularly negative thought, physical illness, or being under the influence of shock, alcohol, or drugs may substantially influence the outcome of this muscle test.]

5. Next, keep your right arm outstretched, while you try to think of a situation, person, past experience, etc., that would make you feel angry, nervous, or uncomfortable in any way, and at the same time repeat Step 3. You will notice you will not be able to resist the pressure applied to your arm, and your arm muscle will immediately give in , and become weak. Then try to think of someone you love or care about and ask your partner to test your arm muscle once more. Your muscle will be strong again.

You may repeat Step 5 of the test while listening to hard rock music, watching a violent movie, or looking at fluorescent light. To test whether a particular shampoo, toothpaste, medical drug, or food item is good for you, place any of these items into one of your hands while you ask your partner to test the muscle of your other arm. Note: If you are left-handed, it is better to test your left arm and place the tested item in your right hand.

You may need to experiment with this technique on each other for a little while before it becomes second nature to you. It is necessary to have an open and innocent mind when you conduct the test. Don't try to influence or manipulate the outcome in one way or the other, as this may lead to false results. Remember that every thought influences the body in a specific way. Ask any questions you may have that can be answered with a "yes" or with a "no." This may concern important decisions you need to make, journeys to take, or foods to eat, etc., (to test food items, it may be enough to just look at or think of the food while applying the test).

The body's own biofeedback system always works – it never lies. The muscles will respond to a particular stimulation either with weakness or with strength, so long as the test is conducted properly. Should a so-called "healthy food" contain anything that your body cannot process or digest properly, it will immediately know about it and send your body cells the appropriate messages. A fearful thought, disruptive noise from the street, or the picture on the television news of a killed person is transmitted to your body cells, too. Your body's response is completely accurate and reflects the exact quality of the information passed on to you.

The cells in your body can detect the frequencies of incoming substances and check whether they are useful or harmful for you. A glass of coke gives off different frequencies than an apple. Because the phosphoric acid, artificial flavours, large quantities of sugar, and other chemicals contained in coke are highly destructive for biological life forms, the cells will consider them to be poisonous and go into a stress response. Their energy production, measured by the amount of ATP molecules, begins to drop abruptly, which means that the tissues in the body are increasingly cut off from the routes of energy supply and hence become weak. In practical terms this means that all the organs, glands, blood vessels, nerves, and muscles are compelled to subsist on minimal energy, which jeopardises the normal functioning of the body. Note: you can obtain more detailed information on the procedure from any book on "Kinesiology."

Stress – and a Shrinking Thymus

The thymus gland, which regulates activation of *T-cells* (white blood or immune cells), is the first organ that is affected by stress. *T-cells* help the body to identify and fight cancer cells and other invading agents. The weakening influence on the thymus gland caused by such factors as negative news, dehydration or consumption of nutritionally poor and processed foods or drinks, reduces *T-cell* activation through thymus hormones and leaves the body without sufficient defence against the spreading of cancer cells and other causes of disease.

The thymus gland shrinks when it is exposed to stress. It is known that after a serious injury, surgery, or sudden illness, millions of white blood cells are destroyed and the thymus gland shrinks to half of its size. It may become very stressful for your thymus gland when you look at a photo of Adolf Hitler, a child abuser, or a wanted terrorist. The next time you look through a magazine, get a friend to test your muscle while you look at the different pictures. You will find that some of them make your muscles strong whereas other pictures make them weak. Our thymus gland has to bear with massive amounts of negative influences, considering the almost daily exposure to radio, television, newspapers, junk foods, chemicals in foods and drinks, indoor and outdoor pollution, and people with negative attitudes, etc. Even advertisements that show people smoking cigarettes or drinking alcoholic drinks have a weakening effect on your thymus.

Most people are not aware how much of their life energy is drained by exposing themselves to stressful situations, unhealthy environments like smoke filled rooms, or energy depleting influences such as driving at night or eating while tired. Only when there is no energy left to function normally, does a person become nervous or begin to panic. The most common expression you can hear in such a case is "I feel so stressed." Stress is nothing but an experience of constant exhaustion of the thymus gland caused by negative or weakening influences in life. Stress ceases to affect us when we stop exposing ourselves to such influences and remove the harm that has been caused by them in the past. You can positively strengthen and recharge your thymus and entire body through uplifting and encouraging activities, eating nutritious foods, and spending more time in nature than indoors or in front of the television. In either case you are practising "mind over matter."

Placebo -- A True Healer

The placebo effect works in a similar way. Placebo is a Latin word and translates as "I shall please." If something pleases me, it triggers the release of pleasure hormones in my body that can lead to a strong healing response. In the medical field, the placebo effect is a phenomenon described in the context of research as an indicator for testing the efficacy of drugs or therapies. There are three possible explanations why healing can take place (please note that shutting down or suppressing a symptom of disease has nothing to do with curing it).

1. A particular treatment has a curative value itself.
2. The healing power of nature is at work. This includes particularly the immune system's natural response to stop and eliminate the causes of illness. While applying to the majority of all medical cases, this "secret ally" of all doctors is hardly ever introduced to a patient. It rarely is the human organism itself that receives the praise for the extraordinary abilities it displays when dealing with infections and physical damage. The body's own remarkable healing ability is behind every success in the healing profession. In many instances healing may occur even despite the side effects that may arise from the use of medical drugs or procedures. If the body's healing response is absent, no medical technology or expertise will have any value.
3. The placebo effect triggers the healing response.

Orthodox medicine originally defined the placebo as an inert substance that for psychological reasons is administered to satisfy or please a patient. However, this definition is no longer considered quite accurate or sufficient. The placebo can also emanate from substances that are *not* inert as much as it can be triggered by procedures that do *not* include medication. The placebo effect implies that the belief in a drug, which may be nothing but a sugar pill or a snake oil, or the trust in a treatment or even the doctor, has the power to stop pain and even cure a disease. A research study is not considered valid or scientific unless it includes a placebo that is applied to a control group.

When the success rate of the drug or treatment is higher than the success rate of the placebo, then the drug has passed the test for effectiveness. The placebo has even been used to study coronary bypass techniques and cancer radiation treatments. In the case of bypass studies, the surgeon opens the chest of the heart patients in the placebo group and immediately stitches it back together again, *without* performing a by-pass operation. After surgery, all the patients are informed that the operation was a success. Some of the placebo group patients confirm that they have relief of chest pain. A number of the heart patients who received the actual by-pass surgery also report relief of pain. If their number of "success" is higher than that of the placebo group, then by-pass operation is considered to be an effective method to relieve chest pain.

An early carefully controlled study with patients suffering from Angina pectoris showed that 5 out of 8 patients who had genuine surgery and 5 out of 9 patients who only received a sham operation felt much better afterwards. Two of the patients with sham operations even experienced a remarkable increase in physical stamina and endurance. A group of sceptics repeated the same experiment with another group of 18 patients. Neither the patients nor the examining cardiologist knew who actually received the surgery. The results were that 10 out 13 patients with surgery and 5 out of 5 patients with the sham operation had improved significantly. This experiment demonstrated that the placebo together with the body's healing system might be in actual fact be the real power behind successful surgery. Surgery, which like every other treatment can work as a placebo for the patient, seems to have no significant advantage over the placebo. It would, however, be very unwise to have a sham operation and continue with a detrimental lifestyle. The survival rate with a sham operation is not more than two years, and with a normal operation not much longer than that either, unless of course the patient makes major changes in his diet, lifestyle, etc.

When the Placebo becomes a Medicine

The mechanics of placebo healing is centred in the belief of the patient that the drug, the operation, or the therapy is going to relieve the pain or cure the disease. Such trust or sure feeling of recovery is all that the patient has at his disposal to initiate a healing response. Through the previously described powerful mind/body connection, he may release natural *opioids* (morphinelike painkillers) from areas of the brain that are activated by certain procedures and thought processes. The corresponding *neurotransmitters* for pain relief are known as *endorphins*. *Endorphins* are about forty thousand times more powerful than the strongest heroin. A patient who suffers from cancer may produce extra amounts of *Interleukin II* or *Interferon* to destroy malignant tumour cells. Being a product of the DNA, the body can make these drugs in every cell and eradicate cancer in a moment (spontaneous remission), provided the patient knows how to trigger their release. To buy these drugs on the pharmaceutical market can cost you up to $40.000 per course of treatment. The "success" rate with these drugs is less than 15 percent and their side effects are so severe that they can destroy the immune system and sow the seeds for future diseases (see section on "Cancer -- who makes it" in Chapter 8).

Your body is capable of manufacturing every drug that could possibly be produced by the pharmaceutical industry. Synthetically derived drugs can only "work" because the cells of our body have receptors for some of the chemicals contained in them. This also means that the body is capable of making these chemicals, too, yet much more eloquently with a much higher precision, proper dosage and perfect timing. The body's own drugs cost us nothing and they have no harmful side effects. Pharmaceutical drugs on the other hand are often very expensive and much less specific and accurate. It is estimated that 35-45% of all prescriptions have no specific effect on the disease for which they are prescribed. The majority of positive results are directly caused by the body's own healing response or triggered by the placebo effect.

The Placebo in Action

Doctors have the power and position to instil in their patients the confidence to believe that the treatment they receive is suitable and effective for them. The hope to find relief and get better may be the main reason behind a patient's visit to the doctor. Also the doctor is most likely to believe that his prescription will produce the desired effect. The belief of the doctor in his treatment and the trust of the patient in his doctor, together may produce a "medicine" that can translate even a useless treatment or a non-specific drug into a definite improvement of the treated condition, and in some cases, into a complete cure. This medicine is nothing more than the placebo effect.

If the doctor himself is completely convinced that the treatment he recommends to his patient will be successful, the patient's perception of the doctor's confidence is likely to produce a placebo response. Dr. K. B. Thomas from Southhamptom, England was able to prove that a doctor doesn't even need a prescription to help his patients. Dr. Thomas selected 200 patients who suffered from such symptoms as headaches, stomach pains, back pains, throat aches, cough, and fatigue and divided them into two groups. One group received a clear diagnosis and a "positive" consultation during which he assured them that they would soon recover. He told the second group that he wasn't completely sure what was wrong with them and asked them to come back again in case there was no improvement. Then he divided each group into two subgroups of which one received a prescription, which was a placebo. After two weeks, 64% of the patients with "positive consultation" had improved considerably compared to 39% of the patients who received uncertain advice. Fifty three percent of the patients who received a prescription had improved compared to 50% of those without prescription. This experiment demonstrates that a medical doctor can have a more powerful healing effect on his patient than a prescription drug.

This may also explain the phenomenon why doctors who really believe what they do is best for their patients -- even though it may defy the logic of scientific understanding -- achieve much better results and their patients do well. If a doctor can motivate a patient to believe that he is going to improve, then he has done a much better job than any sophisticated treatment may be able to accomplish. A leading article in the medical journal *Lancet* asked why should it be wrong to give a placebo when the essential modern therapeutic means have no better effects than placebos. It should be the primary aim of medical training to produce a warm-hearted, honest and optimistic doctor who listens to his intuition and who feels both compassion and love for his fellow human beings. The doctor's very presence can work as medicine. What kind of therapy he uses may be secondary or complimentary. Thus, the doctor as a placebo can be more powerful than his treatment and there won't be any side effects.

The current trend by large proportions of the population to seek alternative practitioners is not so much based on *what* they offer to a patient but *how* they make the patient feel. The very fact that alternative therapists use natural methods and compounds for treatment, makes the natural therapies more humane and potentially more powerful to work as a placebo than medical treatments. We all have a pre-programmed natural instinct, although subdued in many people, which senses a healing effect in natural foods, herbs, or other remedies of nature. An apple or a piece of ginger are more likely to trigger a placebo response in us than the synthetic fat "Olestra" or a chemical drug used to reduce blood pressure. Natural things are naturally pleasing for the body. A naturopath has become a symbol for natural healing. Even if his methods may not be very effective, the symbol may still be powerful enough to trigger a good placebo response.

The placebo is known to be directly responsible for a considerable amount of success in every medical treatment as is confirmed by the results of every controlled study. If there were any other treatment in the system of conventional medicine just as effective and consistent as the placebo effect, it would have most certainly been heralded as the biggest medical breakthrough of all times. However, the placebo effect is not at all or only rarely mentioned in the medical textbooks. This is unfortunate because the placebo plays at least an equally important role in the process of healing and recovery as does an expensive drug or a sophisticated machine.

A typical example for this is *digitalis*, which has been used by doctors for over 200 years to treat heart disease, although its long-term benefits and safety have never been proven. A major three-year double-blind control study (NEJM 1997) conducted by *The Digitalis Investigation Group* showed that out of 3,397 heart patients who received *digitalis* 1,181 patients had died by the end of the study period compared with 1,194 out of 3,403 patients who had received a placebo. This study makes *digitalis* no better than a sugar pill in preventing death through heart disease

During medical training, every would-be doctor has to face the unpleasant fact that drugs themselves cannot induce a healing response. A drug may work in only 35% of the people who receive it. The rest of them may either have no results or become worse because of the drug's side effects. Doctors also know that a patient has a much greater chance of improving with a certain drug if *they guarantee* an improvement. They have learned that a patient can get better by merely looking at a medicine. However, this effect depends more on the imaginative power and the trusting nature of the patient than it does on the medicine itself.

The Miracle of Spontaneous Healing

Modern medicine has unknowingly stumbled over the healing mechanism of the body without having recognised it as such. All the valid scientific research that has been conducted on innumerable drugs and therapies included the "placebo effect" as a necessary element to fulfil the requirement of "objectivity." It is not the placebo effect, however, that has been the subject of research. All the attention has been on drugs or medical procedures that were tested for possible implementation as effective treatments for disease. Drugs by themselves cannot inspire true healing *without* working as a placebo and can therefore only have secondary value if any at all. Moreover, it may be erroneous to assume that a positive change of symptoms resulting from a particular treatment must necessarily be the result of that particular therapy. Treatments have no healing powers of their own and remain ineffective unless they are able to work as triggers for the placebo effect or healing response. If healing does take place it is due to the existing mind/body connection.

This powerful mechanism is illustrated by a study that was conducted on three groups of patients all of whom suffered from bleeding ulcers in their stomachs. All of the patients were told that there was a new drug on the market that could stop the bleeding of their ulcers. One group received the new drug, a second group was given a drug that increases bleeding, and the third group used inert placebo pills. Most of the patients were desperate individuals who hoped that the new drug would help them. The results astonished the researchers. The bleeding stopped in patients from all the groups, even in those who received the drug that was supposed to increase the bleeding. Was the patients' belief in the positive effects of the drug stronger than the destructiveness of the drug?

Obviously, in response to their thoughts and feelings of hope and trust, the patients' bodies did not only produce an internal drug that could effectively stop the bleeding of their ulcers but even neutralise the poisonous substances contained in the drug, which was meant to trigger bleeding.

In one 1950 classic study, pregnant women who were suffering from severe morning sickness were given syrup of *ipecac*, which is an effective compound to induce vomiting, and were told it was a powerful new cure for nausea. To the amazement of the researchers, the women ceased vomiting.

Another intriguing experiment was conducted with the help of medical students. Fifty-six students received either a pink or a blue sugar pill and they were told that the pills were either tranquillisers or stimulants. Only 3 out of the 56 students reported that the pills had no effects on them. Most of the students who received the blue pills assumed that they were tranquillisers and 72% of them felt sleepy. Furthermore, the students who took two blue pills felt sleepier than did those who took only one pill. By contrast, 32% of the students who ingested the pink placebo pills reported that they were less tired and one third of the students stated that they had side effects ranging from headaches, numbness, watery eyes, to stomach cramps, intestinal pains, itching in the extremities, and staggering walk. All responses by the students, except for three of them, were by their caused imaginative beliefs.

The implications of these and similar experiments could have revolutionised the entire medical approach to disease. Unfortunately, the law prohibits the sale of "drugs" that contain nothing but inert substances. Without this law many people could have become their own his own best healer, using only their trust in a drug that in reality isn't one. On the other hand, if placebo sale were made legal, anyone could make a dummy drug and sell it as a real one. But then who is to decide which one is more effective? A former president of the Royal College of Physicians in London once estimated that only 10% of all diseases could be manipulated effectively by modern methods of treatment, including the administration of drugs. Disease manipulation does not necessarily mean drugs have a curative effect, most of them merely suppress symptoms, and they are costly. By contrast, the placebo is very cheap or even cost-free, and if linked with the improvement of health it has no harmful side effects.

Healing Remains with the Patient

Most medical researchers know, that depression, anxiety, negative stress, trauma, emotional crisis, etc. can make the crucial difference whether an administered drug or treatment programme is effective or not. This may explain why drugs have only a very small success rate, on average 35%. A large number of people find no improvement with drugs and many report strong negative side effects. Any drug experiment that tests a drug against a placebo or anyone taking medical drugs should therefore consider the following four crucial questions:

1. Are there fewer subjects who suffer from depression in the experimental group than there are in the placebo group?

2. Would the experiment have ended differently if the control group had received the drug and the experimental group the placebo?

3. Would the results of the experiment be the same if the researchers, who were assigned to administer the drug to the different groups, were asked to switch position?

4. Would any pharmaceutical company risk conducting a similar experiment with different subjects, which may lead to significantly altered or even contrary results?

It may be important to emphasise at this point that the same drug may produce different results in different people and can therefore not be tested for efficacy. A drug may not work for a particular patient unless he allows it to work. It is the patient's state of mind, his subconscious acceptance or resistance, and his emotions that play the major role in determining how successful a therapy is. The type of therapy he receives may, in fact, be secondary. The renowned researcher Dr. Herbert Benson from Harvard University stated once, "Most of the history of medicine is the history of the placebo effect". The ability to cure a disease remains solely with the patient.

An existing or past trauma, sadness, depression, and anger can all lead to unconscious programming of the patient's body cells to shut down their receptor sites to both internal and external drugs. This may render any medical intervention useless and ineffective. It is well known that if a patient is in shock, for example, he cannot be treated or undergo surgery. The same principle applies, although to a lesser degree, to a patient's subjective condition when he receives a particular treatment. With a general drug failure rate of 65% it is obvious that drugs *don't* do the trick, it rather is the recipient of the drugs who determines whether healing takes place or not. True healing requires hope, trust, and the belief that one "deserves" to be healed. Once the body receives the go-ahead signal from his host, which I would like to call "*the bodymind,*" it will trigger a healing response and take care of the necessary details.

The dissimilar levels of trust and belief of different patients in the potency of a drug, as well as the sophisticated procedures and complicated dose instructions, can all trigger a wide range of different responses. They can actually increase the placebo effect from 25% to 75%! For example, the healing rate for duodenal ulcers among the placebo groups in controlled clinical studies range from 20% to 70%. It is very unpredictable who will respond to a placebo positively. Some patients report relief of pain after they are being injected with sterile water. An average 3 to 4 out of 10 surgery patients with serious wounds (caused by ulcers) experience significant pain reduction after they have been injected with a salt solution. There are no reliable methods in modern medicine that can determine or guarantee which ones of the patients will or will not respond to a placebo. It is equally impossible to predict how well a patient will respond to a real drug treatment or surgery. The subjective state of the patient plays indeed a major if not the most important role in curing an illness.

It is well known that wounds may or may not produce pain, depending on whether the wounded considers it a "good" or "bad" wound. Soldiers who were injured during the war often did not even require painkillers when they felt that their wound would help them get into the safety of a hospital and then back home. On the other hand, a serious wound acquired in civil life through an accident can cause tremendous pain and trauma if it is associated with a loss in health, mobility, and financial resources.

Is Today's Medical Practice Trustworthy?

To rely on double blind control studies in order to know whether a particular drug or treatment is useful may be a misleading practice. These studies, which are considered the backbone of medical science, may in fact produce very unrealistic and contrived results. A major research report by the Office of Technology Assessment (OTA), an arm of the United States Congress, came to a similar conclusion. The 1978 report stated: "Only 10 to 20 percent of all procedures currently used in medical practices have been shown to be efficacious by controlled trial." In its October 1991 issue, the British Medical Journal confirmed this report by stating that about 85% of medical procedures and surgery are scientifically unproved. In other words, 80 to 90 percent of the common medical treatments available to the general population have no scientific backing and it is doubtful whether they are justified at all. These findings fall in line with WHO statistics, which conclude that 90 percent of all diseases prevalent today are not treatable with orthodox medical procedures.

However, it would be erroneous to generalise these findings. There are very successful methods in modern medicine which are unmatched by any other form of treatment. They concern mainly acute problems that are caused by accidents, including burns, fractures, heart attacks, as well as matters of hygiene. The high success rate of medical treatment in this field is a truly remarkable and exemplary achievement.

For the other 90 percent of diseases that are in most part chronic in nature, modern research techniques have so far failed to produce any breakthrough results. This is partially due to the fact that the healing mechanism which is triggered by a patient's strong belief in the effectiveness of a drug or treatment does not only take place in the placebo control group but also in the experimental group. It is therefore not scientific to say that a drug produces a higher rate of improvement than a placebo when the placebo effect or the patient's trust in the drug is at work in both the groups. The very fact that the placebo effect has to be included as an essential part of every study shows that the subjective state of the patients in both groups is a major determining factor in the outcome of the experiment. Therefore, medical research cannot be considered objective or scientific.

Who heals -- Who doesn't?

There is no simple way to make a patient believe in the treatment he receives. The success of the placebo response depends mainly on the individual's state of heart and mind, and whether he has a good reason to believe in his doctor. The following three paragraphs describe three major categories of personality which may determine your success in overcoming a serious or life-threatening illness:

1. You feel depressed about everything in your life. You blame others and circumstances for your misery. You are not happy when others are satisfied and joyful because they reflect to you what is missing in your own life. To see other people being happy makes you feel worse. You lack enthusiasm and self esteem and your outlook on life is negative. You get angry even without a reason and you do not like yourself. You say things like "Whatever I try doesn't work" or "I knew from the beginning that the medicine wouldn't help me." You were unhappy most of your life and you try not to remember your past. You give up easily by saying "It's too difficult" or "Nobody cares about me anyway." You feel life has not much to offer and you see no real purpose in living. You only have friends who feel in a similar way as you do.

2. You are a fighter and you are not willing to give up. Your determination gets you through periods of pain and agony. You desperately want to live and you frequently say something like "I am going to beat it" or "I am not allowing this to get me down." However, deep inside, you are scared and you are afraid of not being successful. You often feel alone and create doubts in your mind.

3. You are easygoing and relaxed. You feel that your disease is not a coincidence or even a reason to become angry. You look for important signs or lessons that may enforce major changes in your life that you were not willing to make before. You are not in a desperate hurry to get rid of the disease and prefer to go through the rough periods consciously. Your attitude to the disease is not a negative one even though it makes you feel uncomfortable and suffer. You listen to the "messages" your body is sending you and you learn from them. You accept responsibility for having created this situation yourself but you don't have feelings of guilt. You believe in a higher purpose in life and trust that you are taken care of in one way or another. Death is not a frightening issue for you because you know that there is a purpose in dying as well. You are involved in spiritual practices such as meditation, visualisation, and bodywork. You feel that the disease may disappear by the time you have learnt the accompanying lessons and are ready to embrace the necessary changes in your life.

As you may have guessed, persons who are in category 3 or have similar traits, are better candidates for the placebo effect or for healing themselves than those in categories 1 and 2. A person in category 3 has no reason to believe that a medicine or a treatment would not work, he simply knows within himself that in one way or another he is going to get better. If one approach of healing does not work for him he won't feel disappointed but will have enough motivation to look for alternative solutions.

Whereas a person in category 2 has a good chance of recovery due to his positive attitude, he may nevertheless sabotage the placebo effect by reserving a slight doubt in the background of his feelings, "just in case...;" trying to think positive is not enough to trigger a healing response. He may be sending out two opposite signals to his *bodymind*: "Yes, I am going to get better with this new drug!" and "But what am I going to do if it doesn't work for me?"

A person in category 1 has hardly any self-esteem and wastes all his energy accusing others or blaming fate for his deplorable situation. He is incapable of triggering the placebo response, hence he may remain chronically ill unless he begins to value himself and re-evaluate his life. Disease can be a test to find out how much we value ourselves. You can only have as much faith in a drug, a medical treatment, or even God, as you have in yourself. A low self-esteem lacks in trust. But trust is the necessary element to trigger a placebo response for the cure of any disease.

This connection works also when the healing response is caused by an outer source such as another person, such as a therapist or healer. The success that hands on healing or praying can have for a sick person is the result of a two-way process but largely depends on the patient's receptivity, self-esteem, and deserving ability. If he believes that he deserves to be healed, his body and mind become more receptive for the healing energies. For an increasing number of people, natural forms of healing are much more likely to trigger a placebo or healing response than standard medical procedures, which explains the current tremendous interest in alternative or complimentary forms of medicine.

The Paradigm Shift
There is a definite shift among doctors in the United States and other industrialised nations towards a more holistic approach to health and healing than the one consisting of conducting blood tests, giving EKGs, or using pills or scalpels. A significant number of US medical schools are now adding courses on holistic and alternative medicine, subjects that were considered taboo in medical circles not long ago. Modern high-tech medicine cannot be applied to chronic diseases. It is indispensable during crises when organs have failed, when injuries caused by accidents require surgery, or when someone is fighting a life-threatening infection. Most illnesses, however, are chronic in nature. They include high blood pressure, heart disease, rheumatoid arthritis, diabetes, depression and other acute disorders that become chronic such as cancer and AIDS.

Patients are becoming increasingly disenchanted with the endless high-tech scans and tests of modern medicine that offer none of the personal care or encouragement which are so badly needed when you are ill. This feeling of alienation and helplessness drives many into the hands of alternative practitioners who spend more time with their patients and offer them approaches that include self-help programmes like meditation, yoga, dietary advice, and natural remedies. Americans are already spending approximately $30 million a year on alternative methods of healing. In Australia, 50 percent of all patients opt for exclusively alternative or treatments. In addition, a daily increasing number of medical practitioners are turning "alternative." (Note: Going "alternative" does not necessarily mean it is better than using conventional methods of therapy. Up to 30% of people who visit an alternative practitioner claim to be "very dissatisfied" by the treatment they receive and up to 24% of people using an alternative treatment have reported some adverse reaction to their treatment.)

Consumer demand and the economic crisis of the medical system are probably the most influential reasons that motivate increasing numbers of medical practitioners to turn to the low cost treatments and even to prayer and spirituality. Particularly in the United States where the insurance fees for malpractice are so high, physicians are increasingly interested to attend to their patients' spiritual needs. By building a more personal relationship with the patients, as a bonus to the doctors, they are less likely to be sued by them. This may also restore the doctor's image as an infallible caretaker, a role that used to be the rule rather than the exception. The doctor's role as a friend and guide during the difficult times of sickness can in fact be a very crucial element to lead a patient to his recovery.

The most powerful and continuously occurring trigger for a healing response, however, is the taking of self-responsibility for one's health. This implies the search for and application of natural ways to improve the body as much as avoiding those factors and influences that cause it harm. Once we know what causes disease we will be able to rectify the situation and lay the foundation for optimal health. The following chapters provide an in-depth understanding in what ways we may be contributing to our ill-health, ageing and disabilities and how we can stop and reverse this process for good.

CHAPTER 2

The Laws of Health and Illness

Illness is Unnatural

The main conclusion that can be drawn from the study of health and healing is that there is a natural way of living which prevents diseases from arising. Illness results when we deviate from this way of life and is triggered by a build-up of poisonous substances in the body. To restore health we have to remove the toxins first; a nutritious diet and a natural programme of health care will prevent them from accumulating again.

Disease is the occurrence of a toxicity crisis when toxins in the body have reached a certain level of concentration, which I refer to here as "tolerance." The body signals pain or other forms of discomfort in order to stimulate the immune system for action. The resulting immune response includes the mobilisation of immune cells and antibodies that help to reduce the level of toxicity to below the limit of tolerance (see illustration 1). During this stage of the toxicity crisis we may feel weak and worn out. Under normal circumstances, physical strength, appetite, and good mood will begin to return after several days. This may give a person the impression that his health is back to normal, whereas in many cases he may just have passed the symptom levels of the toxicity crisis.

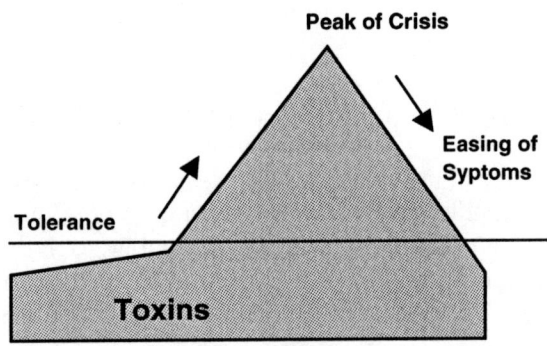

Illustration 1: The Toxicity Crisis

> Toxins gradually rise to the level of tolerance where they produce symptoms of discomfort or disease, i.e., a toxicity crisis. Once the peak level of the crisis is reached, symptoms may begin to ease and the condition reverses.

Unless we have also removed the factors that have led to the build-up of toxins first, they (the toxins) are likely to accumulate again and eventually cause another toxicity crisis. Since immunity becomes progressively weaker with each new crisis, the likelihood of fully recovering again diminishes too. The final outcome of repeated cycles of toxicity crisis may be a chronic illness.

Over one hundred years ago chronic diseases were rare. Then only 10 out of 100 people suffered an ongoing illness. Today, chronic diseases make up over 90 per cent of all health problems. Nowadays, both the general population and the doctors seem to believe that it is correct and good to get rid of the symptoms of a disease through every possible means, which in most cases consists of drugs, surgery, or other means. Although this conveniently bypasses the need for having to detect and attend to the causes of such indicators of toxicity, the net result of such an approach may be depression of the vital organs and systems in the body. Since the body is thus denied the opportunity to remove the accumulated toxins, the toxicity crisis becomes extended in time. This causes further wear and tear to the immune system and makes a person susceptible to develop both acute and chronic forms of illness.

Most of us have made the collective "agreement" that once a sick person recovers after taking medicine his improvement must "obviously" be the result of the medicine. However, this assumption may be wrong. Healing always takes place *in* the body and is controlled *by* the body. If for any reason the body can no longer heal itself, even the most powerful medicine will be not be able to accomplish what the body's failing healing system could not do.

Disease manifests when the body's natural healing responses are weakened or suppressed. The body has a constant tendency to return to its normal balanced state (equilibrium), which is perhaps the only real power of healing that exists. Sometimes the belief in a particular treatment or medicine (placebo) can serve as a trigger for the body to restore equilibrium - an effect that is often (wrongly) attributed to the treatment rather than to the trust or hope that it may be generating in the patient.

In the body, the ultimate law of maintaining perfect balance is undermined by energy depleting influences. A chain smoker, for example, who has developed arteriosclerosis and heart muscle weakness under the constant exposure to carbon monoxide and nicotine, stands only little or no chance to be cured if he continues to smoke. If stockbrokers or gamblers experience constant shocks as part of their business activities, a factor known to cause heart disease, what else can help but giving up the gambling business? Taking them into hospital, away from their jobs, is often enough to help them regain their health. The idea that the applied medical treatment is responsible for their improvement, however, can be misleading.

A Disease is *not* its Symptom

Although you may think that you have found the best medicine there is for your condition, you will not truly heal unless you stop generating its causes. You may succeed in stopping the symptom, but this will only force your body to transfer the toxic substances either to other areas or into "deeper" structures of the body, including the organs and bones. Since this form of suppressing the toxins makes them as if disappear from the general circulation, the body's ability to tolerate toxicity seems to improve. This will allow you to hold on to even more toxins without developing any obvious signs of ill health, which otherwise would naturally manifest in a cold, a fever or an infection. You may in fact believe that you are well again and able to get on with your life in the usual manner, until a much larger wave of toxicity is released. A typical example for such a crisis is the sudden heart attack or stroke in the so-called "perfectly healthy" person.

Most of the serious and life-threatening diseases usually begin with a minor problem such as a simple ***irritation*** of the mucous lining in the stomach caused by overeating or any other poor eating habit. The stomach's hydrochloric acid may be moving up into the oesophagus, which gives rise to the sensation of "heart burn." If the irritation occurs more frequently, caused by the regular consumption of coffee, cokes, sugars, chocolates, meat, nicotine, alcohol, drugs, etc., it may begin to manifest as ***inflammation***. In case the irritating habits continue, an ***ulcer*** may begin to form. Incapable of removing the daily amounting metabolic waste and toxic food particles from the scene of the ulcer lesions, the stomach cells may no longer be able to sustain themselves in this unnatural and toxic environment. This may alter their genetic programme (mutation) and turn them into cancer cells. "Gone out of control" they seem to be no longer aware of being an integral part of the body. This *symptom of disease* is called ***cancer***, which is just another name for constant poisoning and irritation. Thus, stomach cancer is the final result of the continuous irritation of the stomach cells.

Most of the currently used treatment programmes only target the symptoms of disease as if they were the diseases. The idea is to remove the symptoms in the hope that the disease will disappear as well. In many cases sophisticated diagnostic tools can precisely identify the symptoms of a disease, which could be a stomach ulcer, stones in the gallbladder, or a tumour in the uterus. The "treatment" may consist of cutting out the "culprit," often *together with* the inflicted organ. The patient is sent home under the impression that he has been cured. But not being aware of what has caused his problems in the first place, his body may turn into a living time bomb. To date, the purely clinical approach of diagnosis has not been able to identify the causal factors for over 80 percent of all diseases. This is perhaps the biggest drawback in today's medical approach.

Yet we cannot blame the medical professionals for the current crisis in medical care. Doctors are often pressured by their patients to act like "legalised drug pushers" or "symptom hunters." Many patients practically demand from their doctor to remove the symptom by any means and fast so that they can get on with their lives, not realising that this behaviour drives them even closer to the ever intensifying toxicity crises. Added to this dilemma, the side effects that accompany many of the existing treatments for relatively minor problems are often so severe that it is questionable whether they are justified at all.

Miraculous Infection

Infection, for example, is a process of self-defence during which the immune system fights off invading bacteria or viruses that have been "invited" by the host's weakened condition and build-up of poisonous substances. The microbes are often combated with antibiotic drugs in the belief that they are harmful whereas in reality they are quite useful. They are automatically "called" to the scene of a weak organ or an injured part of the body where they help break down toxins and cell debris. The microbes can only get out of control when the level of toxicity in the body is extremely high and short-term medical intervention would be justified.

Infection is one of the body's most effective means to get over a toxicity crisis unless the immune system has already been impaired to a point of no repair, as was common during the Middle Ages when the plague killed millions of immune-deficient people. Trying to suppress an infection with drugs can have severe consequences that sometimes may show up years later as heart disease, rheumatism, diabetes, or cancer. The same applies to the use of painkillers.

Painkillers – the Beginning of a Vicious Circle

Taking painkillers, unless it is absolutely necessary for extremely painful conditions, is an act of suppressing the healing intelligence of the body. When ill, the body may require pain signals to trigger the appropriate immune responses for the removal of toxins from a localised area and also to prevent the individual from further harming himself. Pain is *not* a disease and should therefore not be treated as one. Pain is the body's natural response to congestion and subsequent dehydration of cells and tissues. It occurs in the presence of toxic material and is often accompanied by infection. In most cases, a pain signal occurs when one of the brain's emergency hormones called *histamine* is secreted in large amounts and passes over the pain nerves along the congested area.

The body also uses *histamines* to reject foreign materials such as viral particles or toxic substances and to direct other hormones or systems to regulate water distribution. The latter function of histamine is very important, for where there is a build-up of toxins there is also water shortage or dehydration. When the pain signal becomes suppressed, however, the body is confused over how it to deal with this emergency situation and the dehydration of cells.

Under normal circumstances one can assume that the intensity of pain rises with the concentration of toxins. The brain produces the right amount of natural painkillers, known as *endorphins*, to keep the pain tolerable but also strong enough to maintain a strong and active immune response. Synthetically derived painkillers, on the other hand, cause an electric short circuit of the pain signal that the brain and the immune system need to receive in order to attend the endangered area. The sudden suppression of pain can be likened to cutting the wires of an alarm system that is protecting a house. When a burglar enters the house, nobody will notice him.

Painkillers do not only keep the body ignorant about a particular physical problem; they also sabotage its healing efforts. The regular use of painkillers suppresses *endorphin* production in the brain and thereby causes drug dependency. This also lowers the body's tolerance level for pain, making even minor problems of congestion very painful. Some people have abused their bodies in this way to such an extent that they suffer from excruciating chronic pain, although the causal problem may be a minor one. When painkillers are no longer effective enough, some people may even wish to take their lives to get the desired relief.

How Stimulants Make Strong People Weak

All stimulants are "sweet" when taken but "bitter" in their effect. You can become addicted to them without even recognising your dependency. If you are used to drinking a few cups of coffee a day, try this: Go on a "coffee fast," which means having no coffee for an entire day, and observe how you feel as the day goes on. After a few hours you might notice a dull sensation in your head and a feeling of weakness and lack of energy throughout the body. Some people develop headaches by the afternoon, others begin to yawn and feel downcast due to the weakening effect of the coffee on the heart. Someone may argue "but drinking coffee is normal, everyone does it." Most people in the industrialised nations fall ill at some stage in their lives, which is now considered to be an almost "normal" experience, too.

Stimulants like coffee, tea and cigarettes, seem to be welcome and quick acting substances for those who need a boost of energy, to wake up their mind or to feel lively and strong. But since these substances carry no energy, only stimulants, where is this additional energy coming from? Obviously, it must come from the body itself.

There are also other causes of energy depletion. Food, although it has a stimulating effect, provides balanced doses of physical energy and helps to maintain all the functions in the body. This kind of natural stimulation maintains physiological balance. Overeating, on the other hand, causes overstimulation and so does continual snacking. Excessive sexual activity, overworking, stress and fear can also be causes of continuous overstimulation. Overstimulation occurs when the body, in its attempt to deal with the extra strain and its consequences, begins to over-secrete its own stimulants. They are the stress hormones *adrenaline, cortisol, cortisone, endorphins, prolactin, etc.,* which are needed to sustain the body's most essential activities. Yet the resultant wasting of the body's energy resources takes it toll.

One of the undesirable side effects of abnormal *adrenaline* secretion, for example, is the constriction of blood vessels, particularly those supplying the intestinal tract. This greatly impairs the body's ability to digest food and eliminate toxic waste products. Consequently, abnormal amounts of toxins begin to enter the blood stream. Toxins have a very strong stimulating influence on the body, which may drive someone into a hyperactive mode. The body's energy reserves become even more depleted, which gradually leads towards a toxicity crisis or an acute illness. The toxicity crisis can weaken the body to such an extent that it is forced to rest and waste no more energy. This in turn helps the body to save energy, which it can use to break down the toxins and eliminate them from the system. If the energy-depleting causes are discontinued, the body will regain its balance, but if they are not, it may enter one crisis after the other until it falls seriously ill. Through constant overstimulation even a strong and healthy person may eventually become weak, frail and sick.

Our Constant Need for Cleansing

Since the body is continually renewing itself, that is constructing 30,000,000,000 new cells each day through the process of anabolism, it also needs to destroy the same amount of old cells each day. The breaking down of old cells naturally leaves toxic cell debris behind, which is instantly and automatically removed by the lymphatic system and the blood stream. However, if the body has been weakened, for example, through overstimulation, overeating, or sleep deprivation (all of these have dehydrating effects), the cleansing process is incomplete and toxic remnants remain in the lymph and blood. To keep the blood as pure as possible the body tries to dump the toxins wherever it can, which leads to a build-up of toxic deposits in the connective tissue, the blood vessels and even in the cells of the body. Whichever cell tissue in the body has been saturated with toxins first will suffer from restricted water, oxygen, and nutrient supplies, and trigger a crisis reaction.

Although only one organ or part of the body may have developed a symptom of disease, such as an ulcer, a blocked blood vessel, or a localised tumour, in reality the entire body has fallen ill. To deal with the situation, the body tries to fight for its life by diverting energies from the digestive system, muscles, and other areas towards the afflicted area and the immune system. This provides the immune system with enough energy to counteract the threat of high toxicity. Consequently, during the immune response the afflicted person may feel very weak, tired, and ill. This, however, should *not* be the time to interrupt the body's healing efforts or to stimulate it in any way (through drugs, food, TV, excitement, etc.).

During a toxicity crisis most people tend to panic and try to suppress the symptoms of disease. After a few such interventions, which usually consist of medication, the condition may begin to turn from being acute to becoming chronic. The incidence of chronic illness dramatically increased with the onset of medical intervention when doctors began to interfere with the body's own healing responses through drugs, surgery, radiation, etc. Although medical intervention has saved many people's lives afflicted with acute illness such as a stroke or heart attack, it had little impact on chronic diseases. These diseases are likely to remain chronic unless the mainly *symptom oriented* approach of treatment becomes a *cause oriented* approach of treatment.

Symptoms of Disease are like Sand in the Hand

Symptoms of disease are highly changeable, if not unpredictable and their causes seem to remain obscure. A stomach catarrh may initially show up as an irritation and then become an ulcer. After that it may perceived as a hardening of tissue and eventually be diagnosed as cancer. The course of pathological symptoms may vary from person to person and only few people develop the cancer stage. But the previous stages can be equally life threatening. As a matter of fact there are many more people who die from acute food poisoning and acute digestive problems than from chronic diseases such as cancer and coronary heart disease.

A stomach catarrh may be accompanied by various kinds of complaints, including stomach upsets, nausea, vomiting, gastritis, and cramping of the stomach. In truth, there can never be two people with gastritis who have exactly the same symptoms. One of them may be a very nervous person and his symptoms of gastritis may include headaches and insomnia. The other one may suffer an epileptic attack. As the stages of the disease become more pronounced, some (but not all) of the afflicted people develop anaemia as a result of ulceration and putrefaction of cell protein. A number of people form haemorrhoids when stomach ulcers begin to occur, and some suffer stomach congestion where the food simply is retained and is thrown up every second or third day.

Modern medicine views almost each of these various symptoms as different types of disease that require separate forms of treatment by different specialists. This makes the whole approach of medical diagnosis and treatment so complex that even doctors are confused as to what measures to take. Since each new disease produces different symptoms that may vary from person to person, the specialists are unable to identify the common cause of all these various complaints. Since they haven't been trained to look for the cause of the complaints they tend to deal with the various symptoms as if they were separate diseases. The initial stomach pain seems to have no connection with the inflammation of the catarrh; the thickening of the stomach lining is dissimilar to a stomach ulcer; and the ulcer is certainly not (yet) a malignant tumour.

A physician may be able to stop the initial pain with an antacid or a painkiller, and when the catarrh occurs he may give anti-inflammatory drugs. As the developing ulcer becomes unbearable, a surgeon may decide to cut it out. When the cancer appears, an oncologist may prescribe chemotherapy, radiation, or surgical removal of the tumour and parts of the stomach. Yet none of these symptoms are diseases in themselves, they are all caused by something else and without dealing with that something else the disease will continue to appear in other seemingly unrelated forms and or variations. Symptoms are like sand in the hand. They cannot reveal the true nature of disease. It is therefore in the best interest of the patient *not* to receive treatment for the symptoms of his disorder.

Searching the Cause

Not many people try to find out why their stomach becomes irritated or in what ways they may have contributed to develop the symptoms of ill health. By removing the last symptom, which is the cancer, the physician has done nothing to remove the cause of the first symptom, which is pain. The pain may have been caused by irritating foods, too much salt or hot spices, feeling emotionally upset, smoking, drinking too much alcohol, coffee, or soft drinks, overeating, liver congestion, or just lack of water.

The latter is probably the most common, yet the least known cause of stomach problems and many other illnesses (I am using the example of stomach disorders to describe the basic mechanisms leading to disease). Most stomach pains are signals of advanced dehydration of the mucous lining. Consisting of 98 percent water and 2 per cent physical "scaffolding" which traps water, the mucous layer serves as a natural buffer of protection. The cells below the mucous layer secrete sodium bicarbonate, which is trapped there to neutralise any of the hydrochloric acid that may pass through the mucous lining. The resulting chemical reaction produces salt from the sodium bicarbonate, and chlorine from the hydrochloric acid. Consumption of foods that require secretion of large amounts of hydrochloric acid, such as meat, fish, eggs, cheese, etc., thus causes high salt production, which alters the water-holding properties of the "scaffolding" material of the mucous lining. Regularly eating such foods in large amounts leads to too much acid neutralisation, and accumulation of salt deposits in this layer. This causes "erosion" which will allow the acid to reach the stomach wall; the result is the well-known pain of *dyspepsia*.

As long as the mucous barrier is well hydrated through regular water intake, and protein and fat consumption is moderate, the salt deposits are back-washed, bicarbonate is retained, and the acid is neutralised as it is tries to pass through the mucous layer. Thus, there can be no better acid barrier to the stomach wall than water. Yet the stomach pain, which in most cases is rather a thirst pain, is usually combated with antacids and other medications. The drugs, however, do not offer efficient protection against the (natural) action of the acid. Most people with stomach ulcers and severe abdominal or dyspeptic pain experience an almost instant and total relief of pain after drinking a glass of water or two. Caffeine containing beverages such as cokes, tea, or coffee, on the other hand, have a diuretic effect, and draw the water out of the protective stomach lining. One cup of coffee or an alcoholic drink can easily bring on a pain attack.

The stomach pain is the first signal to tell a person that something is wrong and needs to be changed. The suppression of the first symptom through drugs may prevent the patient from finding out what is causing it. Thus the lack of knowledge about the mechanism of water metabolism -- mistaking the thirst pain for a disease -- may be responsible for the suppression of the initial symptoms that eventually could become a chronic illness such as cancer. Most cancers are the result of repeatedly suppressing mild symptoms of illness such as a cold, pain, an infection, a headache, etc., and treating them as if they were diseases.

The purely clinical approach of treatment focuses on each of the progressive stages of pathological symptoms and keeps producing new findings that promise a cure of each of these problems. Recently, scientists have identified one particular bug, *H pylori*, which is now considered to be the major cause of gastric ulcers. Yet this stomach bug may just as well be a by-product of ulceration rather than being its cause. The antibiotic drugs *omeprazole* and *amoxycillin*, now prescribed for stomach ulcers, destroy the bug and the ulcers disappear, bringing great relief to many sufferers. However, once the drug intake is discontinued, the bug returns and the ulcer too.

This raises the question why the stomach bug returns after the ulcer has been "cured". In reality, the drugs have no curative effects at all because the afflicted person depends on their continual intake. What they *do* "accomplish", however, is to destroy all kinds of bacteria in our gut, including those that help us to break down the toxins which have accumulated in our stomach. The *H pylori* bacteria naturally return to the gut when the antibiotics are no longer there to destroy them. They are attracted there and tend to overpopulate the stomach because there is presence of large amounts of toxins that haven't been removed yet.

These bugs can be found everywhere and in everyone, yet only few people develop stomach ulcers. Why does *H pylori* "cause" a gastric ulcer in one out of 20 people and not in the other 19, although the bacterium is found in all of them? Similarly, a trapped nerve can be seen as a cause of disease in the body but not every trapped nerve results in disease. Instead of looking for an external culprit for such a problem, wouldn't it be far more important to find out *why* some trapped nerves produce pathological changes and others don't? Why does the same frightening situation cause a panic attack or an infarct in one person and not in another? Could it be possible that these external "causes" of disease may simply serve as a trigger to ignite the high toxicity present in a person's body, thus leading to a toxicity crisis, which is known as "disease?"

Defying a Hopeless Prognosis

Jenny was only 25 years old when she came to me with progressive Crohn's disease, a chronic inflammatory condition of the alimentary tract. There was chronic patchy inflammation with oedema of the full thickness of the intestinal wall, causing partial obstruction of the lumen. She had been told that her condition was irreversible and would eventually lead to her death. Despite the many various treatments she received, all of which consisted of painkillers, antibiotics and strong anti-inflammatory drugs, including cortisone, her condition worsened progressively. Since there were no signs of improvement her doctors increased the dosage of the drugs at regular intervals. Her face and body were covered with spots that she scratched to bleeding point during the night. She had several other symptoms including strong menstrual cramps, headaches, and lower back pain.

After examining Jenny through the methods of Ayurveda Pulse Diagnosis and Iridology and listening to her medical history, I pointed out to her that her intestinal troubles were caused by what she ate. Jenny consistently consumed highly acid-forming foods and drinks that had an irritating and dehydrating effect on the intestinal lining. In addition, the strong prescription drugs interfered with her body's attempt to rid itself of the build-up of inadequately digested and therefore toxic food. Apart from impairing the immune system the poisonous compounds of the drugs had also removed large quantities of water from the tissues and cells. Without enough water, which is the principle agent of transport and healing in the body, the body faces a situation of crisis, called body drought or dehydration.

The general dehydration of Jenny's body caused much of her complaints, including the pain in the head, back, and lower abdomen. The drugs led to a massive build-up of toxins and harmful bacteria in the intestines as they effaced almost the entire population of the gut's friendly bacteria. Her irregular sleeping habits and subsequent chronic fatigue made it difficult for her digestive system to cope with any type of food, which further increased the toxicity in the intestinal tract.

I suggested a series of cleansing and re-hydration procedures together with a diet that corresponded to her natural body-type and physical condition as well as a number of changes in her daily routine that would help to rebalance her disturbed biological rhythms. In addition, I recommended that she took up meditation to deal with the underlying patterns of fear and insecurity she had experienced since early childhood.

One month later a check-up with her doctor revealed that the disease had disappeared and so had all her skin problems and other symptoms. Six years later she is still as healthy and radiant as can be. What I have learned from this and similar cases is a simple understanding of healing that can be applied to almost every disease. It can be summarised in the following few words:

A disease is not its own cause and cannot be cured by merely removing its symptoms. One of the most effective ways of dealing with disease is to create a healthy diet and lifestyle and to remove whatever energy depleting factors there may be to impede the body's effort to return to its natural state of balance or equilibrium. It is the weakening influences, i.e., overeating, drugs, stimulants, lack of sleep, lack of water intake, etc., that deplete the body's energy reserves and render it susceptible to disease-causing agents such as bacteria, viruses, or toxins.

Trusting in the Nature of the Body

Every so-called disease is a toxicity crisis caused by the accumulation of toxins beyond the point of tolerance. The body is left with no other choice but to find an outlet for the toxins. The crisis may be accompanied by various symptoms, which could be a cold, a headache, pneumonia, or any other infection, all attempts by the body to rid itself of harmful toxic substances. When the body's immune system has lowered the level of toxicity to a certain degree, which may vary from person to person, the symptoms disappear again. One of the unfortunate side effects of medical intervention is that it prevents this natural response of healing from taking place; hence there are so many diseases today for which the causes remain in the dark.

A simple cold can turn into a chronic catarrh if is not allowed to take its natural course. Further interference with the body's own healing process can turn the catarrh into pneumonia. This can be fatal if the elimination of toxic secretions is obstructed through suppressive drugs. In a similar way, a migraine may suddenly become a mental breakdown, a high blood pressure may turn into a heart attack, and a stomach catarrh may develop into a cancer.

If we were to allow a toxicity crisis to go through its natural stages of development and stopped depleting the body's energy resources, disease would rarely arise nor would it become necessary to fight it. A toxicity crisis may, however, lead to serious complications if we prevent the body from eliminating both metabolic waste and other toxic compounds. Patients who took the seemingly more effective and convenient "shortcut" of medical intervention to have their health restored may remember their illness with apprehension and may continue to live with the subconscious fear of a possible recurrence. But those who were naturally cured by the body's own natural healing powers are most likely to recall their illness as an experience of great emotional relief that increased self-confidence and even psychological success. Having recovered by themselves, they may also have made a quantum leap in self-development. Many people report that their natural recovery has even allowed them to go through a breakthrough of some sort.

A toxicity crisis can be a unique opportunity to neutralise old *karmic debts* and bring about positive changes on the physical, emotional, and spiritual levels of life. By entrusting the healing process to one's own body a new sense of freedom begins to dominate in one's awareness and old fears and anxieties start dissipating. The tactic of *fighting a disease until the end* is not only unnecessary but also reinforces the (false) belief system that true healing occurs only rarely or is subject to luck. Research has confirmed the contrary: Over 80% of all illnesses disappear completely on their own.

To assist the body's healing efforts during a toxicity crisis it is important to take a natural purgative or an enema each day to release accumulated toxic waste in the intestinal tract. It is also good advice to keep one's feet warm, take complete rest, and avoid watching television (too stimulating and dehydrating). Eating food during the crisis interferes with the healing process as this uses up the energy that is meant for the elimination of toxins. But drinking plenty of warm water helps with the much-needed cleansing and re-hydration process in the body. Also recommended is a warm bath before bedtime and, should there be pain, a hot bath as often in the day as is comfortable. To aid the healing process, regular exposure of one's body to fresh air and natural sunlight can be very beneficial too, as both have strong immune stimulating effects. These and similar measures greatly help the body in overcoming a toxicity crisis within the shorted possible time.

All serious diseases are "innocent" in the beginning. Most of them start off as simple colds, headaches, stomach pains, intestinal cramps, fatigue, indigestion, stiffness of joints, etc. These minor seemingly "insignificant" complaints eventually turn "vicious" when they are "cured" too quickly. They can never really be cured in this way because each minor toxicity crisis that is suppressed adds more toxins to the system and depletes constitutional strength and vitality. In addition, if the causes of these relatively small complaints are not removed more serious impairment of the body's functions may result. This may be the starting point of a long-lasting illness. The following section deals with the four most common factors that contribute towards developing a toxicity crisis or disease.

CHAPTER 3

The Four Most Common Causes or Risk Factors of Disease

1. <u>Gallstones in the Liver</u>

The Liver is the largest gland in the body, weighing up to 3 pounds. It is suspended behind the rips on the upper right side of the abdomen and spans almost the entire width of the body. The liver is an extremely active organ with hundreds of different functions. With its dazzlingly intricate labyrinth of special cells, veins and ducts, it resembles an entire city for the variety of its activities.

Because the liver is responsible for processing, converting, distributing, and maintaining the body's "fuel" supply, i.e., energy and nutrients, it literally affects the health of every cell in the body. The liver also influences the secretion of digestive enzymes and produces many hormones that affect the way the body functions, grows, and heals. It makes new amino acids and converts existing ones into proteins, which are the building blocks of cells, hormones, *neurotransmitters*, genes, etc. It also breaks down old cells, recycles iron, and stores blood (during the night) as well as many vitamins and nutrients.

Apart from breaking down alcohol the liver detoxifies noxious substances, bacteria, parasites, and certain drug compounds through enzymes. It filters more than a quart of blood each minute. The liver keeps the body warm, provides the energy for sexual performance, maintains good eyesight, and keeps the mind clear and efficient.

One of the liver's most important functions is to make bile (1 to 1 ½ quarts a day), a bitter, sour fluid which is highly alkaline. Food cannot be properly digested without bile. To enable the small intestines to absorb fat, proteins, and calcium from the food, the food must first be mixed with bile. When fat isn't absorbed it shows that bile flow is inadequate. The fat stays in the intestines and since it is lighter than water it may cause the faeces to float. If fat isn't absorbed properly then calcium isn't absorbed properly either leaving the blood in a deficit. The blood subsequently takes its extra calcium from the bones which leads to teeth, hair, nail and bone disorders.

Apart from breaking down fatty acids contained in our food, bile also removes toxins from the liver and de-acidifies and purifies the intestines. If bile flow in the liver or gallbladder is seriously impeded by hardened bile deposits or gallstones, the colour of the faeces turns tan, orange-yellow or pale as in clay, instead of greenish-brown. Gallstones are an *effect* of an unhealthy diet and lifestyle. Even if all other disease-causing factors are eliminated but gallstones are still present in the liver, they remain a *cause* for future illness. It is for this reason that the subject of gallstones has been included here as a major risk factor or cause of disease.

When the Liver Bile Ducts Become Obstructed...
The most common but rarely recognised health problem today is blockage of the liver's bile ducts through gallstones (see illustration 2).

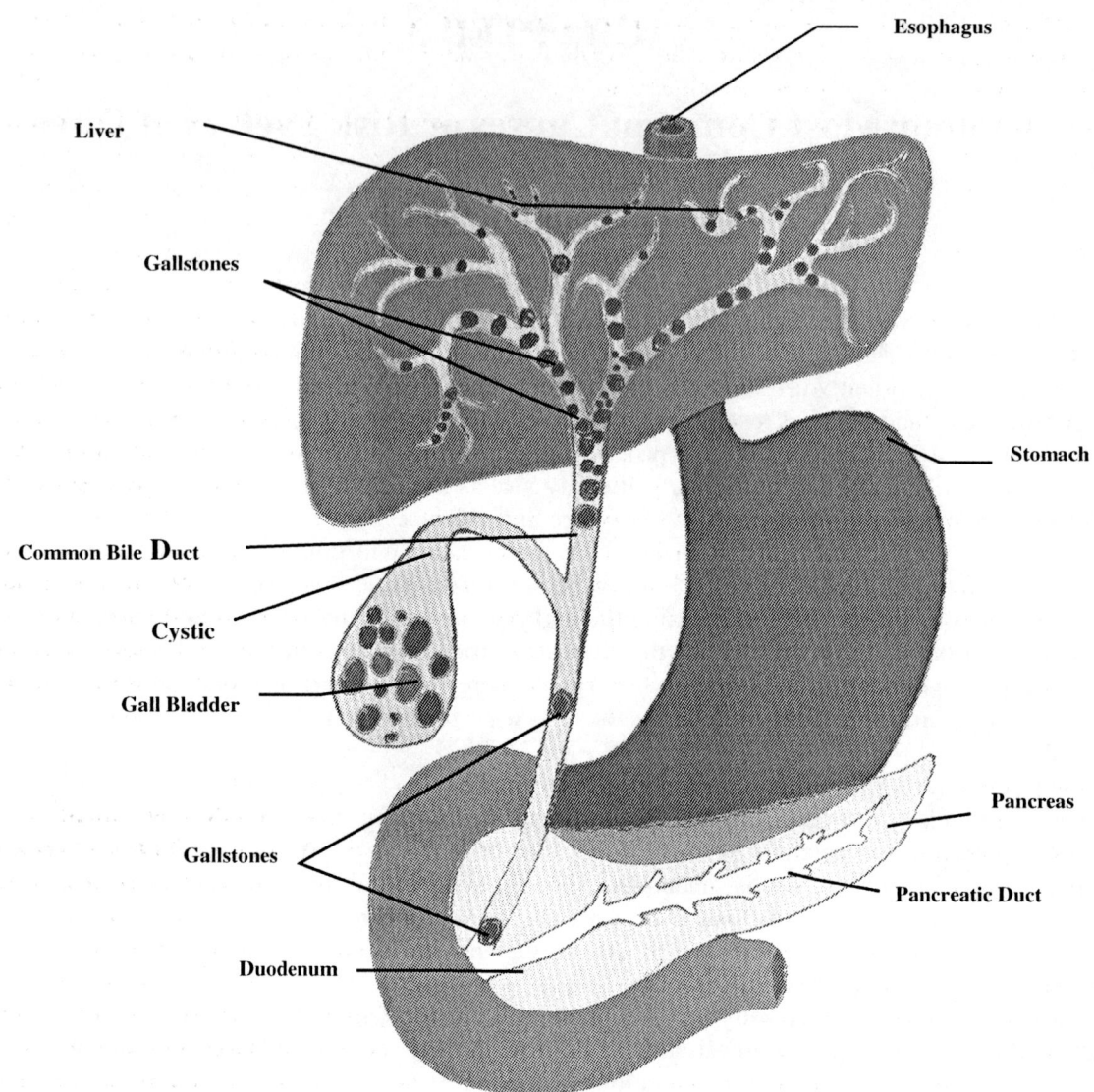

Illustration 2: Gallstones in the Liver and Gall bladder

Obstructed bile flow can directly and indirectly impair the functions of every part of the body and eventually lead to death. If you suffer any of the following symptoms or similar ones you are likely to have numerous gallstones in your liver and gallbladder:

Low appetite, food cravings, all digestive disorders, diarrhoea, constipation, clay coloured stools, hernia, flatulence, haemorrhoids, dull pain in the right side, difficulty of breathing, liver cirrhosis, hepatitis and most other types of infection, high cholesterol, pancreatitis, heart disease, brain disorders, duodenal ulcers, nausea and vomiting, a 'bilious' or angry personality, impotence and other sexual problems, prostate diseases, urinary problems, hormonal imbalances, menstrual and menopausal disorders, problems with vision, puffy eyes, all skin disorders, liver spots especially on the back of the hands and facial area, dizziness and fainting, loss of muscle tone, excessive weight or wasting, strong shoulder and back pain, a pain at the top of the shoulder blade, dark colour under the eyes, morbid complexion, the tongue is glossy or covered with a white or yellow coat, scoliosis, gout, frozen shoulder, stiff neck, asthma, headaches and migraines, tooth and gum problems, yellowness of the eyes and skin, sciatica, numbness and paralysis of legs, joint diseases, knee problems, osteoporosis, obesity, chronic fatigue, kidney diseases, cancer, MS, ME, Alzheimer's disease, cold extremities, excessive heat and perspiration in the upper part of the body, very greasy hair, etc.

People with chronic illnesses have hundreds if not thousands of gallstones congesting the bile ducts of the liver and gallbladder. The liver is able to return to its natural efficiency once the stones have been removed through a series of liver cleanses. And by maintaining a healthy diet and lifestyle most if not all symptoms of discomfort in the body will soon begin to subside. Many allergies will disappear, back pain stop and energy and well being improve dramatically. Cleansing the liver bile ducts from gallstones is one of the most important and powerful procedures to improve your health.

Gallstones – A Constant Source of Disease

Gallstones in the liver consist of mostly *cholesterol* (60%) and other bile constituents as well as toxins, bacteria, and parasites. They are "invisible" to X-rays because most of them are too small and not calcified. The gallbladder may have some bigger stones that are calcified and *can* be detected. Ultrasound technology can spot non-calcified fatty deposits in the liver only if they occur in very large quantities (many thousands of stones). The diagnosis of this condition is often referred to as "fatty liver."

Gallstones may come in all shapes and colours. Most of them are green yet some can be white, red, black or tan coloured. They result from overeating, an unhealthy diet and lifestyle, as well as stress and repressed anger. As the stones grow in size and become more numerous, due to backpressure on the liver, bile production drops. Normally the liver produces over a quart of bile each day. When the major bile ducts are blocked, barely a cup or even less will find its way to the intestines. This does not only impair digestion but also prevent the liver from excreting toxins and pushing the stones out of the bile channels. Consequently, also the liver's blood vessels become increasingly congested preventing *Low Density Lipo Proteins* (bad *cholesterol*) from leaving the blood stream, hence the rise in blood *cholesterol*.

Since gallstones are porous, they can pick up or absorb toxins, bacteria, viruses, parasites and cysts that are passing through the liver, like a fishing net collects fish. The stones can become a constant source of infection, supplying the body with an ever-increasing number of fresh bacteria. The attempt to permanently cure intestinal bloating, cystitis, stomach ulcers, infectious diseases or any of the above conditions is bound to fail if the bacteria harbouring gallstones are not removed from the liver.

If one or several gallstones become impacted in the *cystic duct* - in the channel that links the common bile duct with the gallbladder, or in the *common bile duct* itself - there is a very strong spasmodic contraction of the wall of the duct to try to move the stones onwards. This causes severe pain during contraction of the duct wall. When the gallbladder is packed with gallstones, it too goes into extremely painful spasmodic muscle contractions, a condition known as gallbladder attack. Gallstones can cause irritation and inflammation of the walls of the gallbladder and the cystic and common bile ducts. There may be superimposed microbial infection. Today, over 20 million Americans suffer gallbladder disease and each year about one million of them opt for an expensive gallbladder operation.

If a person has his gallbladder removed surgically, he may feel tremendous relief from the acute pain attacks and his digestion is likely to improve for a short while, as comparatively more bile becomes available for the digestive process. But since he still has many stones left in his liver, the digestive troubles will return and become worse and other possible health problems such as asthma, bursitis, heart disease, arthritis, pain, etc. become intensified too.

If gallstones become stuck in the *ampulla of the bile duct*, where the common bile duct coming from the liver and gallbladder joins the pancreatic duct, jaundice and acute pancreatitis usually develop. This condition may eventually lead to tumours in the pancreas and to a number of other diseases.

Gallstones of any kind and number can be easily and safely removed through the Liver Cleanse described in chapter 7, "Useful self-help programmes." The first positive effects that are commonly noticed soon after the cleanse are pain relief and regained or enhanced energy, vitality, and general well being. Although the Liver Cleanse can be done by people of any age, including children above 10 years (many children today have gallstones in the liver) and the elderly, it is recommended to do the cleanse only after having followed the general guidelines for creating a healthy body for at least four to six weeks, as is described in the following chapters. The colon and kidney cleanses outlined in chapter 7 are an ideal preparation for a liver cleanse, too.

During a series of six liver cleanses, I had passed about 1,600 hundred small pea-sized green stones, hundreds of chickpea sized and a dozen large, over 2cm long ones. A seventh cleanse showed that the liver was almost clean. The effects of each cleanse were often dramatic and added more and more benefits to the previous one(s). The overall results were that my energy and vitality increased by three-fold, all discomfort, stiffness and pain in the body, particularly in the back, ceased and digestion and elimination normalised. For me personally, the liver cleanse is the best thing I have ever done for my physical and mental well being.

You may wonder why in mainstream medicine there is no procedure or medical knowledge to deal with gallstones in the liver. The reason for this extremely important missing link is that the theories of modern medicine suggest that gallstones can only be formed in the gallbladder, not in the liver. The "experimental evidence" of modern medicine supporting this theory is largely based on taking X-rays or ultrasound scans, which can detect only the few stones in the gall bladder that may have grown to a certain size and are calcified (mineral stones). The diagnostic tools are unable to recognise the hundreds or thousands of non-calcified hardened bile deposits in the liver as gallstones. Ultrasound scans can reveal fatty deposits in the liver only when there is an excessive number of large stones (20,000 or more) congesting the liver bile ducts (fatty liver). And even if early deposits are recognised, there is no effective therapy in conventional medicine that can remove them.

The presence of gallstones in the liver can easily be verified by anyone suffering from ill health, especially if his/her gallbladder has been removed. By performing a liver cleanse, the latter's body will release plenty of non-calcified, bile-coated stones. These stones are identical to the green non-calcified stones found in a surgically removed gallbladder. When cut through their middle part, both the "types" of gallstones bear typical "age marks" similar to those seen in cut tree trunks. Proper analysis would reveal their age and the kinds of toxins, chemicals, and bacteria the body had or has to deal with most. Sweeping the liver clean eliminates thousands of bits of poisonous substances that have helped form the stones and plague the thousands of liver bile ducts. Cleansing the liver in this way may be the most efficient and powerful way to help the body heal itself.

For details how cleansing of the liver and gallbladder can make all the difference when it comes to treating disease or improving health and vitality, please refer to my book *"The Amazing Liver Cleanse."* The book describes the indications of gallstones, shows why most diseases originate in gallstones and gives methods to make the cleanse more effective.

2. Dehydration

The human body is composed of 75 percent water and 25 percent solid matter. To provide nourishment, eliminate waste, and regulate all the functions in the body, we need water. Most modern societies, however, no longer stress the importance of drinking water as the most important "nutrient" of all nutrients. Entire population groups are substituting water with tea, coffee, alcohol, and other manufactured beverages. Many people don't recognise the natural thirst signal of the body as a demand for drinking plain water but instead opt for other drinks in the belief that this would satisfy the body's water requirements.

It is true that beverages such as tea, coffee, wine, beer, soft drinks, and juices contain water but they also contain caffeine, alcohol, sugar, artificial sweeteners, and other chemicals that act as intensely dehydrating agents. The more you drink such beverages, the more dehydrated you become because the effects they create in the body are exactly opposite to the ones that are produced by water. Caffeine containing beverages, for example, trigger stress responses that have strong diuretic effects (causing increased urination); beverages with added sugar suddenly raise blood sugar levels, which uses up large quantities of water, too. Regular consumption of such beverages results in chronic dehydration, which is a common factor in every toxicity crisis.

There is no practical or rational reason to treat an illness (toxicity crisis) with synthetic drugs or even with natural medications and methods unless the body's need for hydration has been fulfilled first. Drugs and other forms of medical intervention can be dangerous for the human physiology largely because of their dehydrating effects. Most patients today are suffering from "thirst disease," a progressive state of dehydration in certain areas of the body. Unable to remove toxins from these parts due to insufficient water supply, the body is faced with the consequences of their destructive effects. The lack of recognition of the most basic aspects of water metabolism in our body can be held responsible for seeing a disease when it really is the body's urgent cry for water.

Recognising Dehydration

Those who have lived for many years without proper water intake are the most likely to succumb to the build-up of toxins in the body. Chronic disease is always accompanied and in many cases caused by dehydration. The longer a person lives on a low water ration and/or on a high ration of other beverages or stimulating foods, the more severe and long lasting is the toxicity crisis. Heart disease, obesity, diabetes, rheumatoid arthritis, stomach ulcers, hypertension, cancer, MS, Alzheimer's, and many other chronic forms of disease are precipitated by years of "body drought." Infectious agents such as bacteria and viruses cannot thrive in a well-hydrated body. Drinking enough water is therefore one of the most important preventives for any disease.

People who do not drink enough water or unduly deplete their body's water reserves through overstimulation for a period of time gradually decrease the ratio of the volume of water that is inside the cells to that which is outside the cells. Under dehydrated conditions the cells may lose up to 28% or more of their water volume. This certainly undermines *all* the cellular activities, whether they occur in skin cells, stomach cells, liver cells, kidney cells or heart cells. Whenever there is cellular dehydration, metabolic toxins are retained, causing symptoms that resemble disease but in truth are nothing but signs of disturbed water metabolism. Since more and more water begins to accumulate outside the cells, the dehydration may not be apparent to the afflicted person; he may in fact notice that he retains water, leading to swelling of his legs, feet, arms and face. Also his kidneys may begin to hold on to water, markedly reducing urinary secretion and causing the retention of harmful waste material. Even the enzymes and proteins living in the dehydrated cells become so inefficient that they are no longer able to recognise the dehydrated state of the body; they fail to signal the "thirst alarm."

Eve, a 53 year old woman consulted me to get relief for a painful condition of gallbladder disease. Her skin was dark grey, indicating a high concentration of toxins in her liver and throughout her body. Seeing how dehydrated (and swollen) her body was, I offered her water to drink. She said: "I never drink water, it makes me sick!" I told her that her natural thirst signals no longer worked because of cellular drought and that without drinking water her body could not return to balance. Any water she would drink would instantly be used to remove some of the toxins lurking in her stomach, giving rise to nausea. In her case any other therapy than *drinking water* would have been a waste of time and money.

A dehydrated person may also suffer from lack of energy. Due to the shortage of water inside the cell the normal osmotic flow of water through the cell membrane becomes disrupted or severely disturbed. Like in a stream the movement of water into the cells generates "hydroelectric" energy, which is subsequently stored in form of ATP molecules (the main source of cellular energy). Normally, the water we drink keeps the cell volume balanced and the salt we eat maintains the balanced volume of water that is held outside the cells and in circulation; this generates the right osmotic pressure necessary for cellular nourishment and energy production. During dehydration, this basic process is undermined.

The Pain Connection

Another major indicator of dehydration in the body is pain. In response to increasing water shortage, the brain activates and stores the important neurotransmitter *histamine, which* directs certain subordinate water regulators to redistribute the amount of water that is in circulation. This system helps move water to areas where it is needed for basic metabolic activity and survival (from drought). When *histamine* and its subordinate regulators for water intake and distribution come across pain-sensing nerves in the body, they cause strong and continual pain. These pain signals, as they manifest for example in rheumatoid arthritis, angina, dyspepsia, low back problems, neuralgia, migraine, and hangover headaches, etc., are necessary to alert the person to attend to the problem of general or local dehydration.

Taking analgesics or other pain relieving medications such as *antihistamines* or *antacids* can cause irreversible damage in the body. They not only fail to address the real problem (which may be dehydration) but they also cut the connection between the neurotransmitter *histamine* and its subordinate regulators such as *vasopressin, Renin-Angiotensin (RA), prostaglandin (PG),* and *kinins.* Although the action of the pain killing drugs can relieve local pain for a while, they nevertheless stop the body from knowing the priority areas for water distribution, adding confusion to all its functions. *Antihistamines* -- also known as allergy drugs – effectively prevent the *histamines* from ensuring balanced water supply in the body.

In addition, after reaching a certain pain threshold, painkillers become ineffective because the brain takes over as a direct centre for monitoring pain perpetuation until of course the body is hydrated again. If the body produces pain out of its own accord (not caused through an injury), this should first be interpreted as a cry for water. The use of pain killing drugs, which suppress this cardinal signal of chronic and local dehydration in the body and which "short circuit" its emergency routes, sabotages waste elimination and sows the seeds of chronic illness.

There is enough documentation to show that these drugs can have fatal side effects. They can cause gastrointestinal bleeding, killing thousands each year. Yet the body's natural pain signals are perfectly normal responses to an abnormal situation, which may be simple dehydration. In the case that a pain is simply unbearable, the use of painkillers, however, may be unavoidable. At the same time, the pain afflicted person should drink plenty of fresh water and discontinue all energy depleting factors as they tend to have a strongly dehydrating effect.

"Body Drought" - the Strongest Form of Stress

Our brain, working round the clock, uses more water than any other part of the body. It contains twenty percent of all the blood circulating through the body. It is estimated that brain cells consist of 85 percent water. Their energy requirements are not only met by metabolising glucose (simple sugar), but also by generating "hydroelectric" energy from the water drive through osmosis. The brain depends greatly on this self-generated source of energy to maintain its complex processes and efficiency.

Water deficiency in the brain tissue cut downs its energy supply and thereby depresses many of its vital functions – hence the word depression. With such a lack in brain energy, we are unable to solve our personal and social problems and subsequently succumb to fear, anxiety, anger, and other emotional problems. We may feel drained, lethargic, stressed, and depressed. The chronic fatigue syndrome, which is commonly known as M.E., is mainly a sign of brain dehydration and subsequent retention of its metabolic toxins. The syndrome may disappear on its own when the afflicted person stops stimulating the brain with caffeine, tobacco, or drugs, etc., and begins a consequent programme of re-hydrating the body.

The Stress Response

When dehydrated, the body has to put up the fight of a lifetime - similar to the one experienced in a "fight or flight" situation. It meets a crisis situation by mobilising several strong hormones, *including adrenaline, endorphins, cortisone, prolactin, vasopressin, and Renin-Angiotensin (RA). Endorphins,* for example, help us to withstand pain and stress and allow the body to continue most of its functions. *Cortisone* orders the mobilisation of stored energies and essential raw materials to supply the body with energy and basic nutrients during the crisis, which means that the body is literally feeding off itself. This in itself is a very stressful and damaging situation for the body and is expressed by such emotions as "I can't cope anymore" or "I feel this is eating at me." Many patients with Rheumatoid Arthritis, MS or other degenerative diseases take *cortisone* drugs, which often give them a boost of energy and morale for a relatively short period of time. The "success" of the drug, however, only lasts as long as there are still reserves left in the body that can be mobilised for energy and nutrient distribution. Once the body has used up its emergency reserves the organism can barely function anymore and the symptoms of disease are worse than ever.

Constriction of blood vessels

When the cells in the body are under-supplied with water, the brain's pituitary gland produces the neurotransmitter *vasopressin*, a hormone that has the property of constricting blood vessels in areas where there is cellular dehydration. During dehydration, the quantity of water in the bloodstream is reduced. *Vasopressin*, as its name suggests, squeezes the vascular system, i.e., the capillaries and arteries, to reduce their fluid volume. This manoeuvre is necessary to continue having enough pressure to allow for a steady filtration of water into the cells. This gives *vasopressin* a hypertensive property. High blood pressure is a common experience among people who are dehydrated (for more information on hypertension and heart disease, see chapter 8). A similar situation occurs in the liver's bile ducts, which begin to constrict in response to restricted availability of water. Gallstone formation is a direct result of dehydration.

A person who drinks alcohol suppresses the secretion of *vasopressin* and thereby increases cellular dehydration (if alcohol consumption is excessive, cellular dehydration may reach dangerously high levels). To survive the body "drought" the body has to secrete ever more stress hormones, among them the addictive *endorphins*. With regular consumption of alcohol, meaning every day for several years, dehydration increases even further and *endorphin* production becomes an addictive habit. This may lead to alcoholism, a disease that has devastating consequences on a person's personal and social life.

Water Retention and Kidney Damage

The Renin-Angiotensin (RA) system is activated when there is a water shortage in the body. This system is used to direct the body to hold on to water wherever possible. It instructs the kidneys to inhibit urination and tightens the capillaries and the vascular system, particularly in areas that are not as vital as the brain and the heart muscles. At the same time it stimulates an increase in the absorption of sodium salt which helps the body to retain water. Unless the body returns to its normal level of hydration, the *RA system* remains activated. But this also means that the pressure of the blood against the walls of the blood vessels remains abnormally high, causing the damage that is known as cardiovascular disease.

Hypertension and the retention of urine in the kidneys lead to kidney damage. Conventional treatments for this condition consist mostly of diuretic (urine forming) drugs and restricted salt consumption. Both may have severe drawbacks. Diuretic drugs, which are used to normalise the blood pressure, as well as reduced salt intake strongly undermine the body's emergency efforts to save the little water it has left for cell functions. The resulting stress response causes a further increase in dehydration and the vicious circle is complete. There are so many kidney replacements made today that result from chronic dehydration, caused by something as simple as not drinking enough water or overstimulation of the nervous system.

The Caffeine and Alcohol Drama

The caffeine contained in such beverages as tea, coffee, cacao, or colas not only stimulates the central nervous system but also acts as a strong diuretic. For every cup of coffee or tea you drink you relinquish approximately three cups of water which the body cannot afford to give up without suffering damage. The caffeine containing cola beverages work in a similar way. Caffeine, being a nerve toxin, stimulates the body's stress hormones and triggers a strong immune response that may give a person the (false) impression that his level of energy and vitality has suddenly increased. To remove the nerve toxin caffeine, the body has to come up with extra water, which it takes from its cells, hence the occurrence of cellular dehydration.

Caffeine, which is a major component in most soft drinks, removes water from the body faster than the body can absorb it again, thereby generating constant thirst. People, who frequently take soft drinks, can never really quench their thirst because their bodies continually and increasingly run out of water. There are college students who drink as many as 10-14 cans of cola a day. Eventually they confuse their bodies' never-ending thirst signal with hunger and they begin to overeat, causing even more swelling and excessive weight gain. Apart from its diuretic action and its addictive effects on the brain, regular caffeine intake overstimulates the heart muscles, causing exhaustion and heart disease.

Alcohol has a similar diuretic effect as caffeine containing beverages. For every glass of beer, for example, the body is forced to sacrifice about three glasses of water. A hangover results when due to alcohol abuse the brain suffers severe dehydration. If this occurs repeatedly, a large number of brain cells become damaged and die. Many important brain functions slow down or become depressed. Recovery is possible to a certain extent if alcohol consumption is discontinued.

3. Kidney Stones

From many causes, i.e., overstimulation, dehydration, fatigue, overeating, gallstones, blood pressure disturbance, medical or narcotic drugs, digestive disorders, etc., the kidneys become congested and are unable to secrete from the blood the quantity of urine that is necessary to keep the blood pure and healthy. When the kidneys are incapable of sufficiently separating the urine from the blood, part of it (the urine) continues to circulate throughout the body, depositing urinary waste products in the blood vessels, joints, tissues, and organs. Skin diseases, strong body odour, sweating of palms and feet, water retention, intestinal swelling, high blood pressure, etc. are all signs of toxic blood caused by crystals and stones in the kidneys.

Stones in the kidneys begin as tiny crystals and can eventually become as large as an egg. The tiny crystals are too small to be detected by X-rays and since they do not cause pain they are rarely noticed yet they are big enough to block the flow of liquid through the tiny kidney tubules. Crystals or stones are formed in the kidneys when urinary constituents, which normally in solution, are precipitated, i.e., when they occur in excessive amounts or when urine becomes too concentrated. The crystal particles of the stones are usually full of sharp angles, which may cut and wear away the inner surface of the urinary canal (ureter) during their passage from the kidneys to the bladder, causing great pain in the loins or lower back. There may even be blood in the urine, pain running down the legs, numbness in the thighs and a difficulty in passing urine.

Most crystals or stones originate in the kidneys, although some may be formed in the bladder. If a large stone enters a ureter, urine flow becomes obstructed. This can lead to serious complications, such as kidney infection or kidney failure.

The Types of Stones and their Effects

The most common solutes involved in crystals and stone formation are oxalates, phosphates, urates, uric acid, and the amino acids cystine and cysteine. There are eight varieties of crystals or stones that can be formed from these solutes for various reasons.

Foods or drinks that contain large amounts of oxalic acid cause oxalate stones. A cup of regular tea (not green or herb tea) contains about 20 mg of oxalic acid, which is far too much for the kidneys to excrete. Initially, the body uses calcium to neutralise the acid, which then turns to calcium oxalate. If tea drinking becomes a regular habit, excessive calcium oxalate is deposited in crystal form. Chocolate and cocoa are also high in oxalates. Anyone who has consumed or consumes these foods or drinks regularly has oxalate stones in the kidneys, especially children whose kidneys are still very delicate.

Uric acid crystals are another type of kidney stones that are formed when we consume excessive amounts of animal protein such as meat, fish, eggs, cheese, etc. Uric acid is a waste product that results from breaking down protein in the liver. The strongest uric acid producer among all food products is regular tea, followed by red meat. If the kidneys do not remove all the uric acid, its concentration in the blood rises. As a result, excessive uric acid is deposited first in those areas of the body that have the poorest circulation and oxygen supply, i.e. the toes of the feet. The precipitation of uric acid and other harmful substances in the toes can make the joints rigid, stiff and unbending (check particularly the small toes of your feet, which show the condition of the bladder). If the bacteria feeding on these toxins invade the tissues in sufficient numbers, inflammation and pain may result. Gout and arthritis are the most common symptoms. The uric acid crystals in the toes are essentially made from the same material as the stones formed in the kidneys.

A similar problem can occur in the heels. Heel spurs are due to deposits of uric acid and various phosphates. The uric acid invites bacteria, leading to pain, and the phosphates are responsible for causing rigid and hard structures. Swelling or oedema around the foot or ankle, caused by poor kidney and adrenal function, may accompany this. The kidneys and adrenal glands regulate water and salt levels throughout the body. If their functions are subdued due to stones in the kidneys, you may "hold" on to water in the feet, legs, abdomen, face, arms, organs, etc.

Many kidney stones are caused by insufficient water intake and consumption of foods or drinks that have dehydrating effects, i.e. alcohol, tea, coffee, meat, sodas, artificial sweeteners, sugar. Also smoking cigarettes or watching television for too many hours have a dehydrating effect and cause urine to become concentrated. This increases precipitation of urinary constituents.

Eating lots of acid-forming foods such as meat, dairy products, sugar, etc. forces the body to release many of its valuable minerals, altering the pH (acid/alkaline balance) of the urine. This does not only cause mineral deficiency in the body, e.g., in the bones and teeth, but also turns the normally acidic urine filtrate alkaline. In an alkaline urine, some substances may be precipitated, e.g. phosphates. Phosphate stones are formed particularly from eating too many foods that are high in phosphate and low in calcium, such as meats, cereals, breads, pastas, and nuts as well as from drinking carbonated beverages. To neutralise the highly acidic phosphate which could easily burn the delicate kidneys, the body extracts extra amounts of calcium from the bones and teeth and uses whatever magnesium it can obtain from such foods as green vegetables.

The presence of phosphates generates an acidic environment which effectively dissolves bones, leading to osteoporosis, teeth problems, coronary heart disease, digestive trouble, cancer and any other diseases that are related to calcium deficiency. A person who eliminates more than 150 mg of calcium a day (24 hours) with the urine – an emergency measure of the body to combat excessive acidity -- is in the process of rapidly dissolving his bones. Some of the calcium combines with the phosphates, forming various calcium phosphate crystals, which can lead to the hardening of the arteries and the common arthritis.

The Need for a Kidney Cleanse

The kidneys make a tremendous effort to keep the body clear of toxic substances such as lead, cadmium, mercury, and other impassable pollutants. They also maintain fluid and electrolyte balance and regulate the pressure from the heart to push the blood through their filtering system. Kidney stones greatly impair this ability, which increases the amounts of heavy metals and raises the body's general level of toxicity. This can lead to infection, high blood pressure, heart disease, brain disorders, cancer, and many other diseases.

The following signs indicate the presence of crystals and stones in the kidneys or bladder: *A dark or whitish colour under the eyes; puffy or swollen eyes, particularly in the morning; deep wrinkles under and around the eyes; tiny whitish, tan-coloured or dark lumps under the eyes, which can be felt or made visible when stretching the skin outwards towards the cheekbones; overlapping of the skin of the upper eyelid; chronic pain in the lower back; swelling of feet and legs; constant fear or anxiety.*

There are a number of herbs that can effectively dissolve kidney stones within a period of three to six weeks (see "The Kidney Cleanse" in *Useful Self-help Programmes*, chapter 7). Whether someone has been diagnosed as having kidney stones or not, having a kidney cleanse once or twice a year produces tremendous curative and preventive benefits. It not only improves physical health but also reduces fear and anxieties.

4. Whatever makes us Weak …also makes us Ill

Flu epidemics were rare 100 years ago and when they occurred, once in a while, only a few people became seriously ill. Nowadays, there is a flu epidemic every year, which sometimes lasts all year round. Today's flu epidemics affect a lot more people and with much stronger symptoms than ever before. The viruses from both these eras are very much the same but the natural resistance to them among the general population is much lower now than ever before. Tooth decay and depleted vision among young people are also rapidly growing "epidemics," a phenomenon unheard of a century ago. The fact that our modern societies are plagued with so much chronic disease today shows that there are entire generations with weak constitutions, caused by stress and unhealthy diets and lifestyle. People who lived a hundred years ago and enjoyed good hygienic conditions were much less prone to develop chronic illnesses than we are today.

Our time is characterised by overstimulation, which has a strong energy depleting effect on the body. The following are but a few of the many possible factors that use up or deplete our physical energy: *Watching television too often and for too many hours; stress; time pressure; excessive noise and air pollution; drug, coffee, tea, alcohol, sodas, sugar, sweets, chocolates, meat, and junk food; overeating; sleep deprivation; an irregular daily routine; excessive sex; too little water intake.* All of these factors lead to the retention of toxins in the body.

Toxins are natural products of our metabolism and they act as stimulants. Once formed, they stimulate the body to eliminate them from the system. This, however, can only be happen when the body's life force or vital energy is strong and efficient. On the other hand, when the body is exposed to too much stimulation and cannot return to its equilibrium state through balanced periods of rest and relaxation, its "batteries" can no longer be fully recharged and it is unable to rid itself of all the daily-generated metabolic toxins. As a result, many of the toxins spread throughout the body and provoke a toxicity crisis, which indicates that the body's resistance to disease (immunity) has dropped to a level of low efficiency.

When the blood carries too many of the toxins, it becomes prone to infection. If treated wrongly through suppressive methods rather than supportive ones, a person may develop a chronic illness, which can eventually lead to accelerated ageing and premature death. Each time an infection is suppressed, the subsequent congestion of the deeper structures of the body increases the workload of the heart, making it increasingly weak and defective. Heart disease, which is the biggest killer in developed countries, could largely be prevented if we desisted from suppressing immune responses such as the common infection.

When a virus or bacterium, which normally is rendered harmless by the immune system, infects a "toxic" person it can no longer stop the infection completely. As long as the energy depleting influence is maintained and toxicity and dehydration continue to impair immunity, even the strongest antibiotic drug will not be able to eradicate the harmful microbes. The bacteria and virus particles are ever present, either within the body our outside the body, and if the blood remains toxic they can strike again at any time. A patient can break this vicious cycle through a programme of cleansing and resting, which helps the body to eliminate toxins. Before beginning a cleansing treatment though, the patient has to identify the energy depleting habits and replace them with energy increasing habits.

There are so many young people today who have already developed chronic illnesses and, unless they introduce drastic changes in their lives, they will find it difficult to regain their health because their bodies accumulate new toxins much faster than can remove them again. A doctor friend of mine who was involved in a research study on 721 secondary school children in Cyprus told me that the majority of the children had signs of hardened arteries. Another study showed that 52% of primary school children in Cyprus are obese and have high levels of blood *cholesterol*. Not so many years ago the Mediterranean populations had some of the best health records in the world. The doctor also told me that almost every child in Cyprus has at least once if not many times received a course of antibiotics to suppress an infection. Drugs have a suppressive effect, which means they interfere with the body's attempt to break down the very toxins that make it susceptible to disease-causing agents. To regain its balance again the body has to create a toxicity crisis or disease.

Illness is but a Toxicity Crisis
A toxicity crisis occurs when the body needs to return to the state of balance. The body has built-in mechanisms to remove toxic deposits in a much shorter time than it takes to accumulate them. By interfering with this process we disrupt the body's important cleansing efforts and become vulnerable to external destabilising agents. An inoculation or infectious bacterium can then easily become the trigger for damaging the weakest organ in the body. Any attempt to treat the organ without removing the underlying cause will not restore its functions.

Later in the book I will demonstrate that it is harmful in most cases to give blood transfusions to people with low haemoglobin levels, treat the testicles for impotence, or cut out stones, ulcers, or tumours. The use of drugs, which have nothing in them to remove the toxins in the blood, may even kill a patient, because nobody knows for certain how far the level of toxicity in his body has reached. The toxins generated during an infection in an otherwise healthy person will remain in the body only as long as the toxicity crisis lasts. Provided we support the body in its cleansing efforts by giving it plenty of rest and water to drink, this natural self-regulating process called infection will naturally eliminate all its traces or effects.

We can only reap what we sow; yet we have a choice in what we sow. Almost everyone can choose to develop a state of good health, but only few choose to give up unhealthy habits or a detrimental lifestyle. It is difficult for our body to remain healthy when we overuse it by over-stimulating our mind and senses. Such straining can deplete our energy resources faster than they can be restored. The resulting constant energy deficiency may be the cause of every discomfort and symptom of disease in the body. Although many people know how bad smoking, overeating, drinking alcohol, etc., is for them, they are unable to give up such habits. This indicates a toxic blood and a toxic liver and can be dealt with, for example, through a series of liver cleanses. As liver functions improve, the natural instincts awaken and happiness increases. The enhanced well being and vitality makes it much easier for someone to quit smoking or stop eating junk foods, drinking coffee, or working too many hours.

Symptoms of ill health can occur in a variety of intensities and modifications. To locate the cause of an illness in its effect, that is the symptom, is nearly impossible. Stomach ulcers, appendicitis, or tonsillitis, for example, merely represent various intensities of toxicity in different locations. To diagnose and treat each one of them as a separate disease may not only mislead the patient but also cause further complications. Since over eighty percent of the people who fall ill recover on their own and without any treatment, it is likely that disease is nothing but a toxicity crisis. Once the body has lowered the point of tolerance or saturation of toxins by removing them, the symptoms begin to vanish by themselves. A headache, a cold, a tonsil infection, gastritis, stiffness in the neck or shoulders, all appear and disappear again, following the same law of alternating toxicity build-up and toxicity break-down.

If a physician's treatment turns out to be successful we are likely to thank *him* for having cured us. On the other hand, if we get well without any external help we may say that we were just lucky. Healing, though, does not take place in either case. What *does* happen is the elimination of metabolic toxins and other waste material. Health is the spontaneous occurrence of balance, which is sustained by successfully removing the body's daily amounting toxins and by giving it the nourishment it needs. This makes the creation of health an ongoing process because the generation and elimination of metabolic toxins and the uptake of nutrients are a necessary part of basic metabolism. There may be nothing more mysterious about health and healing than creating and maintaining this fine line of balance.

Are We Consuming Poison?

Most of us were brought up with the belief that disease is caused by external factors. Few people know that germs can only "germinate" in a toxic environment. Parents who see their children catch one infectious disease after another are especially concerned about giving their offspring every possible protection against infection. Giving immunisation jabs seems to be one way of safeguarding their children's lives and in case a child has contracted an infection, antibacterial or anti-viral drugs are considered to be the best option.

Being used to blaming external pathogens (disease causing factors) such as a bacterium or virus for an infection, not many people consider it possible that the problem may have something to do with the food we eat. Could it be possible that children (and also adults) suffering from repeated infections are in fact poisoned by cokes, ice creams, crisps, chocolate, candy, and breakfast cereals (also see chapter 11)? With their immune systems impaired by consuming large amounts of these or similar acid-forming foods, their bodies can hardly stand a chance to fight off the normally harmless microbes that are part of our natural environment.

The situation is worsened if the children haven't been breast-fed long enough to build up their immunity. Many children are fed with milk formulae, which contain rancid (oxidised) *cholesterol* (a result of milk-drying procedures). Rancid fat or rancid *cholesterol* is a cancer-producing substance and the cause of many diseases, including allergies. The British government has recently identified nine brands of commonly used baby milk formulae as containing potentially harmful chemicals. To give formulae milk to babies can be considered a major health risk, particularly when immunity is not fully developed yet. In addition, there may be many other sources of toxins, which when combined, can raise the body's toxicity to such high levels that without a strong immune system a baby cannot ward off infection-causing microbes and consequently falls ill.

Eating foods that are of no use to our body (non-physiological and junk foods) may well be the major cause of infection in the body. Meat, for example, can only be digested partially by the human body. Cellular enzymes and bacteria begin to break down many of the dead meat cells, which consist of mainly protein. The decomposing protein releases *putrescine* and *cadaverine* which are deadly and highly irritating poisons (see also chapter 6 on vegetarianism), enough to leave the body vulnerable to any kind of infection. In most hospitals, patients are given meat, sausages, eggs, and poultry to eat which their already strained digestive and immune systems are unable to handle. Congested bowels are a fertile ground for microbial infection, which is also more likely to occur in the environment of a hospital where germs are present in larger quantities.

The life of a patient may depend on whether he is able to remove most of the decomposing substances in his intestines before they are absorbed into the bloodstream. If gallstones obstruct the liver bile ducts and the toxins that enter the blood via the bowel can no longer be sufficiently detoxified, "food poisoning" occurs. Most so-called epidemics are in reality forms of food poisoning or chemical poisoning. They occur among people with high levels of toxicity and low immunity, i.e., *people who are already ill*. To give such a person any solid food to eat will use his last ounce of energy to attend the new, incoming food instead of overcoming the toxicity crisis. An immune system that has been subdued by the presence of retained toxins is no longer able to ward off any kind of bacteria, parasites, or viruses.

A child who is fed with meat, eggs, and dairy products, including milk, is likely to develop digestive problems and children's diseases that involve external pathogens, but a child who eats fruits, vegetables, grain foods, and salads and who drinks plenty of fresh water is unlikely to get diphtheria, smallpox, or septic fever. Parents are responsible for the health and safety of their children. By becoming more conscious of their own eating habits, they will automatically want to give their children the best and most nutritious foods and drinks available. This can greatly contribute towards creating a generation of healthy young people who will be known for their absence of illness.

To summarise "The Four Most Common Risk Factors of Disease":
The body is made of cells that are turned over at regular intervals, at a rate of 30 billion each day. Cellular enzymes break down old cells, which no longer receive oxygen and nutrients. This results in the generation of toxic waste. Under normal conditions, the lymph and blood stream remove toxic waste materials immediately after they have been created. There are various organs in the body, which are designed to deal with the different kinds of toxins. The liver breaks down toxic cellular components, detoxifies drugs, alcohol and noxious substances. The lungs remove the highly acidic metabolic waste product carbon dioxide and other gases, the kidneys and bladder remove uric acid, urea and other waste matter coming from the liver, and the colon excretes faecal matter. The skin, being the second largest organ of elimination, eliminates sweat and *40-60% of all* the toxins in the body. The lymphatic system, which deals with 18 litres of toxin-loaded lymph fluid, plays a major role in the detoxification process. All this requires copious quantities of water.

During dehydration, the blood becomes too concentrated and consequently draws water from nearby cells. This greatly impairs the body's ability to rid itself of metabolic waste products. (To go on a hydrating programme refer to the guidelines in the section *'Drinking Water – The Greatest Therapy of All,'* chapter 6). By contrast, a well-hydrated body is capable of both nourishing itself and detoxifying its cells. This sustains the body's equilibrium or perfect balance. All the various activities in the body can be conducted in a flawless manner because there is no congestion or hold-up anywhere.

In their naturally occurring amounts, toxins have a slightly stimulating effect. This helps maintain the functions of elimination. However, if the body's energy is depleted and immunity is low due to an excessively stimulating diet and lifestyle as well as insufficient water intake, the continuous process of detoxification is disturbed or obstructed.

All disease is caused by obstruction. If the obstruction occurs in the liver, gallstones are formed, which affects the nourishment and energy distribution throughout the body. Depending on how many toxins, gallstones, or kidney stones are retained, the body will develop various degrees of toxicity crises that are commonly referred to as the different types of disease.

The basic remedy for the most common diseases is to stop all unnecessary 'energy leaks', clear up the blocked bile ducts of the liver, remove kidney stones, clean the passages of the alimentary tract and provide enough fresh air, clean water and nutrient-rich food to sustain all bodily functions, including the elimination of the daily amounting metabolic waste products. The following list gives an overview of the possible factors that can congest the liver, produce kidney stones, dehydrate the body, and sap its energy.

- Not drinking enough water
- Drinking cold beverages or cold water,
- especially when the body is heated
- Overeating
- Insufficient nourishment
- Highly processed and refined foods
- Ill-combined foods
- Coffee, tea, alcohol, other stimulants
- All carbonated beverages
- Tobacco, narcotics
- Medicinal drugs, antibiotics, etc.
- Irregular daily routine
- Insufficient sleep
- Watching too much television
- Exhaustion, strain, stress
- Environmental hazards
- Pollution, both indoor and outdoor
- Anger, rage, envy, greed, fear, jealousy, egotism, anxiety, etc.
- Lack of harmony and happiness
- Extreme and excessive habits
- Sedentary lifestyle
- Overstimulation of the senses
- Injuries

Any of these or similar causes of depleting energy from our body and mind cause a build-up of toxicity in the blood and lead to a toxicity crisis (acute illness). The crisis is necessary to mobilise the immune system, find an outlet for the toxins, and return the body to a state of equilibrium or balance. If the causes remain intact and continue to weaken the body further, it is left with no other choice than to develop a continual toxicity crisis, which is chronic illness. The following section deals with the part of our body where toxins are produced first, i.e. the digestive system.

CHAPTER 4

Most Diseases Start in the Digestive System

To comprehend the next set of reasons why we fall ill, become weak, or age, we must take a closer look at our digestive system, which is not only the "engine" of our body but also a major seat of our emotions and our subconscious. Whenever we look at a physical issue, we need to include its mental and emotional counterparts. Although body and mind seem to appear as separate entities, they are intrinsically one and all events on the physical level like eating food, metabolism, eliminating waste, or exercising, occur at the same time on the mental and emotional planes as well, and vice versa. Please note that whenever I refer to disease or illness I mean toxicity crisis.

To understand the mechanics of disease in greater detail we have to know how the gastrointestinal tract works and in what way its malfunctions contribute to illness in the body and/or in the mind. To get a more complete picture of the mechanics of creating disease, which when reversed become the mechanics of creating health, I have included some of the basic insights of *Ayurvedic Medicine*, which is the most ancient and complete system of natural health care.

AGNI – the "General" of Digestion

When food enters your mouth and touches the taste buds located on the surface of your tongue, your salivary glands secrete saliva to lubricate the food and to pre-digest cooked starches. At the same time, your pancreas is instructed to prepare for the release of the appropriate proportions of digestive enzymes and minerals that are required to help break down the food into the smallest nutrient components.

The first cause of digestive disorders is swallowing the food too fast; it indicates emotional impatience and nervousness. Eating too quickly reduces saliva production in the mouth cavity, which is a major cause of teeth problems. One of the functions of saliva is to keep the mouth and teeth free from harmful substances and bacteria.

When food enters the stomach it mixes with gastric juices which are composed of hydrochloric acid, enzymes, mineral salts, mucous and water. The action of the acid kills most of the harmful microbes, parasites, and noxious substances that accompany the food. Special enzymes begin to act upon proteins that may be present in the food. Once saturated with enough acid, small jets of food are forced into the duodenum, which is the first part of the small intestine.

The pancreas connects to the duodenum and supplies digestive enzymes, minerals, and water to break down starches. The gallbladder, which also leads into the duodenum, delivers bile to help digest fats and protein foods. The duodenum itself releases hormones and digestive juices required for the digestive process. Ayurveda calls the entire activity taking place in this part of the digestive system "AGNI" or digestive fire which "cooks" the food further in order to make it available for the cells and tissues at a later stage (see illustration 3).

The rest of the small intestine, which has a length of about five metres, continues digesting the food and assimilates it through its numerous intestinal folds and villi. The blood takes all the nutrients to the liver for further processing.

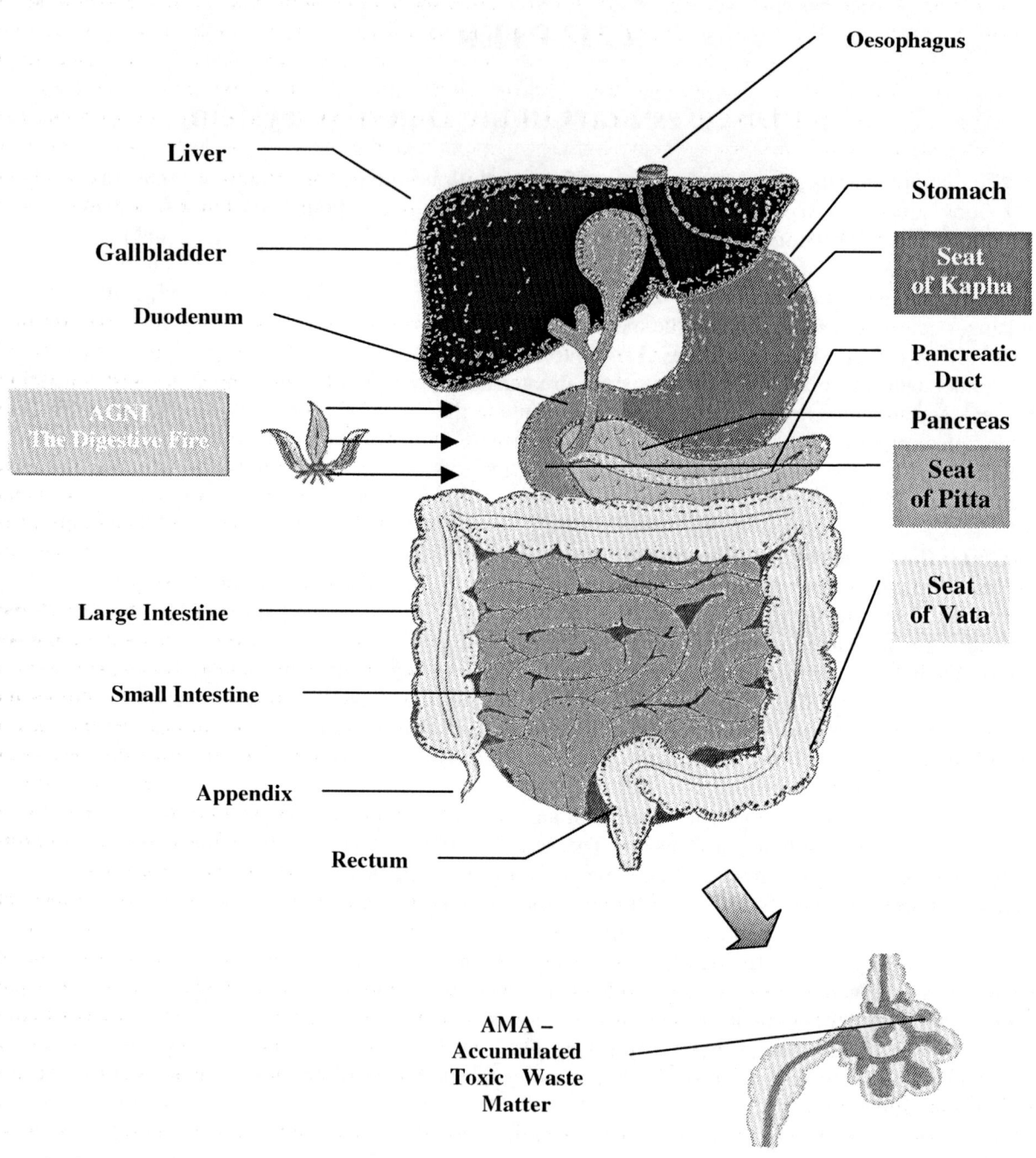

Illustration 3: The Digestive System

The ingested food can only be broken down into its tiny nutrient components and made available for the basic metabolic processes in the body if AGNI, the digestive fire, is strong. AGNI is fuelled by bile, without which none of the other digestive juices would be sufficiently effective to break down food. When bile secretion in the liver is unimpeded good digestion is almost guaranteed, provided the food is fresh and wholesome. The combination of a nutritious diet and a strong AGNI is a partnership that can make sufficient amounts of amino acids, fatty acids, minerals, vitamins, glucose, fructose, trace elements, etc., available throughout the body. This in turn produces healthy blood and healthy tissues and a vital and youthful body. The quality of the blood and the tissues of the body, including those that make up the skin, reflect the condition of the liver and small intestine.

Toxic Body, Toxic Mind

If AGNI is low due to various factors, which are explained below, even wholesome food may become harmful for the body. Much of the ingested food remains undigested and can therefore not pass through the intestinal walls into the bloodstream. It is a target for anaerobic bacteria and starts fermenting and putrefying. The bacteria produce toxins and gases that begin to irritate the intestinal lining and congest the vital intestinal glands and passages. At this point food starts turning into poison.

Today one third of the Western civilisation is diagnosed as suffering from intestinal problems, yet it is estimated that over two thirds are afflicted. The small intestine, having the diameter of a large toe, is the most hidden organ in the body and has no direct contact with the outside world. The mental counterpart of this part of our body is what we may be called "the unconscious." Its stored memories and emotions can exert great influence and power over our present thoughts, emotions, desires, and behaviour.

It is not surprising therefore, that orthodox medicine considers the origin of the "Irritable Bowel Syndrome," which is the general term used for most intestinal diseases, to be psychosomatic, i.e., caused by the mind. In other words, if you feel constantly upset, angry, worried or simply unhappy, you are not only prone to suffering from "mental indigestion" but also from physical indigestion. Imbalances of the small intestines are associated with holding things in our "insides" where nobody can have access to, not even us. Since not only foods but also thoughts need to be digested in order to become useful for us (the cerebral cortex of the brain, which controls thought, is also related to the digestive process), undigested thoughts can have a "poisonous" effect. Anger, shock, anxiety, etc., may be locked up in the intestines for a long time and without any obvious indications of their presence. When they have reached a certain point of concentration, however, they can suddenly erupt and alter one's personality in a negative sense.

But the mind/body connection also works in the reversed order. When you eat highly processed, refined, and denatured foods, or your AGNI is low, the subsequent accumulation of toxic waste in your intestines can give rise to nervousness, hypertension, nervous laughter, and an emotionally volatile condition. As a generalisation, it can be said that retained toxins in the intestines are the physical counterparts of negative thoughts and negative thoughts generate their corresponding toxins. Normally, the immune system, two thirds of which are located in the intestines, takes care of both physical toxins and mental toxins (negative thoughts). It represents both our physical and mental healing system. However, the immune system can easily become overtaxed by overexposing it to non-nutritious foods and negative thoughts (stress), which may make us susceptible to disease, ranging from a simple cold to cancer.

The "Insignificant" Appendix and Its Important Role

In the purely physical sense, the parts of the immune system and lymphatic system that are located in the intestinal tract help detoxify anything harmful that comes along with the food. Through highly sophisticated processes they are able to separate useful nutrients from unusable waste matter. Most nutrients are passed through the walls of the small intestines into the blood stream, which carries them to the liver for further processing (metabolism). There are other specific nutrients, though, that can only be absorbed through the walls of the large intestines. They are meant for nourishing the nervous system and are therefore released, together with waste matter and water, into the ascending part of the large intestine, which is located just above the appendix.

In traditional Indian and Chinese medicine the appendix plays an extremely vital role: It supplies large quantities of friendly bacteria to neutralise harmful substances in faecal matter before its passage through the large intestines. For all practical purposes and supported by the cleansing action of the bile from the liver, the appendix is supposed to keep the colon "neat and clean." If large quantities of undigested and decomposed food reach this part of the intestines, congestion occurs. Congestion is followed by microbial infection, which can cause swelling and ulceration of the protective mucous membrane. If microbial growth increases, the appendix may become inflamed and endanger the healthy performance of the colon altogether.

Through a powerful wave called *peristalsis* faecal matter is moved upwards in the ascending side of the colon and then passes via the transverse and ascending colon into the rectum for excretion. Once there, the faeces stretch the nerve endings in the rectum walls and cause a reflex urge for a bowel movement.

The whole digestive and eliminative process -- from the ingestion of food to the bowel movement -- should approximately take 20-24 hours, depending on the type of food eaten and the time of consumption. However, this is no longer the case with the majority of the population. I have had numerous patients who reportedly had a bowel movement only once every two to five days. By contrast, many people have a bowel movement 3-4 times a day and in some extreme cases there may be up to 16 evacuations; they cannot keep the food in the body longer than from 3 to12 hours. Yet having regular bowel movements once or twice a day by itself does not necessarily indicate good digestion either. The following are descriptions of the main problems that arise from weak digestion and inadequate elimination.

Internal Pollution

Devitalised, processed, refined, canned, and other highly acid-forming foods and drinks such as chocolate, candy, cheese, meat, fish, coffee, alcohol, soft drinks, hallucinogenic and medicinal drugs, etc., can have a strongly irritating effect on the protective mucous lining along the entire alimentary tract, from the mouth to the anus. As these foods or drinks pass through the digestive system parts of them undergo chemical transformations known as fermentation and putrefaction. The resulting poisonous substances may injure the intestinal lining which, like the skin, is designed to protect our blood from becoming polluted.

Regular exposure of our "internal skin" to such acidifying and irritating components as, for example, the phosphoric acid contained in colas and other soft drinks can cause suppurating wounds in the intestines. As a by-product of repairing the damage, pus is formed. If removal of the pus from the wound is obstructed it may become septic and seep into the bloodstream. This is the beginning of an infection which, as in most cases, is *not* caused by bacteria but by the poison that attracts them.

So called *deadly* bacteria, which are involved in infections, can be found everywhere, on your hands, lips, hair, cups, cutlery, door handles, etc., but they remain harmless unless unhealthy habits or suppression of the symptoms of disease turns them into deadly weapons. Immunisation serums, for example, contain highly toxic substances that are meant to heighten our immune response. But instead, the ever-present deadly bacteria in our environment may mingle with the serum and cause such side effects as shock, convulsions, brain damage, and death. The bacteria are totally innocent unless they get something spoilt to "eat." Dogs and cats lick them from their wounds and once in contact with their mouth and stomach secretions, they are digested and are rendered harmless. We too are equipped with more weapons than we normally need to effectively deal with any amount of deadly bacteria. Healthy people kill off all bacteria and parasites before they even get a chance to do any harm.

But the story is very different when waste products from undigested food lingers in our intestinal tract longer than necessary. Food eaten too quickly, in between meals, late at night, or wrongly combined, lower AGNI, the digestive fire, and so do anger and fear. The deadly microbes, normally neutralised or kept in check by the friendly bacteria and the immune system in the gut, are then given the green light to spread freely throughout the digestive tract. After having found a fertile ground for increasing their size of population the harmful microbes turn everything into poison. This includes "cadaverine" and "putrescine" resulting from putrefied proteins, similar to those produced from decomposing cadavers.

This prompts the intestinal lining and intestinal lymph system, which harbour most of our immune cells, to absorb and neutralise the toxins. Yet the constant influx of toxins becomes overwhelming and lymph oedemas begin to occur. This causes swelling of the abdomen and lymphatic congestion in other parts of the body.

The swelling or inflammation of the intestinal lining and intestinal lymph is an emergency measure by the body to prevent the absorption of toxins into the bloodstream, which otherwise could endanger a person's life altogether. By desperately trying to protect the blood from being poisoned the body begins to harden the afflicted tissue. This is the first stage of ulcerative processes. If the unhealthy habits are continued, layer upon layer of hardened mucous creates further rigidity of the intestinal tract, which begins to obstruct blood circulation and slow down intestinal motion (peristalsis). This forces the food to stay longer in the body than it should. In due time it begins to decompose, produce smelly gases and lose moisture. This turns it into a sticky mass, which may in some cases become dry and hard. If large numbers of bacteria invades it, diarrhoea may result. First, there may be alternating constipation and diarrhoea and if the condition persists, frequent bowel movements and chronic diarrhoea may occur.

AMA – the Cause of Congestion in the Body

In the intestinal tract, mucous, toxins, and faecal matter mix into what Ayurveda calls *AMA* or *mucoid faecal matter*. The intestines begin to loose their natural shape as they gradually create pockets layers upon layers of obstructive *AMA* (see illustrations3&4). *AMA* is a breeding ground for parasites, microbes, and cancer cells. The intestinal immune system tries to destroy as much of the destructive material as possible but it eventually succumbs to the overload of toxins. This is when septic poison starts seeping into the blood stream. Appendicitis, diverticulitis, colitis, spastic colon, hernias, Crohn's disease, amoebic dysentery, and tumour formations are but a few symptoms directly related to the build-up and absorption of poisonous waste products in the intestines (see illustrations below).

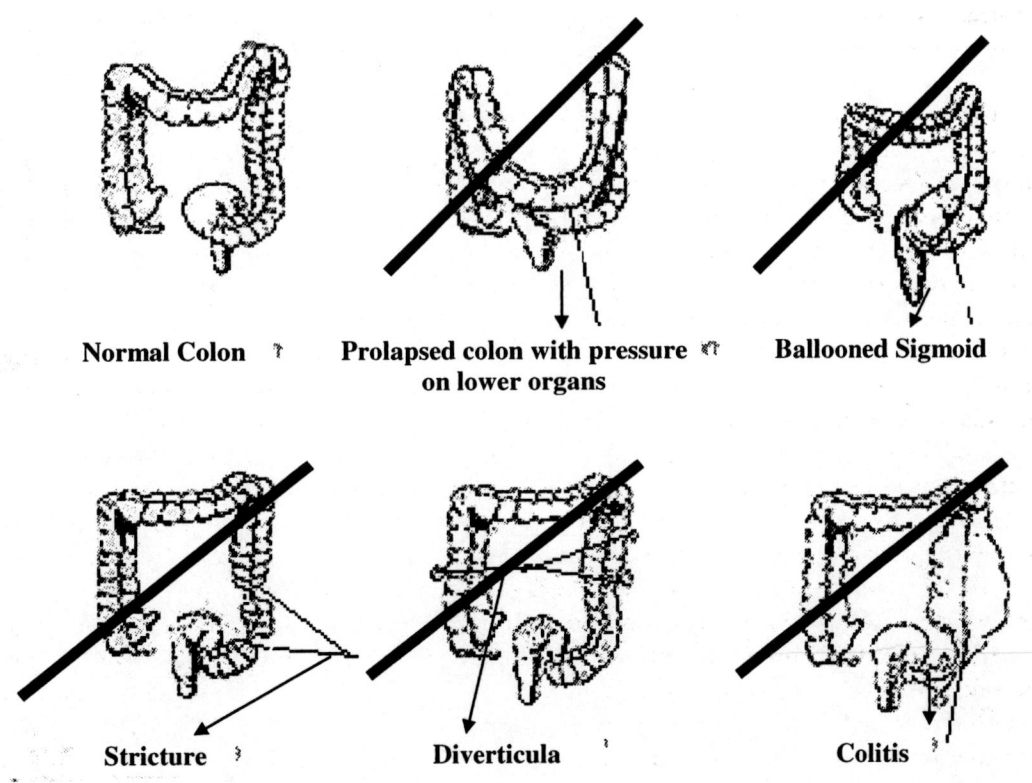

Illustration 4: Abnormal conditions of the colon

Consequences of an Overloaded Colon

The structural changes, which the intestines undergo to accommodate the mass of waste, are truly extraordinary. One particular autopsy revealed a colon of 23cm in diameter, filled with layer upon layer of encrusted old undigested food intermixed with hardened mucous, leaving less than 1cm for passing stool. Today there are numerous men and women who have gathered over 40 pounds of such waste material in the colon alone. Such a condition can be recognised in an enormously extended waste line. The waste accumulation may lead to a *prolapsed transverse colon* (see illustration 4) which in turn puts much pressure on the organs of the lower abdomen, including the bladder, prostrate, or female organs. As a result, these organs may get dislocated which causes them further structural and functional damage.

As toxins begin seeping through the colon walls and into the surrounding organs, more serious problems start to arise. Migraines, pre-menstrual tension, cramps, emotional instability, sexual problems, cysts, kidney and bladder infection, and cancer are but a few complications related to an overloaded colon. In fact, there is practically no chronic illness that isn't linked with an impaired colon function. There are major neural reflex points situated on the bowel, which closely connect this organ with every part of the body (see illustration 5). To whatever part of the colon *AMA* begins to attach itself, its corresponding part in the body becomes afflicted with illness.

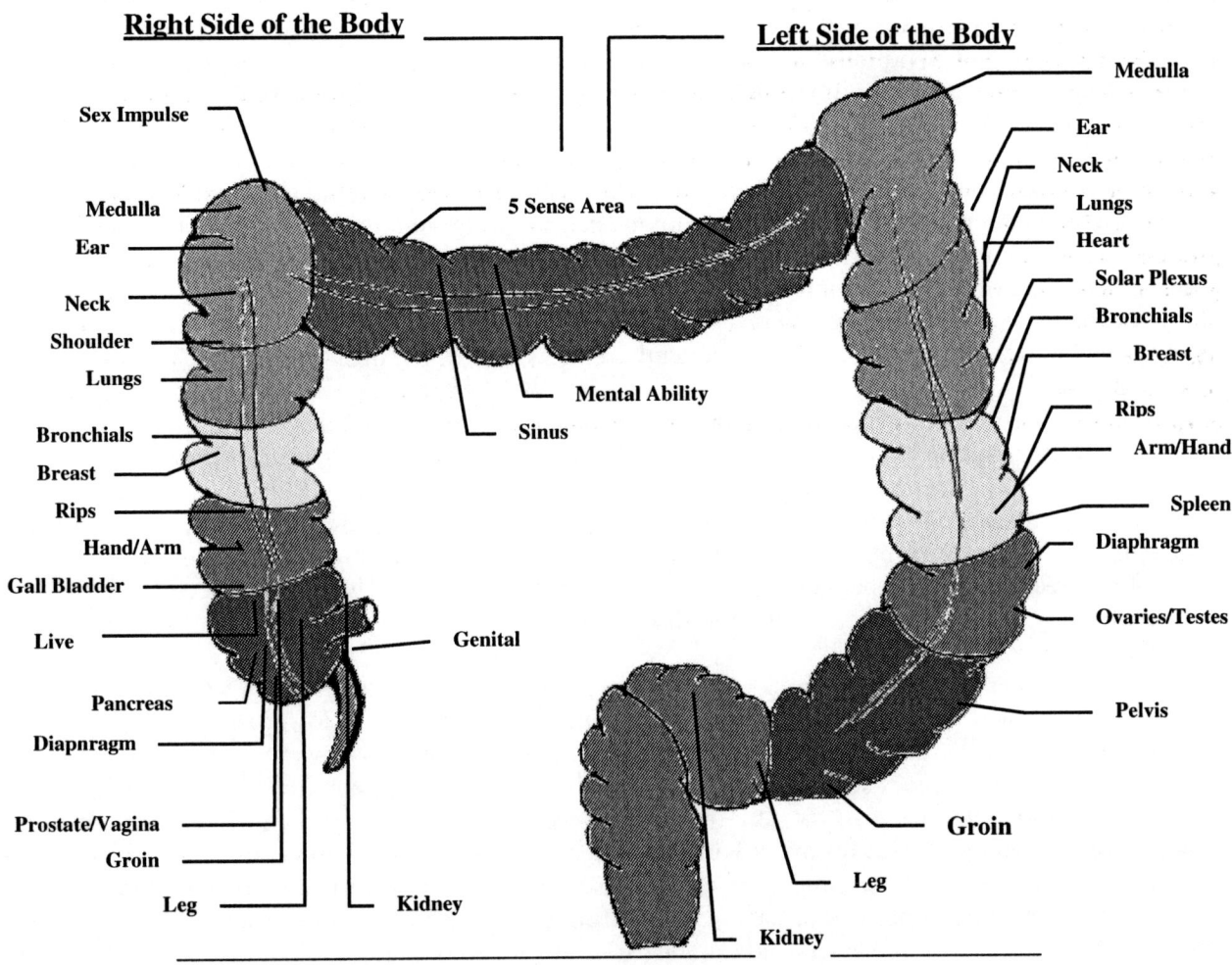

Illustration 5: Bowel Reflex Points

For example, if the middle part of your transverse colon is chronically congested and weakened, sinusitis will result. As a person begins to accumulate toxic waste in the bent area of his ascending/transverse colon the functions of the right lung will be subdued. When this part of the bowel becomes constricted or spastic, the shoulders become rounded, the sex impulse diminishes, and migraines may occur. When irritating substances are present in the nearby area of the *medulla-colon reflex point*, nerve impulses pass to the *medulla oblongata* at the base of the head, stimulating its vital centres, one of which controls constriction and dilation of blood vessels. Initial pain causes constriction of blood vessels, whereas severe pain causes blood vessel dilation, a fall in blood pressure, and fainting. This results in poor circulation, especially in the hands and feet. Up to 80% of women in the first world suffer from mild or severe forms of migraine.

Other vital centres of the *medulla* include the *Cardiac centre* which control the rate and force of cardiac contraction; the *Respiratory centre* which controls rate and depth of respiration; and the *Reflex centre* which initiates the reflex actions of vomiting, coughing and sneezing.

If toxic waste is collected underneath the lung reflex point in the first part of the descending colon then heart problems are likely to manifest. Accumulation of toxic waste in the lower part of the ascending colon irritates the reflex points of liver and gallbladder which can lead to contraction of the bile ducts and formation of gallstones.

The Spreading of Symptoms

Through excessive stimulation of the *bowel neural reflex points* symptoms of discomfort and disease may spread to other parts of the body and intestinal toxins can enter the blood stream. As a result, other organs of elimination and detoxification such as the liver, kidneys skin, lungs, and the lymphatic system may soon become congested and overtaxed, too, which causes further debility and weakness. The blood is meant to eliminate the body's own "natural" toxins generated through the daily destruction of billions of old cells, but this activity may be drastically reduced by an overload and congestion of the eliminative organs, hence the occurrence of a toxicity crisis. The liver happens to be the first organ that succumbs to the flood of toxins from the intestines. The bile flora begins to alter and stones are formed in the bile ducts. This hinders bile secretion and subsequently reduces AGNI, the digestive power. The vicious cycle is closed.

Medical intervention, which usually doesn't include cleansing procedures, can greatly interfere with the body's waste eliminating efforts. Pain reducing medication often leads to further pain and even death. The "alleviation" of the cough in pneumonia through drugs can be fatal, too. Removing a gallbladder that is filled with gallstones does not resolve the problem because the major bile ducts of the liver will remain blocked. This is hardly surprising when, as the medical journal *New Scientist* announced on the cover page of one recent issue, 80 per cent of medical procedures used today have never been properly tested. There are many other factors contributing to disease which cannot be treated away by taking a few drugs or having surgery.

The stress, tension, and exertion, for example, that may accompany a man's incessant drive for success, money, and power can deplete the vital energy of the body and lower the effectiveness of all organs and cells to the degree that they begin to suffocate in their own waste matter. Added to such dilemma, external influences such as changeable weather, change of season, travelling to other countries, mid-life transition, etc., can sap the little energy that is left in the body through its constant efforts to adapt to these changes. These normally harmless external factors may then become a trigger for serious crises in life. It is for these or similar reasons that so many people have respiratory trouble in polluted cities during the summer periods or catch colds during the change of seasons. They may have suffered from low physical energy and a depleted immune system long before falling ill.

All this can accelerate the ageing process quite rapidly since the cells and tissues in the body are no longer supplied with adequate nourishment, water and oxygen. Cancer and all other forms of chronic toxicity are, in most cases, a culmination of years of overuse or "underuse" of mind and senses as well as incomplete elimination of waste from the body. What is needed today, more than ever before, is a balanced lifestyle that helps maintain the vital energy of our body on a continual basis. Vital energy is made available throughout the body by the principal power of movement in our body.

Vata -- The Power of Movement

Ayurvedic medicine has always had a very thorough understanding of the human physiology and declared that the main cause of ill health and premature death is in the intestines. Ayurveda considers the colon to be an extremely important part of the body due to its vital roles of absorbing essential nutrients for the nervous system and eliminating waste material. Vata, one of the three principle forces (doshas) that regulate all the functions in the body, controls both these actions.

Vata translates as "air" or movement and is present in every part of the body. Think of your body being a network of channels, ducts, or pipes through which food, air, water, blood, lymph, and waste are passed continuously. The nervous system, circulatory system, lymphatic system, digestive tract, bronchi and lungs, hormonal pathways, and cellular connections are all part of this enormously complex network, sustained by the movement power of Vata. If movement stops due to an obstruction or blockage in an artery, or due to stones in the liver, gallbladder, or kidneys then symptoms of "dis-ease" are imminent, pain and fatigue being the most apparent ones.

Vata's main seat is in the colon. If the large intestine is clear of obstructions, *Vata* can exert its power in the rest of the body as well and all the systems can function at their best. On the other hand, a build-up of faecal matter and hardened layers of mucous in the colon (*AMA*) drastically slows down *Vata's* eliminative functions. Similarly, the accumulation of gallstones in the liver and gallbladder hinder *Vata's* transportation of bile and thus impair AGNI, the digestive fire. This further increases the retention of harmful substances in the colon. Consequently, healthy cells no longer have enough "space" to breathe and live and are often replaced by toxic undigested food residues.

Solving the Mystery of Back Problems

Waste retention also affects the strong muscles of the ascending and descending colon. One of their functions is to help the body maintain a normal body posture. Insufficient blood and energy supply of the colon muscles makes them loose and weak. Consequently, as the spine begins to curve abnormally, the body posture changes abnormally or collapses altogether. The lower spine in particular is pulled forward by the extra weight of the waste material in the intestines (see illustration 6). These spinal sections become major stress points for the body weight and can therefore cause severe low back problems as well as pain in neck and shoulders. Lifting heavy objects or bending to the floor can then easily dislocate discs. In many cases, the urinary ducts (ureters) are pressed upon by the enlarged colon and pushed out of their normal position. This may lead to retention of urinary deposits causing sharp and excruciating pain.

The second most common cause of back problems is gallstone formation in the liver and gallbladder. AGNI, the digestive fire is fuelled by bile; anyone who accumulates toxic waste in the colon also suffers restricted bile flow due to gallstones. The two disorders go hand in hand. As the gallstones increase in size and number, the liver and gallbladder become enlarged and exert pressure on the surrounding organs and parts of the body. Because the liver spans almost the entire width of the body, when enlarged, it restricts the movement of the diaphragm and reduces the breathing capacity of the lungs. The restricted breathing forces the lungs to retain excessive amounts of the very acidic gas, carbon dioxide. The lungs respond by producing more mucous to deal with the toxins, which causes lung congestion. The resulting accumulation of mucous, dead cells, and metabolic waste eventually expands the lungs towards the back and in some extreme cases also towards the front. The back and shoulders begin to become rounded and hard as is often seen among the elderly and more recently among teenagers. There may be pain in the upper back, neck, and shoulders.

The presence of gallstones in the gallbladder can have an additional effect. If the gallbladder which is attached to the back of the liver, is filled with gallstones the body begins to adjust its posture to ease the pressure that the gallbladder exerts against the surrounding tissue and the spinal column. The result is *scoliosis,* a common phenomenon among both, the young and the old. The right shoulder may drop and the left shoulder move up, and even the left rip cage may begin to protrude. There may be pain between the shoulder blades and a strong but dull ache in the middle upper back area while standing up. The right shoulder and arm may become stiff. Frozen shoulder and tennis elbow are clear indications of gallstones. If gallstones gets stuck in one of the major bile ducts, there is strong, sharp pain around the area of the right shoulder, which may spread towards the entire back region. Breathing becomes difficult at this stage as it can trigger spasmodic pain attacks. All this can produce permanent back problems.

Over 60 percent of Americans are estimated to have back problems. About the same percentage of Americans is overweight, which means that their digestive functions are seriously malfunctioning. If you are among the sufferers of back pain and consider having surgery, you ought to be aware that more than two thirds of back pain sufferers who receive surgery for their condition end up with more pain than before. Unless the chunks of toxic waste are removed from the colon and the liver and gallbladder are free of gallstones, the cause for back pain is most likely to remain the same. These obstructions disrupt the flow of energy up and down the spinal nerves, contributing to problems such as slow circulation, numbness, and pain in the legs.

A third major cause of back problems is dehydration, caused by stimulating (diuretic) foods or drinks, such as meat, coffee, tea, soft drinks, alcohol, etc., and/or inadequate intake of plain water. The water volume that is stored in the disc-core of the spine supports over 75 per cent of the weight of the upper body. Both restricted water supply and increased retention of waste in the intestinal tract deplete the spinal water and the water contained in the disk cartilage and surrounding back muscles, leading to thinning of the intervertebral disks and subsequent muscle spasms.

Back problems are complex problems only as long as we don't take care of the most basic needs of our body. Unless a back injury has occurred due to an accident, back problems can be permanently resolved. The following are simple solutions to the most complex back problems: giving the body sufficient amounts of water to drink; eliminating all gallstones from the liver and gallbladder; dissolving all kidney stones if present; removing all accumulated waste materials from the intestinal tract (how to do all this is explained in the following chapters). Resolving chronic back pain can mean a new lease of life for millions of people.

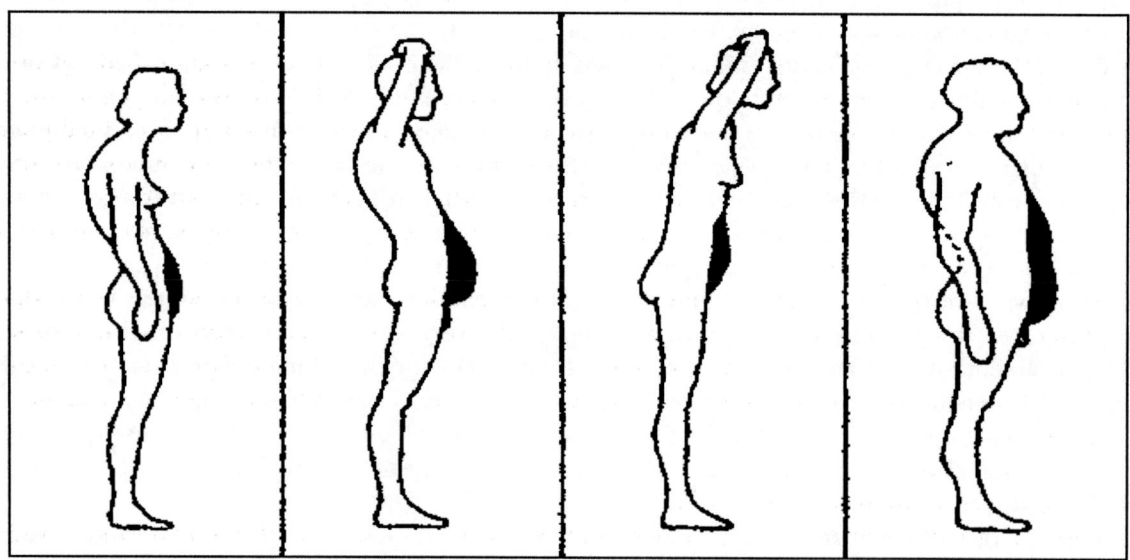

Illustration 6: Abnormal Body Postures

When the River takes a *U-turn*

While digesting a main meal, the body generates 10 litres or more of different kinds of gases to help trigger the peristaltic movements necessary for the transport of food and waste. Once the task has been accomplished the blood stream takes the gases to the lungs for elimination. But if the colon fills up with toxic waste material, the "downward" movement of *Vata* is obstructed and starts reversing. Instead of eliminating all the waste matter through the rectum and anus, *Vata* practically takes a U-turn and moves parts of the toxic mass in the opposite direction.

Any impediment in any section of the intestinal tract acts like a dam that hinders the flow of food, waste, blood, lymph, and gases. The most severe form of obstruction is known as constipation. Constipation leads to a reversed flow of the intestinal content and lymphatic waste. This forces minute toxins, harmful bacteria, mucoid faecal matter and toxic gases all the way into the upper parts of the digestive tract, causing a kind of traffic jam. This chaos can be felt as flatulence or intestinal swelling, cramps or simple discomfort. Flatus is comprised of over 250 gases, of which hydrogen is the most common. It results when bacteria feed off undigested carbohydrates, especially those found in whole grains and beans.

The build-up of internal pressure blocks lymph flow, generates lymph oedema and moves irritating toxins right into the duodenum, gallbladder, and pancreas, thereby disturbing AGNI, the digestive fire even further. Lymph drainage in these organs becomes impaired causing impairment of organs and further digestive problem. This in turn increases the build-up of faecal matter in the colon and gallstones in the liver. Food, instead of providing energy and nutrients, is increasingly converted into fat and waste.

The Force of Pitta Energy

The area between the duodenum and the beginning of the colon is mainly controlled by the energy of *Pitta*, which is the second *dosha*. *Pitta*, which is the Sanskrit word for bile, controls AGNI and is in charge of digestion and metabolism. *Pitta* ensures that food nutrients are properly absorbed and converted into the basic compounds needed to construct new cells and tissues. When *Pitta* (bile flow) is disturbed at its main seat where gallbladder and pancreas meet and connect to the duodenum, then all the metabolic processes in the body are disrupted as well. In such case, nutrient absorption is insufficient and the body suffers malnutrition, although the afflicted person may be eating well or is overweight.

If intestinal toxins and other waste fragments as well some of the bile released by the gallbladder are pressed further up toward the stomach they may seep into the pancreatic duct and from there into different parts of the pancreas. Subsequent blockage of the pancreatic duct may cause pancreatic infection and even diabetes. A continued and drastic reduction in the amounts of secreted of bile and digestive enzymes can lead to obesity, heart disease, and cancer.

Kapha – Cohesion, Structure and Strength

The third principle force that controls our body is *Kapha*, which stands for cohesion, structure, stamina, and strength. *Kapha* governs the digestive fluids and forms the connective tissue, muscles, fat, bones, and sinew. *Kapha* also lubricates the joints, generates the mucous lining in the mouth, throat, lungs, stomach, and intestines, and holds the body together. Without the cohesive properties of *Kapha*, the body would be a pool of disconnected cells spread on the ground.

Kapha becomes aggravated when the reversed movement of the *Vata* force reaches the *pyloric sphincter* -- the "door" between stomach and duodenum. Reflux of bile from the gallbladder, toxins from the intestines, and in some rare cases even faeces, may be pressed through the *pyloric sphincter* and move into the stomach, triggering spasmodic constrictions and pain. There may be various types of stomach disorders depending on the type of toxins and microbes and other factors such as stress and the quality as well as quantity of the food consumed. To protect the blood against the irritating substances, the stomach secretes large quantities of mucous, which is a natural reflex to absorb and remove them.

If the situation continues the stomach lining becomes damaged and dehydrated in places, exposing it to the destructive action of hydrochloric acid. The stomach cells absorb toxic hydrogen ions, which increases their internal acidity, disrupts their metabolic processes, and triggers inflammatory reactions. This is known as acute gastritis, which can become chronic and lead to peptic ulcers and even malignant tumours. The disruption of Kapha in this part of the body can greatly undermine psychological balance and happiness.

Vitiating the *Doshas*

Symptoms include: Bad breath, colds, cough, bronchitis, asthma, pneumonia, low immunity, hay fever, allergies, chronic illness.

The disturbed and restricted movement of *Vata* in the intestines does not only disrupt *Pitta-dosha* residing in the middle of the body, but also *Kapha-dosha* which controls the production of digestive juices (except bile) and mucous. *Kapha's* main seat is in the stomach and the chest. The more toxins build up in the intestinal tract the less efficient becomes the drainage of lymph from the organs of the pelvic area. Suddenly, symptoms of dis-ease may begin to appear everywhere in the body. As the noxious substances, microbes, and harmful bacteria are pressed further upward through the alimentary tract and the main lymphatic duct (thoracic duct) the bacteria acting on the waste begin to produce toxic, bad smelling gases, commonly referred to as "bad breath." Some of the gases may also enter the blood, which takes them to the bronchial system and lungs, causing irritation to their protective mucous lining.

The failure of the (blocked) lymphatic system to remove metabolic waste material from the respiratory organs can cause a variety of symptoms. If the trapped toxins begin mingling with internally residing germs the body's first attempt to remove some of them is through a cold or a cough. However, if such release mechanisms are suppressed through medication or worsened by congesting foods or stress, the mucous lining begins to thicken further. This causes breathing difficulties, bronchitis, and eventually asthma. (**Note**: asthmatics hyperventilate mainly because of the lack of normally present carbon dioxide in the lower lobes of the lungs; by breathing in a very shallow, slow way, the amount of carbon dioxide increases and the asthma attack can be prevented. To cure asthma, however, the whole body must be decongested). Pneumonia and other respiratory infections result when certain microbes, which are permanent and normally harmless residents in the lungs, have found a fertile ground in the congested environment and begin to spread unhindered. The supply of oxygen and water to the lungs, heart, liver, kidneys, stomach, intestines, and all other parts of the body become increasingly scarce. Consequently, the body can no longer guarantee the efficient elimination of carbon dioxide and other metabolic waste as well as decayed cellular components from the cells and organs.

The bronchial system and the lungs attempt to remove some of the excessive mucous by coughing it up into the throat. Chain smokers especially have this problem early in the mornings. Other people may accumulate upward moving or retained toxins in and around the thymus gland, which is in charge of activating immune cells, thus weakening the natural defences of the body against cancer, bacteria, parasites, and viruses. It is to no avail to treat a nose catarrh as a localised disorder. A cold represents the body's need to rid itself of toxins that have spread everywhere. If such toxicity crises occur more frequently, the mucous membranes may become very sensitive to dust and pollen, which can cause sneezing attacks, bronchial spasms and constant watering of the eyes -- typical symptoms of hay fever.

All toxins have a dehydrating effect because the body's cells have to give up precious water to remove them. Allergies (and also asthma) indicate that the body has increased its production of *histamine*, the neurotransmitter responsible for regulating water metabolism, water distribution, as well as antibacterial and anti-viral activities. In a well-hydrated body foreign agents such as bacteria, viruses, chemicals, and proteins as contained in pollen, are neutralised easily without the need to raise *histamine* levels to an exaggerated level.

Histamine activity becomes exaggerated when the body becomes dehydrated, which may occur due to the presence of toxins or insufficient water consumption. This is the time when the body may become sensitive to all sorts of allergens, including the potassium of orange juice. In asthmatics, the exaggerated release of *histamine* promotes bronchial constriction. Once their dehydrated bodies receive the normal daily amount of water, and existing toxins, including gallstones from the liver, are removed, *histamine* production decreases and bronchial constriction begins to lessen. To permanently stop an allergy, though, it may be necessary to delete the memory of the immune cells to produce antibodies upon contacting normally harmless allergens (foreign agents). To restore the body's balance, it may be necessary to neutralise all existing allergies, including the hidden ones, against foods, chemicals, metals, etc. (for details see "Useful Self-help Programmes" in Chapter 7).

If the body continues to accumulate toxins faster than can be removed it may eventually become "tolerant" towards them. In other words, we can "get used" to drinking alcoholic beverages, smoking, eating too much, and wearing ourselves out without developing any signs of major discomfort, but this only means that the body has ceased to respond to the build-up of toxins. Becoming increasingly debilitated, the body may then have fewer (minor) toxicity crises than before; colds and fever now fail to come.

But that's when the real trouble begins. The body is forced to mobilise more and more phlegm to deal with the massive amounts of toxins and begins to congest even more. The natural signals of intact self-defence mechanism fail to alert the person about the imminent danger of permanent damage. This is the beginning of chronic disease. What was an acute cold before may now become chronic bronchitis, pneumonia, a stomach ulcer, chronic cystitis, syphilis, Alzheimer's, MS, heart disease, or cancer. Diagnosing and treating cancer, for example, as an isolated, independent disease is as illogical as blaming a cat's tail for an infection in her ear. Those who keep suppressing their bodies' cleansing reactions such as an infection or a simple cold hurt themselves more than they know. They are sowing the seeds for a vicious cycle of ill health.

When *Vata* "Hits the Top"

Symptoms include: Cardiac Arrhythmia, weight loss, muscle wasting, hot flushes, weight gain, nervousness, mental stress, thyroid problems, protruding eye balls, metabolic disorders, weight gain, ear infection, meningitis, deafness; throat, teeth, and sinus problems; eye trouble, headaches.

When the "river of toxins" reverses into the upper parts of the body its more sensitive areas become afflicted too. With the blocked downward movement of *Vata*, toxins begin to move into the thyroid gland. The lymph ducts in charge of draining metabolic waste from the thyroid fail to do so. Lymph nodes begin to swell up and the thyroid becomes larger. Failing detoxification of the thyroid gland results in *thyrotoxicosis*. High toxicity in the thyroid gland may lead to *cardiac arrhythmia* as the heart becomes over-stressed by trying to supply extra oxygen and nutrition to the hyperactive body cells. Further symptoms may include abnormal weight loss, muscle wasting and weakness, excessive heat production, redness of chest, neck, and face, and hyperactivity of the nervous system, which causes nervousness, physical restlessness, and mental stress. In some cases the eyes begin to protrude due to the deposition of excess fat, dead protein, fibrous tissue, and other toxic material in and behind the eyeballs. The internal pressure causes staring and rigidity of the eyes and other problems of vision. If the thyroid's hormone production is low, as often occurs in unbalanced *Kapha* body-types (see section on body-types), then the metabolic rate drops causing weight gain and slowing of mental activity. In such case, the body feels cold even when the environmental temperature is high.

Most ear problems occur when due to lymphatic blockage metabolic toxins are not properly drained from the chest and head area and other noxious substances from the gastrointestinal tract are pressed into the auditory (Eustachian) tubes. Microbes from an upper respiratory tract infection may then cause painful ear infections, accumulation of pus, and if wrongly treated, tumour formation, meningitis, and other brain disorders, and even loss of hearing. If you experience liquid coming from your ears or a swelling near the ears, then you need to start cleansing procedures straight away (see chapters 6&7).
Note: The ancient technique of *Ear Coning* can quickly drain old wax, fungus, and toxic residues from the ears and open the lymph ducts for improved drainage.

If the body is well hydrated and not interfered with, it will provide extra amounts of liquid and mucous to prevent the toxins from entering the blood stream. Any form of intervention in this very delicate area of the body should be handled with utmost care as it may damage the sense organs of sight, hearing, smell, taste, and touch.

Most people rarely take teeth problems, tonsil infections, sore throat, stiffness of neck and shoulders, hoarse voice, broken speech, nose and sinus congestion very seriously. Yet these "minor" complaints can be the harbingers of circulatory problems and even brain tumours. Constant presence of toxins in the nasal area can lead to the enlargement of nasal bone or cartilage, which can lead to hay fever. Sinus headaches, weak eyesight, sore and swollen or puffy eyes, and general headaches are also directly related to a build-up of toxins caused by lymphatic obstruction and reversed movement of *Vata*. The names that describe these various symptoms are not relevant. But it is important to know that all these symptoms are indications of the body's attempt to eliminate toxins that have accumulated at these various locations. The blockage of *Vata* activity, i.e. the movement of air, water, lymph, blood, waste, etc., is the common factor in every toxicity crisis.

The crisis occurs when none of the three *doshas* are capable of conducting their assigned functions properly. Forced out from their respective abodes, *Vata, Pitta,* and *Kapha* become vicious and destructive. By suppressing or combating the various symptoms of discomfort or disease, they become even more unbalanced. The use of drugs, which aims at relieving a symptom may cause long-term damage to the physiology and is best used only as a last resort.

Any successful approach to healing must be based on balancing the three *doshas Vata, Pitta,* and *Kapha*. Once settled in their respective, rightful places, they ensure that the body operates with utmost precision and efficiency. All the channels of circulation are clear, digestion is strong, and elimination of waste matter is smooth, complete and friction free. This allows the body to give continuous nourishment to all its cells and tissues. The result is uninterrupted health and youthfulness throughout life.

CHAPTER 5

On the Road to Good Health

Wonders of our Biological Rhythms

Our body is run by a large number of "biological clocks." All organs, systems, and cells follow exact, cyclic patterns of rest and activity. For example: Menstrual cycles repeat themselves every 27 ½ days; the stress hormones *adrenaline* and *cortisol* are naturally released into the blood stream at the early morning hours to promote physical activity; immunity and iron levels are lower in women around menstruation and highest during ovulation; the liver is more active during the night than it is during the day; red bone marrow produces more blood cells during the night; most digestive enzymes are secreted during the day; different types of cells have different life-spans and are turned over at specific intervals; the "happiness" hormone *serotonin* is only produced during daylight; by contrast, *melatonin*, the sleep-inducing hormone, is secreted in response to the darkness of the night. Is estimated that there are over 1,000 such biological rhythms in our body.

The Human Body Clock
Each biological clock, which dictates a specific rhythm or cyclic behaviour to a group of cells, an organ, or an endocrine gland, is connected to a common master clock. The master clock co-ordinates all these different individual clocks with each other and makes certain that everything in the body is carried out according to its master plan, which is to maintain perfect equilibrium or balance.

This body's master clock itself is controlled by nature's most influential cycle known as the circadian rhythm, gearing us to become active in the morning and to wind us down in the evening. The sun is the main giver of life on the planet. Both, organic and inorganic life forms require sunlight or sun energy for their existence, and so do human beings. The movements of the Earth around its axis and around the sun create the precise cycles of day and night, as well as the seasonal changes which in turn programme our DNA to conduct all physical activities with perfect precision and at the right time.

All external events that take place in the natural world also take place in the body. A sunrise, for example, triggers a "sunrise" in our body to wake us up and get us going. The morning light begins to enter our eyes as soon as we open them. After the light is broken down into its full colour spectrum (seven colours) by the lenses of our eyes, the various light rays continue to travel to the body's master gland, the hypothalamus. The hypothalamus controls the body's biological clock and dispatches light-encoded messages to the pineal gland, which is often referred to as the "third eye." These messages contain specific instructions for the pineal gland to secrete some of the most important hormones. One of its most powerful hormones is the neurotransmitter *melatonin*. The secretion of *melatonin* follows a regular 24-hour rhythm. *Melatonin* production reaches peak levels between 2am-3am and drops to its lowest levels at midday. The pineal gland secretes this hormone directly into the blood stream, which makes it instantly available to all the cells in the body and informs them about "what time it is."

The brain synthesises another important neurotransmitter, *serotonin*, which relates to our state of well being and has a powerful influence on our day and night rhythms, sexual behaviour, memory, appetite, impulsiveness, fear, and even suicidal tendencies. Unlike *melatonin*, *serotonin* increases with the light of the day, and also through physical exercise and sugar. The increasing and decreasing levels of *melatonin* and *serotonin* indicate to the cells whether it is dark or light outside and whether they should be very active or slow down. This intricate mechanism ensures that all physical functions are synchronised with the rhythmic changes occurring in the natural environment. The health of each cell in the body depends therefore on regular exposure to the cycles of day and night.

Any deviation from the circadian rhythm causes abnormal secretions of the brain hormones *melatonin* and *serotonin*. This in turn leads to erratic biological rhythms, which can subsequently disrupt the harmonious functioning of the entire organism, including metabolism and hormonal balance. Suddenly, we may feel "out of tune" and become susceptible to develop a range of disorders from a simple headache or depression to a fully-grown tumour. The pineal gland controls reproduction, sleep and motor activity, blood pressure, the immune system, the pituitary and thyroid glands, cellular growth, body temperature, and many other vital functions. All of these depend on the regular *melatonin* cycle, which in turn is controlled by our attunement to nature's rhythms. The amount of *melatonin* available to the body depends on the concentration of *serotonin*, which is naturally high during daylight. *Serotonin* is broken down into *melatonin* as daylight diminishes.

If you make a good amount of *serotonin* from exposure to daylight, you will also produce sufficient amounts of *melatonin* during the night, provided your eyes are closed (when exposed to light, the pineal gland does not secrete *melatonin* in sufficient amounts). The secretion of *melatonin* starts between 9.30 - 10.30 P.M. (depending on age), inducing sleepiness. With a sufficiently high level of *melatonin* in the blood, the body is able to regenerate and rejuvenate itself. This sustains good health, vitality and longevity. The cycles of *melatonin* and *serotonin* depend on each other and are precisely controlled by our changing environment.

One of the greatest secrets of good health lies in the discovery of our intimate relationship with the universe. Any sense of separateness between nature and us can only exist in our mind, whereas the body has formed an inseparable and intimate link with the outer world. All its efforts are directed towards staying synchronised with our immediate and distant environment, including the moon.

Secrets of the Lunar Cycles

It is no longer a myth that also the moon has a strong influence on both the human being and nature as a whole. The ebb and flow of the tides, sleep walking, and the menstrual cycles are but a few of the countless phenomena that are stimulated and regulated by this powerful cosmic force. We are meant to use this force for our health, gardening, agriculture, and every area of human concern. Once you have discovered the secrets of the lunar cycles and synchronised your life and activities with them, you will greatly benefit from this newly created harmony with the natural world.

Human beings, other mammals, most birds and insects are subjected to this mysterious force of nature. All natural processes like pregnancy, the growth of plants and their ripeness, as well as the duration of various diseases, depend on the cycles of the moon. Our ancestors were masters of "right timing." Their heightened sensory abilities, perceptiveness, and exact observations of the phenomena in the natural world made them aware of the following points:

- Many events in nature -- ebb and flow of the tides, birth, weather, menstrual cycles in women -- occur in direct relationship with the movements of the moon.
- Animals synchronise their activities, i.e., searching for food, eating, mating, etc., with the position of the moon.
- Effectiveness and success of daily activities such as cutting of wood, cooking, eating, cutting of hair, gardening, applying manure, etc. are subjected to the cycles of the moon.
- Operations and use of medication are successful on some days and useless or even harmful on others -- often independent of dose and quality of the medication and the skills of the attending doctor.
- Plants and healing herbs are exposed to different kinds of energy on different days and contain considerably more active ingredients at certain times than at other times.

At the end of the 19th century, mankind at large was introduced to the clock as a means to know the time. The knowledge of the natural cycles of day and night and the changes in the positions of the moon and the stars was gradually discarded as "no longer necessary." The clock had "successfully" replaced the profound knowledge about these natural cosmic events and their effects on all the life forms on earth. The ancient wisdom that had upheld the natural ways of living throughout the centuries and had been passed on from generation to generation quickly turned into superstition. Yet today, there is a sudden and renewed interest in discovering our relationship to the lunar cycles. In relation to the Earth, the moon passes through the following major phases:

New moon

The moon revolves around the Earth almost every 28 days. While the moon is positioned between the Earth and the sun, we can no longer see it. This is called new moon. New moon can be likened to the phase of exhalation in breathing when we eliminate toxic gases and waste products from the body. You can prevent many diseases by fasting for a day at this time because the body is more than ready to purify itself from accumulated toxins.

New moon also signifies a new beginning and if you wish to give up old habits like smoking or drinking alcohol, this is the best time. You may try as hard as you wish to change such habits at other times of the month, but be disappointed about your inability to do so. The old saying, "well begun is half done" applies to new moon. A sick tree when cut back during new moon can regain its health and vitality.

The waxing moon

Only a few hours after new moon, we begin to see the appearance of its crescent in the sky. The journey to full moon takes about 13 days. Whatever goodness and nourishment is given to the body during this time will be much more beneficial than at other times of the month. This also explains why fertility is much more pronounced and more children are conceived and born during this phase of the moon and at full moon. On the other hand, it is very useful to know that when the moon increases the body's ability to heal after an injury or an operation decreases. (Even the washing of clothes is less successful during this phase despite using the same amounts of detergents.)

Full moon

After having completed half its journey around the Earth, the moon is full, i.e. visible to us at night, and sometimes even during parts of the day. This is the time when the moon exhibits a strong influence on all planetary life forms. Sleep walking, excessive bleeding of wounds, greater potency of herbs collected during full moon night, an increase in the number of accidents and violent crime, and a higher birth rate, are all effects of lunar changes. Cutting trees during full moon can destroy them.

The waning moon

During the following 13 days the moon is gradually overshadowed again. The ancient civilisations knew that this is a good time to have an operation (if needed) as the healing capacity of the body is steadily growing. If possible, book your visit to the dentist during this phase as tooth fillings, crowns, or bridges are less likely to last if they are given during the waxing phase of the moon. Also pulling a tooth should only be performed during the waning moon. In addition, at this time physical activity requires less energy and meets with greater success. The digestive system also works more efficiently, even to the point that eating a little more than usual will not increase weight.

Man's Biological Routine

Ayurveda, which means "The Science of Life," claims that "the Microcosm is as is the Macrocosm." In other words, our body is the mirror of the universe. At every moment the body undergoes profound changes by adjusting to a continually changing environment and recurring cyclic patterns. Ayurveda has a unique understanding of these cycles. It knows of three principal forces or energies, each of which emits a powerful influence on the body and mind for a period of four hours. These forces, which conduct all the complex activities in the human body as well as those that maintain the universe, are known as *Vata*, *Pitta*, and *Kapha*. So let us take a closer look at what happens in our body during a 24-hour cycle (see illustration 7).

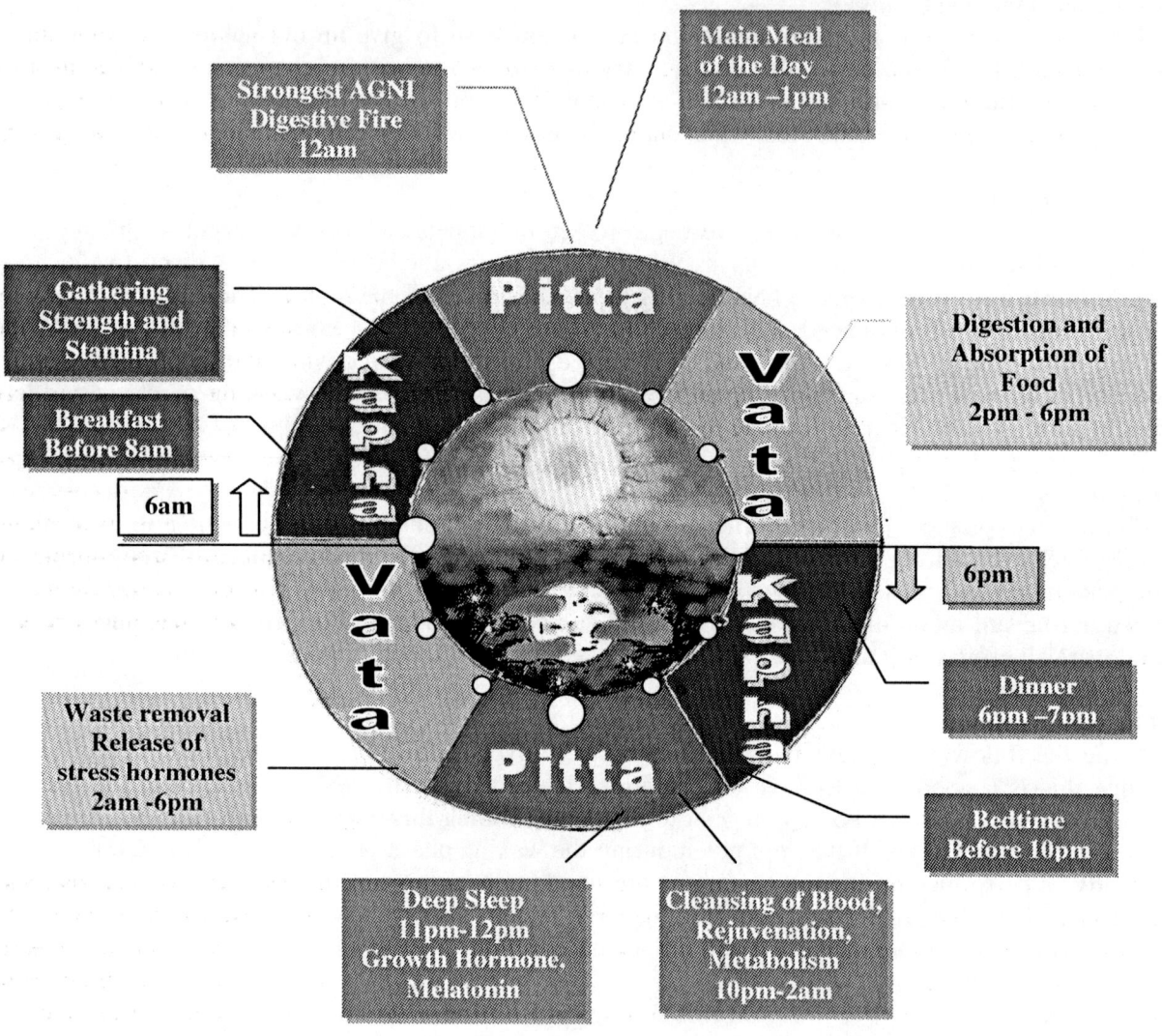

Ideal Routine:
1. Rise between 6am and 7am
2. Eat a light breakfast (optional) between 7am and 8am.
3. Eat the main meal of the day between 12am and 1pm.
4. Eat a light evening meal between 6pm and 7pm.
5. Go to sleep before 10pm

Illustration 7: The Biological Clock

The First *Kapha* Cycle

The first cycle begins with the "birth" of a new day. Let's assume that the sunrise takes place at 6am. At around 4.30-5.00am, nature starts to awaken and become increasingly active and the sun gradually rises to higher positions. Ayurveda calls the period between 6am and 10am "*Kapha* time," which means that our body is still a bit slow, but in the process of gathering strength and stamina. Whether or not you wake with an alarm clock, at around 6am the kidney glands secrete the stress hormones *cortisol* and *adrenaline* to get your body going, similar to a battery starting an engine. This is also the time when the sex hormones in the body reach their peak levels. And, provided your eyes actually see the natural light of the day, the brain increases its production of the powerful hormone *serotonin,* which in turn helps to generate happiness and enthusiasm. Since *Kapha* is composed of the heavier elements of earth and water, we exhibit more of the qualities of "earthiness" and "liquidity" in our mind and body during the early morning hours than, for example, during the afternoon.

The First *Pitta* Cycle

At 10am the heat of the sun begins to increase considerably due to its higher position, and sun energy distribution reaches peak levels at noon. Between 10am and noon we are at our most alert and cognitive best. The *Pitta* period lasts from 10am until 2pm during which the digestive power is at its maximum; its top performance is at around noon. Ayurveda, therefore, advises you to take your main meal of the day between 12pm and 1pm since this is the time of the day when AGNI (the digestive fire) is most pronounced, that is when the digestive juices (bile, hydrochloric acid, enzymes, etc.) are most concentrated and active. Provided the food is wholesome and nourishing, the digestive process will provide you with the energy and vitality you need during the rest of the day. If you feel tired and sleepy after the meal, this indicates that your AGNI is too weak to digest the food properly. Instead of becoming energised and revitalised through eating the body uses up its energy reserves to process the food and consequently remains with little energy for other forms of physical or mental activity. Sleepiness after a meal can have one or more of the following reasons:

1. Your meal is too heavy or consists of ill-combined food items.
2. You are not getting enough sleep during the night.
3. You are eating your lunch much later than one o'clock.

The First *Vata* Cycle

Vata or "movement" controls the hours between 2pm and 6pm. *Vata* conducts the physical transport of food through the intestinal tract and is responsible for absorbing the nutrients as well as taking them to the various tissues of the body. *Vata* can only perform well and on time if *Pitta,* which literally means bile, is allowed to act on the food early enough. If you eat your lunch, for example, as late as 2pm or 3pm *Pitta* becomes disturbed, which creates malabsorption - one of the main causes for nutrient deficiencies.

The *Vata* period in the afternoon is also conducive to efficient mental performance and study due to increased nerve and nerve cell activity. Therefore, this is a good time to absorb and retain information. Studies conducted at the University of Wales showed that students who had afternoon or early evening classes performed better in exams than those who had morning classes.

It may also be useful to know that going to the dentist in the afternoon is less painful than in the morning due to better neural performance. Malabsorption and problems of metabolism, on the other hand, become more apparent at this time. Increased irritability, nervousness, and cravings for sugary foods or other stimulants such as tea, coffee, cokes, chocolate, or cigarettes especially during the afternoon indicate that the body suffers from digestive problems and malnutrition.

The Second *Kapha* Cycle

Sunlight-energy drops considerably after 6pm and so does the *Vata* activity. This also is the beginning of the evening *Kapha* phase, which slows down digestion, metabolism, and physical and mental activities. Those who are in tune with their body cycles feel inclined to slow down when the *Kapha* qualities begin to dominate.

The digestive fire AGNI, which closely follows the positions of the sun, sharply decreases with the onset of darkness and it is for this reason that Ayurveda recommends you to eat only a *light* dinner, preferably at around 6pm. This gives you still enough time to digest before bedtime.

Research has found that most digestive enzymes are no longer produced after 8pm. A late dinner (after 7pm) therefore will not be properly digested and decomposes even while it is still in the stomach. Since the *Kapha* period, when the more "heavy" qualities are dominating in the body and mind, starts at 6pm and ends at 10pm it is best to go to bed and sleep before *Kapha's* influence actually stops. Most people feel sleepy or drowsy between 9pm and 10pm. This sleepiness or drowsiness results from the secretion of a natural tranquilliser that the brain makes when it needs you to sleep. According to researchers from Harvard Medical School, during sleep most of the brain cells are "turned off" by some chemical signal, sent out by a group of cells located in the hypothalamus which is considered to be the brain's brain. This "turning off the lights" lets us go to sleep.

It seems that *melatonin* has a considerable influence over sleep induction, too, since the more we secrete of it the more tired we get. Also, at about 9pm, immunity begins to fall as indicated by a sudden drop in the levels of *endorphins* and *corticosteroids* - the body's weapons against inflammation. During the Kapha period the body tries to save as much energy and physical resources as possible, for a very good reason.

The Second *Pitta* Cycle

The body "tempts" you to go to sleep before *Pitta* time returns for its second round in 24 hours. *Pitta's* influence starts at 10pm and lasts until 2am. During this time, the *Pitta*- energy is mostly in charge of cleansing, rejuvenation, and rebuilding the physiology. Particularly the liver, a *Pitta* organ, receives most of the *Pitta* energy and conducts an astonishing range of activities. By itself it has to cover over 500 different functions, which includes supplying vital nutrients and energy to all parts of the body, breaking down of noxious substances, and keeping the blood clean. The liver cells also produce bile at this time, which is needed to digest food, particularly fats, during the following day. One of the most important of its functions is to synthesise proteins, the building blocks of cells, hormones, and blood constituents. Because it is such an active organ, the liver uses a considerable amount of energy, has a high metabolic rate, and produces a great deal of heat. It is the main heat-producing organ of the body.

The liver requires all the energy it can get to fulfil its responsibilities. This can only happen though if you sleep during this time. Therefore, the *Pitta* energy should not be used for staying awake, eating, digesting, or for mental/physical activity. Instead, most of the available *Pitta*-energy should now be directed to the liver and also to the kidneys (also *Pitta* organs), which helps to keep the blood plasma pure and balanced and maintain normal blood pressure.

Although the brain makes up merely 1/50 of the body mass, it generally contains over one quarter of the body's entire blood content. However, during *Pitta* time at night, most of the blood located at the back of the brain descends into the liver for storage and purification. If you are mentally or physically active at this time, this cannot take place and the liver is unable to cleanse the blood sufficiently. This results in the accumulation of toxic material in the liver and blood stream causing damage to the capillaries, arteries, and eventually the heart muscles. Most heart diseases are the direct result of a sluggish liver, caused by retained toxins.

The most important processes of purification and rejuvenation occur during the two hours of sleep before midnight. Physiologically, there are two very different types of sleep, as verified by brain wave measurements. They are the *before-midnight sleep* and the *after-midnight sleep*. The first one involves deep sleep, often referred to as "Beauty Sleep," which lasts for about an hour from 11pm to midnight. During this time you enter a dreamless state of sleep where oxygen consumption in the body drops by about eight percent. The physiological rest, which you gain during this hour of dreamless sleep, is at least three times deeper than what you can get during the sleep after midnight when oxygen consumption in the body rises again.

Growth factors, commonly known as growth hormones, are also secreted profusely during the hour of deep sleep. They are responsible for cellular growth and rejuvenation. People age faster if they don't produce enough growth hormones. The latest "fashion" in the beauty market is to consume synthetic growth hormones which create "fantastic" rejuvenating results but also have devastating side effects, including heart disease and cancer. On the other hand, if the body makes them, at the right time and in the correct amounts, as it happens during deep sleep, they can keep the body vital and youthful at any age.

Deep sleep never occurs after midnight and it comes only if you go to sleep at least two hours before midnight. If you miss out on deep sleep regularly, your body and mind become overtired. This triggers abnormal stress responses in the form of constant secretions of stress hormones such as *adrenaline*, *cortisol*, or *cholesterol*. To keep these artificially derived energy bursts going, you may feel the urge to use such stimulants as cigarettes, coffee, tea, candy, cokes, alcohol, etc. When the body's energy reserves are exhausted chronic fatigue results.

Fatigue can be considered to be a major causal or contributing factor of today's health problems. When you feel tired not only your mind is tired; your body cells, your organs, your digestive system, etc., all are suffering from the loss of energy and are not able to function properly. When you are tired, your brain no longer receives adequate amounts of water, glucose, oxygen, and amino acids, which serve as its main food. This situation can lead to innumerable problems in mind, body, and behaviour. When you drive a car during the night for example, your body has to keep fighting the "sleepy" hormone *melatonin*, which naturally tries to keep your body at its physical lowest. According to research in the field of *chronobiology*, attention after midnight drops so drastically that your risk for making mistakes is so high as to cause an accident. Most one-way road accidents occur during nighttime and accidents are 20 percent more likely on the night shift in factories.

Doctors at the University of California, San Diego, have found that losing a few hours of sleep not only makes you feel tired during the next day but can also affect the immune system, possibly impairing the body's ability to fight infection. Since immunity diminishes with tiredness, your body is unable to defend itself against bacteria, microbes, and viruses and cannot cope with the build-up of toxic substances in the body.

Tiredness precedes any type of disease, whether it is cancer, heart disease, or AIDS. Most tiredness results from lack of before-midnight sleep. Any treatment of disease that does not include natural "deep sleep therapy" cannot lead to lasting success since the body's healing system itself, the immune system, depends on it to be vital and efficient.

Pitta, which controls *AGNI,* the digestive fire, also becomes disturbed when you regularly eat your dinner late or have snacks during *Pitta* (night) time. Consequently, Pitta will be disrupted also during lunchtime the following day, which causes further complications of the liver, spleen, gallbladder, stomach, and pancreas. The main principle at work here is that when you disturb or use up *Pitta* energy during the night, you disrupt all the *Pitta* functions and *Pitta* organs during the following day as well.

The Second *Vata* Cycle

The time from 2am to 6am is controlled by *Vata* which helps to move the body's waste products from the liver, the cells, the intestines, and all other areas of the body towards the organs and systems of detoxification and elimination. Thus, the lymphatic system neutralises toxic cell debris, microbes, worn out cells, and cells damaged by disease. While the rectum receives faecal matter, which triggers a bowel movement, the kidneys pass urine to the bladder, which causes urination. The skin also receives toxins that begin to surface at this time, hence the importance of washing or showering in the morning. The entire body is geared towards excretion of foreign, useless and toxic material (about 70% of the body's waste is eliminated through the lungs, 20% through the skin, 7% through urine, and 3% through faeces).

At the end of the *Pitta* period the body temperature begins to drop and phase out at 4am. After that it gradually rises again. Towards the end of *Vata* time when nature awakens, body temperature and stress hormone levels (*adrenaline* and *cortisol*, etc.,) have risen enough to start the day's work with a thorough clean out. However, the body has to be awake and in a vertical position to support complete elimination and cleansing. Ayurveda recommends that we get up preferably before sunrise or at dawn, but not after sunrise. Since the times of sunrise vary from season to season and country to country, *Vata* also undergoes certain fluctuations. Still, six o'clock is the most applicable and recommended time to rise for most people (with the exception of teenagers and adolescents whose melatonin cycle is slightly different and who may require about one hour extra sleep in the morning than adults do).

Using an alarm clock to wake up in the morning abruptly cuts down the gradual phasing out of the various, subsequently occurring sleep patterns and can cause irritability, headaches, and nervousness throughout the day. You may feel as if you haven't really woken up. The easiest way of controlling the waking times is to adjust the sleeping times in the evening. For example, if you require 8 hours of sleep to feel refreshed and rested in the morning you would greatly benefit from sleeping at around 10pm. If you need more hours to feel refreshed, then go to bed even earlier. Should you only require 7 hours of sleep then go to bed at 10pm and get up at 5am, an even better time for *Vata* to be effective. The bowel movement is the strongest type of movement in the body and requires a great deal of the body's energy, and needs us to be up and about bright and early. The old saying "early to bed and early to rise keeps a man healthy, wealthy, and wise" is perhaps the best advice available for anyone who seeks to improve his wellbeing.

The Risk of Deviating from Nature's Routine

Deviating from any of the natural rhythms on a long-term basis may disrupt the balance of our body and mind. For example, let us presume that you sleep until 8am. This means that the downward movement of *Vata* is not able to eliminate waste during its final most active moments, which are at around 6am. However, since *Vata* is still very powerful at this time its movement is reversed, similar to a river that is reversed by a dam, and part of the waste is reabsorbed. Also, some of the urine moves back into the kidneys and skin toxins enter the lymph and blood stream. As faecal matter moves back up into the colon, congestion occurs. Lymph ducts become obstructed, leading to oedema in the intestinal tract. Such lymphatic swellings can be felt, for example, as big hard lumps above or around the navel area. This greatly overtaxes the heart in its effort to maintain proper circulation. *Vata* pressure goes all the way up to the respiratory system and brain, leaving toxic deposits in these areas. This causes heaviness, dullness, and swelling of eyes and face.

All these symptoms of discomfort are *Kapha*-related because they occur during the *Kapha* period, which lasts from 6am to 10am. Ayurveda emphasises that sleeping during the *Kapha* period in the morning causes severe congestion, which can lead to respiratory and circulatory problems, both *Kapha* domains. Sleeping during the *Kapha* period can also result in dullness of mind, general heaviness, lethargy, and depression since *serotonin* levels are low due to the lack of exposure to sunlight.

A recent German study confirmed that rising late in the morning may even be a major risk factor for heart attacks. It has been known for a long time that more *people* die from a heart attack *at 9 o'clock on Monday morning* than at any other time. The German study, however, found that most of those who died from heart attacks, got up at around 7.30am, which is the Ayurvedic "danger time." If "oversleeping" becomes habitual, the body cannot efficiently remove waste via the lungs, and other organs of elimination, leading to congestion and exhaustion of the heart.

Remember a weekend when you slept late and woke up late, how bad you felt, as if you were drugged; you felt sluggish enough to spoil the rest of the day. Another side effect that arises from sleeping into the *Kapha* period is that AGNI gets subdued, causing digestive problems. AGNI naturally increases with rising *seretonin* secretions in the morning. It is for this reason that we need to see the light of the sun when it rises. Since *serotonin* is closely linked to happiness and happiness is the main prerequisite of good health, it is obvious that exposure to natural light from dawn to dusk is one of the most important health promoting factors.

There is an old saying that may aptly summarise the reasons why all the ancient cultures in the world adhered to the circadian rhythms: "Early to bed and early to rise, makes a man healthy, wealthy, and wise". And I might add to that: "Early lunch and early dinner makes you a winner." Simply by adjusting these basic aspects of our daily routine to the timing of natural law, we are able to set the preconditions for healing, health, and happiness. Since the cycles of *Vata*, *Pitta*, and *Kapha*, are fixed by the circadian rhythms, we cannot create our own individual rhythms without struggling against the powerful stream of natural law. We may try to, but discomfort, disease, or even death may prevent us from doing so in the long run.

You may have experienced the phenomenon of *jet lag* when you travelled to far away places that are located in different time zones. Sunrise and sunset occurred at different times and upset your biological clock for several days before you were able to adjust to the new rhythms of nature. You might have felt hungry in the middle of the night, tired in the morning, and fully awake in the early morning hours.

There is one basic rule that applies to the experience of jet lag: For every hour of time difference, you require one day for adjusting your biological rhythms to the circadian rhythm in that particular part of the world to which you travel. After a maximum of ten days (for a 10 hour time difference), the cellular functions in your body will have returned to normal, provided you can adhere to the natural cycles of day and night prevalent at the new location.

Most people in the developed world create an "artificial" jet lag in their lives on a daily basis. They allow other factors such as working conditions, television, or social commitments to dictate to them when they should eat, sleep, and wake up, thus disrupting the body's natural links with the circadian rhythms. This in itself may be one of the most energy depleting influences of our time. I recommend every person who has a health problem to begin living in harmony with the natural rhythms of the body, to whatever extends possible. This will greatly aid the healing process and prevent illness from arising in the future. Being in tune with nature's rhythms is also one of the best insurance policies for healthy people to remain healthy. All it requires is to listen to and act upon the constant messages our body is sending us.

Listening to the Body

Like a switched-on radio receiver, our body continuously receives a vast amount of data and information from the external world. The earth, the stars, the sun, and all life forms constantly emit radiation, which our body registers and processes to ensure balanced functioning and a harmonious relationship with the environment. Everything radiates, including light, warmth, air, earth-electric fields, microwaves, magnetic fields, radioactivity, etc. In response to all these visible and invisible influences, the body produces concrete messages, which tell us what to do at what times. Sleep, hunger, thirst, and other natural occurrences in our body indicate that our "radio" is switched on and we are "in tune" with the natural world.

When we are no longer in tune with the outer forces such as the cycles of the sun and moon, we begin to fall ill. This means we need to take more self-responsibility, which requires commitment, self-appreciation, and love. These are the very same qualities perhaps that an illness can unfold in us. Instead of just dealing with the symptoms of a disease we may greatly benefit from locating its origin(s) because it can teach us much about ourselves. Although it is much more convenient to blame a virus for the cold we catch than to acknowledge that our irregular sleeping habits or eating junk foods may have something to do with it, there could be great learning for us in this. In truth, everything has a hidden purpose. It is not a bad stroke of luck that makes you fall ill. All forms of ill health serve as opportunities to learn more about yourself, your body, and your lifestyle. Illness can lead to a heightened state of awareness if seen as a challenge rather than just a nuisance.

It requires an open mind and heart to be able to listen to and follow the rules that nature has laid out for the smooth and effortless functioning of the body. To insist that everything needs to be explained scientifically before it is valid and worthy of consideration is not only impractical but also shows great lack of self-confidence. The messages that we can receive from nature are direct and need no intellectual interpretation.

We do not need to understand the exact mechanisms why the body sends us the signal of hunger when it requires food. All we need to do is to eat and experience how the hunger subsides. By habitually ignoring the natural urge to eat, your stomach, pancreas and small intestines may get "upset" and start adjusting to the new rule by keeping their production of digestive juices low, so as not to waste the body's precious resources. This is a common cause of indigestion.

On the other hand, if your stomach tells you that you are not hungry, i.e., that you don't require any food at the moment, but you still eat out of politeness or curiosity, the digestive system won't process the food. This is another cause of indigestion.

If you feel the natural urge to have a bowel movement, the body sends you in the direction of a toilet. If you disregard this signal because it comes at an inconvenient time, your body has no other choice but to hold on to toxic waste and to reabsorb water. This hardens the stool and leads to constipation, blood poisoning, and many other disturbances of the digestive system.

When your body feels tired and sleepy you have the natural tendency to lie down and sleep. However, a cup of coffee or a cigarette will give you enough *adrenaline* to keep you awake. If you ignore the body's sleep signal as a matter of routine, you may end up becoming hyperactive, unable to relax or sleep properly.

Ignoring the natural messages of the body lies at the basis of most illnesses today. To add to the already existing confusion of health matters, books, radio, television, and especially magazines, bombard us with advice and information on all the numerous diets, routines, and ideal lifestyle programmes that are "so good for us." For example, not long ago we were told that potatoes and pasta were among the most fattening of foods, whereas now nutritionists consider them good for slimming. Torn between various health doctrines, we look for perfect answers to our problems. At the end, when your body is exhausted while trying to adjust to one diet after another, we begin to realise that our requirements are totally unique and undergo constant changes, often from one day to the next.

If you are a sensitive person you must have noticed that at certain days or times you can digest a particular food item more easily than at other days. The same food can make you feel vital and energetic on one day and cause you an upset stomach, bloating and even cramps on another day. You may find that the same pasta dish may leave your stomach quickly after one meal whereas two weeks later the same dish will sit there like a rock and make you put on weight. The answer to this mysterious behaviour of the body lies in the continuous movement of the planets and their various positions.

Health Requires Natural Instinct

In 1984, Nobel laureate Carlo Rubbia proved that the human body is composed of mostly energy and only very little matter. To be exact, for each particle of matter there are 974.600.000 forms of energy (photons). In other words, only one billionth of our body consists of matter, the rest is vibrational energy. Since our body functions essentially in a quantum mechanical way, outer changes, such as sun storms, different weather conditions or the moon's passage through a particular zodiac (all these represent different energy states), can instantly trigger corresponding transformations within the body. As a result, the body sends us subtle signals or intuitive messages to say that its requirements for food, water, rest, exercise, warmth, coolness, etc., have changed. This however, requires sensitivity and wakefulness on our part. Both qualities are absent though, when we suppress our body's natural urges (hunger, thirst, defecation, urination, sleep, etc.), overload our digestive systems, and make ourselves dependent on other people's advice, however useful it may appear to be.

Any good system of health care can be recognised by one characteristic: It teaches you how to listen to your body and how to become self-dependent in knowing what is good for you at every moment in time. In any case, let experience guide you and find out what works for you and what doesn't. A theory alone does not make you healthy. As you begin to listen to your body you will find that its behaviour, activities and natural urges are far from being random or coincidental.

Health trouble begins when we doubt our body's ability to make the right choices, and this is exactly what we have learned to do, almost right from the beginning of life. Much of our natural instincts are subdued by man-made rules. They dictate to us our lifestyle, eating habits and times of eating, sleeping, and elimination of wastes.

If we keep ignoring the body's basic instincts, the mind begins to look for substitutes, which causes (legitimate) food cravings. A little attention on both the mind and body will soon tell you the difference. If, for example, your stomach is still full and you want to eat something, it is not your stomach that wants more food. It rather is your mind that is telling you that your body is no longer able to digest and assimilate foods properly and is consequently suffering from malnutrition. If your stomach is empty, and you feel hungry, ask your stomach what it really would like to eat. Since the body's nutritional requirements shift from day to day in direct response to changes occurring in the near and far environment; a set dietary plan can only confuse the body's unique and individualistic signals. To find out more about your body and its natural instincts it may be useful to discover your unique body-type.

Learning to Take Control

What Body-type am I?

One of the most important steps in the pursuit of good health is first to find out what body-type you are and second how your body-type can benefit from specific guidelines that may help you to recover your balance and vitality. Ayurveda recognises that every person has a unique psycho-physiological body-type that responds to specific foods, medicine, climate, seasons, stressful situations, etc., in a unique and specific way. There are no two people exactly the same because the three *doshas, Vata, Pitta,* and *Kapha* are represented in varied degrees in each person. This creates the individualistic qualities of looks and behaviour and different choices concerning the types of foods, colours, climate, and environment. Before we can restore balance of body and mind, we need to find out who we are in a psycho-physiological sense.

When we identify ourselves as *Vata*, *Pitta*, *Kapha* body-types we should keep in mind that no one constitution is better than another is. The three *doshas* are composed of the great elements of nature, *earth, water, fire, air,* and *space*. These five elements are *proto-elements*, which means they are energies vibrating at different frequencies. For example, the photons (particles of light) that are constantly generated in the air that surrounds you, have a different characteristic pattern of energy than the energy that is created by the particles sitting in a piece of clay or the water that flows in a stream. All existing matter, including your body, is a marvellous intermingling of these five elements or vibrational energies. In your body, these elemental energies are grouped together and represented as the three *doshas*, forming an inseparable link with the environment. The forces of nature work inside and outside and the more we recognise and realise their great powers within us, the more we tend to harmonise with the natural world. This harmony between the natural world and us makes good health a natural phenomenon.

Vata, *Pitta*, and *Kapha*, are the main principle forces or *doshas* that are in control of all life in the universe. At present they are greatly disturbed and cause havoc and turbulence, both within us and in our environment. By restoring balance of the three *doshas* in our body we automatically pacify the great elements that constitute our world. This is very necessary now since we need a healthy environment to become and stay healthy ourselves.

When *Vata* goes out of balance in nature, it causes earthquakes, droughts, hurricanes, and tornadoes. Disturbed *Pitta* generates heat waves and great destruction through fires. Irritated *Kapha* leads to excessive rain and flooding. In the body, an unbalanced *Vata dosha* causes gas, pressure, pain, dryness, shaking, and nervousness. If *Pitta* is disturbed, the body overheats, acidifies, or suffers from inflammatory diseases. An imbalance of the *Kapha dosha* leads to congestion in the stomach, chest and sinuses, as well as water retention. As we begin to create balance in our internal spaces, the external ones will also begin to shine more bright and become vital and fresh. The knowledge of our constitutional make-up will help us to structure a harmonious link with the constitution of our environment and derive all the benefits that nature can bestow on us on our journey to healthy living.

The human constitution is composed of all three *doshas* or dynamic forces of nature. Human consciousness chooses a unique combination of the three *doshas*, to carry out and fulfil its unique purpose in life. Working together in harmony, the *doshas* allow the individual to grow mentally, physically, and spiritually to the highest degree possible. Knowledge of the three *doshas* and their respective concentrations in the body can be very beneficial to self-discovery and health of body and mind.

There are ten basic body-types. Ayurveda defines them as single-*dosha* types, dual-*dosha* types, and sama-*dosha* types. Sama-*dosha* is the rarest of all and occurs when all the three *doshas* are present in equal proportions. Single-*dosha* types are also rare as hardly anyone is influenced by one *dosha* alone. The most common types are the dual-*doshas*. Each dual-*dosha* can contain various proportions of the two components. Thus, a *Vata-Pitta* type exhibits more air energy whereas a *Pitta-Vata* type has more fire energy. A *Kapha-Pitta* type is dominated by water energy with fire energy being the subordinate force. A *Vata-Kapha* type is more controlled by air energy with water and earth energies being secondary, whereas a *Kapha-Vata* type exhibits more water and earth principles with *Vata's* air energy as the subordinate force.

THE TEN BODY TYPES

**Single-*dosha* types*:*
Vata   Air/Space
Pitta   Fire/Water
Kapha   Water/Earth

Sama-*dosha* type
Vata-Pitta-Kapha   all elements equally present

Dual-*dosha* types
<u>*Vata-Pitta*</u>   1. <u>Air/Space</u>   2. Fire/water

Pitta-Vata	1. Fire/Water	2. Air/Space
Pitta-Kapha	1. Fire/Water	2. Water/Earth
Kapha Pitta	1. Water/Earth	2. Fire/Water
Kapha-Vata	1. Water/Earth	2. Air/Space
Vata-Kapha	1. Air/Space	2. Water/Earth

The following questionnaire will give you an idea of your particular traits and characteristics and the possible imbalances in mind and body. From there onwards you will be able to understand why each one of us has special needs and requirements and what we can do to meet all of them. Begin by answering all the questions for all the three *doshas*, then add up the numbers, and study the characteristics of the corresponding body-type. Keep in mind that your current diet and lifestyle may somewhat influence your evaluation. So to give more accurate results when answering the questions, take into account the past 10-20 years. You may also want to repeat the assessment after six months of implementing the Ayurvedic programmes. The results of your second evaluation will be more in line with your true body-type.

BODY TYPE QUIZ

Vata

1. I am generally a very active person, and my body movements are quick.
2. My memory retention is quite poor.
3. I am very quick to learn new things.
4. I am naturally enthusiastic, vibrant, and vivacious.
5. I am very tall (or very short), very thin, and I have difficulty in putting on weight.
6. My joints protrude and the tendons and veins in my hands and forearms are clearly visible.
7. My hair is generally dry, wiry, thin and dull.
8. I tend to be indecisive and hesitant when it comes to making choices.
9. I get easily constipated and cannot tolerate gas-forming foods such as beans.
10. I worry a lot even when there is no reason.
11. Under stress, I am nervous, agitated, restless, and even paranoid.
12. I tend to have cold hands and cold feet.
13. I love hot weather and sunbathing.
14. My skin is generally dry, dark, cold, leathery, and rough.
15. My eyes are narrow, small, and dull and tend to be dry and itchy.
16. My sleep is often disturbed and interrupted and I have difficulty in falling asleep.
17. I speak quickly and others may call me talkative.
18. Left on my own, I tend to skip meals and sleep at irregular times.
19. Being in midst of nature makes me calm, happy, and relaxed.
20. I make a good counsellor or teacher.

*Vata score*_____

Pitta

1. I am generally a very efficient, precise and organised person.
2. I tend to perspire profusely and sometimes have a strong, unpleasant body odour.
3. I prefer cool foods and drinks, heat irritates me.
4. I may retain water and have a puffy face, or swollen eyes.
5. I am quick to loose my temper and can be irritable, acidic and cynical.

6. I can get angry very easily but calm down quickly again.
7. I have a strong appetite and I often eat more than I need.
8. I feel uncomfortable when I skip a meal or if it is delayed.
9. I have very regular bowel movements and it is more likely for me to have loose stools than be constipated.
10. Impatience is one of my greatest weaknesses.
11. My body is medium built, athletically toned and of medium height.
12. My skin is yellowish/reddish, and is prone to freckles, moles, rashes, pimples, and sunburn.
13. I generally cannot tolerate foods that are hot and spicy but under stress I crave them as well as other intoxicating foods and drinks.
14. I am susceptible to early greying and baldness; my hair is thin, fine and straight and is red, blond, or sandy coloured.
15. My eyes are almond shaped, green, light brown, or hazel. My sclera (white of the eye) are sometimes yellow and bloodshed.
16. I am very competitive, success-oriented, and somewhat forceful.
17. I sleep for about six to eight hours and my dreams can be of violent contents.
18. Under stress I have the tendency toward ulcers, insomnia, diarrhoea, weight loss.
19. I tend to be critical of others and myself.
20. I believe myself to be endowed with intelligence, charisma, reliability, and even brilliance. I feel very comfortable in the role of leadership and I think am quite good at it.

*Pitta score*_____

Kapha

1. My body build is large, compact, and wide. My thighs, arms, buttocks, chest, and hips are big.
2. I prefer doing thinks slowly and methodically.
3. Although I have a soft, gentle and mellifluous voice, but it is often congested with mucous.
4. Friends refer to me as calm, placid, easygoing, or even "laid-back."
5. My sleep is deep, uninterrupted, and profound and I need eight to twelve hours to feel comfortable during the next day.
6. My skin is thick, oily, soft, smooth, clear, gleaming, cool, and has a somewhat pale complexion.
7. I feel better when I skip a meal occasionally.
8. I love hot weather and sunny days. Cold, damp weather bothers me.
9. My eyes are round, large, and clear with thick eyelashes. They are sensual pools of black or blue.
10. I walk slowly, with a measured gait.
11. I am a sweet-natured, affectionate, and forgiving person.
12. My hair is abundant, thick, blond, or black, and wavy.
13. I am physically strong, have good stamina, long endurance, and a steady level of energy.
14. When I am under stress, I tend to overeat, oversleep, feel groggy upon awakening, and am slow to get going in the morning.
15. My digestion and metabolism seem to be slow and I tend to feel heavy after eating.
16. I have a tendency toward mucous aggravation, phlegm, chronic congestion, asthma, and sinus problems.
17. I do not learn as quickly and as easily as some people but whatever I have learnt and understood is retained in my memory for a long time.
18. When I feel unhappy or stressed, I become narrow-minded, stubborn, neglectful, possessive, or attached.
19. I would love to do nothing and be lazy, but I am hard working.
20. I hold on to many things, including money, relationships, and excessive weight.

Kapha score _____

After adding up the numbers for all the applicable attributes in each section, compare the total scores for *Vata*, *Pitta*, and *Kapha*. If, for example, your totals are *Vata* 15, *Pitta* 12, and *Kapha* 4, then your body-type is <u>*Vata-Pitta*</u>. Should *Vata* be 3, *Pitta* 4, and *Kapha* 11, then you can consider yourself a *Kapha* type. It may be that your score for *Vata* turns out to be 10, for *Pitta* 19, and for *Kapha* 10, then your second *dosha* is not yet clear. Treat yourself as a *Pitta* type and take the test again six month later; you will then find that either *Vata* or *Kapha* has taken a clearer position due to the removal of impurities. In the rare case that your scores are something like *Vata* 13, *Pitta* 14, and *Kapha* 14, then your body-type is SAMA.

It is good to know that no one particular body-type is more advantageous than another is. A SAMA or *Kapha* type may have a stronger constitution, which seems to be more favourable, but he doesn't realise when he steps over the line; and when he is out of balance he is more slow to restore his health. By contrast, those with a weaker constitution like the *Vata* type are kept from making too many mistakes because of their aches, pains, and other minor problems.

The emphasis lies on making each body-type perfectly balanced and bringing out all its inherent, good characteristics. The different percentages and associations of *Vata*, *Pitta*, and *Kapha* in each person are responsible for structuring a unique individual. To give you an idea of the main characteristics of a *Vata*, *Pitta*, or *Kapha* dominated body-type, please see the corresponding lists below. Please try to remember that you are always a combination of *all* three *doshas*.

CHARACTERISTICS OF THE BODY TYPES

The *Vata* Type

Light, thin physique, narrow body frame; bent or irregularly shaped nose
Moves and performs activity quickly
Tendency toward dry, rough, cold, and dark skin
Aversion to cold weather
Irregular hunger and digestion
Light, interrupted sleep, insomnia
Enthusiasm, vivaciousness, imagination, perceptiveness,
spiritually inclined
Excitability, changing moods, unpredictable
Quick to grasp information, but also quick to forget
Tendency toward worry, anxiety, and restlessness
Tendency toward bloating and constipation
Tires easily, tendency to overexertion and hyperactivity
Mental and physical energy comes in bursts
Low tolerance to pain, noise, bright light

Illustration 8: The Vata Type

The basic theme of the *Vata*-type is "**changeable.**" This characteristic is natural to *Vata* as it is composed of the elements of air and space. *Vata*s dislike any form of status quo. They love excitement and constant change and if that is not available to them, they create an irregular lifestyle, e.g., each day a different bedtime, skipping meals, etc. Their unpredictable nature makes them among the least stereotyped people.

Vata types often feel isolated and awkward when they have to stand up against the earthy *Kapha* type or the intensive *Pitta* type. But their "airy" flair, mobility and vivacious nature inspires particularly *Pitta*s and *Kapha*s who lack these qualities. *Vata*s look elegant when they are dressed-up. Clothes fill their need for insulation and confidence; their dry, lean, and "hungry" look is ideal for modelling, a reason why most high-fashion models are *Vata*s. Physically, *Vata*s are the thinnest of all the body-types; their shoulders and hips are narrow and often rounded. Some *Vata*s are chronically underweight, and despite eating large amounts of food, they do not put on any weight at all. Other *Vata* types are thin in their youth and become overweight in middle age.

*Vata*s are the most likely to have physical irregularities among all the body-types. Some *Vata* types have hands or feet that are too large for their small body, or too small; their teeth may be protruding or very small. *Vata*s may be well shaped but under stress and when constipated they are prone to develop spinal curvature (scoliosis) or other skeletal problems. Some *Vata*s come with very light bones, others with very heavy but long bones. You can recognise a *Vata* by his visible joints, tendons, and veins. This is due to low fat content under their skin. Another typical indication of a *Vata* physiology is the audible cracking of joints.

A balanced *Vata* type is enthusiastic, energetic, and uplifting in spirit. His clear mind and exalted sense of awareness makes him the best candidate for spiritual development. *Vata*s are ruled by their heightened sense of touch and hearing. They feel and hear the world more than they see it, a reason why they need frequent cuddles and words of encouragement. Sex in itself is not so important to the *Vata*s, but the feeling of being loved and cared for is. They have no difficulties in going for long stretches without sex but once they have found a partner who truly accepts and loves them for who they are, they are very fulfilling sexual partners. *Vata* types need matured *Kapha-Pitta* or *Pitta-Kapha* types to give their best in a relationship.

Since *Vata* is the principal force of movement in the body, it regulates everything from the bowel activities, absorption of food, inhalation and exhalation, transport of blood, lymph, and nerve impulses to the movement of the muscles and the entire body. *Vata* is especially in charge of the nervous system. *Vata* imbalances are likely to show up as nervous disorders, including tremors, spasms, seizures, anxiety, depression, and clinical mental disorders. Once *Vata* is returned to balance, such disorders, which otherwise may defy conventional treatment, often disappear spontaneously.

*Vata*s who are out of balance tend to worry a lot even when there is really nothing to worry about. This may lead to restlessness, insomnia, and fear. Fear, which is *Vata*'s most typical emotion, affects their digestion and particularly the elimination of waste. *Vata's* main seat is in the colon. When disturbed it causes constipation and gas. Also the stomach and intestines may cramp when Vata is deranged. Irregular menstrual cycles, PMT, and menstrual cramps are more often found among *Vata* types. *Vata*s easily get unbalanced when they don't get enough rest and sleep, and particularly if they miss out on the two hours sleep before midnight. By pushing themselves too hard and having an irregular lifestyle, they easily overexert themselves, which can lead to chronic fatigue and any of the above mental or physical problems. The main key to balancing *Vata* is "regularity."

The following factors are the most irritating for the Vata type:

Excessive exercise and physical strain
Sleep deprivation (especially lack of before midnight sleep)
Falling
Irregular mealtimes
Sitting for many hours
Tuberculosis
Suppression of natural urges

Cold
Cold foods and drinks
Stimulants of any kind
Excessive noise
Fear and grief
Fasting
Pungent, astringent and bitter foods
Late autumn and winter

The *Pitta* Type

Medium build, well-shaped, and athletically toned
Medium strength and endurance
Sharp hunger and thirst, strong digestion
Tendency towards anger and irritability when under stress
Can be arrogant, self-centred
Adaptable, intelligent, and bright
Tendency toward reddish skin and hair, moles, freckles, skin problems
If out of balance, prematurely bald and/or grey
Pointed, reddish nose
Piercing, sometimes bloodshot eyes
Aversion to sun, hot weather
Prefers cool food and drink
Enterprising character, likes challenges, good organiser
Sharp intellect
Good, precise, articulate speaker
Can't skip meals
Medium memory
Successful leader

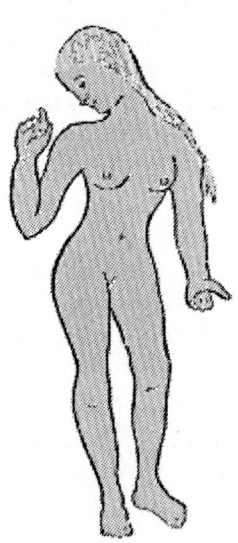

Illustration 9: The Pitta Type

The main theme that describes the *Pitta* type is **"intense"** since he is mostly dominated by the fire element and its qualities. Fire represents the dynamic force of nature and is responsible for all transformational processes in the body and mind. The mental body, i.e., thoughts, emotions, and feelings are functions of *Pitta*. The *Pitta* energies are located in the central region of the body, that is the solar plexus. The solar plexus serves as a "switchboard" for both, psychological and physiological activities. The "gut feeling" we sometimes have about such and such is locked into the *Pitta* force. It gives us the natural instinct to search for pure foods, clean air, fresh water, etc., so that we can remain in physical, mental, and emotional balance. *Pitta dosha* also helps us to be moderate in eating, drinking, sexual activity, and other needs. This instinctive quality is highly developed in a balanced *Pitta* type, which makes him a symbol of "*Sattva*," i.e., purity of mind. A disturbance of *Pitta*, however, will result in the loss of knowing what is right or wrong and lead to excessive use of stimulants such as alcohol, tobacco, drugs, as well as of power and influence.

To translate ideas into concrete realities we require the *Pitta* energy. Since it is mostly available in the *Pitta* type, he exhibits a very dynamic, ambitious, and perhaps even aggressive personality. *Pittas* get things done. Their great vision and foresight is due to the fire element that gives them a clear inner and outer vision. However, if a *Pitta* person abuses his power and irritates his energies, he is the first to develop eye problems and difficulties with both his inner and outer vision.

Pitta dosha, being located in the most central position in the body, keeps *Vata* and *Kapha* in check. This too is represented in the *Pitta* type's personality, as he is one who always wants to be in control in every situation. When his *Pitta dosha* is balanced, he is indeed the most successful of all body-types. His one-pointed focus and brilliance nearly always finds a solution to every problem and he can be good at almost anything. His real expertise though lies in the mental field where he exerts his true power and skills. He makes an eloquent and articulate speaker and a good leader of society.

Because of *Pitta dosha's* strategic position in the body, *Pitta* types are excellent at playing central roles in life. The solar plexus is related to sun energy, which controls life on the planet. *Pittas* are aware of their solar plexus power and are therefore naturally self-confident. If they are able to transcend the excesses, indulgence, and arrogance, which they may have acquired, they have access to the most profound knowledge of self. They are also very good in passing on what they have learnt through their insights and experiences.

When his *Pitta* energies move outside their main centre and enter other parts of the body, the *Pitta* type becomes fiery, jealous, cynical, angry, and egotistic. He rapidly begins to lose control, like a forest fire that quickly spreads through strong winds. If his sense of "I-ness" becomes exaggerated, he may try to subdue his *Vata* and *Kapha* counterparts, especially in the area of sexuality. *Pitta's* overwhelming passion for always wanting to be a winner in every field of life may leave very little room for a wholesome sexual interplay. He may not have the necessary patience and humility that is required during the most intimate moments of sharing and equality. The unbalanced *Pitta* type also tries to use every means to avoid admitting defeat. The most suitable partners for *Pittas* are the strong *Kapha* types; or else *Kapha-Vata* or *Vata-Kapha* types.

In physical terms, the dispersion of excessive *Pitta* energy can lead to heartburn, stomach ulcers, burning sensations in the intestines, and haemorrhoids. This destructive *Pitta* energy may also affect his skin, which becomes prone to rashes, pimples, inflammation, and acne. The skin, particularly of the face and chest, may begin to redden and become hot. Hot flushes are a typical sign of *Pitta* imbalance. Unbalanced Pitta women who go through the menopause frequently experience them.

The *Pitta's* eyes can easily become bloodshot and blurry and are often oversensitive to light, a reason why *Pittas* whose *doshas* are out of balance insist on wearing sunglasses. Their natural internal heat makes them the worst candidates for sunbathing. They prefer the cool and shady places, and they love taking cold showers when outside temperatures begin to rise. If they don't follow their natural instincts about the sun and heat, they quickly burn their skin and develop heat fatigue.

Physically, *Pitta*s are well proportioned, athletically built and of medium size. The same applies to their face. Their eyes are medium in size with a sometimes penetrating glance. You easily can recognise a typical *Pitta* type from far away, as he is likely to have red, blond, or sandy coloured hair. He is also the first among the body-types to have grey hair or go bald. *Pitta*s rarely feel cold, even during winter. When the sun comes out, they are the first to complain that is it too warm. Their skin is fair, warm, and soft, and is most likely marked by freckles and moles or other skin blemishes (some of these *Pitta* characteristics do not apply to racial groups with dark hair and dark skins).

Pitta types have only medium physical energy, which prevents them from over-exercising or going beyond their limits. Their stamina is moderate but their digestive energy is abundant. However, overeating can lead to sudden intestinal problems. For this reason they greatly benefit from moderate food intake and a pure lifestyle. Impure foods, polluted water and air, alcohol, coffee, cigarettes, soft drinks etc., are particularly upsetting to *Pitta* types and often cause very uncomfortable cleansing reactions such as skin eruptions, stomach problems or emotional distress. *Pitta*s also get affected by wearing clothes that are made from synthetic materials. *Pitta*'s main warning signal that he is out of balance is anger, which may fuel his fire energy to the extent that his body becomes toxic and diseased. The main key to balancing *Pitta* is "moderation."

<u>*The following factors are the most irritating for the Pitta type:*</u>

Anger	*Vinegar*
Insufficient sleep	*Impure foods*
Strong sunshine	*Unripe fruits*
Fasting	*Linseed*
Sesame seeds and sesame products	*Yoghurt*
Wine and other alcoholic beverages,	*Pungent, salty, and sour foods*
Coffee and other stimulants	*Late summer and autumn*

The *Kapha* Type

Compact, strong and heavier build
Well developed and lubricated joints
Great physical strength and endurance
Hair may be black, blond, dark brown, thick, wavy, oily
Stable and reliable personality
Steady energy; slow and graceful in action
Tranquil, relaxed personality, slow to anger
Cool, smooth, pale, often oily skin
Hidden veins and tendons
Slow to grasp new information, slow to forget
Heavy, prolonged sleep
Tendency to excessive weight, obesity
Slow digestion, mild hunger
Excessive need for sleep
Calm, affectionate, complacent, tolerant, forgiving, nurturing, maternal
Tendency to be possessive, stubborn, attached, narrow-minded

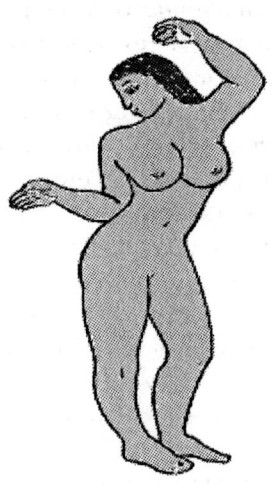

llustration 10: The Kapha Type

The *Kapha* type is controlled by the elements of earth and water, which makes him the most grounded and stable of all the body-types. One word that describes him most is "**slow**." The force of *Kapha* pervades the food element and in the body it is mainly located in the upper thoracic cavity. Both stomach and lungs are central areas of *Kapha* activity. Proper lubrication of the mucous lining and joints plays a major role in keeping his body strong and resistant to disease.

Since *Kapha* types imbibe the material elements of earth and water, they are the most attuned to the pace of earthly survival. It is therefore not surprising that they have the longest life spans of all three types. In a way, they represent Mother Earth and her qualities of nurturing, vitality, and stability.

*Kapha*s, who represent the *food force*, are the complete opposites of the *Vata*s, who represent the *mobile force*. *Pitta* is the *dynamic force* between them. A *Kapha* person is affectionate, sensual, calm and forgiving. He makes an excellent parent because he is naturally tolerant and does not become irritable even when there is a lot of noise or turbulence around him. *Kapha* types exist mainly on the physical and astral planes. They feel more at home on planet earth than *Vata*s or *Pitta*s do, since the earth and water elements are most concentrated in their bodies. Their dominating senses are smell and taste, which makes food one of their favourite things. This naturally makes them good cooks, a characteristic that is rarely found among *Vata*s.

Physically, *Kapha*s have great strength and stamina. Most weight lifters are *Kapha*s who can access and utilise huge energy reserves. Their bones and joints are heavy and well built but are hidden under a fat protective skin. They have wide hips and broad shoulders, as often found among rugby players and heavyweight boxers. Their compact and heavy bodies thrive on athletic performance and physical activities. They are very willing to perform strenuous physical labour because they feel so much more alive afterwards.

Too much sitting or sleeping, on the other hand, can make *Kapha*s lethargic and lazy, which slows their already low metabolic rate. A sedentary lifestyle predisposes them to putting on weight very easily; this may sometimes even happen by merely looking at food. They tend to deal with unresolved emotional issues through eating, because eating gives them the most pleasure. Unbalanced *Kapha*s can be recognised by their excessive weight. They often become obese if "things don't move" in their lives.

*Kapha*s have the biggest eyes of all the body-types. Their dark or blue pupils stand in clear contrast to the milky white sclera, which makes them very attractive. A typical *Kapha* trait is their skin, which is silky smooth, soft, cool, thick, and pale, without a sign of freckles or moles. Even at an advanced age, their skin tends to be clear and without wrinkles. Its natural oiliness gives the skin a shiny glow.

Kapha types do everything slowly, including eating, walking, and talking. They are slow to anger and slow to react. Calm and self-contained, they love peaceful environments. They are the most relaxed and the most romantic of all body-types, and a romantic dinner for two is one of the most pleasing things for them. *Kaphas* tend to flirt innocently with everyone and rely on bodily feelings, which makes them ideal lovers. They rarely feel obstructed in their flow of sexual energy and they have plenty of it. *Kapha* types make wonderful partners for all body-types, especially for those who have vital sexual prowess and a need for many offspring. *Kaphas* find fulfilment in caring for a family.

When *Kapha types* are unable to deal with inner conflicts they tend to keep them inside the body, unlike *Vata* types who spurt out whatever they think and feel. This is when stored unrest and antagonism can disturb the *Kapha's* basic metabolism and cause congestion, stagnation, and a heavy form of depression. Depression and melancholia are the vibrations that transform *Kaphas'* most precious assets into very destructive forces. Most cancers are caused by an imbalance of *Kapha dosha* and *Kapha* types are the most likely to develop *Kapha* imbalances; hence they are more prone to develop cancers than other body-types.

Because *Kapha dosha* controls the moist tissues of the body, the mucous lining is the first one to show signs of imbalance. Unbalanced *Kapha*s frequently complain of chest colds, wet coughs, asthma, sinus congestion, allergies, and painful joints, especially during late winter and spring times (*Kapha* season).

Another indication of an unbalanced *Kapha* type is his tendency to hold on to possessions, positions at work, money, food, energy, and relationships. He would prefer everything to remain as it is. And to keep it that way he tries very hard to please everyone, except himself, which again makes him a possible candidate for cancer (also see "Cancer -- Who Makes It," Chapter 8).

Even though it is not necessarily a part of their nature, *Kapha* types benefit greatly from excitement in their lives. Status quo situations turn the *Kapha's* stability into inertia, which turns out to be their greatest enemy. *Kaphas* thrive physically, emotionally, and spiritually if they focus is on having enough stimulation in life. Exercising, going out, travelling, singing, dancing, playing musical instruments, etc, "keeps them alive." They need to progress in life to feel good. By contrast, watching television makes them passive and depressed. Also lack of exercise, cold and heavy food, overeating, and receptive work slows them right down. They only recognise their great assets of inner security and steadiness when they are in action. This keeps them youthful and healthy. The main key to balancing *Kapha* therefore is **stimulation**.

<u>The following factors are the most irritating for the Kapha type:</u>

Sleeping during daytime	*Spring and early summer*
Heavy food	*Sugar and sweets*
Sweet, sour and salty food	*Laziness*
Milk and dairy products	*Lack of exercise and physical activity*
Cold and damp	*Too much sleep*

CHAPTER 6

A Life of Balance

This chapter is dedicated to the main insights and methods that can help you create a life of balance. Once balance is achieved, good health results quite spontaneously. This applies to every living being and to nature as a whole. Yet creating balance is not something we need to do just once in life, it rather is on ongoing process that allows the body and mind to function in perfect co-ordination and harmony with each other. That's when we will be ready to take up the challenges of our time, endowed with physical and mental strength, creativity, and wisdom.

We require a life of balance more now than we ever did before because the factors that could possibly disrupt our health have increased manifold within the relatively short period of the last few decades. Balance or good health of mind, body and spirit is an option most of us can choose to develop now by implementing the following simple steps. To some extent, the guidelines presented here are derived from the ancient medical science of Ayurveda but they have been updated and improved as a result of regular feedback that was given to me by thousands of patients who followed them.

Guidelines for Daily Routine and Diet

Regularity -- *follow the rhythms of nature as described in the previous chapter. This ensures that your body and mind can operate at ease and with perfect precision.*

Regular rest and sleep: Bedtime: 9-10pm
- Don't worry if you have difficulties with falling asleep, just lie with your eyes closed and relax; you will still get 90% of the benefit from sleep. This programme can help eliminate the causes of sleep disturbance.

Regular exercise and physical activity
- Morning and /or evening walk.
- Surya Namaskara or sun salutation -- the most ancient and comprehensive exercise
- programme (see illustration 9).
- Chose any other form of physical exercise that suits your body-type (see section on "Balancing the Doshas"). Whenever you exercise always breathe through your nose and keep your mouth closed to avoid harmful 'adrenaline breathing.' Aerobic exercises are good as long as one maintains nose breathing (versus mouth breathing).
- Exercise only up to 50% of your capacity; do not allow yourself to become tired. For example, if you can swim for 30 minutes before feeling tired, swim only for 15 minutes, etc. In time, your capacity for more exercise will unfold. Over-exercising weakens the immune system and floods the blood with harmful acidic chemicals.
- Exposure to fresh air at least once or twice each day is important for proper circulation and oxygen supply to the trillions of cells in the body.
- Regularly practice of Yoga, Tai Chi, or Chi Kung, etc. is highly recommended for maintaining energy and flexibility.
- PranaYama: 5-minute breathing exercises to increase Prana energy, as explained below, best done twice daily before meditation and before eating.
- Meditation according to your choice. I recommend the "Technique of Conscious Breathing," as described in my book "It's Time to Wake Up."

Regular Mealtimes
- Lunch should be the main meal of the day, best time is around 12,00 - 12,30pm (if summer time applies to your country, 1pm is still fine).
- Dinner should be light as digestive power is low in the evening
- Take dinner between 6-7pm so that the main digestion is completed before bedtime and does not interfere with your sleep.
- Take food at the same time every day, so that the digestive system functions at its best.
- Eat according to your hunger level; if you are not hungry don't eat; wait until your appetite (digestive power) has returned. Note: food cravings have nothing to do with hunger and should be treated like an addiction (see chapter 7).
- Drink a minimum of 6-8 eight glasses of water a day. Pure and fresh water is best. Distilled water, which is the closest to natural rain water, is excellent for hydrating the body cells (adding 3-4 grains or rice to one gallon of distilled water gives it plenty of minerals and vitamins; exposing it to direct sunlight for an hour will re-energise it). Make it a daily habit of drinking one glass of water ½ hour before each meal and one glass of water 2 ½ hours after each meal (for exact instructions see section on 'Drinking Water – The Greatest Therapy of All').
- Make certain you always sit down when you eat, even if it is for a small snack. The digestive system is better able to secrete balanced amounts of digestive juices when eating in the sitting position.
- Eat in a settled environment without radio, television, or reading. Any distraction from eating impairs the enjoyment of food and the ability of the body to supply the appropriate enzymes for digestion.
- Sit quietly for 5-10 minutes after the meal so that the food has a chance to settle in the stomach before getting up from the table. Lying on your left side for a few minutes is good, too. If you possibly can, go for a 15-minute walk afterwards, this aids digestion of food.

Morning

Bowel Movement:
- For optimum health, the bowel movement should occur regularly in the morning after rising, best at the end of the Vata period (around 6am) while Vata is still strong enough to eliminate waste materials from the system. Give yourself that extra time but do not force a bowel movement. Never suppress natural urges as this leads to great disturbance of Vata in the body.
- Every morning after rising drink one or two glasses of warm water. This will help to end the "drought" of the night and regularise the bowel movement apart from cleansing the gastrointestinal tract from AMA and harmful bacteria. Drinking a glass of warm water with a teaspoon of honey and a little juice of fresh lemon after that further helps to cleanse the intestines from unwanted debris. Wait for at least 30 minutes before eating breakfast.

Regular Dry Brushing and Oil Massage:
- Quickly brush your whole body with a dry body brush made of natural bristle or a good natural loofah. This will improve circulation, strengthen and rejuvenate the skin, and help with lymph drainage. The brushing of the skin also opens the pores and increases effectiveness of the oil massage.
- Abyanga or oil massage: Massage yourself with sesame oil or else with coconut or olive oil (all cold pressed and unrefined, available from health food stores) to draw out toxins and improve circulation, followed by a warm bath or shower (see guidelines below for oil massage). Sesame oil, in particular, penetrates all the layers of the skin quickly, binds to and removes toxins of various kinds (incl. harmful fatty acids) and cleanses the blood vessels of debris. This helps prevent and reverse hardening of the arteries. It also stimulates growth hormone production and improves immunity (one third of the immune system is located in the skin).

Breakfast

- If you are not hungry, skip breakfast (Kapha types rarely need breakfast).
- If hungry, eat a light breakfast, which may consist of light wholemeal products (check for wheat allergy!). Toasted wholemeal bread with butter, porridge, or other natural cereals, are fine, too. If you use milk, make sure it is not skimmed and it is boiled before consumption (see chapter 11 for further details on milk). Avoid animal protein such as cheese, ham, or eggs as well as sour foods, including yoghurt and citrus fruits, as these quickly subdue AGNI, which is naturally low in the morning hours. Breakfast consisting of only fruit (other than citrus) is fine.

Lunch

- Make lunch to be the main meal of the day
- Avoid drinking beverages during the meal as this will dilute the concentrated digestive juices and thus become a cause of indigestion and weight gain. Sipping a cup of hot water during the meal, however, can help increase the digestive power. To maintain thinness of blood and bile, it is best to drink a glass of water ½ hour before lunch and again 2½ hours after lunch.
- Yoghurt, which serves as a good digestive aid, can be added during or towards the end of the meal. However, this applies only to freshly prepared yoghurt that is not older than one day, i.e., that has been started the night before. Commercial yoghurt is too old and contains toxin-producing bacteria that counteract the digestive process. Yoghurt can also be taken as lassi (i.e. yoghurt blended with the same amount of water to which is added honey or ginger, cardamom and honey, or ginger, cumin and salt).
- Eat salad as a starter at the beginning of the meal, before eating any cooked food. Since raw foods require different enzymes than cooked foods, eating these foot items separately, one after the other, makes it easier on the digestive system. (During cold days and in the winter, eat fewer salads since they have strong cooling effects.)

Dinner

- In the evening, Ayurveda recommends not to eat meat, pork, chicken, fish, ham, eggs, nuts, as AGNI is too low by then to digest protein foods (note: the production of digestive enzymes stops at around 8pm). Yoghurt, cheese, fruits, and salads are also best to be avoided. Their natural bacteria content is very high, which, when exposed to the warm and humid environment of the stomach during the night, causes indigestion and fermentation (low quality alcohol). Oily and oil-fried foods, as well as root vegetables, with the exception of cooked carrots, beetroot, or white radish, are also difficult to digest at night.
- An example of a light dinner is freshly prepared vegetable soup with toast or light wholemeal crackers; or cooked vegetables with rice, pasta, or couscous, etc.

General Guidelines

- It is best to avoid: heavy, oily, and fried food, aged cheeses, large amounts of yoghurt, onion and garlic, highly processed and refined foods, soft drinks, alcohol, coffee, black tea, etc.
- Try to include at least one or two pieces of fresh fruit every day and/or freshly prepared fruit juices (best diluted with water) in your diet. Packaged fruit juices are pasteurised, which makes them acid forming, deprives them of natural enzymes, and depletes the body of important minerals and vitamins. Many brands contain artificial sweeteners, which dehydrate the body and may cause damage to the nervous system and immune system. Fruit or fruit juices should always be taken on an

empty stomach and on their own, and preferably of one type at a time. Since fruits leave the stomach within 20-40 minutes without requiring digestion there, it is better not to eat them with or after food, which otherwise may cause fermentation and bloating. The best times for eating fruit are mid-morning and mid-afternoon, or for breakfast with nothing else. Fruits should preferably be consumed when in season. Since they have a cooling influence, they are less suitable during the cold season when we need more warming foods. The best types of fruit are the ones that naturally grow in your environment. To properly digest fruits from another country we require different digestive enzymes. We can only produce these enzymes if we have lived there for some time and our bodies have adapted to the new environment.

- You may take soaked dried fruit, e.g., sultanas, figs, dates, prunes, either for breakfast or as a snack like other fruit. "Muscle test" which ones are the most suitable for you! Dried fruits contain enzyme inhibitors that can make them gas- forming and constipating; soaking them makes them easily digestible.
- Take 6-10 almonds without the skin on a daily basis. This provides vital nutrients to eyes and bones. Remove the skin by placing the almonds in boiled water for 10-15 minutes and then peel them. Note: the skin contains harmful acids.
- It is best to avoid leftover and frozen foods, only rice and beans are OK to be kept and to be reheated. One hour after cooking food, its life force (Prana energy) and important enzymes and vitamins have dissipated. Frozen food is void of the life force, and so is microwave food. Without Prana, food cannot be digested and assimilated properly.
- For deep cleansing, drink hot (ionised) water frequently: Boil water for about 15 minutes. Keep it in a thermos flask and every ½ hour, take 1-2 sips or more according to thirst. To have cleansing effects, the water must be boiled this long and be taken as hot as one takes tea. You may put a small piece of fresh ginger in the flask. By boiling it continuously for 15 minutes, large numbers of (negatively charged) oxygen ions are generated. When these are ingested through frequent sips throughout the day, they start to systematically cleanse the tissues of the body and help rid them of (positively charged) hydrogen ions, those associated with high acidity and toxins. If you have excessive body weight, this technique alone can help you to shed many pounds of body-waste without any undesirable side effects.
- Try to avoid cold foods or drinks as they can "extinguish" AGNI, the digestive fire, for many hours. They may also damage the nerve endings of the stomach. A hand, held in icy water, becomes numb. Similarly, cold things make the stomach cells contract and prevent them from secreting proper amounts of digestive juices; they also make the stomach insensitive to potentially harmful foods or drinks and effectively disrupt its warning signals to the brain. In addition, digestive enzymes require a certain environmental temperature to operate. By cooling down the enzymes' environment, their digestive and anti-cancer properties begin to diminish too, predisposing a person to excessive weight gain and even cancer. Also the sudden cold influence, as caused, for example, by ice cream or iced drinks, forces the body to increase its internal heat production in order to compensate the otherwise harmful drop in temperature. This response wastes the body's energy reserves and may make it feel even hotter and thirstier than before, particularly during the summer period. Foods and drinks that are of room temperature or warm are the most suitable and natural ones for the human body.
- Use the spices in your foods that are suitable for your body-type (see Ayurvedic diet section). Spices not only enhance the flavour of food, but also contain vital nutrients and aromas that help with the digestion and metabolism of food. People who have a low metabolism (mainly Kapha types) can speed up their metabolic rate by as much as 30 percent by using spices in their food. Chilli peppers or chilli containing spice mixes should be avoided, though, as they affect the chest and cause mucous irritation in the stomach and intestines. If you like it hot, Cheyenne pepper is the best option.
- If available, take ¼-½ glass of freshly prepared carrot juice before lunch. Note: Pitta types should do the muscle testing for carrot juice.
- For one day a week take only a liquid diet (soups, freshly made juices, water, herbal teas, ionised water, etc.). Then gradually build up to a normal diet again. This will greatly relieve the digestive system and improve its ability to remove any accumulated toxic waste. Women benefit greatly if they

have a "liquid day" about one or two days before menstruation; it helps to make the menstrual period more comfortable and effective.

Drinking Water -- The Greatest Therapy of All

Dehydration is perhaps the most common yet mostly unrecognised problem prevalent in modern societies. Alcohol, coffee, tea, and soft drinks, have become the primary choices of satisfying thirst, especially among the younger generations. Their principal effect, however, is to remove water -- the most important substance in the body -- from the cells and the blood. If you wish to avoid disease and slow the ageing process, drinking fresh water is an essential prerequisite. Anyone who is healthy and wants to stay that way needs to drink a minimum of 6-8 eight-ounce glasses of fresh water a day. This will ensure that the 60 trillion or so cells in the body receive their daily-required ration of water in order to maintain efficiency of metabolism and waste removal.

Suggestions:
- Start the day by drinking one or two glasses of warm water to end the "drought" of the night and remove accumulated wastes from the excretory organs (this can be followed by a glass of warm water with lemon and honey water).
- Half an hour before each meal drink one glass of water. This will keep your blood thin so that it can readily pick up food nutrients and distribute them to the cells after digesting food. The water also helps increase the secretion of digestive juices and prevents bile from becoming too viscous. [By contrast, drinking a lot of water or other beverages with the meal dilutes the digestive juices, which impairs digestion].
- Drinking another glass of water approximately 2 ½ hours after each meal restores the blood's water requirements. [Following a meal, the blood uses up a considerable amount of water to distribute nutrients to the cells and can therefore become water deficient quite quickly.]

These simple instructions can help prevent the most serious major diseases that are prevalent in modern societies today. Drinking sufficient amounts of water at the right times can and should be part of every other therapy used in the treatment of disease.

A note of caution: The attempt to restore complete hydration of the body should take place gradually, otherwise this may cause serious harm to the body! A dehydrated person, i.e., one who has not taken the minimum required amount of water and/or has removed cellular water by consuming caffeine or sugar containing foods or drinks for a considerable length of time, is susceptible to becoming ill. The tissue cells are no longer able to function efficiently. To protect themselves against further loss of water they make their membranes less penetrable to water diffusion by pulling in extra amounts of fats, including *cholesterol*. This, however, prevents metabolic waste from leaving the cells which consequently begin to suffocate in the their own waste; some of them, in order to survive in the toxic environment, may even undergo genetic mutation and become cancerous.

During dehydration, the kidneys hold onto water and so does the rest of the body. At this stage many people start overeating salt or salty foods because the body needs more salt to hold on to the little water it has left. This, however, causes the kidneys to contract and filter even less water than before. Urine becomes more and more concentrated and scarce. In this condition of extreme dehydration it would be unwise to suddenly start drinking gallons of water. Since the cells have created a barrier in order to save water, they are in no position to absorb this much water all at once. The water would simply stagnate outside the cells and lead to water retention and weight gain. The sudden intake of large amounts of water can indeed cause severe congestion and swelling in the body, since the kidneys are not able to filter much of it. The transition from a state of severe dehydration to improved hydration therefore should be very gradual and is best monitored by a health practitioner who knows about the basics of water metabolism.

This is the procedure of gradual hydration of the body: Add *only* about one glass of water a day to the amount of water you usually drink and check whether urination increases. When it does, drink another 1-2 glasses. It is of principle importance that your kidneys begin to filter more water when you drink more water. You don't want to create a "dam" in your kidneys, which could even flood your lungs. In time, the kidneys will recognise that water is no longer a scarcity in the body and make the necessary adjustments to increase urination. At the same time there will be a decrease of salt production and salt retention in the body. The urge to eat a lot of salt or salty foods will also subside. This response is caused by the water's own natural diuretic effects.

If you are on diuretic drugs it is important for you to know that water is a much more efficient diuretic than any other drug can possibly be, and it has no harmful side effects. Diuretic drugs should be decreased gradually and under supervision of a health practitioner. Once the kidneys have no more difficulties with eliminating urine, you can increase your water intake to the natural minimum daily requirement of 6-8 glasses a day. This will drastically reduce the health risks imposed by an illness. To undo years of dehydration and be completely hydrated again, however, it may take up to a year, and sometimes even longer.

A note of caution: When the body is dehydrated, it tries to *keep* its salt in order to hold onto water. When urination increases following improved hydration, these salts are gradually passed out with the urine. If the hydration attempts are implemented too fast, those areas with most salt retention may form oedema. Puffiness of the eyes or swelling of the ankles indicates that the hydration process should be done more gradually. As the swellings decrease, normal quantities of water can be taken. With increased water intake, your body will also be able to remove excessive salt. You should therefore make sure to take some salt as an important part of your diet. If your untrained muscles start to cramp, particularly during the night, your body is most likely not getting enough salt.

Both water and salt are absolutely essential for keeping the water metabolism balanced and for generating enough hydroelectric energy to maintain cellular activities. *Drinking water* can be considered to be the most important therapy of all therapies because there is simply nothing in the body that doesn't depend on it. Drinking water and cutting down energy depleting (over-stimulating) influences should be the very first treatment in the case of an illness, before anything else. In most cases, the problems will disappear by themselves.

Exercise Programmes

The Purpose of Exercising

Under normal circumstances, exercising one's body would not be necessary. Man, like every other animal, was meant to live in nature, have plenty of fresh air, and be involved in enough physical activity to keep the body vital and fit. Technological and economic advancement, however, has led to an increasingly sedentary lifestyle, which requires additional forms of physical movement to keep our bodies healthy and strong.

The purpose of exercise is not only to prove to ourselves that we are able to defy the ageing process, look good, or prevent a heart attack. Exercise also helps us to enhance our capacity to digest food, eliminate physical and emotional impurities, and increase firmness and suppleness, as well as our ability to deal with stressful situations. Especially the lymphatic system, which drains toxic and noxious substances from the connective tissues of the organs and muscles, depends on the daily movement of all the parts of the body. Unlike blood, lymph fluid has no pumping device to push it round the body.

Exercise is a great immune stimulant if done in moderation and improves neuromuscular integration in all age groups. Its effect of boosting self-confidence and self-esteem stems from the improved oxygen supply to the cells and the resulting well being in all parts of the body and in the mind. Foremost of all, exercise is an excellent means of increasing happiness in life.

The conventional approach to exercise, however, believes a good workout to be something that takes you right to your limits, leaving you exhausted and tired afterwards. This is a form of violence to the body, a kind of "punishment" for not performing well enough. The pain that shows in people's faces when they struggle through a set workout programme is an indication that the body is suffering from overexertion. This sort of exercise defeats its very purpose. Any form of physical exertion upsets *Vata* and causes the secretion of abnormal amounts of stress hormones such as *adrenaline*; this leaves the body restless and shaky. The body, thus depleted of energy, is unable to do the repair work that arises from the strenuous workout, leaving the cardiovascular system weak and vulnerable to other stress factors.

In the excitement of competitive sports, you may not be aware at first how strenuously you are exerting yourself, but once the *adrenaline rush* is over, the side effects step in. Many professional athletes suffer a range of problems, including immune deficiency, which makes the body prone to infections of all sorts. Athletes consume a lot more prescribed drugs than the average person does. The thymus gland, which activates *lymphocytes* and controls energy supplies, may actually shrink in size and leave the body weak and debilitated as a direct result of over-conditioning.

Exercise According to *Doshas*

Exercise is best done according to one's capacity and psycho-physiological body-type. A *Vata* type, who has the lowest capacity for exercise, benefits mostly from such light forms of exercise as walking, dancing, bicycling, short hikes, balancing and stretching. *Vata*s generally like yoga, Tai Chi, and Chi Kung. Since *Vata* types experience energy in bursts, they should particularity be careful of not overdoing it, because when their energy suddenly drops they can feel depleted for a long time afterwards.

Pitta types, being competitive by nature, are equipped with more drive and energy than *Vata*s. They generally are not satisfied with the more ordinary forms of working out. To achieve physical satisfaction they need a goal-oriented exercise programme. However, they, too don't have boundless energy and are better off exercising in moderation. *Pitta*s feel challenged by hiking in the mountains, skiing, jogging, swimming, playing tennis, or other sports that create in them a sensation of achievement.

Unbalanced *Pitta* types are often bad losers and may get angry if they feel they are "not good enough." *Pitta*s, who get angry while performing should look for a less competitive exercise programme to increase their level of satisfaction. Because excessive heat is a sign of unbalanced *Pitta*, swimming, which has a cooling influence, is one of the best forms of exercise for them. A walk in the cool forest is another excellent way to pacify an unbalanced *Pitta* type.

Kapha types are the ideal candidates for a good or moderately heavy workout. Weight training, running, rowing, aerobics, long distance bicycling, dancing for a long time, and playing football, basket ball, or tennis are all suitable for a *Kapha*. The *Kapha* type's steady energy gives him the necessary endurance and stamina to last through long competitive games without feeling tired. Exercise will clear out possible *Kapha* congestion, remove excessive water and fat, and improve general circulation. This will leave him feeling refreshed and buoyant afterwards.

There are a few basic precautions regarding exercise that apply to all the body-types:
- It is best not to exercise more than 50% of your capacity, whatever that means to you. The purpose of exercising is not to prove to others how capable you are but to derive personal benefit and satisfaction from it. If you are able to run for 30 minutes before you are tired, then make the choice to run only for 15 minutes. Getting tired during exercising defeats the very purpose of exercise. Feeling refreshed, revitalised and energetic afterwards indicates that the workout has been successful. In due time your capacity for exercise will naturally increase on its own.
- Stop exercising when you feel the need to breathe through the mouth. Once your are forced to breathe with the mouth rather than with the nose you have gone beyond the 50% threshold of your capacity for exercise. This is a sign that your body has moved into the adrenaline-breathing mode, which uses up your basic energy reserves. You have reached your limits when you feel your heart pounding violently or when you begin to sweat profusely or your body shakes. In that case it is good to finish off with a short period of walking and breathing normally. The basic rule is to always breathe through the nose and not through the mouth.

- Exercise to the point of light perspiration once a day.
- It is best to exercise during daylight. The best capacity for exercise is available during the Kapha period in the morning (6am to 10 am) and at the end of the Vata period in the afternoon at around 5pm-6pm.
- Ayurveda discourages exercising after sundown, so instead the body can slow down in the evening and prepare itself for a restful and rejuvenating sleep.
- Never exercise just before or after a meal, as this impairs AGNI, the digestive fire, and cause indigestion. However, walking for 15 minutes after meals works as a good digestive aid.
- Always drink water before and after exercising to prevent the blood from thickening.

Surya Namaskara (Sun Salutation)

Surya Namaskara is the most ancient and comprehensive single exercise programme. It is an integral part of Yoga and benefits both the mind and the body. It is unique in the sense that it strengthens and stretches all the major muscle groups, massages all the internal organs, supports lymph drainage from every part of the body and enlivens the energy centres and acupuncture points of the body. This exercise programme increases blood flow and circulation, conditions the spine, and improves flexibility of the joints. Grace, suppleness, as well as physical stability are the natural results arising from daily practice.

SURYANAMASKARA

Illustration 11: Surya Namaskara

Surya Namaskara consists of two cycles of twelve postures each. They are performed one after another in fluid sequence and co-ordinated with the breath. It is important not to strain with this exercise because benefits can only be felt when it is done easily and effortlessly. When you feel tired, lie down and rest, and breathe freely. Begin with one or two complete cycles and see how you feel afterwards. This way, the exercise will gradually increase your capacity for more. As a general guideline, men can eventually do as many as twelve complete (double) rounds, ladies as many as six.

Breathing should be co-ordinated with the movements of the body. Whenever you extend the spine or elongate the body, inhale and when you bend or fold the body, exhale. You will find that after a few cycles your breath will naturally adjust itself to the different movements (see illustration 12). After having done this exercise for a few days, the sequence of movements will be automatic and you will no longer need to look at the instruction pictures.

Breathing Exercises (PranaYama)

Ayurveda recommends simple breathing exercises or *PranaYama* that help to refresh energy and restore vitality to both mind and body within minutes. The word *PranaYama* is composed of two Sanskrit words. *Prana* means "the life force" or "the breath of life"; it carries vital energy from the surroundings into the body. *Prana Yama* can cause an extraordinary balance in consciousness. *Yama* is the exercise that increases the flow of *Prana* and thereby stimulates all the functions of body and mind. *PranaYama* has a deep cleansing effect and it purifies the "nadis," which are the pranic currents of energy in the body.

The benefits of *PranaYama* include reduction of stress and tension, improved respiration and circulation, as well as heightened awareness and clarity of mind. Especially those suffering from lung problems, headaches or migraines, and depression, may derive great relief from *PranaYama*. For maximum results, any of the following three types of *PranaYama* (according to body type) should be performed twice a day for five minutes each, preferably on an empty stomach in the morning and in the evening, or when under stress. There is one *PranaYama* suitable for each of the different body-types. Breathing should be normal and effortless. For maximum benefit, one should sit straight but comfortably, and with eyes closed.

Vata PranaYama

A person of *Vata* constitution or *Vata* imbalance benefits most from *alternative nostril breathing* which brings balance on all levels of mind and body. For this exercise, **close your right nostril with the thumb of your right hand and inhale through the left nostril. Then close the left nostril with the middle or ring finger of the same hand and exhale through your right nostril. Hold your finger there and inhale. Release, and once again close the right nostril with your thumb and exhale through your left nostril. Remain there and breathe in again.** Repeat this sequence for five minutes. Make sure to breathe in a relaxed and natural way while sitting straight and comfortably. This *PranaYama* supplies larger and equal amounts of oxygen to both hemispheres of the brain, empties the lower lobes of the lungs from excessive carbon dioxide, and makes room for more oxygen to be taken to the cells, giving them an "oxygen bath." *Vata*s who feel tense, restless, and stressed can quickly return to balance by practising this *PranaYama*.

Pitta-PranaYama

A person of *Pitta* constitution or *Pitta* imbalance can "cool down" and enhance female energies in the body by performing *left nostril breathing*. The left nostril corresponds to the cooling system in the body. If it is blocked, the body is overheating. For this exercise, **close your right nostril with the thumb of your right hand and inhale through your left one. Then close your left nostril with your middle or ring finger and exhale through your right one.** Repeat for five minutes, breathing normally and naturally, and sitting upright and comfortably.

Kapha-PranaYama

A person of *Kapha* constitution can "warm up" and increase male energies in the body by performing *right nostril breathing*. The right nostril corresponds to the heating system in our body. If it is blocked the body becomes too cold. For this exercise, **close your left nostril with the middle or index finger of your right hand and inhale through your right nostril. Then close the right nostril with your thumb and exhale with your left one.** Repeat for five minutes, breathing effortlessly and sitting upright and comfortably.

Obese-*Pranayama*

A person who suffers from obesity should perform a fast *PranaYama*. **Sit in a comfortable position, take a deep breath and exhale quickly and forcefully through the nose. You will naturally inhale after each exhalation. Repeat for one minute, then rest for one minute. Do this exercise for a total of five times, resting for one minute after each time.** This exercise speeds up the metabolic rate and is the *equivalent of running two miles*. You will begin to feel hot and start sweating excessively. It is important at this stage not to take cold or chilled drinks, as they shut down AGNI and increase the build-up of fat in the body. Drink water of room temperature.

Abyanga - Daily Oil Massage

The main purpose of Abyanga or daily oil massage as part of the Ayurvedic daily routine is to assist in preventing the accumulation of physiological toxins (*AMA*) and to lubricate and promote flexibility of the muscles, tissues, and joints. The classical texts of Ayurveda indicate that daily massage promotes softness and lustre of the skin as well as youthfulness. The skin is a major producer of endocrine hormones and is connected to every part of the body through thousands of cutaneous nerves. A daily oil massage can therefore balance the two master systems of the body - the nervous system and the endocrine system. The following are some simple instructions to assist you in learning the Ayurvedic daily do-it-yourself oil massage.

- Unless a specific oil has been recommended for you, cold-pressed and unrefined sesame oil (not the Chinese roasted sesame oil) should be the preference. Sesame oil is suitable for all body-types but if you find it irritating to the skin, you may try olive oil or coconut oil as an alternative. To purify the massage oil "cure" it by heating it to about 100 degrees centigrade, the boiling point of water. Add a drop of water to the oil at the beginning and when the water begins to splutter you will know that the proper temperature has been reached. You may prepare the entire content of the bottle in one go or as needed.
- Before beginning the massage, the oil should be at or slightly above body temperature, especially during winter. Start by massaging the head if you intend to shampoo afterwards. Place a small amount of oil on the fingertips and palms and begin to massage the scalp vigorously. Since the head and feet are considered to be the most important parts to be emphasised during Abyanga, spend proportionally more time on the head and feet than on other body parts.
- After massaging the head, apply oil gently with your hands to your face and outer part of your ears.
- Massage both the front and back of the neck, and the upper part of the spine.
- You may want to apply a small amount of oil to your entire body and then continue with the massage of each area.
- Next massage your arms. The proper motion is back and forth over the long bones and circular over the joints. Also massage hands and fingers.
- Now apply oil to the chest and abdomen. A very gentle circular motion should be used over your heart. Repeat this circular motion, following the "bowel pattern" from the right lower part of the abdomen, moving clockwise towards the left lower part of the abdomen.
- Massage the back and spine. Some areas are probably more difficult to reach, so you may want to ask your partner to help you.
- Massage the legs. Like the arms, use a back and forth motion over the long bones and circular over the joints.
- Lastly, massage the soles of the feet. Since all body reflex points are situated in the feet, a good amount of time should be spent on massaging the feet.
- Ideally, one should spend about 5-10 minutes on the massage every morning. If there is not enough time for a full body massage, then a mini-massage of 1-2 minutes on the head and feet is second best. After your massage take a warm shower or bath. Use soap only on the genital area and under the arms. This will leave a thin film of oil on the skin that is very beneficial for toning the skin and keeping the body muscles warm throughout the day. Sesame oil in particular has a disinfecting action,

which helps to ward off harmful microbes. If, however, you have applied too much oil, a mild soap made from natural ingredients can be used to wash it off.

Diet According to Body Types

To know which diet is good for *you*, you need to know your body-type first. As discussed earlier, different people digest and utilise the same food in a different way. If a *Vata* and a *Pitta* type go to a restaurant and order the same meal, one of them may feel invigorated afterwards and the other one dull and heavy. The following food charts give a summary of the foods, which are more suitable for each body-type. Ideally you would not require any lists to know what foods are good for you since your natural instinct would make the right choices for you. But most people's *doshas* are out of balance today. Our natural instincts often fail us because we generally orient our tastes towards nutritional information, time schedules, and the promises of advertisements. In addition, once a *dosha* is out of balance, we tend to eat exactly those types of foods that maintain the imbalance. For example, an unbalanced *Pitta* type may choose spicy, sour and salty foods, and an unbalanced *Kapha* type prefers cakes, candy, and oily foods.

Since the *doshas* are represented in our body in a unique and individual way, each one of us has different requirements for the various nutrients contained in food. *Our* body is only able to utilise the nutrients of those foods that are suitable to *our* body-type just as certain feeds are only suitable for certain animals and not others. Once you have determined your body-type, or the prevailing *dosha*, look up the charts and chose the foods that pacify this *dosha*. For example, if you have scored *Vata* 6, *Pitta* 15, and *Kapha* 8 in the Body Type Quiz, look up the section for *Pitta Pacifying Diet*.

So in order to know yourself better, familiarise yourself with the food charts that are applicable to your body-type, and choose to eat more of those foods that are on your "favour" list. You don't need to become fanatical about sticking to the list, especially if you are not just one clear body-type, but you will find it very helpful in your efforts to return to a balanced state of body and mind. If you feel attracted to a particular food that is not on your list, double check with the muscle test and you will know for sure whether your body can benefit from it or not. Both the food lists and the muscle test help you to get to know yourself better and to re-establish your natural instincts. If you are an experienced dowser, you can also use this technique to confirm the correctness of your choice of foods. Both methods can also be used to determine your exact body-type. If most items on the *Vata* list, for example, test positive for you, you are most likely a *Vata* type or this *dosha* is right out of balance.

Note: Whenever I have used the word *Reduce* in the food charts, I suggest that you use the corresponding food items only in moderation, that means, not every day and only sparingly.

VATA PACIFYING DIET

Favour: Warm foods and drinks; moderately heavy; added *ghee*, butter, oil; mostly high liquid containing and nourishing foods. Foods that are of sweet, sour, and salty tastes.

The *Vata* type, influenced mainly by the elements of air and space, is naturally sensitive to foods that are light, dry, and cold. He lacks the qualities of *heavy, oily* and *hot,* which when taken in form of food and drinks can keep him balanced. Also foods that have the dominant tastes of *sweet, sour* and *salty* pacify *Vata*, but those that are *pungent* as in spicy foods, *bitter* as in bitter greens, and *astringent* as in tea or beans, greatly upset it. A meal consisting of lettuce salad, hot vegetable curry with steamed potatoes, kidney beans, and ice cream, can derange *Vata* for many days, whereas an avocado with lemon and salt, stir fried asparagus, Basmati rice cooked with raisins, and almonds, and fresh home-made yoghurt can keep *Vata* balanced and strong.

Vata dosha is cold, dry, and light by nature, which are the qualities dominant in autumn and early winter. Especially during this time, *Vata* needs to be soothed and nourished by foods such as hearty stews and soups, long cooked vegetable casseroles, freshly prepared bread, puddings, and hot cereals. Butter, oils, and cream, too, keep *Vata* in check. Since sensitivity is one of his characteristics, the *Vata* type becomes upset when there is too much noise and disturbance around meal times.

Vata types are the most likely to need a more nourishing breakfast. Hot cereals such as porridge cooked with whole milk or soymilk and raisins soothe *Vata*, so does cream of rice or wheat. *Vata*, however, gets severely irritated by caffeinated drinks such as coffee or tea, due to their bitter and astringent tastes and stimulating effects.

Vata types tend to suffer from constipation with dry and hard stools if they have too much rice, pasta, or other wheat products but if eaten with plenty of well-cooked juicy vegetables they are *Vata* pacifying, too. Potatoes in any form are likely to cause *Vata* problems since they have a drying effect. *Vata*'s rule regarding starch-containing foods, often referred to as carbohydrates, is to add good amounts of fats, otherwise they tend to cause bloating and fermentation in the large intestines.

*Vata*s also benefit from spices that are mild, soothing, sweet, and heavy, as listed below. Since their digestive fire tends to fluctuate and be irregular, ginger, cardamom, fennel, and cinnamon can stimulate the appetite and improve digestion. They help to reduce gas, a problem that *Vata*s are particularly prone to develop.

The *Vata* type is the only body-type that requires more salt in his body and can benefit from adding it to his food, although it is always better to use it during the cooking. Care is to be taken, however, when the salt is eaten as dry, salted snacks, such as crisps.

It is better for the *Vata* type to choose unprocessed foods such as unsalted nuts, which are sweet, heavy, and oily, all qualities that pacify *Vata*. Be aware that nuts and seeds are very concentrated and rich foods, which means they should be consumed only in small quantities. *Vata*s can digest them more easily when they are ground or made into butters. One of the best nuts for pacifying *Vata* are almonds (8-10 a day), without the skin.

Ripe and sweet fruits are also very beneficial to the *Vata*, provided they are eaten on an empty stomach and not in the evening. *Vata* types should avoid fruits that have an astringent taste as in unripe bananas or persimmons, whereas the sour taste of grapefruit helps to pacify *Vata*.

The drying, cooling, and light elements of Air and Space dominate the *Vata* type and in a balanced state he shows a natural aversion to the following foods:

AIR/SPACE FOODS

- All cabbage families
- All dry, rough, and stale foods
- Bitter vegetables
- Hollow vegetable with tiny seeds (except peppers)
- Greens and lettuce
- Most nightshade fruits and vegetables
- Most dry and compact legumes

===

Vata Food Chart

Fruits
Favour

Apricots	Grapefruit	Papaya
Avocado	Grapes	Peaches
Bananas	Lemons	Pineapple
Berries	Mango	Plums
Cherries	Stewed fruits	Rhubarb
Coconut	Soaked dried fruits	Tangerines
Dates, fresh	Melons (sweet)	
Figs, fresh	Oranges	

Reduce

Apples	Dried Fruits, cooked	Pomegranate
Cranberries	Pears	Quince

Avoid

Persimmon	Prunes	Watermelon

Note: all fruits should be ripe, sweet, and be consumed on an empty stomach. Apples and pears should be cooked.

Vegetables
Favour

Artichokes	Green beans	Summer squash (yellow
Asparagus	Leeks, cooked	crookneck, zucchini)
Beetroot	Okra (lady fingers), with fat	Watercress
Carrots	Pumpkin, orange and white	Winter squash (acorn,
Celery (cooked)	Radishes, cooked	buttercup, butternut)
Cucumber, seedless	Sweet potatoes with fat	

Reduce

Broccoli	Lettuce	Plantain
Collards	Mustard greens	Radishes
Corn, fresh	Onion, cooked	Spinach
Jerusalem artichoke	Parsnips	Turnip greens

Avoid

Bell peppers	Eggplant	Peas
Brussels sprouts	Endive	Potatoes, white
Cabbage	Kohlrabi	Swiss chard
Cauliflower	Mushrooms	Sprouts
Celery, raw	Onion, raw	Tomatoes

Note: These vegetables are acceptable if cooked well, with oil and *Vata* spices, except for cabbage and sprouts. Potatoes require much fat to be digestible for *Vata* types. Raw vegetables should be avoided altogether.

Grains
Favour

Basmati rice, white	Whole rice, well	Wheat cereal, not dry
Oats, cooked	cooked,	Wild rice

Reduce

Amaranth	Pasta	Unbleached white flour,
Barley	Quinoa	Whole wheat flour
Bulgur	Rice flour	
Couscous	Udon noodles	

Avoid

Buckwheat	Cereals, dried	Oats, dry
Corn	Millet	Rye

Legumes, Beans, Peas, Soybean products
Favour

Aduki beans	Pink lentils	Toor dhal
Mung beans (split or whole)	Soy milk	
	Tofu, cooked	

Reduce

Black chickpeas	Muth beans	Urad dhal

Avoid

Black beans	Kidney beans	Soybeans
Black-eyes beans	Lima beans	Split peas
Chick peas	Navy beans	White beans
Lentils, brown	Pinto beans	

Dairy
Favour

Buttermilk	Cow's milk, certified raw	*Yoghurt,*
Cottage cheese	*Ghee*	*home-made*

Note: all of these can be taken in moderation

Reduce

Cheeses, hard and soft	Goats milk	Sour cream

Avoid

All commercially produced dairy products, including low fat milk and ice cream

Nuts and seeds
Favour

Almonds	Pecans	Sesame seeds, roasted
Brazil nuts	Pine nuts	Sunflower seeds
Cashews	Pistachios	Walnuts
Chestnuts	Pumpkin seeds	

Note: all these nuts and seeds are OK in moderation; peanuts should be avoided.

Sweeteners
Favour

Brown rice syrup	Palm sugar	Unrefined sugar
Date syrup	Rock sugar	Cane products
Honey, raw	Sugar cane juice	

Reduce

Barley malt	Maple syrup	Molasses

Avoid

Honey, heated or cooked	Sugar substitutes, (aspartame,	
White sugar	saccharin, Sweet'n Low,	
	NutraSweet)	

Oils/Fats
Favour

Almond	*Ghee*	Sunflower
Butter	Sesame	

Reduce

Coconut	Olive	Soy
Mustard	Safflower	Walnut

Avoid

Animal fats, except butter and *ghee*	Corn Mixed vegetable oils	Light fat products Synthetically derived fats

Herbs, Spices, Condiments
Favour

Allspice	Cilantro	Olives, black or green
Almond extract	Cumin	Oregano
Anise	Dill, leaves or seed	Paprika
Asafoetida	Fennel	Peppermint
Basil	Gomasio	Rock salt
Bay leaf	Ginger, dried or fresh	Rosemary
Black cumin	Lemon juice	Sage
Black pepper	Liquorice root	Sea salt
Caraway	Mace	Savory
Chutney, coconut or mango	Marjoram	Spearmint
	Mango powder	Tamarind
Cardamom	Mustard seeds, black and yellow	Tarragon
Cinnamon		Thyme
Cloves	Nutmeg	Vanilla

Reduce

Cayenne	Fenugreek	Parsley
Chilli peppers	Garlic, cooked	Saffron
Coriander seed	Horseradish	Turmeric
Curry, leaves and powder	Mint	

Note: Use all spices in moderation but avoid raw garlic and all extremely bitter and astringent tasting spices and herbs.

Brews, Beverages, Teas
All are acceptable except for:

Alcohol	Cranberry juice	Blackberry tea
Apple juice	Pear juice	Burdock tea
Caffeinated drinks	Prune juice	Dandelion tea
Carbonated drinks	Pungent drinks	
Cold drinks	Tomato juice	

PITTA PACIFYING DIET

Favour: Cool or warm foods and drinks; moderately heavy; less added butter and fats except for *ghee*; foods that are of sweet, bitter and astringent tastes.

The *Pitta* type is naturally equipped with a strong digestive power that allows him to choose from a larger variety of foods than the other body-types. His main adversary, however, is overeating. As long as he does not abuse his strong digestive power, it is hard to throw him off balance. The dominating elements in his body are fire and water. Therefore, pungent and sour foods (both are heating) as well as salty food (retaining water) upset *Pitta* and should only be used sparingly. The dominating presence of the fire element makes the *Pitta* type prefer cooling, refreshing foods and drinks, especially during the hot summer season.

Unlike the *Vata* types who benefit from oily, sour, salty, and heating foods, the *Pitta types* are greatly disturbed by them. (**Note:** if you are a *Vata/Pitta* type and not sure which one of the two *doshas* dominates one in your body, apply the muscle test for a couple of major food items from the *Pitta* list and see whether the results match with your body-type score). The *Pitta* types benefit more from bitter and astringent tastes, both of which are contained in salads. Legumes are mainly astringent and are generally liked by all *Pitta* types. Foods that have cold, heavy, and dry qualities are generally more suitable for the *Pitta* type. Mint, for example, has cooling properties whereas honey is heating. Wheat is both cooling and heavy compared to the light and heating properties of buckwheat or millet; and potatoes or cabbage are drying compared to the oiliness of eggs or peanuts. The *Pitta's* strong AGNI faces no problem in digesting them and they are therefore also not gas-forming for him. Grain foods, on the other hand, cause him trouble if they are left whole. Brown rice and heavy wholemeal bread can upset *Pitta dosha*, so does brown unrefined cane sugar. The *Pitta* type is the only one that can afford white sugar if taken in moderation and together with cereals such as oats. Maple and carob syrups, too, are easily digested by the *Pitta* type.

The fats that are contained in meat, eggs, pork, etc. strongly irritate *Pitta* types. Fried and oily foods, too, perturb a *Pitta's* stomach, causing heartburn and even ulcers. He also has great difficulties in digesting meat and fish proteins. These foods tend to heat up his body and cause circulatory problems. Most of the *Pitta* types who eat large quantities of meat on a regular basis develop coronary heart disease. *Pitta* types benefit more from a purely vegetarian diet than the other body-types. Starchy foods, plenty of vegetables, grains, and pulses greatly satisfy a *Pitta's* stomach.

A steak can make a balanced *Pitta* bad-tempered and aggressive. So can alcohol, tobacco, and coffee. They are too acidic for the already "sour-taste" dominated *Pitta* type. Mint, liquorice, and fennel teas are all pacifying *Pitta*, whereas regular tea aggravates it. The tea is broken down into large amounts of uric acid by the liver and tends to cause sluggishness and thickening of the blood. Fresh, cool water is the best drink for this body type.

*Pitta*s are better off staying away from Indian or Mexican restaurants whereas Chinese and Japanese foods suit them better. Salty snacks, like crisps, can also upset their sensitive stomach lining. *Pitta* types thrive on fresh and unprocessed foods, preferably organically grown. The remnants of pesticides or other impurities contained in foods are more likely to be felt by the *Pitta* type and can even cause "food" allergies. **Note:** to test food allergies, take your pulse; then place a small piece of the food under your tongue and take your pulse again; if it is higher than before you may be allergic to that particular food. *Ghee (clarified butter)* is one of the main foods to pacify irritated *Pitta* and can be used for cooking, and on breads. It pacifies imbalances resulting from excessive secretions of bile and stomach acid.

Pitta types should be particularly careful not to eat unripe and prematurely picked fruits, they tend to ferment in the intestines and cause loose stools or diarrhoea. Since the heating properties of the fire element are dominating in the *Pitta* type, in a balanced state he has a natural aversion to Fire Foods, which can be summarised as follows:

FIRE FOODS

- Acidic foods/medicines
- Meat and its products
- Heating grains
- Hot spices
- Nuts
- Salt and salty foods

- Sour/pungent fruits and vegetables
- Oily foods
- Pickles, vinegar.
- Red looking
- foods

Pitta Food Chart

Fruits
Favour

Apples	Mangoes	Plums, sweet
Coconut	Melons	Pomegranate
Dates, fresh	Oranges, sweet	Prunes, soaked
Figs, fresh	Pears	Raisins, soaked
Grapes, dark	Pineapple, sweet	Watermelon

Reduce

Apricots	Kiwi, sweet	Quince, sweet
Avocado	Lemons	Strawberries, sweet
Dried fruits, sweet	Limes	

Avoid

Bananas	Grapes, green	Pineapples, sour
Berries	Papaya	Persimmon
Cherries	Oranges, sour	Plums, sour
Grapefruit	Peaches	Rhubarb

Note: *Pitta* types are very sensitive to unripe, sour, and chemically treated fruits, which can cause fermentation, based diarrhoea and bloating.

Vegetables
Favour

Artichokes	Cucumber	Peas
Asparagus	Dandelion greens	Potatoes, white
Bitter and	Endive	Pumpkin, white
sweet vegetables	Green beans	Sprouts
Broccoli	Jerusalem artichoke	Sweet peppers
Brussels Sprouts	Leafy green vegetables	Winter squash
Cabbage	Lettuce	(acorn, buttercup,
Cauliflower	Mushrooms	butternut, spaghetti)
Chicory	Okra	Watercress
Collards	Parsnips	Zucchini

Reduce

Bamboo shoots	Kohlrabi	Pumpkin, orange
Carrots, cooked	Leeks, cooked	Spinach
Celery	Mustard greens	Tomatoes, in salad
Corn, fresh	Parsley	Turnip greens

Avoid

Beets	Horseradish	Swiss chard
Beet greens	Hot chilli peppers	Tomatoes, cooked
Carrots, raw	Onions, raw and cooked	Turnips
Eggplant	Radishes	

Grains
Favour

Barley	Oats, cooked	Wheat
Basmati rice, white	Pasta	

Reduce

Barley flour	Couscous	Wheat bran
Bulgur	Pasta, whole wheat	Whole wheat flour
Cereals, barley or wheat	Unbleached white flour	

Avoid

Amaranth	Corn	Quinoa
Buckwheat	Millet	Rice in excess
Brown rice	Oats, dry	Rye

Legumes, beans, peas, soybean products

Favour

Aduki beans	Mung beans, split or whole	Split peas, all kinds
Black beans	Navy beans	Tofu, cooked
Black-eyes beans	Pinto beans	Urad dhal
Chickpeas	Soybeans	
Lima beans		

Note: Consume not more than 1-2 times a week, and *avoid* lentils, brown and pink.

Dairy

Favour

Butter, unsalted	*Ghee*
Cottage cheese	Milk, certified raw

Reduce

Fresh cream cheese	Yoghurt, home-made
Lassi, sweet	

Avoid

Buttermilk	products,	Sour cream
Cheeses, hard	Goat's cheese	
Commercial dairy	Ice cream	

Nuts and Seeds

Favour

Almonds (8-10 a day)	Pumpkin seeds, raw or roasted	roasted
Coconut	Sunflower seeds, raw or	Water chestnuts, cooked
Poppy seeds		

Avoid

All other nuts and seeds

Oils/Fats

Favour

Coconut	Soy	Sunflower

Reduce

Avocado	Olive	Safflower

Avoid

Almond	Corn	Vegetable, mixed
Animal fats	Mustard	
Apricot	Sesame, dark	

Sweeteners

Favour

Barley malt	Maple syrup	White sugar, in moderation
Date syrup	Rock sugar	
Fructose	Palm sugar	

Avoid

Brown, unrefined cane sugar	Honey (except for small amounts)	Sugar substitutes (aspartame, saccharin, Sweet'n Low, NutraSweet)
Brown rice syrup	Molasses	

Herbs, spices, condiments
Favour

Apple cider vinegar	Coconut milk	Peppermint
Black cumin	Coriander	Rose water
Cilantro (green coriander)	Curry leaves	Saffron
	Dill leaves	Spearmint
Coconut, grated or roasted	Fennel	Turmeric
	Mint	Wintergreen

Reduce

Almond extract	Black pepper	Cinnamon
Basil, fresh	Caraway	Cloves
Black mustard seeds	Cardamom	Dill seed
Ginger	Mace	Olives, black
Lemon juice	Nutmeg	Orange peel
Parsley	Salt	Tamarind
Vanilla		

Avoid

Allspice	Gomasio	Preservatives and additives, chemical
Barbecue sauce	Horseradish	
Anise	Mango powder	Pickles
Asafoetida (hing)	Mustard	Rosemary
Basil	Marjoram	Sage
Bay leaves	Mayonnaise	Salt, iodised
Catsup	Yellow mustard seeds	Salty foods
Cayenne	Onion, raw	Soy Sauce
Fenugreek	Oregano	Thyme
Garlic	Paprika	Vinegar

Brews, Beverages, Teas
All are OK except:

Alcohol	Clove tea	Grapefruit juice
Banana shake	Commercially produced juices	Papaya juice
Caffeinated drinks (coffee, tea)		Sour fruit juices
	Cranberry juice	Tomato juice
Carbonated drinks	Ginger tea	Sage tea
Chocolate drinks	Ginseng tea	

KAPHA PACIFYING DIET

Favour: Warm foods; light and dry in texture; cooked without much water; only small amounts of butter, oil, and sugar; foods of pungent, bitter, and astringent tastes; foods and drinks that have a naturally stimulating influence.

The *Kapha* type has imbibed profuse amounts of the water and earth elements. This makes him naturally strong, heavy, and stable. The qualities present in the air energies, however, are not well represented in his body, which makes him look for foods that can give him the drive, movement, and the agility he requires maintaining his balance. The *Kapha dosha* has the exact opposite properties of the *Vata dosha*, which tempts him to eat mostly *Vata* increasing foods. They are the dry, light, and heating foods. Honey, beans, and barley, for example, are foods that have a drying effect and are therefore able to remove excessive fluids from the *Kapha's* system. Potatoes, too, have a similar effect.

An ideal food for the *Kapha* type is the astringent legumes that help to cleanse his intestinal tract from excessive mucous. Combined with hot spices, they stimulate his digestion and help with the removal of waste material. Most vegetarian Mexican and Indian foods are good for the *Kapha* type. The exotic smell of herbs and spices satisfies him since his sense of smell is highly developed. His often sluggish and slow metabolism can benefit greatly from an eye-watering spicy meal. A spicy and bitter appetiser like romaine lettuce with added pepper can kindle his AGNI, so can chewing on a piece of fresh ginger. *Kapha*s don't need or even want much of a salad dressing that is sour and oily.

Generally, *Kapha* types should make sure that there are enough pungent, bitter, and astringent tastes present in each meal. Spices such as cumin, fenugreek, and turmeric are both astringent and bitter. Green leafy vegetables such as spinach cooked with plenty of spices also help to pacify *Kapha*, but care should be taken not to add too much water during cooking.

During the summer, the *Kapha's* body is warm enough to eat fruits, salads, and raw vegetables. These foods, however, can greatly upset his balance in the winter, when his body requires mainly cooked foods with hot spices. Cayenne pepper is especially beneficial for him. Cooling foods such as dairy products, milk shakes, ice cream, cream, butter, sugary sweets, cakes, etc. make the *Kapha's* system cold, cause mucous congestion, and lead to heaviness, lethargy, and depression. Besides the dulling effect on the *Kapha* type, they also increase his body weight, whereas the heating influence of pungent, bitter, and astringent foods keeps his weight in check.

Fats and oils are far too heavy for the *Kapha* type and should be used sparingly. Deep fried foods quickly suppress his AGNI, which is the lowest among all the body-types. However, corn oil, sunflower oil or safflower oil are more digestible for him since they possess heating qualities (use in small quantities only). *Ghee* is a good choice, too, when used in cooking.

Salt or salty foods quickly imbalance the *Kapha* type because they tend to retain water. Many *Kapha*s suffer from swollen feet and arms because of too much salt consumption.

Since the balanced *Kapha* type is mainly influenced by the elements of Earth and Water, he has a natural aversion to Earth/Water foods, which are listed below:

EARTH/WATER FOODS

- *Salty tasting foods*
- *Sweet, juicy fruits*
- *Sweets and sweet tasting foods*
- *Sweet, watery vegetables*
- *Cool, milky foods*
- *Oily foods*
- *Sticky and cold foods*

Kapha Food Chart

Fruits

Favour

Apples	Dried fruits	Pomegranate
Apricots	Figs, dried	Quince
Berries	Peaches	Prunes
Cranberries	Pears	Raisins
Cherries	Persimmon	

Reduce

Grapes	Limes	Strawberries
Kiwi	Mango	Tangerine
Lemons	Oranges	Tamarind

Avoid

Avocado	Grapefruit	Plums
Bananas	Melons	Rhubarb
Coconut	Papaya	Watermelon
Figs, fresh	Pineapple	

Vegetables

Favour

Asparagus	Endive	Parsley
Beets	Garlic	Peas
Bell peppers	Green beans	Potatoes, white
Broccoli	Jerusalem artichoke	Radishes
Brussels sprouts	Leafy green vegetables	Spinach
Cabbage	Leeks	Sprouts
Carrots	Lettuce	Turnips
Cauliflower	Mushrooms	Turnip greens
Celery	Mustard greens	Watercress
Corn, fresh	Okra	
Eggplant	Onions	

Reduce

Artichoke	Plantain	Zucchini
Parsnips	Summer Squash	

Avoid

Cucumber	Tomatoes	Winter squash (acorn, buttercup, butternut, spaghetti)
Pumpkin, all kinds		
Sweet potatoes		

Grains

Favour

Barley	Corn	Rye
Buckwheat	Millet	

Reduce

Amaranth	Cornmeal	Quinoa
Basmati rice, white	Millet cereals	Rye cereals
(small amount)	Oats, dry	Rye flakes
Barley cereals	Oat bran	
Couscous	Pasta, rye	

Avoid

Brown rice	Steamed grains	Wheat
Oats, cooked	Rice flour	Whole wheat flour

Legumes, Beans, Peas, Soybean products

Favour

Aduki Beans	Lentils, pink	Pinto beans
Black beans	Lima beans	Split peas
Chickpeas	Navy beans	

Reduce

Black-eyes beans	Urad dhal	
Mung beans	White beans	

Avoid

Kidney beans	Soybeans	
Lentils, brown	Tofu	

Dairy
Favour

Dairy foods are best used only occasionally and in small amounts as they cause congestion in the *Kapha* type.

Reduce

Ghee	Goat's milk	
Goat's cheese, unsalted	Lassi, spiced and with honey	

Avoid

Butter	Cow's milk	Sour cream
Buttermilk	Dairy products, commercial	Yoghurt
Cheese	Ice cream	

Nuts and Seeds
Reduce

Coconut	Pumpkin seeds, roasted	Sunflower seeds, roasted
Poppy seeds	Sesame seeds	

Avoid

All nuts

Oils/Fats
Reduce

Almond	Mustard	Sunflower
Corn	Safflower	

Note: all in small amounts

Avoid

Apricot	Olive	Walnut
Avocado	Sesame	
Coconut	Soy	

Sweeteners
Favour

Honey, raw and unheated (but not more than one tablespoon a day)

Reduce

Barley malt	Dates syrup
Brown rice syrup	Maple Syrup

Avoid

Brown cane sugar, unrefined	Honey, cooked	Sugar substitutes of all kinds
Fructose	Molasses	White sugar
Glucose	Palm sugar	
	Sugarcane juice	

Herbs, Spices, Condiments
Favour

All are good for K-types except mango powder, miso, olives, salt, tamari, vinegar

Brews, Beverages, Teas
Favour

Aloe Vera juice	Carrot juice	Pomegranate juice
Apple juice	Cherry juice	Prune juice
Apricot juice	Mixed vegetable juice	Soy milk
Berry juice	Pear juice	
Carob drinks	Pineapple juice	

Note: all fruit juices should be freshly pressed, diluted with water, and taken on an empty stomach.

Reduce

Almond drink	Grape juice	Lassi, spiced and with honey
Almond milk	Mango juice	
Caffeinated drinks	Vegetable broth, salted	

Avoid

Alcohol	Cold drinks	Milk shakes
Banana shake	Comfrey teas	Orange juice
Carbonated drinks	Grapefruit juice	Papaya juice
Chocolate drinks	Lemonade	Sour drinks
Coconut milk	Liquorice tea	Tomato juice

A note with respect to all body types

In the above food charts I have omitted beef, pork, poultry, fish, and eggs as they can create major imbalances in all body-types (see section on vegetarianism). Although chicken, turkey and shrimps are the least disturbing among the animal foods, they nevertheless reduce *Ojas* in the body, which is the chemical equivalent of bliss. The following foods have a similar effect: Heavy, and oily foods, hard cheese, leftover and processed foods, and excessively sour and salty tasting foods. Also overeating prevents the body from producing *Ojas*.

Ghee – Its Importance and Preparation

Ghee is clarified butter. Although it is prepared completely from butter, its properties, according to Ayurveda, are very different from butter itself. In many cases *ghee* is recommended in the diet. *Ghee* is particularly useful for the *Pitta* constitution; it helps to digest and absorb food better and makes food tastier. Its great advantage over other forms of fat lies in the fact that it stimulates AGNI without fuelling *Pitta dosha*. Also *Vata* and even *Kapha* types benefit from *ghee*. Unless you have access to an Indian Health Food store that sells *ghee*, you have to prepare it yourself, using the following recipe.

How to Prepare Ghee

Place any amount of unsalted butter in a deep Porcelain or Pyrex type glass pan over medium-low heat (be sure that the butter does not scorch while melting). Allow melting completely and then reduce heat to low.

In the next 30-40 minutes the water in the butter will boil away (approximately 20% of the butter is composed of water). Milk solids will appear on the surface of the liquid and at the bottom of the pan.

Be alert to remove the liquid from the heat as the milk solids turn golden brown on the bottom of the pan (otherwise, the *ghee* may burn). At this point, you may notice that the *ghee* smells like popcorn and you can see tiny bubbles in the *ghee* rising from the bottom.

Strain the *ghee* while still hot or warm, pouring it through a cotton cloth into a stainless steel or Pyrex-type container. At this point it is very hot, so you should always be cautious. Another way is to let the *ghee* cool down and then strain it by pouring it through a cotton cloth or handkerchief directly into clean glass jars or bowls.

Ghee can be stored at room temperature for several weeks and it keeps indefinitely when kept in the refrigerator. Every time you cook, put a teaspoon full (per person) into food or on food afterwards. *Ghee* can be used in the same way as cooking oil, in the place of butter, or as a *digestive aid* dripped over food. If not available the best alternative is olive oil, or butter.

Note: Caution should always be observed when handling hot liquids. Ghee should never be left unattended during the heating process.

How to Make Fresh Yoghurt

1. Boil raw milk (full fat) for five to ten minutes.
2. Let milk cool to around 40 degrees centigrade.
3. Place milk in yoghurt machine (if not available, an ordinary thermos flask can be used instead).
4. Add yoghurt starter (1/2-1 teaspoon of ordinary commercial yoghurt is OK).
5. Leave yoghurt undisturbed for at least 5-7 hours. (If a thermos is used, it may take 12 hours or more).
6. Unplug yoghurt machine. Leave yoghurt at room temperature.

Perfect yoghurt is well formed (a semisolid consistency that easily breaks up) and tastes only mildly sour. Fresh yoghurt helps to improve digestion and restore the natural intestinal flora. Yoghurt, which is stored longer than one day becomes thick and sticky and has a distinct sour taste. It is damaging to the friendly bacteria in the colon and irritates the mucous lining along the entire gastrointestinal tract. Fresh yoghurt is best consumed during lunch, or as *lassi* in between meals.

Note: *Avoid yoghurt if it causes mucous irritation or leaves a white coating on the tongue.*

A Summary of General Principles Regarding Diet

1. Half a teaspoon of grated ginger taken with a pinch of salt is an excellent appetiser and kindles AGNI, the digestive fire. Splashing of cool water over face, neck, and hands before meals also stimulates AGNI.
2. Eat in a settled environment and quiet atmosphere and with a settled mind. Company and environment should be pleasant. Do not work, listen to music, read, or watch TV during meals.
3. Always sit down to eat. Eat at roughly the same times each day.
4. Eat neither too quickly nor too slowly (about 20 minutes) and without interruption.
5. Eat to about ¾ of your stomach capacity, which equals the amount of two hands full (your hands). Ideally one third of the meal should consists of liquid food.
6. Avoid taking a meal before the previous meal has been digested. Allow approximately 3 to 6 hours between meals, depending upon the kind of food you have eaten.
7. If you desire to drink anything with your meals it is best to sip hot water. Avoid drinking large quantities of liquids before, during, or within the first two 2½ hours after meals. Lassi, however, may be taken toward the end of the meal to aid digestion (it counts as liquid food).

8. Drinking excessive amounts of water (3-4 litres a day) may produce obesity and kidney disorders, drinking to little causes dehydration. To meet the minimum requirements for water take 6-8 glasses of water (at room temperature or warm) a day. Increase the amount during hot weather, when exercising, or during stress.
9. Cold foods and drinks may reduce resistance to disease, impair AGNI, and create mucous congestion.
10. Avoid taking milk with meals that have mixed tastes (e.g., vegetables, meats, fish, eggs, and sour foods such as fruit and yoghurt; radish, garlic, salt). Milk should be boiled before consumption and may be taken with toast, cereals, or sweet tasting food, or separate from a meal. Avoid altogether if it generates mucous.
11. Diet should be balanced by including all six tastes in at least one meal a day. However, you may need to consider specific recommendations regarding your particular body-type and physiological needs or imbalances
12. It is best not to heat or cook with honey; heat destroys it and makes it toxic.
13. Never eat just before going to bed. There should be at least three hours between eating and sleeping.
14. Chew well -- the digestive process starts in the mouth.
15. Ayurveda does not favour the intake of too much raw food like raw vegetables, uncooked oat flakes, uncooked grains, etc. Fruits are an exception as they are already "cooked" or ripened by nature (see also about raw food diets in chapter 10).
16. It is better not to eat when the mind is dominated by strong emotions like anger, worry, sorrow, etc., but to wait until it has become more settled.
17. Sleeping after meals causes sluggishness, and increases *Kapha* and body weight. It is best to rest for 10-15 minutes after a meal and then go for a 15-minute walk.
18. Food should always be delicious and pleasing to the senses and be prepared by a happy cook.

Sequence of Dishes during Lunch

Before you eat, be sure that your stomach is empty and that you feel hungry. If you feel you need to kindle your AGNI, take ½ teaspoon of grated ginger with a pinch of salt before eating and/or apply cool water to your face, neck, and hands.

Food that is more difficult to digest requires more digestive power and should therefore be eaten at the beginning of the meal. To improve digestion, Ayurveda recommends the following sequence of dishes:

Stage A
Sweet and heavy dishes such as whipped cream with honey, cake, cookies, other sweets, nuts, carob, milk puddings, bread and butter, etc. *Note: Sweet desserts can no longer be digested at the end of the meal when AGNI is depleted.*

Stage B
Salads composed of such raw food items as sprouts, grated carrots and beetroot, young white radish, chopped cucumber, celery stalk, lettuces and endive, etc.

Stage C
Dhal and beans, including Mung beans, lentils, chickpeas, kidney beans, etc., or else protein foods such as fresh cottage cheese, poultry or fish. *Note: Make sure that you eat only one type of protein during a meal.*

Stage D
Cooked vegetables such as asparagus, artichokes, broccoli, carrots, cauliflower, okra, butternut, zucchini, spinach, green beans, or any other wholesome fresh vegetable. *Note: Vegetables should be cooked exactly tender, not too little, and not too much. Overcooked vegetables create toxins, bloating, and dullness.*

Stage E
Basmati rice or any other wholesome type of white rice (brown rice is too heavy at this stage), pasta, couscous, barley, millet, or other grains. *Yoghurt or lassi can be taken at this stage if acceptable for your body-type and condition. Yoghurt is most beneficial when freshly prepared, i.e., started the night before, and consumed at lunchtime only.* ***Note: Stage E should be omitted if you have included animal protein in your meal because animal protein and starches cannot be digested when eaten in the same meal.***

The amounts of food at stages A, B, C should be small, at stages D and E more substantial. The latter two stages can be eaten together. The total amount should not exceed more than two cupped hands full.

Lunch does not have to consist of all the stages. In fact, it is easier on the digestive system to have not more than 3-4 basic ingredients in one meal. Try to avoid eating two concentrated food items in one meal such as rice with potatoes, rice with bread, beans with cheese, pasta with cheese, chicken with bread or other starchy foods. The only exception is beans eaten together with rice. Cooked vegetables, however, should be part of every lunch, as they help with proper bowel activities.

Ideal Daily Routine – Dinacharya

The following outline summarises an ideal daily routine, which can help anyone to restore his health or prevent illness from arising. Many people find that they can stick to some of the points but not to all of them. This is fine. Begin implementing those first that seem to be the easiest for you. As they become a natural part of your way of life, you may discover that you can implement more and more of them in your daily routine.

Morning:
- Arise early in the morning (around six o'clock)
- Drink a glass of warm water
- Drink another glass of warm water, but this time with lemon and honey
- Evacuate bowels and bladder
- Clean teeth, scrape and clean tongue
- Dry brushing of the body
- Oil massage to head, body and soles of feet
- While massaging, swish 1-2 tablespoons of cold-pressed sunflower or sesame oil in your mouth for 3-4 minutes and then spit it into the toilet
- Warm bath or shower, ideally followed by a cold shower
- Yoga Asanas (postures) and *PranaYama* (breathing exercise)
- Meditation
- Light breakfast before 8am (optional)
- Work or study

Afternoon:
- Lunch: At noon time; balanced diet according to body-type and season
- Brief rest after lunch, ideally followed by a walk of 10-15 minutes
- Work or study
- Yoga Asanas and *PranaYama*
- Meditation

Evening:
- Dinner: Light diet according to body-type, between 6pm-7pm.
- Brief walk for 10-15 minutes
- Pleasant relaxing activity such as listening to music

- Early to bed (before 10pm)

Note: Exercise should be done on a daily basis, away from meals (1/2 hour before or 2-3 hours after) according to body-type. The best time for exercise is in the morning during the *Kapha* period or else during the late afternoon.

Vegetarian Diet – One Solution to Many Health Problems

Vegetarians Live Longer and Healthier Lives

It is not necessary to be a vegetarian to enjoy benefits from an Ayurvedic diet and lifestyle. However, a balanced vegetarian diet is often considered necessary, particularly when the body is afflicted with disease. Vegetarians have believed all along that living on a purely vegetarian diet can improve health and quality of life. More recently, medical research has found that a properly balanced vegetarian diet may in fact be the healthiest diet. This was demonstrated by the over 11,000 volunteers who participated in the *Oxford Vegetarian Study* which for a period of 15 years had analysed the effects of vegetarian diet on longevity, heart disease, cancer, and various other diseases.

The results of the study stunned the vegetarian community as much as the meat producing industry: "Meat eaters are twice as likely to die from heart disease, have a 60 percent greater risk of dying from cancer and a 30 percent higher risk of death from other causes." In addition, the incidence of obesity, which is a major risk factor in many diseases, including gallbladder disease, hypertension, and adult onset diabetes, has been found to be much lower in those following a vegetarian diet. Those who take less meat in their diet have also been found to have fewer problems with *cholesterol*. The American National Institute of Health, in a study of 50,000 vegetarians, found that the vegetarians live longer and also have an impressively lower incidence of heart disease and a significantly lower rate of cancer than meat-eating Americans.

Our diet is very important for our health. According to the *American Cancer Society*, up to 35% of the 900,000 new cases of cancer each year in the United States could be prevented by following proper dietary recommendation. Researcher Rollo Russell writes in his *Notes on the Causation of Cancer:* "I have found of twenty-five nations eating flesh largely, nineteen had a high cancer rate and only one had a low rate, and that of thirty-five nations eating little or no flesh, none had a high rate."

Could cancer loose its grip on modern societies if they turned to a balanced vegetarian diet? The answer is "yes" according to two major reports, one by the World Cancer Research Fund and the other by the Committee on the Medical Aspects of Food and Nutrition Policy in the UK. The reports conclude that a diet rich in plant foods and the maintenance of a healthy body weight could prevent four million cases of cancer worldwide. Both reports stress the need for increasing intake of plant fibre, fruits and vegetables and reducing daily red and processed meat consumption to less than 80-90g.

If you are currently eating meat on a regular basis and wish to change over to a vegetarian diet, *do not give up all flesh foods at once!* Start by reducing the number of meals in which you include red meat, beef, pork, veal, etc., and substituting poultry and fish during these meals. In time, you will find that you are able to take less poultry and fish also, without creating strain on the physiology. **Note:** experts say that 40 per cent of North Sea fish have cancerous tumours caused by sea pollution, others suffer from various other illnesses; this means that healthy fish are rare today.

But isn't Meat Natural for Humans?

Vegetarians have been warned that they are not getting enough of the essential proteins humans are supposed to eat on a daily basis. Although it is known that the eight amino acids making up these proteins can be found in as simple a meal as beans and rice, meat as a source of protein is still considered to be the better option. Yet there are many more meat-free foods that contain these proteins than there are types of meat. The fact that eating *too much* protein is linked to many more serious health problems than eating too *little* protein is only rarely or not all considered in the protein discussion.

Typical disorders caused by overconsumption of protein are osteoporosis, heart disease, rheumatoid arthritis, and cancer. By contrast, those who never eat animal protein as contained in meat, fish, eggs, or dairy products, have very low rates of these diseases and don't suffer from protein deficiency either, provided they eat plenty of fruits, vegetables, grains, etc. There is no scientific evidence as yet that might indicate a protein deficiency in persons who never eat animal protein. By contrast, our modern civilisation consumes at least 50 per cent more than it actually needs to sustain itself. We may not be suffering from lack of protein at all, regardless whether essential or nonessential, but from overconsumption of protein. By filling up the connective tissues of our body with unused protein, we turn the body into an overflowing pool of acids, thereby laying a fertile ground for disease, including arteriosclerosis and bacterial or viral infection.

Research has also shown that *all* meat eaters have worms and a high incidence of parasites in the intestines. This is hardly surprising given the fact that dead flesh is a favourite target for micro-organisms of all sort. Parasites weaken the immune system and are the source of many diseases. In fact, most food poisonings today are related to meat eating. During a mass outbreak near Glasgow, 16 out of over 200 infected people died from the consequences of eating *E. coli contaminated meat*. There are frequent outbreaks reported in Scotland and many other parts of the world. Not all parasites act so swiftly as *E.koli* though. Most of them have long term effects that are noticed only after many years of eating meat.

At the root of the problem lies man's inability to properly break down meat protein into amino acids. Chunks of undigested meat pass into the intestinal tract and with them parasites. Most of the ingested parasites, also known as intestinal flukes, can neither be destroyed by the cooking process or by human stomach acid. Carnivorous animals, on the other hand, kill them instantly while passing through the stomach. Their stomachs produce twenty times more hydrochloric acid than we do. This massive amount of stomach acid helps them break down the meat proteins into their essential components. Carnivorous animals can even digest bones and fibrous tissue. Parasites and other bugs cannot survive the acid "assault."

The animals' main digestive work takes place in their stomach, which explains why they only require a relatively short intestinal tract, about three times the length of their bodies. Meat stays in their intestinal tract for only a very short while. By contrast, our small intestine is about five metres long, which is approximately twelve times the length of our body, and food is forced to stay there for many hours. If the food happens to be meat, it may remain in the small intestine from 20-48 hours by which time much of it is putrefied or decayed. The resulting meat poisons *cadaverine, putrescine,* and other toxic substances begin to act as pathogens (causal factors) of disease in the body. Since the remnants of undigested meat can be held in the large intestinal walls of humans for 20-30 years or longer, it is not surprising to find colon cancers to be highly prevalent among meat-eaters, but virtually non-existent among carnivorous animals and vegetarians. Colon cancer, in most cases, is just another name for constant food poisoning through putrefying meat. While being digested, meat is known to generate *steroid metabolites* possessing *carcinogenic* (cancer producing) properties.

The kidneys, which extract waste products from the blood, also suffer from the overload of meat poisons consisting mostly of nitrogenous wastes. Even moderate meat-eaters demand three times more work from their kidneys than do vegetarians. Young people generally may still be able to cope with this form of stress, but as one grows older the risk of kidney damage greatly increases.

After many years of regularly consuming meat the body may suddenly succumb to the floods of poisonous substances emanating from undigested meat. A recent study conducted in Germany showed that middle-aged persons who consumed meat in the evening were more prone to suffer a heart attack during the next morning. Too many proteins entering the blood can thicken it and drastically cut oxygen supplies to the heart and other organs such as the brain.

Animal cells, unlike plant cells which have a rigid cell wall and a simple circulatory system, die very rapidly once the they are cut off their blood supply. When the animal dies, its cell proteins coagulate and self-destruct enzymes begin to break down the cells. This in turn results in the formation of a denatured substance called *ptomaine,* which is a known cause of many diseases. Cellular destruction applies to the cells of all types of dead animal flesh, as well as chicken and fish; all meat is poisoned with decomposed and putrefied protein. A dead animal, bird, or fish is no longer "fresh." Putrefaction and bacterial growth start immediately after death and are very advanced when the meat is several days or weeks old, as is in most cases.

Whether it is *E.koli,* other bacteria, or enzymes acting on the dead protein, they effectively send the immune system on a "mission of war," hence the stimulating effect of meat. Depending on one's physical resources and immune capacity, the body may eventually get overwhelmed by the influx of virulent poisons and begin to signal "dis-ease." Those with the weakest immune system are usually the first ones to suffer from meat poisoning.

Man's entire anatomy (jaw, teeth, and digestive system, hands and feet) shows that he must have evolved for millions of years living on fruits, grains, vegetables, nuts, and seeds, etc. Non-carnivorous animals, including the human animal, have long bowels, designed for the slow digestion of nutrient-rich vegetables and fruits. Our dental structure is only conducive to cutting vegetables with incisors and to grinding vegetables and fruits with molars. Our short, dull canines have no capacity for slashing or tearing meat. We have indeed nothing in our anatomy that compares with the sharp claws of a tiger or an eagle. The human hand with its opposable thumb is better suited for harvesting fruits and vegetables than to killing prey. Had it been in our nature to eat flesh, we, too, would have been equipped with the same or similar hunting faculties as carnivorous animals.

It is also worth noting that carnivorous animals have an unlimited capacity to handle saturated fats and *cholesterol*. Dogs, for example, who receive one half pound of butterfat with their daily ratio of meat for two years, show no signs of damage to their arteries or change of serum *cholesterol*. By contrast, the purely vegetarian rabbits quickly develop arteriosclerosis if they are fed with meat or if 2 grams of *cholesterol* is added daily to their food. Meat eating humans too have a very limited capacity to digest and process meat proteins and meat fats. If we listened to our basic instincts, we would discover that meat is not meant for humans.

Meat -- A Major Cause of Disease and Ageing

Populations who eat meat regularly have the shortest life spans and the highest incidence of degenerative diseases. According to published reports on national health statistics from around the world, one out of two people in the industrialised world will die from heart disease or related blood vessel disease. This makes heart disease the leading killer disease in the world. The American Medical Association reported in June 1961 that a vegetarian diet could prevent 90% of our thrombo-embolic disease and 97% of our coronary occlusions. In other words, adopting a vegetarian diet could nearly eradicate heart disease altogether. Compared with meat eating, smoking seems to be only a minor risk factor for heart disease.

Heart disease is virtually unheard of in societies where meat consumption is low and the majority of the population eats mostly traditional foods. A group of Harvard doctors and research scientists examined 400 people in a remote mountain village in Ecuador and were surprised to find that except for two men none of the people above 75, including all the centenarians and a 121 year-old man, showed any signs of heart disease. The villagers were all vegetarians. Such examination of a similar population in the United States would show 95 per cent with heart disease.

Cancer, the second most common killer disease, may largely be caused by meat eating, too. Modern cancer research claims to have found specific protein compounds responsible for certain types of cancers. This in itself may be a very important finding but it is even more important to find out where these protein particles come from. Putrefying meat is one answer and decaying protein of dead human cells another. Meat consumption slows or hinders the complete removal of dead cells in the body by using up its resources of energy, enzymes, minerals, and vitamins. Both, undigested meat proteins and decaying cell protein can therefore damage the human cells and impair genetic programming.

Another reason why meat-eaters have more cancers than vegetarians may be that they ingest large quantities of sodium nitrates and sodium nitrites, which are *carcinogenic* preservatives that are used to make the meat look "fresh." But meat is no longer fresh after the animal is dead. If untreated, within a few days animal flesh turns into a sickly grey-green colour. Since nobody would buy the meat in that condition, the meat industry uses these toxic chemicals to make it look red and palatable, whereas in reality it is already decomposed and poisoned.

The most appalling news from cancer research, however, is that secondary *amines*, prevalent in beer, wine, tea, and tobacco, react with chemical preservatives in meat and form *nitrosamines*. The American Food and Drug Administration (FDA) has labelled *nitrosamines* to be "one of the most formidable and versatile groups of *carcinogens* yet discovered." In other words, if you are a smoker or if you drink beer, wine, or tea *and* eat meat, you produce one of the most deadly toxins that can be found anywhere. As it turns out, most meat-eaters also drink wine or beer and many of them smoke, too. When fed to test animals, *nitrosamines* produced malignant tumours in *one hundred percent* of the animals; the cancers appeared everywhere, including the lungs, pancreas, stomach, adrenals, intestines, and the brain.

There are many other cancer-producing agents that a meat-eater's immune system has to combat. Farm animals are regularly injected with hormones to stimulate growth, are fed appetite stimulants to "force" them to eat non-stop, and are given antibiotics, sedatives, and chemical feed mixtures. There are already over 2,500 drugs routinely given to animals to fatten them and to keep them alive. Although these drugs given to the live animals and many others that are added after the animal has been slaughtered will still be present in the meat when it is eaten, the law does not require that they be listed on the package.

One of the chemicals added to animal feed in the United States is the growth hormone *diethylstilbestrol* (DES). The FDA estimates it saves meat producers in the United States $500 million annually. DES is highly carcinogenic and is banned as a serious health hazard in thirty-two countries. According to another report by the FDA, the antibiotics *penicillin* and *tetracycline* alone save the meat industry $1,9 billion a year. Yet the drugs may be breeding deadly antibiotic resistant organisms in the consumer's body.

Perhaps some of the worst effects that can emanate from eating meat are generated by the tragic conditions farm animals are exposed to today. Most animals never see the light of day. They spend their entire lives in cramped and cruel surroundings, merely to die a brutal death. High rise chicken farms breed animals without giving them fresh air or allowing them to even take one step. This not only greatly upsets their body chemistry but also causes malformations and growth of malignant tumours. The sick animals are slaughtered and sold to unsuspecting customers. Examples of common diseases include cows with eye cancer and abscessed livers. In the United States, chicken with *airsacculitis* (a pneumonia-like disease), which causes pus-laden mucous to collect in the lungs, are permitted for sale. Carcasses contaminated with rodent faeces, cockroaches, and rust are routinely found in meat-packing companies, but meat inspectors feel very lax about enforcing regulations because this would effectively close down the whole business.

Modern cancer research is mostly focused on how to combat the *effects* of a disruptive lifestyle and unhealthy eating habits. Billions of dollars are spend on discovering everything about the symptoms of disease, with little or no attention on their underlying causes. By contrast, some parts of the population in our western society have adopted vegetarianism as a way of life and subsequently shown to have significantly lower cancer rates. These groups have no advanced medical knowledge or treatment to deal with cancer.

Benefits of a Vegetarian Diet

A recent study conducted in California revealed that the cancer rate among Mormons, who are known to eat only very little meat, was 50 per cent lower than in the normal population. A more comprehensive controlled study on 50,000 vegetarians of the *Seventh Day Adventists*, compared with the same number of non-vegetarians of the same sex and age, produced similar results as *the Oxford Vegetarian Study*. The members of the vegetarian group had an astonishingly low rate of cancer of all types, their life expectancy was significantly longer, and they suffered significantly less from cardiovascular disease than those in the control group.

In the same context, the "forced" vegetarianism of the Danes due to the allied blockage of Denmark in World War I, led to a 17 per cent reduction of mortality rates in the first year of meat rationing. Norway had a similar experience during the years of World War II (1940-1945). There was an immediate drop in national mortality rates from circulatory diseases during the period of meat shortage; the rates returned to pre-war levels when the population resumed meat consumption.

Studies from the University of Belgium, testing endurance, strength, and quickness of recovery (from physical exhaustion) in vegetarians, clearly showed that vegetarians were far superior in all three categories. A study at Yale University proved that vegetarians have nearly twice the stamina of meat eaters. Other findings confirmed that during endurance tests, the vegetarians were able to perform two to three times longer than the meat eaters before reaching the point of complete exhaustion, and took only one fifth the time to recover from fatigue after each test than their meat-eating counterparts.

The common belief that eating meat makes you strong is unfounded and misleading. Such super strong animals as the elephant, gorilla, rhinoceros, and the bull sustain their physical power by eating only vegetation. On present evidence there is nothing to suggest that meat is beneficial to our health. That populations like the Eskimos can survive on a meat diet without suffering heart disease is known. But it is less known that they also drink the blood of the animal, which is alkaline and capable of neutralising the toxic effect of the meat. Still, the Eskimo's average life span is not more than 40 years.

Another major benefit of the vegetarian diet is that, statistically, vegetarians are thinner and healthier. On average, vegetarians weight about 20 pounds less than their meat eating counterparts. Harvard research showed that a vegetarian diet reduces colds and allergies. Also children greatly benefit from meat abstinence. Studies show that vegetarian children have better teeth and much less incidence of children's diseases than non-vegetarian children have, and are less prone to obesity, high cholesterol, and heart disease.

Food For Thought
- According to Harvard nutritionist Jean Mayer, we would have enough food for the entire developing world if we ate half as much meat. Reducing meat production by merely 10 per cent could release enough grain to feed 60 million people!
- Only 10 per cent of the protein and calories we feed to our livestock are recovered in the meat we eat. In the case of the United States, for the 20 million tons of humanly edible and nutritious protein that is fed to livestock yearly, only about 2 million tons of meat protein is obtained; and out of that amount less than 27 per cent can be utilised by the human body. The wasted protein could fill the protein deficit around the world three times over.
- One acre of grain produces five times more protein than an acre of pasture set aside for meat production. An acre of beans or peas produces ten times more, and an acre of spinach twenty-eight times more protein.
- One portion of meat contains only 20 grams of protein, whereas a 100-gram portion of soybeans yields 35 grams of protein. The meat, however, costs about 20 times more than the beans do. Being vegetarian saves not only lives but also money.
- The food energy supplied by meat production uses 10 times more fossil fuel than the food energy supplied by plant production.
- Eighty-five percent of the topsoil lost in the USA alone each year is directly associated with the raising of livestock. In this way, 4 million acres of cropland get destroyed every year. In the same way, precious rain forests have to give way to satisfy the demand for more meat in the world.
- To grow one pound of wheat requires only sixty pounds of water, whereas production of one pound of meat requires anywhere from 2,500 to 6,000 pounds of water. In addition, large chicken slaughtering plants use up to 100 million gallons of water daily, enough to supply a city of 25,000 people!
- The meat production process is so wasteful and costly that the industry needs hundreds of millions in tax subsidies to survive. You never pay just for the meat you eat. In 1977, the governments of Western Europe spent almost half a billion dollars purchasing the farmer's overproduction of meat and spent additional millions for the cost of storing it. This is precious money lost, heavily burdening every national economy. In this sense, meat consumption is directly impoverishing the wealthy nations.

CHAPTER 7

Useful Self-help Programmes

1. The Liver Cleanse

Cleansing the liver and gall bladder from gallstones is one of the most important and powerful tools to improve your health. To remove gallstones you need the following things:

Apple juice	6-12 one litre boxes
Epsom salts	4 tablespoons
Olive oil, cold pressed and pure	half cup
Fresh grapefruit (pink is best)	1 large or 2 small, enough to squeeze 2/3 to ¾ cup juice
Black Walnut Hull Tincture	10 drops
2 pint jars, one with lid	

Note: The 10 drops Black Walnut Hull Tincture in the cleanse-recipe are used to kill bacteria and viruses as they come out of the bile ducts. (If your local herb or health food shop/pharmacy doesn't have it you can order it from the "Self Help Resource Center," USA or Nutri Centre, London; see Useful Addresses).

Preparation

- Drink 1-2 litres of packaged apple juice a day for a period of six days. This will soften the stones and make their passage through the bile ducts easier. The apple juice has a strong cleansing effect and may cause bloating and even diarrhoea during the first few days. The fermentation of the juice helps the expansion of the bile ducts. If this becomes somewhat uncomfortable, mix the apple juice with water. Drink the juice slowly throughout the day, in between meals (**avoid** during, just before, 2 hours after meals, or in the evening). This is in addition to your normal water intake. **Note:** although packaged apple juice (possibly of organic source) is normally not recommended, it works best for this type of cleanse. Eat regular meals but reduce or avoid protein foods and heavy items.

- The main part of the cleanse is best done over a weekend, when you have enough time to rest, and preferably during the days of full moon or waning moon. During the cleanse avoid taking any medicine, vitamins, or pills that are not absolutely necessary; this includes sleeping pills. [If you are on medication consult your doctor.]

- On the sixth day of drinking apple juice, if you feel hungry in the morning eat a light breakfast such as cooked cereal, fruit, or fruit juice (no milk, butter, yoghurt cheese, ham, eggs, etc.). For lunch eat plain cooked vegetables with rice (a little salt may be added). <u>Don't eat or drink anything (except water) after 2 PM!</u> The timing given below is essential for the success of the cleanse.

Doing the Cleanse
Evening
6:00 PM: Mix four tablespoons of Epsom salts in 3 cups of water and keep it in a jar. This makes four servings, ¾ cup each or 185 ml. Drink your first portion now. You may take a few sips of water afterwards to get rid of the bitter taste in the mouth (it may be easier to take it with a large plastic straw, as this will bypass the taste buds on the tongue).

8:00 PM: Drink your second ¾ cup of Epsom salts.

9:30 PM: If you haven't had a bowel movement until now, take a water enema (see section on Enema treatments below); this will trigger a series of bowel movements.

9:45 PM: Squeeze the grapefruit(s); you will need ¾ cup of juice; remove pulp. Pour the juice and ½ cup olive oil into the pint jar. Add the 10 drops of Black Walnut Hull Tincture. Close the jar tightly and shake hard about twenty times, or until watery. You want to drink this mixture at 10pm, but if you feel you still need to visit the bathroom a few more times you may delay for 10-15 minutes.

10:00 PM: Stand next to your bed (don't sit) and drink the concoction, if possible in one go or otherwise with a large plastic straw. You may use brown sugar to chase it down between sips. Don't take more than 5 minutes for this procedure.

LIE DOWN STRAIGHTAWAY, otherwise you may not be able to release the stones. Turn off the lights and lie flat on your back with your head up high on a pillow or two. Put your attention on the liver and, if you can, visualise the mixture moving the stones out of its numerous bile ducts. *Keep perfectly still for at least 20 minutes!* This gives the stones a chance to move freely along the bile ducts. There won't be any pain because the Epsom salts will keep the bile duct valves wide open. Go to sleep if you can.

If at any time during the night, you feel the need to have a bowel movement, do so. Check if there are already small gallstones (pea green or tan coloured) floating in the toilet. You may feel nauseous during the night and in the early morning hours. This will pass as the morning progresses.

The Following Morning
6:00 - 6:30 AM: Upon awakening, but not before 6am, drink your third ¾ cup of Epsom salts (in case you feel very thirsty drink a glass of warm water before taking the salts). Rest or meditate. If you are very sleepy you may go back to bed.

8:00 - 8:30 AM: Drink your fourth and last ¾ cup of Epsom salts and rest.

10:00 - 10:30 AM: Take freshly pressed fruit juice, preferably apple or orange juice, water it down and drink very slowly.

Half an hour later eat 1-2 pieces of fruit. One hour later you may eat regular (but light) food.

The Results you can expect
You will have a number of bowel movements in the form of diarrhoea, consisting of gallstones mixed first with food residue and then with only water. Look for gallstones floating in the toilet (they float because they contain cholesterol). You will see mostly green ones of all sizes and shapes, some pea-sized or smaller and others as big as 2-3 centimetres. There may be hundreds of stones coming out at once. Also watch out for tan-coloured and white ones. Some of the larger tan-coloured stones may sink with the stool because they are calcified and contain heavier toxic substances and only small amounts of cholesterol. All the green stones are as soft as putty, thanks to the apple juice.

You may also find a layer of white or tan coloured scum or foam floating in the toilet. The scum consists of millions of tiny white, sharp-edged cholesterol crystals, which can easily rupture small bile ducts; they are equally important to get rid of.

It is most likely that some stones will get caught in the colon. They can quickly be removed through colonic irrigation (see next section). If they remain in the colon, they can cause irritation, headaches, skin problems, and abdominal discomfort. So make sure that you **have a colonic irrigation after each liver cleanse!** If colonics are not available where you live, take a coffee enema followed by a water enema (see next section). Although this may take out most of the remaining stones, there is no guarantee that it will. Only colonics are 100% effective. It certainly is not recommended to attempt a liver cleanse without taking a colonic afterwards.

Try to make a rough estimate of how many stones you have eliminated. To permanently cure bursitis, back pain, allergies, or other health problems, you need to remove **all** the stones. This may require at least six cleanses which can be performed at 2-3 week intervals (don't cleanse more frequently than that). If you cannot manage or don't feel like it, take more time between the cleanses. The main thing is that once you have started cleansing the liver you must continue until it is clean. The liver as a whole will begin to function more efficiently soon after the first cleanse and you may notice sudden improvements, sometimes within a few hours. Pains will be less, energy will increase, and clarity of mind will improve considerably.

However, within a few days, stones from the rear of the liver will have travelled "forward" towards the two main bile ducts exiting the liver, which may cause some of the previous symptoms of discomfort to return. In fact, you might feel disappointed because the recovery seems so short-lived. But all this shows that there are still stones left behind, ready to be removed with the next round of elimination. Nevertheless, the liver's self-repair and cleansing responses will have greatly increased, adding a great deal of effectiveness to this all-important organ of the body.

As long as there are still a few small stones moving from some of the thousands of small bile ducts towards the hundreds of larger bile ducts, they may combine to form larger stones and produce such previously experienced symptoms as backache, headache, earache, digestive trouble, bloating, irritability, anger, etc., although they may be less severe than they were before. If a new cleanse no longer produces more than a few very small pale-coloured stones, which usually happens after the sixth cleanse, you can consider your liver to be in excellent condition. Still, it is recommended to repeat the liver cleanse every six months. Each cleanse will give a further boost to the liver and take care of any toxins that may have accumulated there in the meanwhile. **Note:** Never cleanse when you are a suffering an acute illness, even if it is just a cold.

Making the Liver Cleanse more Effective

A more effective version of the Liver Cleanse includes taking one tablespoon of pure, cold pressed olive oil mixed with one table spoon of lemon juice on an empty stomach in the morning, during the six days of preparation. Start by drinking one or two glasses of warm water first thing in the morning and wait for 10-15 minutes. Mix the olive oil with the lemon juice until watery and drink the mixture; otherwise take them separately, one after the other. You may have breakfast after one hour. Although the Liver Cleanse is very effective without this addition to the pre-treatment, it can add more success to the cleanse. If your body doesn't agree with the oil, you may instead eat two medium size ripe, sweet pears on an empty stomach in the morning, at least half an hour before eating breakfast. Drinking pear juice is equally effective, especially for Vata and Pitta body types. Kapha types benefit from eating 1-2 grapefruits a day during the six days of preparation.

Although the liver cleanse by itself can produce dramatic results, for maximum benefit it is best done *after* a colon and kidney cleanse. Cleansing the colon and the kidneys first will ensure that the stones and toxins coming out of the liver are more easily eliminated without causing too much extra burden on the vital organs of elimination. The ideal pre-treatment for the first liver cleanse consists of 2-3 sessions of *colonic irrigation*, which is best preceded by 3-4 four weeks of cleansing the kidneys (see "The Kidney Cleanse").

To re-emphasise: Removing gallstones from the liver and gallbladder may leave some of the stones and other toxic residues in the colon. It is therefore very important that you have a colonic after each liver cleanse. To give the best possible results, the colonic is best taken within three days after the cleanse. Also, drinking one cup of any kidney/bladder tea ½ hour before meals for three days after each cleanse helps the kidneys to dispose of any harmful substances that may have moved there as a result of the liver cleanse.

Note: If there is severe congestion in both the major liver bile ducts and/or the gallbladder, it may take one or even two cleanses to break through the obstruction. In such a case, only a few smaller stones may come out at first. With the following cleanses larger quantities of stones are released, including large dark green (old) stones. Although such cases are extremely rare, they do occur. The important thing is to continue cleansing until the results are satisfactory. To recognise the signs and indications of gallstones in the liver and gallbladder refer to my book "The Amazing Liver Cleanse."

2. Intestinal Cleansing - For Prevention and Cure

The body's health greatly depends on the effortless and complete elimination of waste products from the intestinal tract. Most physical problems are caused by a build-up of toxic substances, which may first accumulate in the intestines and then spread to other parts of the body, such as the liver and kidneys. Retained waste material in the large intestine may consist of impacted faeces, hardened mucous, dead cellular tissue, gallstones that were released from the gallbladder, microbes, parasites, worms, etc. Parts of the waste matter may enter the general circulation, causing a person to feel tired, sluggish, or ill. The toxic waste also impairs the colon's function to absorb important minerals and bacteria-produced vitamins.

Colon-related complaints include constipation, diarrhoea, bloating, headaches, dizziness, nausea, sinusitis, backaches, bad breath, body odour, sciatica, skin blemishes and skin diseases, abdominal gas, low energy, problems of the nervous system, etc. A clean colon is a prerequisite for the balanced functioning of the rest of the body. To cleanse the intestines should therefore be part of every therapy. I recommend three methods to aid intestinal cleansing; they are *Colonic Irrigation, Magnesium Oxides,* and *Enema* treatments.

Colonic Irrigation or Colon Hydrotherapy

Colonic irrigation is perhaps one of the most effective colon therapies since it can eliminate within a short passage of time large amounts of trapped waste that took many years to accumulate. During a 30-50 minute session of colonic irrigation, a total of 2-6 litres of distilled water is used to gently flush the colon. Through gentle abdominal massage old deposits of mucoid faecal matter are loosened and subsequently removed by the water.

A Colonic removes not only toxins but also tones, strengthens, and rejuvenates the colon muscles. The gentle emptying and filling of the entire colon with water improves the colon's peristaltic action and reduces the transit time of faecal material. In addition, colonic irrigation helps restore the colon's natural shape, and stimulates the reflex points that connect the colon with all the parts of the body. This form of colon cleansing can detach old crusted layers of waste from the colon walls, which permits better water absorption and hydration of the colon and the body as a whole.

Colonic irrigation can also help with emotional problems. It is no coincidence that the transverse colon passes right through the solar plexus, which is the body's emotional centre. All uncompleted and "undigested" emotional issues are stored in the solar plexus and result in the tightening of the colon muscle, which may slow bowel movement and cause constipation. Colonics can help clear the physical obstruction and release the tension that caused the emotional repression in the first place.

Colonics have a truly relieving effect. Although during a colonic you may feel a slight discomfort from time to time whenever larger quantities of toxic waste detach themselves from the intestinal walls and move towards the rectum, but the feeling of lightness, cleanness, and clarity of mind soon afterwards make up for that.

Colonic irrigation is a completely save and hygienic system of cleansing the colon. Rubber tubing carries water into the colon and waste out of the colon. The released waste material can be seen floating through a tube, showing the type and quantity of waste eliminated.

Colonic cleansing is best done when the stomach is empty. It is beneficial to drink 1-2 glasses of water afterwards and eat fruit or have fruit juice ½ hour later. The first one or two meals after the treatment should be light and not contain heavy food items such as meat, eggs, cheese, fried food, etc. To help restore the friendly bacterial population of the colon, it is best to have a cup of freshly prepared yoghurt or kefir towards the end of lunch for at least three days after the cleanse and let the colon do the rest rather than taking extra bacteria in capsule form (omit this advice if yoghurt causes mucous aggravation or white coating on the tongue).

It is much easier for the friendly colon bacteria to multiply in a clean environment than in a putrefied one. The bowel movement will become naturally restored within 1-2 days. If it takes longer than that it indicates that the colon has accumulated unduly large amounts of waste over a period of many years, which may require more colonics to clear them.

Once the colon has been thoroughly cleansed through 2-3 or more colonics, then diet, exercise, or other health programmes will become many times more effective. Since an estimated 80 per cent of the immune tissue resides in the intestines, cleansing the colon from immune-suppressive toxic waste in addition to removing gallstones from the liver can make all the difference in the treatment of cancer, heart disease, AIDS, and other illnesses.

Colosan Treatment

Colosan (formerly known as *Colo Zone*) is a proprietary blend of various oxides of magnesium designed to gently release oxygen in the digestive tract for cleansing. In my practice I have found it to be a very useful product to counteract the following problems (please note that there may be similar brands of magnesium oxides available that have similar effects, "Oxy-Cleanse" being one of them):

Build-up of undigested material in the intestines and colon
Impeded assimilation of nutrients
Presence of pathogens and parasites that breed in the putrefaction of the digestive tact
Detox or healing crisis associated with many health regimens
Insufficient oxygen to maintain homeostasis

The main actions of Colosan:
It releases oxygen in the intestines and colon to help speed the elimination of wastes.
It provides needed oxygen for proper digestion and cleanses digestive membranes to allow better uptake of nutrients.
It eliminates the unwanted build-up of toxins, creating a clean and healthful environment where there is no room or "food" for disease causing microbes.

How does Colosan Work?
The various oxides of magnesium contained in *Colosan* involve the bonding of oxygen and ozone to magnesium. This alkaline compound requires an extremely low pH in order to liberate its oxygen. For this reason the hydrochloric acid in the stomach is commonly assisted with the juice of a lemon or apple cider vinegar. The average size tablespoon of approximately 7-10g of pure magnesium oxide would produce a total volume of 3.85 cubic meters of oxygen. In the use of *Colosan*, one tsp. would provide approximately 7.5 litres of available oxygen. This oxygen is made bio-available to the stomach which is 40 per cent more efficient at assimilating oxygen than the lungs are. It also assists in oxidising the undigested putrefaction that is known to be impacting the intestines and the colon. The average person has six to twelve pounds of putrefaction rotting away in their gut, breeding pathogens and creating a welcome home far parasites, germs, bacteria, and viruses.

Digestion is known to be a process of oxidation. By introducing oxygen into the intestines and the colon, one can assist the process of assimilating nutrients, as well as oxidising the undigested material. It is common for *Colosan* to turn undigested material into CO_2 and water. For this reason, *Colosan* is a cathartic. It is not unusual to have very liquid stools during the use of *Colosan*; this is a sign that the product is working. If the stools are not liquid during the first 1-2 treatments, it shows that most of the magnesium is absorbed straight away, indicating a mineral deficiency. After a few treatments, the situation returns to normal and stools become liquid and more frequent following each dose of *Colosan*.

Digestion is known to be a process of oxidation. By introducing oxygen into the intestines and the colon, one can assist the process of assimilating nutrients, as well as oxidising the undigested material. It is common for *Colosan* to turn undigested material into CO_2 and water. For this reason, *Colosan* is a cathartic. It is not unusual to have very liquid stools during the use of *Colosan*; this is a sign that the product is working. If the stools are not liquid during the first 1-2 treatments, it shows that most of the magnesium is absorbed straight away, indicating a mineral deficiency. After a few treatments, the situation returns to normal and stools become liquid and more frequent following each dose of *Colosan*.

Many people use *Colosan* once or twice weekly as a maintenance product for staying clean and maintaining regularity. The most common health problem besides irregular bowel movement that *Colosan* has shown tremendous benefit for is *Candida* (also see chapter 10). *Colosan* provides an aerobic environment in the intestines and colon. Therefore, it is beneficial to the friendly aerobic bacteria, which are desirable and inhibitory toward anaerobic undesirable bacteria. In other words, it helps beneficial intestinal flora flourish.

Colosan can be used to prevent any type of healing crises or detox reaction that those persons undertaking a cleansing regimen will frequently come across. Anyone versed in natural therapies is usually familiar with these occurrences. These incidences stem from attempting to clean out the body before the organs of elimination have been cleansed. This results in a backup of wastes and the body frequently attempts to get rid of these wastes through the skin. This backup can result in feelings of nausea, headaches, tiredness, or pain in the liver and kidneys.

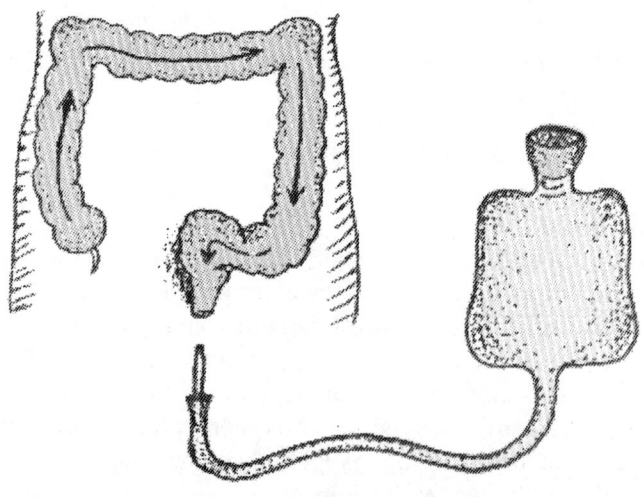

Illustration 12: Enema Treatment

By cleaning out the organs of elimination through the use of *Colosan*, one can avoid detox reactions associated with the use of herbal cleansing programmes or other regimens that are practised for this purpose. *Colosan* is available from "The Family News" in the United States (see "Useful Addresses" at the end of the book).

Three Major Enema Treatments

Enema treatments involve introduction of liquids into the rectum for the purpose of cleansing and nourishment (see illustration 12). Since the colon is the seat of *Vata*, an enema has an immediate effect on all the functions of *Vata*. It alleviates constipation, distension, chronic fever, the common cold, headache, sexual disorders, kidney stones, pain in the heart area, vomiting, low back ache, stiffness and pain in neck and shoulders, nervous disorders, hyperacidity, and tiredness. Also disorders such as arthritis, rheumatism, sciatica, and gout greatly benefit from an enema. (If you have access to a *Colon-hydrotherapy* treatment, this is still the best and fastest means to balance disturbed *Vata* functions)

Digestion is known to be a process of oxidation. By introducing oxygen into the intestines and the colon, one can assist the process of assimilating nutrients, as well as oxidising the undigested material. It is common for *Colosan* to turn undigested material into CO_2 and water. For this reason, *Colosan* is a cathartic. It is not unusual to have very liquid stools during the use of *Colosan*; this is a sign that the product is working. If the stools are not liquid during the first 1-2 treatments, it shows that most of the magnesium is absorbed straight away, indicating a mineral deficiency. After a few treatments, the situation returns to normal and stools become liquid and more frequent following each dose of *Colosan*.

1. Oil enema: Half a cup of warm sesame oil for above problems and chronic constipation once or twice a week. The oil should be retained for at least 30 minutes or longer. To make it a nourishing enema, add 3 tablespoons each of honey and ghee and half a cup of milk (unless you have a milk allergy). **Note**: Those with diabetes, obesity, indigestion, low AGNI, and enlarged spleen should opt for the second type enema.

2. Decoction or water enema: Up to half a litre of lapacho, comfrey, or chaparral tea, or plain water, at room temperature. This enema is indicated for acute constipation and above problems, but should not be taken more often than once or twice a week. **Note**: avoid if you suffer from debility, haemorrhoids, inflammation of anus, diarrhoea, or if pregnant. If you are diabetic, consult your physician. The effects increase if an enema type 2 is followed by an enema type1. Patients who are lying in bed and are constipated can take enemas type 1 and 2 alternately, one every day.

3. Coffee enema: Place 3 heaped tablespoons of ground coffee (not instant coffee) into 16 ounces (2 glasses) of boiling water. Boil for 3 minutes and let simmer (on a low flame) for a further 15 minutes. Then filter the decoction through a coffee filter or cotton cloth. Make sure that no coffee substance is left at the bottom. Let it cool to about body temperature and perform the enema while lying on your back with your legs elevated. Hold the coffee solution as long as possible; turning to your right side may help make this easier. This enema is indicated when you feel very sluggish and tired, and particularly when you feel pain in your middle/upper back, all indications of a toxic liver. Although ground coffee is a major toxin for the body, triggered by a nerve reflex it can open the bile ducts of the liver and releases poisonous substances and even a few gallstones from the liver. The effect is often immediate. This enema can be taken if time or circumstances, or feeling ill don't permit a person to apply the liver cleanse. When seriously ill with cancer, liver or heart disease, it can be taken more frequently, as often as every other day.

3. The Kidney Cleanse

To remove crystals and stones from the kidneys and bladder you need the following dried roots and herbs:

> Marjoram
> Uva Ursi
> Hydrangea Root
> Gravel Root
> Marshmallow root
> Comfrey Root
> Golden Rod Herb
> Cat's Claw
> Fennel Seed
> Chicory Herb
> Lemon Seed
> (if Available)

Preparation: Mix the herbs together in equal parts. Soak 3-4 heaped tablespoons in two large cups of water overnight. In the morning bring to a boil and let simmer for 10-15 minutes. Strain and drink this concoction in 4-6 divided doses each day, warm or at room temperature.

Further instructions: To dissolve most crystals and stones in the kidneys and bladder takes about four weeks, in severe conditions six weeks. Drinking ½ cup of parsley water each day of the cleanse adds effectiveness and so does taking a capsule of ginger root powder before every meal. To prepare parsley water, boil a small bunch of fresh parsley in ¾ cup of water for three minutes; drink when cool enough.

While on the kidney cleanse follow a light Ayurvedic diet with little or no protein foods. Avoid all carbonated beverages, tea, coffee, chocolate, etc. as these can form new stones within a few days and prevent the herbs from dissolving the old ones. Drink plenty of water (not refrigerated) to help flush out the crystal residues.

Try following the Ayurvedic daily routine. Many kidney stones result from sleeping during the *Kapha* period in the morning (6-10am, or after sunrise). When urine is forced to stay in the body longer than is normal, some of its constituents begin precipitating and forming crystals. If sleeping until 8am or later becomes a regular habit there may be urinary infection, accompanied by pain in the joints, headache, or heaviness.

The kidney cleanse is perfectly safe and there is no pain involved, although there may be slight discomfort from time to time in the lower back area. While you are on the cleanse look for crystal sediments in the urine. At some stage the urine may give off an unpleasant odour. There may also be increased body odour for a day or two. Such or similar cleansing reactions usually do not occur but they can. So if anything unusual happens, it may be related to normalising kidney functions.

To keep the kidneys clean, you require two cleanses a year. The ingredients for the cleanse can be obtained from any nutrition or herb centre. In the UK, they are available from the Nutri Centre (see Useful Addresses).

Important note: If you are over 70 or very sick do the cleanse for six weeks. If you have a history of kidney stones, or have been diagnosed as having large kidney or bladder stones, or have chronic pain or stiffness in the loin areas, toes or fingers, you may need to add the following alkalisation procedure to the kidney cleanse. If you are not sure whether you need this addition, then do it anyway, it can help many other problems, including allergies:

1. Check the acidity of your urine with a pH-indicator, a special paper used for measuring urinary pH (available at the chemist). First thing in the morning hold a small piece of this paper (Nitrazine™ paper) in the urine stream. If it indicates a pH of 5,5 or below, the acidity level is too high which shows that you require an alkalising treatment. You need to have a morning urine of about 6,0 acidity. Most people with painful joints have a morning urine pH of 4,5, which means that more uric acid is precipitated during the night which can cause extreme pain in the morning hours. During the day, the urinary pH tends to be less acidic and sufferers tend to feel better as some of the acid deposits are neutralised.

2. To alkalise the body, mix two parts *sodium bicarbonate* (bicarbonate of soda) and one part *sodium potassium* in a glass jar. Take one level teaspoon of this mixture in one large glass of water (not cold) at bedtime (at least 2 hours away from dinner); if possible, drink it in one go. The next morning your urine pH should be at about six; if not, increase the dose to a heaped teaspoon. Check you pH from time to time as you may need to cut the dose to maintain a pH of six. By alkalising yourself at bedtime you prevent the urinary pH from dropping too low in the night. This will reduce the deposits in the joints and at the same time prevent dissolved kidney crystals from reassembling themselves into new stones. Continue this alkalising procedure throughout the kidney cleanse or as long as there is pain in toes or fingers. *Note:* if sodium potassium is not available use just sodium bicarbonate; the dose is ½ teaspoon (or more if need be) in a glass of water at bedtime.

4. **Removing Allergies**

Although the liver cleanse helps remove the main cause of allergies in the body, it may take a long time before the cells of the immune system stop producing antibodies against certain antigens contained in dust, pollen, duck feathers, cats hair, or such foods as milk, wheat, oranges, tomatoes, etc. In fact, allergic reactions, which might have had their root cause in a congested liver and impaired digestive system and have not disappeared, may be responsible for causing gallstones over again. As to my knowledge and experience one of the most effective methods to deal with and nullify any remaining antibody complexes in the blood responsible for allergic reactions, is *Bio-resonance Therapy*.

It is known that every person suffering an illness or long-term complaint has one or several major allergies. An allergy results when repeated exposure of the body to a normally harmless substance or antigen stimulates the immune system to produce antibodies. In whichever part of the body the defence reaction is most pronounced that's where the symptoms of disruption and discomfort will occur more intensely. If it is in the nose, sinus cavities, or chest area, mucous congestion may arise. A similar immune response in an ovary or the prostate gland may lead to a cyst or enlargement respectively. In some instances, the reaction may cause anaphylactic shock, nausea, skin rashes, breathing difficulties, fainting, diarrhoea, and death. There may be more diseases linked to allergic reactions than is currently known.

Research in the field of *Radionics* has shown that there may be four main allergies, which cover all the other possible allergies. They include the body's reactions to *duck feathers, milk, wheat, and mint*. If you happen to be allergic to duck feathers you may also be allergic to numerous allergens belonging in the category of duck feathers, including, for example, certain fruits, vegetables, dust particles, metals, pollutants, etc. There may, in fact, be hundreds of such substances. By annulling your body's allergic response to duck feathers through *Bio-resonance Therapy*, all these allergies are likely to disappear as well. Similarly, when a wheat allergy is terminated, the body's immune system stops reacting to all the antigens that fall in the wheat category. The same principle applies to the milk and mint allergy groups.

Most people with health problems have at least one major allergy, which may, for example, be against wheat and its subordinates. Almost everyone who has teeth fillings that are made with mercury-containing amalgam is allergic to milk, as well as to its products and subordinates. Research has shown that all AIDS patients, who have been tested for all the four allergy categories, are allergic to each one of them. Cancer patients have allergies to at least three groups.

Those *Bio-resonance* therapists who not just test the body as a whole for existing allergies but each energy centre (chakra) separately, seem to have the best results. Subsequent tests show no further allergies against anything; that is provided, a balanced diet and lifestyle are an integral part of daily life. Recent research conducted in Germany on the value of *Bio-resonance Therapy* in the treatment of the severest forms of allergy showed that of out of 200 tested patients 83 per cent were completely cured of all allergies and 11% had improved significantly. Although *Bio-resonance Therapy* is effective even without a liver cleanse, the benefits are many times more pronounced if it is done after cleansing the liver. Each person will be able to proof for himself that his allergies have ceased when coming into contact with former antigens such as orange juice, flower pollen, or gluten that is contained in wheat, etc.

5. Replacing all Metal Tooth Fillings

Metal dental ware is a constant source of poisoning and allergic reaction in the body (especially to milk and its products). All metal corrodes in time, especially in the mouth where there is high concentration of air and moisture. Mercury amalgam fillings release their extremely toxic compounds and vapour into the body, the main reason why German dentists are prohibited by a recently passed federal law to give them to their patients. For the same reason, most North-European countries have limited the use of amalgam, and Sweden, Spain, Austria, Denmark, among others will ban it altogether by the year 2000. The amalgam compounds are so toxic that dentists are instructed not to touch amalgam with bare hands and store excess amalgam in tightly sealed containers. If it is so dangerous to touch amalgam it certainly is dangerous to keep it in the mouth 24 hours a day and year after year!

The World Health Organisation issued a report showing that mercury absorbed from amalgam fillings is up to 10 times higher than mercury absorbed from environmental and dietary sources. It is noteworthy to point out that Multiple Sclerosis (MS) and Alzheimer patients have up to 10 times the normal mercury levels in their brains. Post-mortem studies show that the mercury level in some organs is directly proportional to the number of amalgam fillings in a diseased person. The most vulnerable of all to mercury poisoning seems to be the foetus in a pregnant mother: he accumulates more mercury than the mother herself, and in amounts directly proportional to the number of her amalgam fillings.

The gradual but continuous release of mercury and other toxic metals from metal fillings into the body affects particularly the liver, kidneys, lungs and brain. Cadmium, for example, which is used to make the pink colour in dentures, is five times as toxic as lead. It does not take much of it to raise the blood pressure to abnormal levels. Thallium, which is also found in mercury amalgam fillings, causes leg pain and paraplegia. It affects the nervous system, skin, and cardiovascular system. All wheelchair patients who have been tested for metal poisoning tested positive for thallium. Many people who were in a wheelchair several years after they received metal fillings completely recovered after removing all metal from the mouth. Thallium is lethal at a dose of 0.5-1,0 gram.

Other metals contained in dental fillings are known for their cancer-producing (carcinogenic) effects. They include nickel, which is used in gold crowns, braces, and children's crowns. Chromium is also extremely carcinogenic. All metals corrode, (including gold, silver, and platinum) and the body absorbs it. Women with breast cancer have accumulated large amounts of dissolved metals in their breasts. When the mouth is cleared of all metals, they will also leave the breasts and the metal-caused cysts will shrink and disappear by themselves.

The body's immune system naturally responds to the presence of toxic metals in the body and eventually develops allergic reactions which may show up as a sinus condition, tinnitus, enlarged neck and glands, bloating, enlarged spleen, arthritic conditions, headaches and migraine, eye diseases, and more serious complications such as paralysis or heart attacks. The only effective way to improve these conditions is to replace all metal fillings with *plastic fillings* that contain *no* metals.

If you decide to replace your amalgam fillings make certain that your dentist provides for protection (through a special plastic device) against absorbing or inhaling the generated amalgam "dust", otherwise you may end up having severe migraine attacks, memory loss, weakening of eyesight, etc. Before attempting to have any larger fillings removed you may need to take selenium for several months. Eat plenty of Vitamin C containing foods (oranges, red peppers, etc.) and green leafy vegetables for about 10 days to help clear mercury and other metal deposits from the body. Also drinking lapacho tea or taking it in capsule form helps detoxify the blood, liver, and kidneys (see section 7). It is also beneficial to remove all allergies through the *Bio-resonance Therapy* as described above, although milk allergies tend to remain until all amalgam fillings have been removed. An excellent alternative to amalgam is plastic for fillings called "composites." Porcelain can be toxic, too. It is made of aluminium oxide with other metals added. The fillings should be replaced cautiously and gradually, one at a time. Leave about two months time in between each removal.

6. How to give up Smoking and other Addictions

Smoking - An Unconscious Act of not Being in Control

Any form of addiction may be accompanied or caused by the inability to fulfil one or more of our deepest desires. We begin to unconsciously accept the idea that there is a power beyond our control that stops us from achieving our dreams, big or small. We may even admit self-defeat by maintaining the belief that it is too difficult to give up old habits like smoking, drinking, or eating addictive foods.

Many smokers argue that they cannot quit smoking if they constantly see other people smoking. Others do not want to face the possibly unbearable withdrawal symptoms that may accompany a sudden abstinence from smoking. Most smokers who wish to quit the habit feel that they don't have enough willpower to stop smoking. We give a small cigarette such great power that it is able to rule over our freedom to make conscious choices in our life. Smoking, like any other addictive habit, is merely a symptom of an underlying deficiency of some kind. What is it that is missing in our lives that we feel so dominated by outer influences and continue to desire for substitutes?

This is a question, which is impossible to answer in this context due to an almost infinite number of possible answers. But the desire to smoke in itself may be very useful in as much as it can reveal this inner lack, whatever it may be. Instead of criticising or judging yourself for giving your power to a habit that has the potential of making you ill or even kill you, you can learn a great deal from it and make yourself feel complete again. Because you may not be able to understand the underlying message that smoking entails, you tend to resign to the idea that quitting the habit is a difficult and frustrating task. Yet smoking can make you aware that you are no longer completely in control of your life.

The excuse that "I cannot give up smoking because...," is an unconscious recognition that I am a victim of some kind of inner weakness or low self-esteem. The act of smoking makes me admit in a way that my desire for a cigarette is greater than my desire to stay healthy or, in other words, to love myself. It is only difficult to give up smoking or other addictions as long as I preserve this underlying weakness by projecting such convictions as "I can't give it up," or "I go crazy if I don't have my fags."

Recovering Your Free Will

Similar to using a thorn to pull out another thorn, learning to give up the habit of smoking may be one of the most effective ways to uproot any incompetence and dependency in your life. By suppressing or fighting the habitual desire to smoke you only feed it with greater power; this all but increases the addiction. Desires want to be fulfilled, or at least we should be able to decide whether we want to fulfil them or not. Smoking, which is an expression of lacking inner completeness, can become a means to regain control over your life. Smoking is not the problem you need to combat; it rather is the lack of freedom in making your own choices that needs to be corrected.

If understood and dealt with properly, smoking can be one of the most important things that ever happened to you. It can lead you to adopt an entire new way of thinking, and thus reshape your destiny. If you are a smoker and wish to give up the habit you first need to understand that your addiction is not an accidental mistake. You have created this habit in your life to learn from it and it will stay with you or change into another addictive habit unless you have acquired the ability to refer all power of fulfilling your desires back to yourself. Giving up smoking is not about quitting one addictive habit just to adopt another one; it is about recovering your free will.

The purpose of willpower is not to fight an undesirable habit but to learn how to make conscious choices. Addictions stick like glue to everyone who wishes to overcome them. They are the "ghosts of memory" which live in our subconscious and pop up every time the addictive substance is in sight or is imagined. The subsequent urge is not under conscious control, hence the feeling of "dying" for a fag, a cup of coffee, or a bar of chocolate. It is important to realise that **you always have a choice**. This is all you need to learn when it comes to overcoming an addiction.

You cannot exorcise the ghost of memory by throwing away your cigarettes, avoiding your smoking friends, or living in a smoke-free environment. Society has condemned the act of smoking so much that many smokers already feel deprived of their personal freedom to make their own choices in life. A nagging spouse, a doctor, and the warning written on cigarette packs that smoking is dangerous to your health, may make you ridden with guilt, if you are a sensitive person. When all this external pressure succeeds in making you give up smoking, you will still feel deprived of your free will and look for other forms of addiction.

Making Smoking Your Conscious Choice

We all remember our childhood days when our parents told us not to eat chocolate before lunch or watch television when we wanted to. The subconscious mind reacts negatively when he is deprived of his ability to make choices or when he feels forced to do something against his will. The many occasions of disappointment that arose from unfulfilled desires in the past lead to an inner vacuum or emptiness that wants to be filled. Smoking is simply a subconscious rebellion against the external manipulation of our freedom to choose what we want, and it fills that uncomfortable space within for a little while. However, this inner lack will only subside when the mind has regained its freedom of choice making. You must know that you are free to smoke whenever you like and how ever much you like. If you have a cigarette and a match to light it, you will certainly find a way to smoke it, too.

The unconscious association of smoking with all the other "don'ts" of your past will be cut asunder by accepting your desire to smoke. I had my first cigarette when I entered high school at age ten. I felt like a criminal because the law said I was only allowed to smoke when I was sixteen years old. Years of hiding my "secret" from my parents and my teachers left me with no choice but to continue smoking until I *had* a choice. When I finally got the legal permission to smoke I lost interest and chose to quit. I was able to give up the habit at once, without any withdrawal symptoms.

The first and most important step to quit smoking is to give yourself full permission to smoke. Guilt in the act will only stop you from gaining satisfaction and urge you to have another cigarette that may "at last" give you what you have been looking for. But you are not really looking for the short sensation of satisfaction that smoking provides but for the lost freedom to make choices in your life. If you deprive yourself of this possible satisfaction by avoiding smoking you may create psychosomatic side effects, which are nothing other but the so-called withdrawal symptoms. Symptoms may include depression, lack of interest in life, sleeplessness, anger, nausea, ravenous hunger, lack of concentration, and shaking. However, they can only manifest if you believe that you have been deprived of your freedom to smoke.

Choosing not to Smoke

Contrary to general belief, to give up smoking you *do not* need to abolish your desire to smoke. **You will give up automatically when you learn to choose not to follow your desire to smoke**. This will take the fuel out of your subconscious rebellious mind and stop you from being a victim of outer forces or other people. A master of yourself, you can choose to smoke or choose not to smoke. Keep your cigarettes with you as long as you feel you want to have this choice. It may even be a good idea to encourage your desire to smoke by keeping your cigarette pack in front of you, smelling it from time to time. Watch other people around you light up and inhale, imagining that you inhale deeply too. Do not count the days that pass without you smoking and do not look ahead in time either. You do not have to prove to yourself or to anyone that you can beat this addiction. You are free to stop smoking today and begin again tomorrow. You will always have this choice, and you will always be only a puff away from being a smoker.

Choice making or training our free will takes place in the now and has to be done anew repeatedly. Though the longer you keep making the choice not to smoke, the faster your desire for a cigarette will fade, becoming less intense each day. Whenever the desire to smoke returns, which is possible through the ghost of memory, you are again compelled to make a new choice. This time, however, your conscious mind finds it much easier to stick with its previous successful choice because of the newly improved self-confidence and self-esteem.

The conscious retraining of your mind will benefit your entire life. It will restore your power of free will and remove the "victim" within you. Because you have been told so many times in your life that *you cannot do this* or *cannot do that*, you began to use this formula to accept your addiction as being too difficult to quit as well. By reclaiming your power of conscious choice making you will be able to break the "I can't" pattern in your life for good.

Quitting the Habit

Before you decide to stop smoking (or any other addiction), make sure that you are aware of the following points:

- Make stopping smoking a priority in your life.
- Don't try to make too many other changes in your life at the same time.
- Don't reward yourself for quitting the habit, quitting is enough of a reward.
- It's good not to tell anyone about your intention to stop smoking because this only undermines your freedom to choose to smoke.
- Carry your cigarettes or tobacco with you, so people will assume you are still smoking; this way you don't have to prove to anyone that you are capable of quitting the habit.
- Unless for health reasons, don't try to avoid places where other people smoke; you want to remain in charge under all circumstances.
- You are always free to smoke whenever you wish to, even if you have to do it in a toilet or out in the cold air.
- Avoid substituting things like tea, coffee, chocolate, chewing gum, more exercise, drinking mineral water, etc. for cigarettes, as they won't satisfy your desire to smoke in the long run.
- Choose a starting time of your programme to stop smoking that does not coincide with an emotional upheaval or stressful situation. It is best to link the starting date with a positive event in your life. New moon day is one of the best days to quit.
- Think about all the benefits that will come to you when you stop smoking, i.e., better health, less mucous discharge from the lungs, cleaner breath, saving money, etc.
- Acknowledge your desire to smoke when it comes up by saying to yourself: "I really have the desire to smoke now and I feel free to do so but right now I decide not to smoke." When the desire to smoke returns in an hour or so, you may choose to fulfil it this time. This will teach you to consciously accept your desire to smoke but not always fulfil it. By choosing not to smoke each time the desire emerges, you train your mind to make conscious choices.
- Often your desire to smoke is coupled with clues like drinking a cup of coffee, the ringing of the telephone, waiting for a bus or a taxi, or switching on the television set. Your addiction is a "programme" that you have written in your subconscious mind and associated with such clues. As the clues occur, your desire to smoke pops up too. The next time you want to smoke when the telephone rings, while you drink a cup of coffee, or after you switch on the TV, make the conscious choice to wait for a few minutes until you have the time or opportunity to smoke consciously. Another suggestion is to smoke somewhere in the house or garden where you usually don't smoke. This will sever the ties to your subconscious and make your decision whether to smoke or not a conscious one.
- Allow your desire of smoking to become quite strong before you actually reach for the cigarette; in other words, you will still have the freedom to smoke but postpone your decision for a while until you feel discomfort. Notice where in your body you feel tense, irritable, or nervous. It is important to feel how strong your desire to smoke becomes before you light up. Most smokers give into the slightest urge to smoke and do not even notice when they light up. You want to break the pattern of doing things unconsciously.
- To make it easy to quit smoking (or any other addiciton) drink half a glass of water (not from the fridge!) every time before you decide to smoke a cigarette. Physiologically, the urge to smoke is directly linked to toxins that were deposited in the connective tissues of the body and are now entering the blood, increasing its thickness. This causes irritation, nervousness, and fear. Instead of pushing the toxins back into the connective tissues (they will surely re-emerge!), by drinking half a

glass or one glass of water you cause thinning of the blood, which helps the removal of the toxins from the body. Thus the urge to smoke lessens each time you do this and eventually disappears altogether.
- Finally, your addiction to smoking is not something terrible you need to get rid of; it rather is a unique opportunity to train yourself to become the master of your destiny. In this sense, your addiction can be one of your very best teachers.

Summary of the Technique to Stop Smoking:

Whenever you feel the urge to smoke, repeat to yourself: **"I want to smoke now."** This will bring your desire to smoke from your subconscious into your conscious mind and allow you enough time to make the conscious choice of whether to smoke or not to smoke. Drinking half a glass of water also brings the desire into your conscious mind.

Then say to yourself: **"I have the free choice to smoke now."** If you do not remind yourself of your inherent freedom of choice, your subconscious, addicted mind may believe that you can't smoke anymore and may go into a state of rebellion. This may cause severe withdrawal symptoms.

If you feel a desperate need to smoke, acknowledge your desire by saying: **"I choose to begin smoking again."** Before you reach for a cigarette check whether this is what you really want. Or you may repeat to yourself: **"For the moment I accept that I want to smoke but I will give it a miss this time."** Think about how you would feel if you stopped smoking altogether?

Follow this simple sequence every time you have the desire to smoke. The technique is fool proof because you cannot go wrong, whatever the outcome. Whether you decide to continue smoking or not, you have begun to become "aware," a prerequisite to consciously taking charge of your life. The majority of people who follow this simple programme give up smoking within one week, others take a little longer. But all report a major positive shift in their thinking and their entire personality.

All the research studies that show that smoking is a hazard to your health have missed the point. Instead of condemning people who smoke we should show them ways to learn from this addictive habit as we can learn from any other problem in life. This technique works equally well for any other addiction, including coffee, alcohol, drugs, sleeping pills, sugar, salt, and even work. I suggest that you read this section as often as it takes to familiarise yourself with the major points, or at least once a week.

7. The Amazing Lapacho

South American physicians are using a recipe derived from the ancient civilisation of the *Incas* to successfully treat various forms of cancer -- including leukaemia and other life-threatening diseases. They use the inner bark of the lapacho colorado tree, or *red lapacho* - called so because of its scarlet flowers. Also known as Pau d'Arco, Ipe Roxa and Taheebo, the *red lapacho* tree grows in the warmer parts of South America: Brazil, northern Argentina, Paraguay, Bolivia, etc. The tree apparently only grows where there is high ozone content in the air, with high concentrations of vital negative oxygen ions. It is virtually free of contaminants caused by pollutants such as pesticides or exhaust fumes.

The tree has vibrant, trumpet-shaped flowers -- pink, purple, or yellow, depending on the species. The *lapacho* tree with the purple flowers has the most potency. The unusual thing about the flowers is that they are carnivorous and eat insects, protecting the tree against pests, parasites, viral infections, and fungal growth.

The power of the tree lies in the inner bark, which can be removed without damage, dried, and an extract obtained. The tree renews its bark and therefore serves as a continuous source of supply. The active ingredient is known as *lapachol* and the herbal remedy is valued for its ability to strengthen and balance the body's immune system. With all the herbal cures and the treasures the *Incas* left us there appears to be none as precious as *lapacho*, which their descendants -- the Callawaya -- are still using today.

Lapacho is used in the alternative treatment of cancer, AIDS, and Candida albicans overgrowth and fungal problems as well as other diseases of the immune system. Moreover, *lapacho* is highly valued for its ability to detoxify the body, particularly the liver, kidneys, and intestinal tract. It also helps babies cope with food allergies and intestinal cramps. Research on *lapacho* in South America claims that it helps reduce counter-reactions to antibiotics, allowing other medicines to work effectively in reducing the danger of toxic effects upon the liver. In other words, in can be used with other medicines and minimise their side effects.

Issues of Life and Death

Dr. Orlando dei Santi, medical doctor from Santo Andre, Brazil, heard about the miraculous properties of *Lapacho*, took the bark, boiled it, and took the brew to the Santo Andre Municipal Hospital where his brother was dying of cancer. The cancer patient had just undergone a second operation and his condition had been declared "inoperable and terminal."

Immediately after drinking the *lapacho* tea, dei Santi's his brother noticed that his pain began to disappear and he was able to sleep soundly. After taking *lapacho* for a month, he was discharged from the hospital. A thorough examination found that he had no trace of cancer remaining.

The cancer-curing properties of the tropical bark were discovered already over twenty-five years ago. The story began when a Sao Paulo family reported the miraculous cure of a young relative of theirs -- a girl who was afflicted with cancer.

The girl's doctors had given up on her and told her parents that her death was imminent. Her great aunt, however, contacted an Indian tribal doctor who claimed that the cancer could be cured with the brew made from the bark of a certain tree. The medicine man gave her a little bag of the bark.

The young girl and the parents at first disdained the medicine man's concoction, but then the sick girl had a strange dream. She saw a friar who told her: "Drink tea brewed with the bark the Indian gave you, and you will get well." At first she paid no attention to the dream, but her pain increased and the dream repeated itself. But when she eventually tried the tea, all pain vanished miraculously. Encouraged by the results, she continued to take the medicine every morning. Within a month, she was well, and her regular doctor told her parents that no trace of cancer could be found.

Since then, the physicians at the small provincial town hospital of Santo Andre began to notice that the pain suffered by patients with leukaemia or other cancers disappeared within hours after they received the brew made from the inner bark of the red *lapacho* tree. They also found, that within 30 days of treatment with this herbal medication, most patients no longer had any signs of cancer in their body.

The physicians noticed that many other afflictions from which some of the cancer patients suffered -- such as diabetes -- would disappear even more quickly than cancer. Since the early 1970s, the bark has been used regularly at the Municipal Hospital of Santo Andre to treat leukaemia as well as numerous diseases where viruses were suspected to be the cause. Both the herb stores and the "legitimate" pharmacies of Brazil now carry this bark. One of the doctors from Santo Andre, Professor Walet Accorst, reported: "From my first experiments with it [lapacho], I learned two important things that greatly encouraged me in regard to cancer. Firstly, red *lapacho* eliminated the pains caused by the disease; and secondly, it multiplied the amount of red corpuscles." He continued: "Our amazement grew. This bark cured everything! Ulcers, diabetes and rheumatism, the medicine cured them all. And what impressed us most was the time it took to achieve the cure, which was almost always less than three months!"

Other physicians at the hospital have also seen cases of diabetes, osteomyelitis, cancer, ulcers and anaemia improve very rapidly. Dr. Octavionao Gaiarsa, another resident physician at the hospital treated a case of advanced leukaemia with 240,000 leukocytes (white cells) per cubic millimetre (of blood). After one month of treatment with *lapacho*, the number of white cells was down to 20,000 and the patient recovered.

At another hospital (*Concepcion*) five-year-old Maria Adela *Vera* was treated for leukaemia. Her cytological counts had worsened continuously and indicated the imminent death of the little girl. The doctors of the hospital told the parents of the girl that there was no hope for her but mentioned a small clinic where they could treat her with *lapacho* tea. So the parents transferred her to the clinic of Dr. Ruiz. After only 6 days she had improved considerably. Six weeks later she was released from hospital with normal blood counts.

Medicine of the Highest Calibre

The following is a list of ailments that the doctors at the Municipal Hospital of Santo Andre found were helped by *lapacho*:

Anaemia Tonic	Gastritis	Parkinson's disease
Asthma Ulcers	Hernias	Ringworm
Arteriosclerosis	Infectious diseases	Rheumatism
Blood builder	Luekaemia	Skin problems
Bronchitis	Liver ailments	Varicose veins
Cancer	Osteomyelitis	Venereal diseases
Cystitis	Psoriasis	Wounds
Diabetes	Pyorrhoea	

Further research showed that *lapacho* is also helpful in colds, influenza, gonorrhoea, polyps, prostate infection and enlargement, tuberculosis, growths, multiple sclerosis, typhus, dizziness, impotence, alopecia, boils, snake bites, food allergies, chemical allergies, and when applied topically it can help against dandruff, eczema and skin cancer. Scientists believe that *lapacho* may even have potential in the treatment of AIDS. *Aveloz* is a herbal remedy which when used in combination with *lapacho* is capable of practically tearing cancer cells apart while *lapacho* itself addresses more the cause of the disease.

The fascinating revelation about the properties of *lapacho* is that there has never been any record in medical research of an antibiotic chemical agent capable of destroying both bacteria and viruses. Any other known type of vegetation when exposed to water and the weather is eventually covered with spores that lead to the formation of fungus. This does not occur in the case of *lapacho*, indicating an uncommon resistance. Following are the known properties of *lapacho*:

ANALGESIC - agent which diminishes pain without the loss of consciousness.
SEDATIVE - agent which alleviates nervousness, irritation and distress.
DECONGESTANT - agent that relieves congestion throughout the body.
DIURETIC - agent used to stimulate secretion and the flow of urine.
HYPOTENSIVE - powerful nervine relaxant that induces sleep when necessary.
VIRUCIDAL - agent capable of destroying a virus.

The dramatic cures caused by *lapacho* were so astounding that the government of Brazil began to study and confirm its healing properties. Research at the University of Illinois, USA, supports the research in Brazil, and the claim that *lapacho* does indeed contain a substance to be highly effective against cancers. Dr. Teodoro Meyer of the State University of Tucuman, Argentina, was the first researcher to discover an antibiotic substance, called *Zyloiden*, which he found is capable of killing viruses. *Lapachol*, the main ingredient of the herb, also was discovered to have powerful antitumoral action without toxic side effects. The antineoplastic activity was confirmed in 1968 when the use of *lapachol* on rats carrying *Yashida's Sarcoma* inhibited the growth of the tumours in 84 percent of the animals treated with high doses.

Professor Accorsi of Sao Paulo University also found *lapacho* to be of excellent therapeutic value in the treatment of various forms of cancer including leukaemia. A Japanese research group led by doctors from the National Cancer Center confirmed Professor Accorsi's findings. The researchers were able to extract an anti-cancer substance from *lapacho*, which they found acted against leukaemia and malignant tumours including those in stomach cancer.

Besides its powerful healing properties, *lapacho* is a powerful tonic and blood builder that increases the haemoglobin content and the number of red corpuscles. This is not surprising because *lapacho* contains easily absorbable (colloidal) iron. It also assists with the proper assimilation of nutrients and the elimination of wastes, which is essential for recovery from any illness. *Lapacho* seems to be capable of revitalising the body, by creating new vital elements and normal cell growth. It permits control of "incurable" diseases, lengthening life span and enhancing the quality of life both at the same time. *Lapacho* is a gift of nature to us humans and we may greatly benefit from accepting this gift.

8. Guarana - A Super Herb
(+ other useful plant products)

There is another plant that has unusual and very beneficial properties for man's health. It has become very popular around the world and like *lapacho* it can be found in most health food stores. The plant is known as Paullinia cupana and its seeds as *Guarana*.

Guarana is regarded as an elixir, a natural energy booster. Often the Indians would eat only *Guarana* when they went into the jungle. They would grind the seeds, mix them with water, and drink the concoction. This alone would sustain them on their long treks. They also used *Guarana* to combat fever, headaches, and pain.

Research has shown that *Guarana* gently stimulates the adrenal system to combat fatigue without producing the harmful *adrenaline* shots. The large amount of bulk prevents its natural caffeine from being released in bursts, as is the case with coffee or tea. The gradual release of caffeine makes much energy available to the body without using up its own energy resources. *Guarana* soothes the nervous system and is therefore useful for stress related conditions including anxiety and depression. It has become highly valued as a tonic herb, improving both concentration and physical stamina. Many professional sportsmen and gymnasts use it regularly. Recommended uses are:

- When you need an energy boost (take it instead of coffee which exhausts the nervous system).
- As a general tonic and stress reliever.
- For those who live an active lifestyle or have a demanding day ahead.
- During periods of hard work, either mental or physical.
- As a gentle stimulant and to remove fatigue.
- When recovering from an illness or feeling weak.
- To combat signs of ageing.
- To help relieve headaches and migraine.
- As a natural diuretic, to rid the body of excess fluid.
- To relieve period pain.
- As a non-addictive anti-depressant.

Whatever brand you use, be sure it is 100% pure *Guarana* and not mixed with any other ingredients or preservatives. Beware of chewing gums or similar products that claim to contain *Guarana*. The large amount of chemicals and preservatives, colourings, artificial sweeteners, etc. in them turns them into pure poison for the body, which you can confirm by using the muscle test. I recommend the Rio *Amazon Guarana* made by Rio Trading Company Ltd in the United Kingdom (see "Useful Addresses"). Their *Rio range* also includes *lapacho* and other very useful plant products, such as *Cat's Claw* and *Pfaffia* (also known as Brazilian Ginseng or Suma). The latter one is very effective for menstrual problems, menopausal symptoms, diabetes, and any other hormonal problems.

I also recommend *Gingko Biloba*, available at most health food stores. Guarana and Gingko seem to complement each other. Gingko is brain food. It increases blood flow to the brain, thereby improving memory and brain function. It is very effective in improving all kinds of circulatory problems and it especially increases blood flow to the heart, extremities, skin, eyes, inner ear, and other vital organs. Gingko is a strong antioxidant and relieves anxiety and depression, vertigo, headaches, tinnitus, PMS, asthma, allergy symptoms, and hepatitis. It is also a natural mood-enhancer.

9. Aloe Vera -- An Ancient Healer

Aloe Vera has been known throughout the ages as the "Medicine plant," "Burn plant", "First-aid plant" or "Miracle plant". Even today, *Aloe Vera* is one of the most effective plants for treating burns, healing wounds, and relieving aches and pains, including psoriasis, where, when used regularly, it reduces scaling and itching and greatly improves appearance.

Aloe Vera became very popular for its use in combating the severe burning effects caused by X-rays and nuclear disasters. Radiation burns cause skin ulceration which had been nearly incurable until physicians began trying the old folk remedy of the *Aloe Vera* leaf.

Today *Aloe Vera* has gained such great popularity that it is being used in many cosmetics and health products. Particularly *Aloe Vera* juice which is taken internally, has been found to be effective in almost every illness, including cancer, heart disease, and AIDS. In fact, there is hardly any disease or health problem for which *Aloe Vera* has not been proved successful. It is helpful for all kinds of allergies, skin diseases, blood disorders, arthritis, infections, candida, cysts, diabetes, eye problems, digestive problems, ulcers, liver diseases, haemorrhoids, high blood pressure, kidney stones, or strokes, to name a few. Effects are most beneficial if treatments are applied both internally and externally. *Aloe Vera* contains over 200 nutrients, including the vitamins B1, B2, B3, B6, C, E, Folic acid, iron, calcium, magnesium, zinc, kalium, manganese, copper, barium, sulphate, 18 amino acids, important enzymes, glycosides, polysaccharides, etc.

Caution: With regular drinking of *Aloe Vera*, diabetics may improve the ability of the pancreas to produce more of its own insulin. Therefore, diabetics should consult their physician to monitor their need for extra insulin, since too much insulin is dangerous. Many diabetics report a reduction in the amount of insulin required.

Watch out for the frauds

Since the market has created a great demand for *Aloe Vera* juice, production is increasing rapidly. Unfortunately, many brands contain inadequate amounts of *Aloe Vera* juice to be effective. According to the law, if you take a 10,000-gallon vat and put 9,999 gallons of water in it and then add one gallon of *Aloe Vera* juice you are allowed to advertise that it contains "100% pure stabilised *Aloe Vera*." You are not required to mention how much extra water has been added to the 100% *Aloe* juice. Hence many people are disappointed because they do not receive the acclaimed benefits. Before using any brand it is good to check out the exact table of contents as mentioned in a company's brochure or better ask the company to give you the exact figures of contents.

Also don't be tempted to buy the cheapest *Aloe* juice. *Aloe Vera* juice *is* expensive. If you are not getting any benefits from it, you may have chosen the wrong product. Try other brands until you are satisfied. Tests have shown that less than one percent of readily available brands contain acceptable levels of *Aloe Vera* to be of any medicinal value. From the over 1,000 brands of *Aloe Vera* available on the market today, some hardly have a trace of *Aloe Vera* in them. Their labels contain such phrases "it tastes like mineral water" and "no additives or preservatives." Chemical analysis reveals that these "products" contain almost nothing but plain mineral water.

I found two reliable brands sold by British companies, one is called *Biogenic Aloe Vera* from *Life Stream,* and the other one is *Aloe Juice* from *Pro-Ma*. Since more and more people have begun to see through the fraud business, many other companies are now also introducing the real thing.

10. Green Tea -- A Tea for Life

The countries with a long tea tradition have much to contribute to health. However, regular or black tea, which is very popular now almost everywhere, has not much to do with the *real tea*. Real tea is derived from the tea plant *Thea sinensis* or *Thea asoncica,* not to be confused with herb teas such as peppermint, camomile, or fennel.

Both, black and green teas, originate from the same tea plant, only their methods of processing are different. Breaking the leaves of the plants and exposing them to the oxygen of the air produces black tea. The resulting fermentation destroys the most important biological ingredients (*tannins*) of the tea. By contrast, during the production of green tea, the leaves are stabilised through exposure to both humid and dry heat. This eliminates fermentation producing enzymes and safeguards the nutrients.

Because of fermentation, black tea becomes a drug. Since the *tannins* or important nutrients are no longer present, the caffeine contained in the tea appears now in free and unbound form. This causes the addictive effect of black tea. It triggers a "fight or flight response" in the body. Since the ingested caffeine is considered to be a poisonous nerve toxin by the body the adrenal glands counteract by secreting the antidote *adrenaline*. This defence reaction by the body has a stimulating and enlivening effect. However, as the effects of the caffeine and *adrenaline* begin to decrease, the body feels tired and exhausted.

Green tea works very differently. The large amounts of *tannins* in green tea make certain that the caffeine is taken to the brain in only small and well-dosed amounts, which help to harmonise the energies in the body. Unlike black tea, the green version makes the body's energies active. This helps the drinker of green tea improve his vitality and life force without experiencing the "up and down" effect accompanied by black tea. In truth, the more green tea you drink, the more energy you are able to produce.

The value of *tannin* has been studied for centuries all over the world. Besides its effect of binding the caffeine, it has healing properties. Problems of the intestines and high blood pressure can particularly benefit from green tea. Green tea has been shown to be 20 times more effective in slowing the ageing process than vitamin E is. Studies have demonstrated that the success rate of green tea in reducing oxidants in the body (considered responsible for ageing) is 74% compared to 4% with vitamin E. Its vitamin C content is four times higher than in lemon juice and it contains more B-vitamins than any other known plant.

Since green tea is highly alkaline it helps combat hyperacidity. People who drink green tea suffer less from arteriosclerosis. It keeps the blood thin and prevents coronary heart disease, heart attacks, and strokes. Furthermore, Japanese researchers from the University of Osaka have proved that green tea kills microbes that are responsible for cholera, tooth decay, and salmonella infection before they even get the chance to enter the stomach. A substance called "EGCG" has been found to retard tumour growth. The Botikin Hospital in Moscow reported that green tea is more effective against infection than antibiotics, without producing any harmful side effects.

Green tea has over 100 ingredients that have been found useful for a number of conditions; It inhibits

- cell mutations leading to cancer
- reduces blood fats
- balances cholesterol levels
- prevents high blood pressure
- increases heart efficiency
- improves brain functions
- enhances metabolism
- improves vision
- supports secretion of saliva
- increases growth of hair
- reduces body fat and weight
- stimulates digestion

The best green tea comes from the *Shizuoka* area in Japan; it grows organically and has no additives. People living in this area have a much lower cancer rate than those living in other areas of Japan. A reliable brand is *Sencha* sold by Kurimoto Trading Co., Japan. With over 130 ingredients it is the richest of all green teas. Other brands are *Ocha* or *Bancha*; you should be able to find at least one of them at a good health food store.

Note: The effectiveness of green tea depends on how you prepare it. Take 1½ teaspoons of green tea for two cups of tea. While you bring water to the boil, put the tea into a pot and pour the water over the tea when the bubbles disappear. After no longer than 35-45 seconds pour the tea through a sieve into a teapot, otherwise the tea loses its effectiveness. You may use the same leaves a second time by applying the same procedure.

11. Ener-Chi Art

Ener-Chi Art is a unique method of rejuvenation that helps to restore a balanced flow of Chi (vital energy) through the organs and systems in the body. When seen in the context of the liver cleanse, I consider this healing approach to be a very basic and useful tool in facilitating a successful outcome of other natural healing methods. When Chi flows again through the cells of the body, they can remove toxic wastes better, absorb all the oxygen, water, and nutrients they need, do the necessary repair work and increase their health and vitality. Although I consider the liver cleanse to be one of the most effective tools to help the body return to balanced functioning, by itself it may not be able to restore its overall vital energy due to many years of congestion and deterioration. Test results have shown that Ener-Chi Art may very well fill this gap. Its rate of effectiveness so far has been 100% for every person who has been exposed to it. (For more information on *Ener-Chi Art* see "Other Books and Products by the Author" at the end of this book.)

12. Body Odour? A Good Reason for *not* Using Deodorants

Most people are not aware why they sweat. Antiperspirants and perfumes have become so much part of our lives that we rarely think about why we need them or whether we really need them. It may even be more important to find out if they can be harmful.

Deodorants and antiperspirants have been invented because more and more people began to sweat abnormally and develop body odour. Today it is the normal thing to do to give the underarms a spray in the morning and forget about this "nuisance" for the rest of the day. But sweating is not a nuisance, it is the body's natural way of ridding itself of toxins and keeping cool. Like the bowels, urinary system and lungs, our sweat glands too are meant to help purify and keep the body clean, why else do we have them? To make your body sweat once a day even for a few minutes is a good way to stay healthy. But trying to prevent the body from doing its cleansing job by inhibiting the sweat glands from releasing the toxins is rather like trying to run a car whilst blocking its exhaust pipe.

Many people today feel that they "need" chemical products to control their body odour. This is because the other eliminative organs of the body, such as colon, liver, lungs, and kidneys, are badly blocked or overtaxed which increases the dumping of toxins into the skin. The chemical products block their excretion through the skin, which seems desirable but causes a build up of more toxins and increases bacterial development.

Body odour is not caused by sweat itself, which is just an odourless fluid consisting of 99 per cent water. Normal sweat evaporates from the skin very quickly. Bad smell under the armpits or on the skin occurs only when *bacteria* are required to eliminate excessive sweat that could not be removed by fresh air. There can be as many as ½ million of bacteria per square inch. In addition, when there are excessive amounts of toxins that need to be *digested* by the bacteria, a strong and penetrating smell occurs. This may be a sign of constipation accompanied by bad breath, or kidney and liver problems. The body is crying out for help as toxins are "bursting at the seams." But instead of reading the body's symptoms as a sign of imbalance we merely shut down the symptom.

To combat the bacteria, we use deodorants and to tackle the amount of wetness, we apply antiperspirants. Deodorants contain germicides that kill the microbes and, as is the case with most of the brands, a synthetic perfume to mask the smell of the germicide. Antiperspirants contain the active ingredient -- *aluminium chlorohydrate* or *aluminium zirconium chlorohydrate; it* reacts with the protein contained in the sweat. This forms a gel that can partially block the sweat glands from excreting liquid. There is increasing evidence that people who suffer from Alzheimer's disease have high amounts of aluminium in their bodies.

Aluminium that is contained in fruits and vegetables is "colloidal" which means that it is synthesised by the plants and essential for our body. By contrast, synthetically derived aluminium is highly toxic for the body. The argument by the industry that aluminium can be found almost everywhere is therefore misleading because these two types of aluminium have completely opposite effects on the body. The same applies of course to all minerals and trace elements, including gold, silver, lead, mercury, and even arsenic. In colloidal form, i.e., processed by plants, these substances are essential for our bodies but when taken in their inorganic forms they can lead to poisoning. By applying the latter chemicals to our skin they enter the blood which may deposit them in the brain or other tissues.

Tips to effectively deal with body odour:
- Pitta and Pitta-Vata types are the most prone to develop body odour. Follow the Ayurvedic regimen and cleansing procedures. Remove all gallstones from your liver and cleanse your kidneys. Avoid too many acid-forming foods such animal proteins, fats and starches; the

more refined and processed the foods are, the worse is the effect. The digestion of the toxins by bacteria causes an unpleasant smell of skin and breath. Meat eaters especially have a tendency to develop bad body odour. Stick to fruits, vegetables, and salads as your main source of alkaline-forming foods. They also work as natural cleansers.
- Stop using deodorants and antiperspirants, they only reinforce the problem by blocking off part of your lymphatic system and dispersing the toxins together with the chemicals contained in these products into other parts of your body, including the breasts. This can cause lumps and cancer of the breast!
- Wash the afflicted areas in the morning with a natural soap that contains no harmful chemicals and finish off with a splash of cold water on your underarms.
- Make sure to wear loose-fitting cotton cloth. Synthetics will prevent your skin from breathing and eliminating toxins.
- You may want to make a solution of your most favourite essential oil (1-2 drops in an ounce of water; shake well to disperse the oil!) and dab it on your underarms (use the muscle test to determine which oil or oils are most suitable for you).
- I recommend deodorant stones (without aluminium!) made from non-toxic and natural materials such as potassium sulphate and other colloidal minerals. They are pure and harmless and stop bacteria from spreading if applied right after washing. I found an excellent brand sold by The Family News in the United States (see useful addresses). It is called "EnGarde Crystal Deodorant" and lasts for at least three years! And it is very effective. Those who use it regularly, no longer complain about body odour. Neal's Yard in London also has a pure deodorant stone. Another good brand is Thai Deodorant Stone.

13. Magnotherapy

Applied magnet therapy or *Magnotherapy*, dating back to the ancient Egyptians, has been shown to help restore the body's magnetic field and prevent and treat many chronic and acute problems. The correct use of magnets applied to specific parts of the body increases oxygenation of the blood, boosts energy levels, and speeds up oxygen and nutrient supplies to the cells, all factors that can greatly accelerate the healing process. *Magnotherapy* has also been proved effective in reducing inflammation, bruising, and stiffness. Initial carefully controlled studies at *St. Petersburg Petrov Research Institute of Oncology* and at *Bordeaux University, France*, have shown that *Magnotherapy* may even have a role to play in the regression of solid tumours.

Since the industrial revolution, the earth has lost much of its magnetic energy. Most of it is absorbed in construction steel, in railway lines running across large areas in almost every country in the world, in concrete buildings, in metal cars, trains, buses, etc. The majority of the world's population lives in cities. Encapsulated within these structures for prolonged periods of time, a person is unable to absorb enough of earth's natural magnetic energy necessary to maintain balance of body, mind, and nervous system. Artificial electromagnetic fields produced by high voltage power lines, and by the electric cables and machines in our homes, offices, and factories further reduce the body's magnetic field.

The body's requirement for a static magnetic field was highlighted when early pioneers in space (where there is no magnetic field) suffered from what became known as "Space Sickness." By providing the astronauts with a magnetic field that imitated the earth's natural field *space sickness* was prevented.

Also footwear that is made of rubber or other insulating plastic materials deprives us of the contact with the Earth's magnetic energy. If you spend long periods of time in high buildings you may lose your "groundedness" and begin to feel unstable. Our immune system in particular requires a balanced magnetic field to withstand all kinds of stress factors, microbial, mental, and physical.

Physiotherapists in most hospitals now actively promote and use magnetic fields not only to help reduce pain but also to accelerate the healing of muscular and osteo complaints. By correctly applying low-strength magnets it is possible to rebalance the energy within the body and realign the skeletal system, gradually and without pain. Many football clubs, fitness centres, and rehabilitation centres are now using what they call "magnetotherapy massage units" to ease sprains and speed up recovery of damaged tissue and fractured bones with astonishing results. Magnetotherapy increases the blood's ability to absorb and carry larger amounts of oxygen and nutrients as well as waste products. Healing can be accelerated and pain reduced by an improved circulation and nutrient supply in the body. So far many thousands of people have benefited from *Magnotherapy* and enjoy a better life as a result.

Bioflow – A Timely Invention

The *Magnotherapy* performed by many physiotherapists uses a pulsed magnetic field which is not only expensive but would not be practical to use on a personal basis. The manufacturers of *Bioflow*, Ecoflow Ltd., England, use their unique "Central Reverse Polarity" and apply it to the strongest magnetic material available to produce a product that is small and light and yet mimics the pulsed magnetic equipment. For general body maintenance the *Bioflow* is worn discreetly on the wrist just like a wristwatch. For areas of the body requiring special attention the *Bioflow* may be positioned locally. Because the *Bioflow* provides the natural balance of a static magnetic field it is completely safe, with the exception of persons who have a pacemaker fitted. It is waterproof and will retain its magnetic properties for a lifetime.

I have tested a number of devices that claim to be beneficial for balancing our EM field and I found *Bioflow* to yield the most profound and quickest results. There are people who have suffered from arthritis and rheumatism for years and even within days of using *Bioflow* were free of pains. Others regained 85% of mobility of their hands and feet. Sufferers from high blood pressure report that it has returned to nearly normal levels and even diabetics have improved or recovered altogether. Some even have their hair growth restored, others their energy. *Bioflow* has also been helpful with headaches, cramps, and other problems of the nervous system. Since removal of toxic waste is so essential with every physical problem, *Magnotherapy* may benefit them all. I personally have been using *Bioflow* to keep my own magnetic field intact while driving long hours in a car, sitting in an aeroplane or in front of the computer and have noticed a significant reduction in their energy draining effects.

The manufacturers of *Bioflow* offer an interesting range of other products based on the same principle. Their fuel and emission control products have been independently tested and are used around the world by individuals, companies and governments. The water treatment product *H2flow,* for example, helps to keep plumbing free of hard scaling. It does this by keeping salts in suspension instead of building on the inner walls of pipes. Depending on the thickness of the build-up of limescale, heating systems can loose up to 40% of energy. The waste of energy is enormous when considering a nation like Great Britain. Ecoflow Ltd. also has a product for pets to help them remove pain and arthritic conditions (to order Ecoflow products see Useful Addresses). There are many other distributors in England and around the world.

There are a number of other kinds of magnotherapies available, which bear different names. One is *biomagnetic therapy*, which is a combination of acupuncture without needles and osteopathy without manipulation. It is offered by an increasing number of acupuncturists and osteopaths, both in Europe and North America.

For more information on *Magnotherapy* and related self-help products, you may contact the British Biomagnetic Association (see Useful Addresses).

14. How to Deal with Electro-pollution

Not only do we suffer from low intake of magnetic energy, we are also exposed to the harmful low frequency Electromagnetic (EM) fields of 50-60 cycles per second (HZ) that are generated by electricity. This man-made electric current produces "electro-pollution" when utilised by computer equipment, TV transmissions, AM radio waves, mobile telephones, and the various home and industrial appliances such as hairdryers, electric toasters, and microwave ovens.

While you sleep in a room that has a TV connected to the power circuit, an electronic alarm clock, a bedside light, or an electric blanket switched on, you may be building up an electric charge of up to 105 Volts! Since your feet are not in direct contact with the floor while lying in bed, you are not able to disperse that charge which may create chaos in the body's electric circuitry and even cause diseases like cancer. Badly shielded electric cables within the walls or under the floor can have similar effects. It is best to move all electric equipment out of the bedroom, or simply turn off the fuse for the entire room during the night. If you are not sure whether your electric cables are safe or not, choose the latter solution, or otherwise you may want to hire an expert who can measure the safety of your most immediate environment. When I tested electro-pollution in my own house I was surprised that the worst culprit wasn't my computer but the unearthed electrical strip lights.

Electromagnetic imbalance is also caused by chemical pollution, which occurs indoors more than it does outdoors. Add to the above mentioned pollutants the harmful chemicals contained in the cosmetics, deodorants, and perfumes that cover and penetrate into our bodies, and any biological system will eventually succumb such an overdose of stress and duress. Although most of us cannot completely avoid living in a toxic environment, we still can reduce our direct exposure to it to the minimum possible.

15. How to Avoid the Negative Effects of Ley Lines

If you suffer from recurring problems such as headaches, irritability, or depression without any apparent reason or from any other persistent physical problem, you may be working or sleeping on a ley line, which is a source of harmful slow frequency energy.

Slow frequency energies can infiltrate and distort our personal electromagnetic fields from various sources. Some are generated outside our home and others originate from within our home and work environment. They include geographic stress points, ley lines and distorted ground energies.

Sleeping on a ley line can be particularly harmful since such a source of constant negative energy has a chance to disrupt our body's biochemical processes and energy systems for many hours each night. Disharmony and diseases are more likely to occur if you are exposed to such negative energies for a periodic length of time. Genetic weaknesses or latent physical problems can suddenly manifest in the form of migraines, ulcers, varicose veins, or cancer. Placing a mirror, which should face the current of a ley line or better even moving the bed away from such a stress line can lead to sudden recovery. The following are some examples of ley line problems that were resolved simply by moving the bed:

- A 55-year-old widow experienced an unexplainable loss of weight from 70 to 44 kg within two years. She suffered from severe diarrhoea, which became very painful and was accompanied with blood. All medical treatments failed. Her condition became life threatening. After her house was searched for ley lines, two of which crossed her bed, the bed was moved by two metres. One week later her intestinal bleeding stopped. After one month all pain ceased and she steadily began to put on weight again.

- A young women suffered from severe nightmares and sleeping problems for many years. After her bed was moved 50cm, her nightmares stopped and sleep returned back to normal.
- A 40-year-old businessman had a chronic heart complaint with heart cramping, panic attacks, and circulatory problems. All complaints spontaneously disappeared within two weeks after his bed was moved away from a ley line.

Over the past few years I have visited many homes and offices where ley lines have caused physical and psychological problems. In most cases putting a mirror at the right place or slightly shifting the bed or office chair led to marked improvements of the condition and in many cases even to complete cures. I consider it essential to have one's home or working place checked for such disturbances as they may not only contribute to ill health but also cause it. There is an increasing number of experts who are able to identify the exact position of ley lines, although the method of mirror placement is less known. You may contact your nearest centre for alternative therapies; they may be able to put you in touch with a reliable and trustworthy ley line specialist.

16. Sunlight – Medicine of Nature

The Sun –Source of all Life on Earth

Regular exposure to the germicidal wavelength of ultraviolet light of the sun effectively controls germs, mites, mould, bacteria, and viruses, thus helping the immune system to maintain physiological balance. But this is only one of the many effects sunlight has on human physiology.

The electromagnetic waves generated by the sun have throughout the ages kept the planet in a habitable condition for humans, and animals and plants. The sun is in fact the only true source of energy on Earth. It provides the right amount of energy for the plants to photosynthesise all the products necessary for growth. Sun energy is stored in the plants as carbohydrates, proteins, and fat, which when ingested provides us with the vital energy we need to live. The processes of digestion, assimilation, and metabolism in animals and humans are concerned with breaking down, transferring, storing, and utilising these various forms of solar energies. The lowest level of the food chain, where foods are manufactured directly by sunlight, makes available the most sun energy. By contrast, products that are high on the food chain such as animal products, junk and microwave foods, or fast, frozen, irradiated, genetically engineered[1], and highly processed foods contain only little or no sun energy and are useless if not harmful for the body.

Wood, fuel, and minerals, too, are merely different forms of locked-up sun energy. In fact all matter is "frozen" light. Our body cells are nothing but bundles of sun energy. The glucose and oxygen we feed them with are products of the sun. We couldn't even think a thought without the molecules of sun energised glucose and oxygen.

Air, which is warmed by the sun, is capable of absorbing water from the oceans while passing over them. As the air moves over the land masses up to higher elevations, it cools down and thereby releases some of the absorbed water which falls as rain, or snow at higher altitudes. This feeds the rivers and through them the land and the vegetation. Depending on its position in relation to earth rotation, the position of the moon, and internal cyclic activities (sun spot cycles), the sun masterminds the entire climate and the seasonal changes down to the minutest details, including right temperature, amount of rainfall, cloud formation, periods of dryness, etc.

---

[1] In 1998 scientists have found the first evidence that genetically-modified food may damage human health. Researchers at the prestigious Rowett Institute in Aberdeen found that genetically-modified foods could damage the immune systems of rats. Around 60 percent of the processed food products found in supermarkets – from hamburgers to ice cream – may contain ingredients which have been genetically tampered with.

The planet is not only a home for human beings. The sun has to support the growth of all the species; that includes plants, insects, animals, humans and especially microbes without which life could not be possible. The mathematical complexity that stands behind a system of organisation so infinitely diverse and intricate as planetary life cannot be fathomed by even trillions of computers. But the sun, without making mistakes, "calculates" what each species, whether it is an ant, a tree or a human being, needs to fulfil its evolutionary purpose.

The electromagnetic waves generated by the sun come in a variety of lengths, which determine their specific course of action and responsibility. They range from 0.00001 nanometer for cosmic rays (a nanometer is one billionth of a meter) to about 4,990 kilometres for electric waves. There are cosmic rays, gamma rays, x-rays, various types of Ultraviolet rays, the visible light consisting of seven colour rays, short-wave infrared, infrared, radio waves and electric waves. Most of these energy waves are absorbed and used for various processes in the layers of atmosphere that surround the earth.

Only a small portion of them, the electromagnetic spectrum, reaches the surface of the earth, of which the human eye can perceive just about 1 percent. We cannot see any of the ultraviolet and infrared waves yet they influence us. In fact, ultraviolet light has proved to be the most biologically active. Depending on the location of the earth and the season, ultraviolet light and of course all the other portions of light, vary in intensity. This permits all life forms to go through constant cycles of change necessary for growth and renewal.

The Miraculous Healing Powers of UV light

Unfortunately, it is the ultraviolet light that is the most easily eliminated by windows, houses, spectacles, sunglasses, sun lotions, and clothing. Before antibiotic drugs were discovered in the 1930s, penicillin being the first one, the healing power of sunlight was the favoured interest of the medical world. Sunlight therapy was the most successful treatment for infectious diseases.

Studies revealed that single exposures of a large area of the body to ultraviolet light were found to dramatically lower elevated blood pressure (up to 40 mm Hg drop), decrease *cholesterol* in the blood stream, lower abnormally high blood sugars, as found in diabetics, and increase the number of white blood cells, which help us to resist disease. Patients suffering from gout, rheumatoid arthritis, colitis, arteriosclerosis, anaemia, cystitis, eczema, acne, psoriasis, herpes, lupus, sciatica, kidney problems, asthma, as well as burns received great help from the healing rays of the sun.

The renowned medical doctor and author, Dr. Auguste Rollier treated his patients with sunlight at a clinic that was situated 5,000 feet above sea level. This allowed them to catch a lot more of UV light than was possible at the lower levels of the atmosphere. The "miraculous" complete cures of tuberculosis and other diseases made headlines at the time. What surprised the medical community most was the fact that the sun's healing rays remained ineffective if the patients wore sunglasses. By the year 1933, there were over 165 different diseases that clearly benefited from sunlight.

But soon, man-made drugs replaced medicine's fascination with the sun's healing powers, which consequently were believed to be dangerous to health. Today, the sun is considered to be the main culprit for causing skin cancer, certain cataracts leading to blindness, and even ageing. Only those who "risk" exposing themselves to the ultraviolet light for short periods of time, find that the sun makes them feel better, provided they don't use sunscreens or burn their skin. UV light stimulates the thyroid gland to increase hormone production, which in turn increases the body's basal metabolic rate. This assists both in weight loss and improved muscle development. Farm animals fatten much faster when kept indoors, so do people who stay out of the sun. So if you want to lose weight or increase your muscle tone, expose your body to the sun on a regular basis.

The use of antibiotics has led to the development of drug resistant strains of bacteria, which defy any other treatment than balanced use of sun, water, air, and food. Separation from any of these basic constituents of life result in disease, for we are made up of all of them. The four elements fire, water, air, earth are connected in space and are essential for everything that exists.

Life without adequate exposure to sunlight remains incomplete and is bound to suffer from lack of energy. The populations in northern European countries like Norway and Finland, which experience months of darkness every year, have a higher incidence of irritability, fatigue, illness, insomnia, depression, alcoholism, and suicide than those living in the sunny parts of the world.

UV light is known to activate an important skin hormone called *solitrol*. *Solitrol* influences our immune system and many of our body's regulatory centres, and, in conjunction with the pineal hormone *melatonin*, causes changes in mood and daily biological rhythms. *The haemoglobin* in our red blood cells require ultraviolet (UV) light to bind to the oxygen needed for all cellular functions. Lack of sunlight can therefore be held responsible for almost any illness, including skin cancer. In other words, it may be highly detrimental to our health to miss out on sunlight.

Sunlight and Exercise
Both sunlight and exercise seem to have similar benefits on health and physical fitness but when used together, the effects are multiplied. Tuberculosis patients, for example, who have been treated with sunlight therapy alone (regular exposure to sunlight) have experienced a considerable increase in muscle tone with very little fat, even though they have not exercised their bodies at all. The same happens to a person who is on a regular fitness programme. But if sun exposure and exercise are combined, muscular strength increases much more than if either of the two are used alone.

In the male physiology, muscular development is linked to the production of the male hormone, *testosterone*. The old Greek practice of exercising nude on a warm sandy beach was used to develop a healthy muscular body. When sunlight falls on any part of the body, *testosterone* production increases substantially, but when it strikes the male genitals directly, secretion of the hormone is greatest. A study at Boston State Hospital has proved that ultraviolet light increases the level of *testosterone* by 120% when the chest or back is exposed to sunlight! The hormone, however, increases by 200% when genital skin is exposed to the sun. Regular sunbathing increases strength and size of all muscle groups in the male physique. The combination of sun and exercise is therefore ideal to develop a strong and healthy body with ideal reproductive abilities. It may well be that constant lack of sun exposure is the main cause of the increased infertility problems among the city populations in the world. If you want to improve your sex life or fertility rates, rather than using one of the currently available costly treatments and risk your health due to their serious side effects, I would recommend that you first try the sun.

Women of course benefit from sunlight, too. Their levels of female hormones rise when they are exposed to particularly one specific portion of UV light, i.e., 290 nanometers, which is *assumed* to be dangerous and useless. Women, who have only very little exposure to sunlight, are often suffering from menstrual problems or have no menstrual periods at all. They can re-establish a healthy menstrual cycle by sunbathing regularly and spending several hours of the day outdoors. Normalisation of the menstrual cycle can occur within a few weeks after starting sunlight therapy.

Several independent studies demonstrated that hypertensive patients who followed a vigorous exercise programme for six months lowered their blood pressure by 15 percent, whereas those who had one single exposure to the ultraviolet light of the sun, had a markedly lower blood pressure for five or six days. Exercising in the sun, therefore could be one of the best non-medical treatments for hypertension, cost-free and without any side effects. At the same time, both exercise and sunbathing increase the heart's efficiency, which is measured by the amount of blood pumped by the heart at each beat. A single exposure to the ultraviolet rays of the sun alone has shown to increase heart efficiency by an average of 39 percent, again lasting for as long as five to six days. Such an approach could effectively replace drugs currently used to stimulate the heart. It should be noted that sunlight acts not like a drug that merely suppresses the symptoms of disease, but rather restores balance in body and mind.

Diabetics, too, can benefit from exercise and sunlight. Their blood sugar drops when exercising as well as when sunbathing. One single exposure to sunlight first stimulates the production of the enzyme *phosphorylase*, which decreases the amount of stored glycogen. Two hours later, another enzyme, *glycogen synthesise*, increases storage of glycogen in the tissues while lowering blood sugar levels. Thus sunlight works like insulin. The effect may last for days. It is important for diabetics to know that they may need to adjust their insulin dose and should therefore regularly consult their doctor while gradually increasing their body's exposure to sunlight.

Both sunlight and exercise have beneficial effects on reducing stress levels. These include decrease of nervousness, anxiety, emotional imbalance; increase of stress tolerance, self-confidence, imagination and creativity; positive changes in personality and moods; reduction of unhealthy habits such as cigarette smoking and alcoholism. Studies from Russia showed that also duodenal ulcers are greatly improved through regular exposure to the sun.

American research found that when exposure to ultraviolet light is added to fitness programmes, subjects have a 19 percent increase in performance as measured by physical fitness tests. In addition, those exposed to UV light, had 50 percent fewer incidences of colds than those who didn't. Their immune systems were maintained on a high level of efficiency. Also children who receive extra UV light during wintertime have a marked increase in physical fitness.

What makes the Sun so "Dangerous" – The Fat Connection

Sunlight is most beneficial for those who eat a balanced diet according to their individual requirements and body type. Sunbathing may be dangerous, however, for those who live on a diet rich in acid forming, highly processed foods, and refined fats or their products. Also alcohol, cigarettes, and other mineral and vitamin depleting substances such as allopathic and hallucinogenic drugs can make the skin highly vulnerable to ultraviolet radiation. In particular, polyunsaturated fats as contained in highly refined and vitamin E depleted products such as thin vegetable oil, mayonnaise, dressings, and most brands of margarine pose a high risk in the development of skin cancer and most other cancers. According to *Archives of Internal Medicine*, 1998, polyunsaturated fats increase your risk of breast cancer by 69 per cent (by contrast, monounsaturated fats as found in olive oil and canola oils reduce your breast cancer risk by 45 per cent).

This is due to the fact that, once in contact with air, these fats quickly attract oxygen free radicals and become oxidised, i.e., rancid. Oxygen radicals get generated when oxygen molecules lose an electron. This makes them highly reactive. They quickly bind to almost anything around and can cause damage to cells, tissues, and organs. Free radicals can be formed in polyunsaturated fats if they are exposed to sunlight before consumption. Otherwise the radicals form in the tissues after the oil has been eaten. Polyunsaturated fats are difficult to digest, since they are deprived of their natural bulk and are no longer protected against free radicals by their natural protector vitamin E, a powerful antioxidant. Hence large numbers of radicals can enter the tissues.

Saturated fats are solid and found in products such as lard and butter. They contain large quantities of natural antioxidants, which makes them much more safe against oxidation by free radicals. Since polyunsaturated fats are man-made and do not exist in natural form, they are indigestible and considered dangerous by the body. Free radicals, the natural cleansers of the body, try to get rid of the culprit, but as a harmful side effect they cause damage to the walls of the cells as well. This is considered to be the main cause of ageing. Research has shown that out of 100 people who consumed large quantities of polyunsaturated fats, 78 showed marked clinical signs of premature ageing, plus they looked much older than others of the same age did.

Tissue cells that are damaged by abnormal free radical activity are unable to reproduce properly and can impair major functions in the body, including those of the immune, digestive, nervous, and endocrine systems. Ever since polyunsaturated fats have been introduced to the population on a large scale, degenerative diseases have increased dramatically, skin cancer being one of them. In fact, polyunsaturated fats have made sunlight "dangerous," something that would have never been the case if foods hadn't been so altered and manipulated as they are today. When polyunsaturated fats are removed from their natural foods, they need to be refined, deodorised, and even be hydrogenated, depending on the food product they are used for. During this process some of the polyunsaturated fats undergo chemical transformations, which turns them into *trans fats* or *trans fatty acids*, often referred to as "hydrogenated vegetable oils." Margarine can contain up to 54 percent of them, vegetable shortening up to 58 percent.

You can detect hydrogenated vegetable oils in foods by reading the labels. Most processed foods contain them, including breads, chips, doughnuts, crackers, biscuits, pastries, all baked goods, cake and frosting mixes, baking mixes, frozen dinners, sauces, frozen vegetables, and breakfast cereals. In other words, nearly all foods that are shelved, processed, refined, preserved, and not fresh can contain *trans* fats. *Trans* fats inhibit the cell's ability to use oxygen, which is required to burn foodstuffs to carbon dioxide and water. Cells, which are inhibited in completing their metabolic processes, may become cancerous.

The trans fats also make the blood thicker by increasing stickiness of platelets. This multiplies the chances of blood clots and build up of fatty deposits, which can lead to heart disease. Research at Harvard Medical School, observing 85,000 women over eight years, found that those eating margarine had an increased risk of coronary heart disease. Further studies have shown that trans fatty acids prevent the body from processing Low Density Lipo Protein (LDL) or bad *cholesterol*, thereby raising blood *cholesterol* to abnormal levels. A Welsh study linked the concentration of these artificial trans fats in body fat with death from heart disease. The Dutch Government has already banned any products containing trans fatty acids.

Polyunsaturated fats have also been shown to suppress immunity. For this reason, they are used today in patients who have undergone kidney transplant operations or skin grafts taken from other people. This helps the patients to prevent the immune system from rejecting the foreign tissue but of course leaves them vulnerable to infection and other disorders. The same approach is used in the so-called *autoimmune diseases* where the immune system attempts to kill off some of the body's own cells, i.e. those that have become toxic. But the tragic in all this is that such treatments don't change overall mortality rates, only the cause of death is altered.

What Really Burns and Damages the Skin

A person who consumes polyunsaturated fats in his diet and exposes his skin to ultraviolet light to the point of reddening produces hormone-like substances called *prostaglandins* from the linoleic acid contained in the fats. *Prostraglandins* suppress the immune system, thereby contributing to tumour growth. In addition, polyunsaturated fats are accompanied by free radical production, which can damage cells. If you add suntan oils to the skin you have the right combination of chemicals to produce skin cancer, especially on areas that are more exposed to the sun than others.

In nature, oils never occur in large quantities. To obtain one tablespoon of corn oil in natural form you would have to eat 12-18 ears of corn. Since oil extraction from corn, grains, and seeds became possible 80-90 years ago, consumption of polyunsaturated and unsaturated fats (thicker oils) as salad and cooking oils has increased dramatically in the industrialised world. The average person today consumes 16 times more of these fats than a person did 90 years ago. That does not include all the other fats contained in today's foods. The lack of exercise, fresh air, and foods rich in nutrients make it even less possible for a human being to cope with such large amounts of unnatural fats. They impair the digestive power and lead to a build-up of toxins and subsequent crises of toxicity. The presence of excessive amounts of free radicals indicates that the body is full up with toxins. Once they enter the skin tissue, even short-term exposure to ultraviolet light can burn and damage skin cells.

If your eyes and skin are sensitive to sunlight, this indicates that your body is toxic. Your subsequent effort to avoid the sun may result in serious light deficiency, which can lead to serious health problems. The fact that cancer of all kinds increased when sunscreen was introduced is hardly surprising. The UV light entering the eyes stimulates the immune system. Today, more than 50% of the U.S. population wear prescription or sun-protective glasses, which are able to block out most UV light. The latest fashion is to wear plastic glasses; they also block out all UV light. Indoor activities, sun tan lotions, clothing, UV-repelling windows, etc., make certain that we hardly get any of it. Without regular exposure to sunlight, however, the immune system decreases its effectiveness with every year of age. With sunlight the use of oxygen in the body tissues increases, without it our cells begin to starve of oxygen. This leads to cellular malfunction and premature ageing and even death.

Starved of a balanced sunlight diet, we tend to look for help elsewhere even though nature is ready to cure us at any time. It is very unfortunate that sick people are mostly kept indoors, often with curtains drawn and windows closed. One of nature's most potent preventive and curative powers is there for everyone to use.

Guidelines for Increasing Sun Exposure

If you wish to benefit from the sun but cannot afford much time to be outdoors, there are several ways to increase your exposure to UV light. Windows should consist of glass that permits UV light to enter. Have as many such windows as possible. Keep your curtains pushed back so that you have maximum exposure. If possible, depending on weather and season, keep your windows open. Install as many full spectrum lights as possible, they are the next best alternative to natural sunlight.

Those living in a moderate climate can sunbathe regularly. It is best to avoid the sun between 10.00 a.m. and 3.00 p.m. during summer, whereas during winter and spring this time is OK, too. During winter you can sunbathe if you lie in a totally wind protected place. You can build your own sunbathing area against a wall facing the sun. The sidewalls should be made of material that can serve as a good windbreak. The wall pointing toward the sun should be at an angle slanted toward the sun so that the low winter rays can shine into the sunbathing area. Lying on a blanket, you will be warmer than if you were indoors.

For maximum benefits it is best to take a shower before sunbathing. Start your sunlight treatment by exposing your entire body (if possible) for a few minutes to begin with and then increase the time each day by a few more minutes until you reach 20-30 minutes. Alternatively, walking in the sun for an hour has similar benefits. This will give you enough sunlight to keep your body and mind healthy, provided you incorporate the basic measures of a balanced diet, lifestyle, and daily routine as outlined in earlier chapters.

CHAPTER 8

Man's Foremost Killer Diseases

I. Heart Disease – A Symptom of Ill Health

Less than a hundred years ago heart disease was an extremely rare disease. Today it kills more people in the developed world than all other causes of death taken together. In several industrialised nations mortality rates from heart attacks have slightly decreased due to a generation of breakthroughs in heart care - the new medicines, the bypass operations, the angioplasties. Now the beneficiaries of this care are living with the consequences: Their damaged hearts still beat, but not strong enough to enjoy a decent quality of life. Many wish they had died swiftly than suffering a slow and torturous death.

The unintended result of better cardiac care is an unprecedented increase in a chronic, debilitating disease called *heart failure*, which could very well be described as a virtual epidemic. Heart failure is a *gradual* ebbing of the heart's power to pump blood and supply the body with oxygen. "Heart failure is a product of our success in dealing with heart disease and hypertension," said Dr. Michael Bristow of the University of Colorado. Treating the symptoms of heart disease and hypertension rather than their causes has lead to more hardship and suffering than anticipated. It is the call of our time to take a more holistic look at the causes of this greatest killer disease in the modern world and to apply natural methods to restore heart functions swiftly and permanently, without side effects.

The Beginning of Heart Disease

Our Cardiovascular System is composed of a central pumping device – the heart muscles – and a blood vessel pipeline, consisting of arteries, veins and capillaries. The heart muscles pump blood through the blood vessel system to deliver oxygen and nutrients to all parts of the body. The blood vessel system is over 60.000 miles long and has a surface of more than half an acre. The cells in the body depend on the frictionless flow of blood through this vast network of channels.

The tiny capillaries, which are only one tenth as thick as a human hair, are of particular importance for the body. Unlike arteries, the capillaries permit oxygen, water, and nutrients to filter through their thin walls in order to nourish the surrounding tissues. At the same time, they have to allow for cellular waste to return to the blood so that it can be excreted from the body. If the capillary network becomes congested, the heart has to pump the blood with greater pressure to reach all the different parts of the body. This increases its workload considerably and makes its muscles tense and tired. In due time, the exertion of the heart leads to stress and fatigue and impairs all major functions in the body.

Since the capillaries are also responsible for nourishing the muscle cells of the arteries, a reduced supply of oxygen, water, and nutrients will gradually injure and destroy them. The resulting lesions in the arteries cause the development of arteriosclerotic deposits, which are considered to be the major cause of heart attacks.

The Major Contributing Factors

While most heart attacks are believed to be triggered by the clogging of the heart arteries, which destroys millions of heart cells, strokes are caused by the clogging of the brain arteries, which causes the death of millions of brain cells. Since brain cells co-ordinate the activities and movements of every part of the body, their death can lead to partial or complete paralysis, and death. A stroke is just another form of cardiovascular disease.

The brain arteries are located in close proximity to the heart. The blood pressure in both the brain and heart arteries is relatively higher than in those arteries that are located in other parts of the body, hence the difference of blood pressure in the different arteries of the circulatory system. If turbulence and congestion occur in the branching areas of the arteries, the blood pressure begins to rise. This particularly stresses the coronary, carotid (neck), and cerebral (brain) arteries to the point of damage. Damage occurs first in those blood vessels that are already weakened by nutrient deficiencies. This makes high blood pressure a major risk factor for strokes and heart disease.

Lowering an elevated blood pressure through medication, however, is not a solution but a mere postponement of the problem, and, as recent research has shown, it can lead to chronic heart failure. Without removing the cause(s) of elevated blood pressure the standard treatment for hypertension can cause severe cellular dehydration and sharply reduce the blood's capacity to deliver oxygen to the heart muscles and remove toxic waste from the cells and tissues of the body. All this further increases the risk of heart disease and many other physical problems, including kidney and liver disorders.

The Western Hemisphere is heading the global list of heart disease. Doctors blame the wrong type of food, overeating, too little exercise, smoking, and stress as the major risk factors. Latest research has added a few more, such as free radicals, pollution, poor circulation, certain drugs and chemicals, and a decreased ability of the blood to digest protein, which may form into blood clots. When the proteolytic enzymes mromelain, trypsin, and chymotrypsin are no longer sufficiently available to help break down the blood clots, heart attacks, phlebitis, and stokes are the most likely consequences. The major cause of coronary heart disease, however, is overeating of animal proteins. When stored in the body, protein becomes one of the greatest risk factors for heart disease and for most other diseases as well.

Meat Consumption and Heart Disease

In 1800 meat consumption in Germany was 13 kg per person a year. One hundred years later, meat consumption was nearly three times as high at 38 kg. By 1979 it had reached 94,2 kg, which is an increase of 725 per cent in less than 180 years. These figures do not include fats. During the period of 1946-1978 meat consumption in Germany increased by 90% and heart attacks rose by 20 times. During the same period fat consumption remained the same, whereas consumption of cereals and potatoes, which are major suppliers of vegetable protein, decreased by 45%. Therefore, fats and carbohydrates as well as vegetable proteins cannot be considered to be causes of coronary heart disease. This leaves meat as the main factor responsible for this degenerative blood vessel disease.

In consideration of the fact that 50 percent of the German population are overweight and most overweight people eat much more meat than those with normal weight do, meat consumption among the overweight must have at least quadrupled in the 33 years after World War II. Being overweight is considered to be a major risk for high blood pressure and heart disease.

According to statistics published by the World Health Organisation in 1978, the yearly increases of heart attacks in Western European countries were accompanied by a continuous yearly increase in meat consumption by as much as 4kg per person. This practically means that eating habits after World War II have shifted from a healthy mixed diet to one rich in animal protein but poor in carbohydrates. Yet fat consumption remained virtually unchanged. Heart attacks and arteriosclerosis began to increase dramatically in Germany and in Western industrialised nations soon after the war, today they cause 50 percent of all deaths.

Although fat consumption among vegetarians is not lower than among meat eaters, the vegetarians have the lowest death rates from heart disease. The Journal of the American Medical Association reported that a vegetarian diet could prevent 97% of all coronary occlusions. The reason for the virtual absence of coronary heart disease among vegetarians is their low intake of animal protein. Fat consumption is therefore only an accomplice of the disease but not its cause. The current mass hysteria that sees fat, which is generally associated with cholesterol, as the main dietary culprit of heart disease, is completely unfounded and has no scientific basis.

The Body *Does* Store Protein

Meat and meat products have a five to ten times higher concentration of protein than most vegetable foods. It is therefore easily possible to overeat animal protein but it not possible to overeat vegetable protein because man's intestinal capacity is not sufficient to handle 5-10 times more food than is normal for the body. It is common knowledge that the body is able to store unused sugar and carbohydrates in the form of fat but it is hardly known that it also has a large storage capacity for protein. The body's protein stores are the *connective tissues* (the fluids between the capillaries and the cells) and the *basement membranes*, which hold together and support the cells of the capillaries. When these protein stores are filled to their full storage capacity, the organs and arteries that are supplied by such protein-congested capillaries starve of oxygen and nutrients and suffocate in their own metabolic waste products. The result is a toxicity crisis. If it occurs in the coronary arteries, it is called coronary heart disease.

A person who overeats carbohydrates such as sugar, bread, pasta, and fats in a particular meal has high concentrations of carbohydrates, fats, and the *cholesterol* containing lipo proteins in his blood. But blood tests also show that if he overeats protein his blood contains higher concentrations of protein. Nutritional science assumes[2] that protein is completely burned during the digestive process. Whatever protein the body cells don't use or need, says the argument, continues to circulate in the blood until it is broken down by liver enzymes and excreted as urea.

But a problem arises when a person's urea-producing enzymes are not sufficiently effective to clear the blood from excessive protein, as naturally is the case in the typical *Kapha* constitution and to a large extent in the *Pitta* constitution. The same applies to people who regularly overeat proteins. The excessive proteins, which are not eliminated in this way, are then absorbed partly by the connective tissue under the skin (which is harmless) and to some extent by the connective intercellular tissue of the organs (which can be harmful). If the supply of large quantities of food protein continues, the intercellular connective tissue and basement membranes of the capillaries become saturated with protein and begin to thicken. Unless protein intake is discontinued, the capillary cells become damaged. This is the beginning stage of diet-caused arteriosclerosis.

On the other hand, as already discovered in 1955, people who live on a protein-free diet for a certain length of time do not produce urea after their first protein meals. Their connective tissues contain no excessive protein. This is the case in all vegetarians whose sole source of protein is of vegetarian origin. They can never develop a surplus of protein in the connective tissues and are therefore not at risk of developing arteriosclerotic deposits, as has been confirmed by the American Medical Association.

---

[2] There is no scientific study to support this assumption

It is a commonly accepted medical theory that all unused calories, whether they occur in the form of carbohydrates, fat, or protein, are converted into fat and deposited in the body's fat cells. This would make fat to be the only storage molecule responsible for obesity and related illnesses, including coronary heart disease and diabetes mellitus. Yet there is overwhelming evidence that stored fat cannot be held responsible for causing coronary heart disease. The only other substance the body can store in large amounts is protein.

Protein Storage – The Body's Time Bomb
Obese people have both high concentrations of fats and excessive amounts of protein in the blood. The blood's tendency towards clotting, which is considered to be the greatest risk for suffering a heart attack or stroke, stems almost exclusively from the saturation of the blood with proteins (also smoking increases protein concentrations, as shown below). Fats, on the other hand, have no blood clotting ability. In their attempt to avoid a heart attack, the capillary cells absorb the excessive protein, convert it into *collagen-fibre,* and store it in their basement membranes. This thins the blood again but also thickens the blood vessel walls. Examinations of connective tissue in obese people have proved that it contains not only plump fat cells but also large amounts of thickened collagen-fibre.

Collagen is 100 percent pure protein. Building more collagen-fibre is the body's emergency measure to deal with dangerously high protein concentrations in the blood. Hence the blood becomes thin and the crisis is avoided. But if the body's protein stores are filled up and protein consumption continues, the blood once again becomes saturated with protein. That's when the blood begins to permanently thicken and develops a tendency towards clotting. Unless the afflicted person takes aspirin, which has a blood thinning effect, a stroke or a heart attack may occur. Yet in the long run the drug also fails to prevent such an incidence.

Examinations have shown that by abstaining from food for a periodic length of time, both fat cells and collagen fibre begin to reduce in size. This clearly demonstrates that overeating protein *does* increase protein tissue in the body; the sites of the protein deposits are the basement membranes of the capillary walls and the connective tissues that surround the cells. As a direct consequence of this development, the thickened blood vessels are no longer capable of absorbing sufficient amounts of oxygen, water, and nutrients and removing their own metabolic waste products. Hence the cells that make up the blood vessels become injured and eventually die from malnutrition, suffocation, and dehydration.

In a young person, the blood vessels of the heart have a diameter of about 3mm. By regularly overeating protein foods, the normally smooth and polished inner wall of a blood vessel becomes uneven, and the blood vessel as a whole thickens and loses its elasticity. This leads to deterioration of the blood flow throughout the circulatory system, and may culminate in a complete blockage. People whose coronary arteries are totally blocked resemble an old rusty, damaged, and calcified water pipe. Their walls are brownish-red and are clogged up with yellowish calcified material. Researchers discovered that the toxic, sulphur-containing amino acid homocysteine (HC) promotes the tiny clots that initiate arterial damage and the catastrophic ones that precipitate most heart attacks and strokes (Ann Clin & Lab Sci, 1991 and Lancet 1981). HC results from normal metabolism of the amino acid methionine – which is abundant in red meat, milk, and dairy products.

Conclusion: If we regularly consume large quantities of animal protein, including meat, pork, poultry, eggs, milk, cheese, etc., our body's ability to break down all the protein becomes increasingly impaired (if it is not already naturally inefficient by constitution). Since excessive protein consumption thickens the blood and increases its risk of clotting, the body is forced to store the protein and the by-products of protein metabolism in the connective tissues under the skin as well as in the connective tissue of the organs and in the basement membranes of the capillary network. When the storage capacity of the basement membranes is exhausted, no more protein can be deposited in the capillaries. A continued overconsumption of animal protein is then met with storage of the excessive protein in the walls of the arteries themselves. At this stage the main heart arteries become thickened, damaged, and inefficient. As they occlude and cut off the oxygen supply to the heart, a heart attack occurs. Thus the storage of excessive protein in the body becomes a "time bomb" ready to explode at any moment.

How and Why do Heart Attacks Occur?

When the basement membranes of the capillaries and arteries can no longer guarantee sufficient supply of oxygen, sugar, and insulin to the heart muscles, their ability to contract and pump blood is greatly reduced. To continue their work even without enough oxygen, the heart cells begin to ferment glucose to produce energy, but this (anaerobic) process produces lactic acid, which acidifies the muscle tissues. The heart employs an additional emergency measure to gain energy, which is to mobilise and break down fats. Yet, without using oxygen in the process, these fats turn into harmful acids. Proteins too begin to be used to provide energy; the by-products are harmful fatty acids. Since the thickening of the connective tissues, and the lymph and blood capillaries in the heart obstruct normal waste elimination, the heart muscles become intensely saturated with acidic waste material. This may cause intense pain.

If uric acid, which is a waste product resulting from the braking down of old cells is retained in the tissues, gout occurs. The muscle cells become severely dehydrated and a group of cells known as mast cells secrete the hormone *histamine*. When *histamine* passes over the sensitive pain nerves in the tissues, strong muscle pain results. If this form of muscle rheumatism occurs in the heart it is called *Angina pectoris* pain. Both the acid accumulation and lack of oxygen lead to the death of the heart cells.

Heart attacks can occur in a number of ways. The connective tissues surrounding the heart cells may become so thick that the heart cells simply die a painless death. In the case of an angina attack, it is acidification and low oxygenation of the heart muscles that destroy the heart. If the basement membranes of the capillaries and arteries are blocked and can no longer supply oxygen to the heart, then the heart attack is caused by their occlusion. The area where the storage capacity for protein has been exhausted first becomes the cause of the infarct. Another possible cause for an attack is a blood clot that breaks lose from a congested and injured blood vessel and enters the heart, blocking off its oxygen supply.

Risk Indications of a Heart Attack

Food-related blood vessel diseases, heart attacks, stroke, rheumatism, angina pectoris are not disorders of sugar and fat metabolism, but are diseases resulting from protein storage. Eating too much protein food can be considered to be one of the greatest risk factors for developing any kind of disease. The thickening of the basement membranes and connective tissues caused by the storage of protein affects the lives of all body cells. Wherever in the body the thickening occurs, complications and ageing arise. Wherever the capillary walls maintain their porous nature and original thinness, continued nourishment and vitality result.

Fat and *cholesterol* are not primary blocking agents of blood vessel walls and can therefore not be considered to be the cause of heart disease or any other disease in the body. Storage of protein in the blood vessel walls, on the other hand, is the common factor in all patients who suffer from alimentary (food-caused) arteriosclerosis. Since most people in the advanced nations have consistently been consuming too large quantities of protein, particularly since World War II, coronary heart disease has become the leading cause of death in the developed world. The following are indications of being at risk of suffering a heart attack.

1. *Thickening of blood as measured by Haemocrit or packed cell volume.*

The *Haemocrit* is the volume of red blood cells in 1 litre of whole blood and can be determined by a simple and cheap blood test. If it is above 42%, the risk of a heart attack increases. A healthy person has a *Haemocrit* of 35% to 40%. In the assumption that the presence of larger quantities of protein in the blood is harmless, a volume of 44-50% has been considered to be the normal level; research, however, has shown that heart attacks were twice as high when the *Haemocrit* reached 49% compared to when it was 42%. The higher the *Haemocrit* rises the greater is the risk of suffering a heart attack.

When the basement membranes and the intercellular tissues become thickened due to storage of excessive protein, blood flow slows down and becomes obstructed. This "naturally" increases the concentration of all blood values, including proteins, fats, and sugar. The thickening of the blood poses a great risk for all parts of the body. To deal with the dangerously high concentration of protein in the blood, the capillary cells begin to absorb the excessive protein, convert it into collagen, and deposit it in their basement membranes. This thins the blood again but also reduces nutrient transport to the cells. When the cells signal malnutrition, the blood nutrient levels begin to rise until the pressure of diffusion is high enough to again deliver enough nutrients to the cells.

In the meanwhile, this constant manoeuvring raises the number of red blood cells, which contain the red coloured *haemoglobin*. *Haemoglobin* combines with oxygen in the lungs and transports it to all the body cells. With increased thickness of the basement membranes also the oxygen supply to the cells becomes restricted. The increased need for oxygen in the cells raises *haemoglobin* concentrations in the red blood cells. But this makes the red blood cells swell up. Now they are to too big to pass through the tiny capillaries, blocking them altogether.

This drastically cuts down the nutrient supply to the cells, which subsequently begin to suffer dehydration. To signal dehydration, the cells release their water deficiency enzyme *renin* into the tissue fluid, which through a myriad of chemical events leads to an increase of heart beat and cardiac output. This emergency measure increases water supply to the cells and prevents their death but it also raises the blood pressure, called *essential hypertension,* which causes further damage to the blood vessels. The vicious circle is closed.

<u>Conclusion</u>: Both factors - the increased *Haemocrit* (blood thickening) and *haemoglobin* concentration in the red cells - reduce blood circulation. A round, red-coloured face and chest are typical indications of increased blood volume and decreased blood circulation in the adult hypertensive and diabetic patient. The cell tissues begin to dehydrate, as water distribution becomes increasingly difficult. The rate and force of contraction of the heart muscles increase to maintain the cardiac output against a sustained rise in congestion throughout the circulatory system. Eventually, the heart can no longer sustain such strenuous activity and collapses.

2. *Eating too much Animal Protein*

The majority of heart attack patients confirm that they have been eating large quantities of animal protein, including, meat, chicken, fish, eggs, or cheese for many years in a row.

3. Cigarette Smoking

The risk of cardiovascular diseases increases greatly with smoking. This, however, is not so much due to the nerve toxin *nicotine*, which is completely broken down within a few hours after smoking, but is rather caused by the *carbon oxide* (CO) contained in cigarette smoke. *Carbon oxide* or *monoxide* diffuses from the lungs into the blood where it attaches itself to the *haemoglobin* of the red cells, about 300 times faster and tighter than oxygen does. All the CO of the inhaled smoke combines with *haemoglobin* and thereby blocks off oxygen transport to the cells. The red blood cells, which are loaded with *carbon monoxide-haemoglobin,* begin to burst and shed their defective protein particles into the plasma of the blood from where they are absorbed by the capillary cells and eventually deposited in the basement membranes. When the capillaries' storage capacity has reached the saturation point, also the arteries begin to deposit the protein debris in their walls.

This makes the *carbon monoxide* of cigarette smoke a slow working poison that, by forming excessive amounts of protein debris, destroys the body's circulatory network and heart muscles. Also *passive* smokers inhale large amounts of *carbon monoxide,* which explains why they too are at risk of developing coronary heart disease.

4. Constitutional (genetic) Disposition towards Reduced Protein Destruction

People whose constitution does not require large quantities of food protein (mostly the *Kapha* and *Pitta* types) in order to be to be healthy don't have an efficient enzyme system for breaking down or dissolving protein. Since constitutional body-types are mostly hereditary, this genetically determined "deficiency" is passed on from parents to children. Those with a family history of heart attacks are not necessarily at risk because heart disease is hereditary but because the family members, who share or shared a similar constitutional body-type, diet, and lifestyle may have the same "inefficient" enzyme systems for destroying excessive proteins.

5. Women during and after Menopause

Women who consume large quantities of protein foods and/or smoke cigarettes are at risk after their menstrual cycles stop. The regular loss of menstrual blood protects a woman (before menopause) from accumulating dangerous amounts of protein in the body. This may explain why menstruating women before age 40 are generally not at risk of suffering heart attacks, whereas men of that age are. All the blood values in women under 40 years are lower than among men in the same age group, including red blood cells, *haemoglobin*, *Haemocrit*, and the total amount of protein. Research has shown that men aged between 30 and 40 years are six times more likely to die from a heart attack than women of the same age are. In fact, heart attacks among menstruating women are extremely rare.

Once a woman's menstrual bleeding cycles subside, if she continues eating animal protein, the level of protein concentration in the blood begins to rise. By the time she is about 50 years old her risk of suffering a heart attack is nearly the same as it is for a man of the same age. The earlier the menopause begins the greater the risk. Women, whose ovaries have been removed before age 35, have a seven times greater risk of a heart attack than those who have yet to enter menopause.

The hot flushes and reddening of the face, which many women experience during menopause, are signs of risen blood values. They indicate that the body has stored excessive amounts of protein, which it can no longer expel with the menstrual blood. It has now been found that the so often recommended diet consisting of a lot of dairy products hastens the forming of arteriosclerotic deposits in a woman's body even further, and, as will be seen later, causes osteoporosis.

Solving the Cholesterol-Heart Disease Mystery

Cholesterol is *not* the Culprit after all

For the past thirty years, *cholesterol* has been stigmatised to be the number one cause for most deaths in the rich nations – heart disease. *Cholesterol* is known to increase in the blood stream of many people today, stick to the walls of arteries, and eventually starve the heart muscles of oxygen and nutrients, at least this is what the theory says. We are generally advised to reduce or ban fats from our diet plan so that we can live without the fear of dying from a heart attack. This concern has finally led to innovative technologies that can extract *cholesterol* from cheese, eggs, and sausages, thus making these "deadly" foods "consumer-safe." Products that claim to be low in *cholesterol* such as margarine and light-foods have become a popular choice of "healthy eating."

A recent study that was sponsored by the German Ministry of Research and Technology proved, however, that there is no link between food *cholesterol* and blood *cholesterol*. In Japan, the *cholesterol* levels have risen during the past few years, yet the number of heart attacks has dropped. The largest-ever health study was conducted in China, which found no connection between heart disease and the consumption of animal fats. All the other major European long-term *cholesterol* studies confirmed that a low fat diet couldn't reduce *cholesterol* levels by more than 4% percent, in most cases by 1-2%. Since measurement mistakes are usually higher than 4% and *cholesterol* levels naturally increase by 20% in autumn and drop again in winter, the anti-*cholesterol* campaigns of the past ten or more years have been misleading, to say the least. A recent study from Denmark involving 20,000 men and women in fact demonstrated that most heart patients have normal *cholesterol* levels. The bottom line is that *cholesterol* hasn't been proved a risk factor for anything.

The current medical understanding of the *cholesterol* issue is more than incomplete. The argument that animal tests on rabbits have proved that fatty foods cause hardening of the arteries sounds reasonable *only* when the following facts are omitted:

1. Rabbits respond 3.000 times more sensitively to *cholesterol* than humans do.
2. Rabbits, which are non-carnivorous animals by nature, are forced to eat excessive quantities of egg yolk and brain for the sake of proving that *cholesterol*-containing foods are harmful.
3. The DNA and enzyme systems of rabbits are not designed for consumption of fatty foods and if given a choice these animals would never eat eggs or brains.

It is obvious that the arteries of these animals have only an extremely limited ability to respond to the damage caused by such unsuitable diets. For over three decades the Western civilisation assumed that animal fats are the main cause of dietary heart disease. This misinformation is highlighted by the fact that heart attacks began to rise when consumption of animal fats actually decreased. This was also testified by British research, which revealed that those areas in the UK where people consumed more margarine and less butter had the highest numbers of heart attacks. Further studies revealed that heart attack patients had consumed the least amounts of animal fats. As explained before, those who died from an attack were found to have many more of the harmful fatty acids, which are derived from the partially hydrogenated vegetable oils of margarine, in their fat tissue than those who survived. These so-called "faulty" fats (trans fatty acids) envelop the cellular membranes, including those of the heart and the heart arteries. This practically starves the cells of oxygen, nutrients, and water, and eventually kills them. In another more comprehensive study, 85.000 nurses working in American hospitals observed a higher risk for heart disease in patients who consumed margarine, crisps, biscuits, cakes, and white bread, all of which contain "faulty" fatty acids.

There is also much confusion about how much *cholesterol* in the blood is supposed to be bad for you. The claim that 200 mg% (200mg per 100 ml) blood *serum cholesterol* is normal and everything above is dangerous is scientifically unfounded. What about 84% of all the men and 93% of all the women aged 50-59 whose *cholesterol* levels are 220 mg% and more, do they all need treatment for heart disease? This theory would make most of us patients for a disease that we probably will never develop. It is considered completely normal for a 55-year-old woman to have a *cholesterol* level of 260 mg%. In a 1995-issue the Journal of the American Medical Association reported that there was no evidence linking high cholesterol levels in women with heart conditions later in life. Also healthy employees are found to have an average of 250 mg% with high fluctuations in both directions.

It seems we need to be more concerned about low *cholesterol*, which is a major risk for cancer, mental illness, suidcide, liver diseases, anaemia, and AIDS. Studies conducted in major German hospitals verified that low *cholesterol* levels are linked to high mortality rates. When *cholesterol* levels dropped to 150 mg%, two out of three patients died. Most of the patients whose *cholesterol* levels were high recovered from whatever they suffered. Also longevity in old homes is linked with higher levels of *cholesterol*. Recent studies published in the British Medical Journal (BMJ) indicate that a low level of blood *cholesterol* could increase a person's risk of suicide.

Another study published in the Lancet in 1997 showed that particularly among the elderly, high total cholesterol levels are associated with longevity. The research suggests that elderly people with elevated cholesterol levels live longer and are less likely to die from cancer or infection.

After so many years of researching heart disease and its risk factors, there is no evidence to date linking high *cholesterol* levels to heart disease as a cause-and-effect reaction, although both *can* occur together. On the other hand, there is increasing evidence to show that a diet high in animal proteins poses the greatest risk for increasing blood fats to life-endangering concentrations.

Cholesterol -- Our Life and Blood

A newborn baby, who is being breast-fed by its mother, receives a high dose of *cholesterol* right from the beginning of its life. Mother's milk contains twice as much *cholesterol* as cow's milk! Nature certainly has no intention of destroying a baby's heart by giving it such high amounts of *cholesterol*. On the contrary, a healthy heart consists of 10% pure *cholesterol* (all water removed). Our brain is made of even more *cholesterol* than the heart is and half of our adrenal glands consist of this lipid. *Cholesterol* is an essential building block of all our body cells and is needed for every metabolic process. Because *cholesterol* is such an important substance for the body every single cell is capable of producing it. We simply could not survive without it. *Cholesterol...*

- is important for brain development
- protects the nerves against damage or injury
- supports immune functions
- gives elasticity to red blood cells
- stabilises and protects cell membranes
- is the basic ingredient of most sexual hormones
- helps to form the skin
- is the essential substance which the skin uses to make vitamin D
- is the basic ingredient used to manufacture the body's stress hormones
- is needed to form bile acids to help digestion of fats and keep us lean
- helps to prevent kidney damage in diabetes

Cholesterol plays a vital role in every living being. Microbes, bacteria, viruses, plants, animals, or human beings, all depend on it. Since *cholesterol* is so important for our body, we cannot solely depend on its supply from outside but must be able to produce it independently as well. Normally, our body produces about half a gram to one gram of *cholesterol* a day, depending on how much the body requires at the time. The main *cholesterol* producers are the liver and the small intestines; they release it into the blood stream where it is instantly tied to blood proteins that are in charge of transporting *cholesterol* to their destinations. They are called "Lipo Proteins." But only 5 percent of our *cholesterol* circulates in the blood, the rest is used for numerous activities in the body's cells.

If a healthy person consumed 100g butter a day (the average European eats 18g a day), he would ingest 240-mg *cholesterol* of which only 30-60% could be absorbed through his intestines. This would give him about 90 mg *cholesterol* a day but of this amount only 12 mg would eventually end up in his blood and raise the *cholesterol* level by as much as 0.2%. In comparison, our body is able to produce 400 times more *cholesterol* a day than what we can get from eating 100g butter. If you eat more than the usual amount of *cholesterol* with your food, *Serum cholesterol* levels will rise, which causes the body to automatically reduce its own *cholesterol* production. This self-regulating mechanism ensures that *cholesterol* remains on the individually required stable level.

If eating fatty foods does not significantly increase *cholesterol* levels then what does? Stress, for example, triggers *cholesterol* production in the body. Since *cholesterol* is the basic ingredient of stress hormones in the body, stressful situations use up large quantities of *cholesterol* which stimulates the liver to produce more of it, to make up for the loss.

Research has shown that watching television for several hours alone can drive up blood *cholesterol* more dramatically than any other so called risk factor, including diet, sedentary lifestyle, or genetic disposition. Exposure to television is a great challenge for the brain. It is far beyond its capacity to process the flood of incoming stimuli that emanate from the overwhelming number of picture frames appearing on the TV screen every second. The resulting strain takes its toll. Blood pressure rises to help move more oxygen, glucose, *cholesterol*, vitamins, and other nutrients, around the body and to the brain, all of which are used up rapidly by the heavy brainwork. Add violence, suspense and the noise of gunshots etc., to the spectacle and the adrenal glands respond with *shots* of *adrenaline* to prepare the body for a "fight or flight". This causes contraction of many large and small blood vessels in the body, leading to shortage of water, sugar, and other nutrients in the cells.

The signs for such an effect can be several. You may feel shattered, exhausted, and stiff in neck and shoulders, very thirsty, lethargic, depressed, and even too tired to go to sleep. If the body did not bother to increase *cholesterol* levels during such stress encounters, we would have millions of television deaths by now.

When *Cholesterol* Becomes Dangerous

The self-regulating *cholesterol* mechanism is disrupted when the body has stored excessive amounts of protein in the liver capillaries. The liver capillaries called *sinusoids* are shaped like a grid and their thin basement membranes have large pores, which permit large molecules and even the relatively blood cells to leave the blood stream and enter the fluid surrounding the liver cells. The Low Density Lipoprotein (LDL) and the Very Low Density Lipoprotein (VLDL) are quite large *cholesterol* molecules when compared to those of the High Density Lipoprotein (HDL). Yet they are still able to pass through the *sinusoids* to reach the liver cells where they are rebuilt, sent to the gallbladder for storage, or excreted into the intestines. In fact, most of these large cholesterol molecules cannot "escape" the blood stream anywhere else but through the liver *sinusoids*. Only the small HDL molecules, which make up 80% of all lipoproteins, are tiny enough to leave the blood by penetrating the ordinary capillaries. For this reason HDL, also known as *good cholesterol*, is hardly ever found to reach abnormally high levels in the blood.

Under normal circumstances, all the *cholesterol* eaten in a meal is absorbed into the blood stream through the intestines. The larger LDL and VLDL molecules enter the liver and are removed there in the manner described above. This mechanism, which keeps the *cholesterol* concentration of the blood balanced, becomes faulty when the normal outlets for *cholesterol*, namely the grid fibres of the *sinusoids*, become blocked through storage of excessive amounts of protein. Consequently LDL and VLDL concentrations (considered to be the *bad cholesterol*) begin to rise in the blood to levels that may be harmful for the body. They are trapped in the circulatory system because their escape routes, the liver *sinusoids*, are blocked. This forces the capillary network and arteries to absorb as much of the bad *cholesterol* as they possibly can, mixing it with the stored proteins. Subsequently the arteries begin to become hard, rigid, and occluded.

The vicious circle closes when the liver cells no longer receive enough of the LDL and VLDL *cholesterol*, assuming that the blood doesn't have enough of it. The liver cells subsequently begin to produce large amounts of the "bad" *cholesterol*, which is combined with bile. The product is then dispatched to the intestines to combine with fats and enter the blood stream. This raises the levels of "bad" *cholesterol* in the blood even further. Such a patient produces often twice as much LDL as a healthy person does. In the presence of toxic substances and due to a lack of bile salts some of the excessive cholesterol gets locked into gallstones, which decreases bile flow and further reduces the body's ability to digest protein foods. Every meal that contains *cholesterol*, which is a natural part of almost all foods, adds more bad *cholesterol* to the one that is already trapped in the blood stream. The body's last attempt to stay alive is to pack the *cholesterol* into the walls of the blood vessels until they finally become occluded altogether.

In many cases, the liver's *sinusoids* become so congested with proteins that they do not even allow enough water and sugar to reach the liver cells; many of them simply die off. The dead liver cells get replaced with fibrous tissue, leading to portal hypertension, as well as to diabetes, and eventually to liver failure. But since the protein storage does not only occur in the liver *sinusoids* but also in the entire blood vessel system of the body, a heart attack or a stroke is likely, too.

Cholesterol is *not* the culprit of heart disease. The liver cells are cut off from the blood stream and begin to synthesise more and more *cholesterol* due to excessive protein consumption. To restrict *cholesterol* by cutting out fats in the diet has little or no benefits in the control of heart disease. What helps most is cutting out animal protein from the diet plan until the condition has been normalised. At the same time, all gallstones should be removed from the liver and gallbladder, and the colon should be cleansed from existing waste deposits. Additional essential measures include drinking plenty of water, maintaining a healthy diet and lifestyle, and giving blood to reduce excessive amounts of protein from the blood and lower the *Haemocrit* value. All this can effectively reverse arteriosclerosis and effectively prevent a heart attack or stroke.

An Encouraging Testimony
Over the years I have seen hundreds of patients with "heart" problems that in fact were not heart problems at all. Most of them turned out to be cases of simple indigestion, causing strong sensations of pain in the chest and stomach. Their stomachs were usually hard and swollen, exerting great pressure on the diaphragm and heart. Trapped gas and "heart burn" led to the false alarm of a heart condition.

Other patients, however, did have serious heart trouble, in addition to suffering chronic indigestion, or, as I would see it, because of it. George was one of them. He had been treated for thirty years for progressive heart disease. During the same period he had been on a large variety of drugs to relieve the symptoms. One of them was an anti-hypertensive drug. The drug's diuretic effects helped to drain excess fluids from his body but caused severe cellular dehydration and damaged his kidneys and liver. Other side effects included impotence, increase of angina, stomach upset, eye pains, muscle weakness, depression, and nightmares.

Despite taking the drugs regularly he was advised to have a bypass operation since several of his heart arteries were almost completely blocked. A few years after the operation, at age 62, his "new" heart arteries also showed strong signs of damage, causing chest pain and severe tiredness. His heart was no longer able to perform sufficiently and he was informed that only a heart replacement could save his life. That was the time I saw George for the first time. He said: "I feel more dead than alive. My energy level is only a fraction of what it used to be. There is not much I can do now except wait for a heart transplant, but considering my general condition I am not sure whether I can make it through such an operation."

After applying the diagnostic tools of Ayurvedic Pulse Reading and Eye Interpretation, I explained to him that his real problem was the amassed and toxic undigested food in his intestines, pointing to his large belly, and the storage of unused animal protein throughout his blood vessel system. The toxic material was suffocating the cells of his body and causing slow poisoning of the liver, kidneys, and heart. His liver bile ducts were congested with thousands of gallstones. I suggested that he removed all the toxic waste, which his body had collected over the past 40 years in his small and large intestines, and stimulated the digestive power through a series of liver cleanses. Thereby he could directly relieve his heart from the heavy burden of having to give nourishment to a body that was blocked and overtaxed with harmful material. His heart was obviously tired from pumping blood through a congested body.

George quickly began to implement a programme that included instructions for a specific body-type diet, cleansing of his intestines and liver, the daily and seasonal Ayurvedic routine, regular full body oil massage, a gentle yoga and exercise programme, and meditation.

Already three days later, George felt a huge burden had been taken off his heart. His energy began to return although he did not yet feel strong enough yet to go back to work. After 2 weeks he was back at work. Being a director of his own successful company, he no longer felt as stressed at work as he used to feel before the treatment. Both the before-midnight sleep and the meditation, which he practised every morning and evening, made him feel refreshed and calm and he was able to handle the difficulties at work with a more relaxed attitude, more creativity, and increased willingness.

Three months later, he visited his cardiologist who took him through a series of tests to determine the condition of his heart. George was not surprised to hear his doctor confirm that he no longer needed a heart transplant operation. This saved him $750.000, which is the amount of money a heart transplant would have cost him. Over a period of time he was able to reduce and finally stop his medication. Seven years later he is still very active and enjoys an excellent state of health.

Non-dietary Causes of Heart Disease

Lack of Social Support System

Traditionally, Japanese people have very low rates of heart disease and cancer. But when they began immigrating in large numbers to United States, their newly adopted "lifestyle" and diet often proved disastrous for their health. By the second generation in the new world there was no advantage left. First it was hypothesised that the typical American diet rich in fats, was responsible for this development. But then the *heart disease-diet-cholesterol* explanation received a severe blow.

There was one subgroup among the Japanese immigrants in California who continued to have very low rates of heart disease, irrespective of whether their blood *cholesterol* levels were high or low. The group consisted of males who retained their sense of being Japanese by growing up in a Japanese neighbourhood, by participating in traditional Japanese cultural and social events, and by learning and speaking their mother tongue. The close family ties and social support system were the only factors that prevented them from developing degenerative heart disease. Even if they had personal problems at home or financial difficulties there was a large family to lean on and to receive moral and often financial help and support.

The feeling of being rejected, left behind, and lonely can be a "heart breaking" event, which can turn a healthy heart into a sick heart. It is well known that women are in greater need for support and understanding while being pregnant. An epidemiological study on pregnant women showed that 91 percent of those who felt unsupported by family and friends suffered serious complications during pregnancy. The women reported that they were leading stressful lives with little or no social support. Similar studies on unemployed men have revealed that those men who felt strong support from family, relatives, and friends were less likely to develop physical or mental problems.

Greatest Risk Factors: Job Satisfaction and Happiness Rating

What is rarely mentioned in reports on heart disease and their contributing risk factors is one the most important discovery that was ever made about man's number one killer disease: *The greatest risks of developing heart disease are job satisfaction and happiness rating.* These unexpected risk factors turned up when American researchers looked once more at clues of what could cause heart disease.

If you ask a man on the street whether he is satisfied with his job and happy, depending on his answer, you will be able to make a prognosis about whether he is at risk of developing heart disease or not. It would be too simplistic to assume that heart disease is *only* caused by stress, cigarette smoking, overeating, alcohol abuse, etc. These risk factors are not the ultimate causes of a dysfunctional heart but rather the effects or symptoms of plain dissatisfaction in life. The cause of the major causes of heart disease, which basically is just lack of happiness, may still be there after all the other risk factors or causes have been eliminated. A large number of people have died from heart attacks with perfectly clean arteries. Many of them have never smoked, abused alcohol, or led a particularly stressful life. But they were unhappy within themselves.

One 1998 study by the Johns Hopkins School of Medicine has confirmed what 10 other surveys have found: Men who are clinically depressed are twice as likely as those who aren't to suffer heart attacks or develop other heart illnesses. If a "heartache" is severe enough, there are several ways to shut down the arteries and in fact the entire energy system in the body. By applying the procedure of Kinesiology muscling testing on an unhappy person you can find that all the muscles in his body are weak, especially while he ponders over his personal problems. This affects also the muscles of his heart and arteries. If unhappiness persists, disease is inevitable, and whatever part of his body is weakest will succumb first to the chronic shortage of energy. If it happens to be the heart, then heart disease may result.

Even if such a person doses himself with antioxidants, which are believed to protect the arteries against oxygen radical attacks, they will neither be digested and assimilated, nor be transported to the damaged arteries. Lack of satisfaction in life paralyses the body's functions of digestion, metabolism, and elimination. This causes congestion, high toxicity, and damage to all cell tissues. People who have blocked coronary arteries are not just sick in the area of the heart, they are sick throughout the body and what seems to be the most important determinant, they are not happy.

The reason modern medicine is so helpless in providing lasting cures of heart disease is because there is not much in the current medical approach that can increase happiness in a patient. Yet there is hardly any other primary risk factor for disease, including coronary heart disease, than its absence. It is the lack of lasting happiness and peace of heart and mind that makes a person feel stressed, take drugs, overeat protein and other foods, abuse alcohol and cigarettes, drink excessive amounts of coffee, become a workaholic, or dislike his job or himself.

The Need to Love
Satisfaction in life increases spontaneously when we devote time to meet our spiritual needs, apart from developing our physical and mental aspects. The self cries out to be recognised as a spiritual being whose nature is unconditioned happiness. A truly happy person finds deep inner satisfaction in sharing whatever he likes in himself with others; it is called love. Love is the most basic characteristic of a human being, although it can at times be overshadowed or remain unexpressed. If it is unable to flow, it causes deep sadness and frustration in the heart centre.

The need to open one's heart to others and to oneself cannot be met by identifying a few risks of disease and "treating them away." Such an approach is futile because it ignores the fact that feelings are far more powerful than any physical effect can be. If unhappiness continues to prevail in a patient's life, no amount of vitamin C or E will stop free radicals from creating havoc in the body.

The continual emphasis on the risk factors for disease today may divert people's attention from the real issues in life. That happiness rating and job satisfaction are the leading causes of heart disease is hardly publicised because there doesn't seem to be a *magic formula* to deal with them. The pharmaceutical industry possesses no drugs that can make people truly happy; all it can offer is drugs that deal with the physical symptoms of the disease. If you suffer from heart trouble, you may need to ask yourself a few basic questions such as the following ones:

Am I living a lifestyle that is detrimental to my health? Do I feel that no one really loves me? Am I afraid of being rejected by my partner? Do I believe that I have a deeper purpose in your life but can't find it? Am I feeling frustrated because I am not able to get out of life what I really want?

What a Loving Wife can do
Major research on male heart attack patients has shown that the men's feeling of being loved by their wives was the most crucial element that determined whether they survived an attack or not. Heart attacks often become an eye-opener for estranged couples who have forgotten how to love and care about each other. The sudden closeness which couples often experience after one partner suffers a heart attack can serve as an incentive for many of the patients to continue wanting to live, and the chances are that they *will* live.

Surveys of male heart attack victims revealed that most men felt lonely or misunderstood before their attack. Minor attacks led to death only in those men who felt that their wives no longer loved them. If a relationship was brought back to "life" as a result of the attack then even a massive heart attack could not take the person's life. Most men are quite sensitive at heart, even though they may not necessarily admit it. They generally tend to put on a brave face and suffer silently when they have a "heartache." Most men tend to consider it a sign of weakness to shed tears, especially if it is in front of a woman. Yet the male's tendency to repress feelings of weakness makes him a likely candidate for heart disease. A heart attack can reveal his deep vulnerability and yearning for support and comfort. His partner is allowed to see this "new" side of him, which can trigger love, compassion, a new sense of intimacy, and give a new lease of life to both of them.

The Loving Touch

Every time someone touches us with loving care or we do the same for someone else, an emotional exchange takes place, which nourishes the heart. The expressions "He touched my heart", "I felt so touched by his words," or "It was so touching to see my old friend again", show that the sense of touch is closely related to our physical and emotional heart, which is also the centre of our being. To touch and to be touched is as essential to health as a balanced diet, if not more.

When American researchers discovered that prematurely born babies who are stroked three times a day increased their weight by 49 percent, they had unintentionally discovered the *loving touch*. As it turned out *loving touch* - the scientific expression is *kinaesthetic tactile stimulation* - became recognised as an effective method to reduce the time and cost of a baby's stay in hospital. The *loving touch* (I prefer to use the non- scientific term for this gift of God) stimulated the babies' production of growth hormones and thereby improved utilisation of nutrients from the daily food ratio. The researchers did not realise that they had stumbled over a major technique of healing that could be applied successfully to both the young and the old, the healthy and the sick, not only for prevention but also for cure.

In the human body, the sense of touch is so highly developed that it can detect or sense everything it comes into contact with, like radar. By (unconsciously) picking up other people's *pheromones* and/or "touching" their aura, your body can identify who is friendly, honest and loving or cold-hearted, deceitful, and aggressive. The body instantly translates all that information into powerful chemical responses that can make you either well or fall ill. This response, however, may also depend on your interpretation of the experience. Muscle testing can verify whether your interpretation is correct. You may think of a person and check with your muscles whether this person has a good influence on you or not. A weak muscle indicates that your relationship with this person disturbs your balance and energy field. Merely thinking of a person gives you enough physical responses top decide whether you want to be with that person or not.

The Ayurvedic oil massage has been proven to open clogged arteries because of its deeply penetrating and detoxifying action, but this is only a minor part of the phenomenon. By touching your body with the intention to improve its health it senses that you love and appreciate yourself and your life. Love carries the highest frequency of energy, and, when present in the depth of one's heart, it triggers a strong healing response by releasing *endorphins* and other healing drugs throughout the body, similar to the ones a breast-fed baby receives from its mother.

If you want to help a sick person but do not know how, hold his/her hand in yours, or gently hold or massage his/her feet. This does more to help the person's condition than any amount of consoling words can do. The body remembers a *loving touch* more vividly than spoken words and it reproduces the same drugs whenever it links into the "touching" feeling through remembering. Heart patients especially need to feel that they are loved and cared for because their hearts have lost the sweetness of life that is mostly present in a committed and loving relationship where emotional exchange is most common. Many heart disease victims have isolated themselves from such intimacy before they became ill, by overloading themselves with work, commitments, deadlines, and social engagements. By rediscovering the *loving touch*, they can once again connect to the circuit of love that supplies the only frequency the heart needs to function properly and efficiently, i.e., the frequency of love.

Loving touch opens the heart. It is the kind of touch that gives without expecting anything in return. It is the kind of touch than can cause miracles. Each one of us has this power; it is only a matter of acknowledging that you have it, which is a prerequisite for being able to use it. Give it freely and without reservations, for it is one of the few gifts that can make you truly happy, too.

2. Cancer - Who makes It?

Cancer appears to be a very confusing and unpredictable disease. It seems to strike the very happy and the very sad, the rich and the poor, the smokers and the non-smokers, the healthy and the not so healthy. People from all backgrounds and occupations can have cancer. But if we begin to look behind the mask of physical appearance and behaviour, we will find that there are certain types of people who are more vulnerable to develop the disease than others do.

After I had seen numerable cancer patients with cancer over the years, I began to recognise a certain pattern of thinking and feeling that was common to most of them. To be more specific, I have not met a single cancer patient who didn't feel burdened by a history of unresolved conflicts or emotional trauma. The following two cases may provide the insight that cancer always occurs in two forms, i.e., as a visible physical cancer and as an invisible "mental cancer." Cancer as a concrete physical illness cannot occur unless there is an underlying pattern of deep-seated frustration and lack of self-respect or "unfinished business" in life. Cancer can be a way to reveal the source of such an inner conflict, come to terms with it, and even heal it.

The Cancer's Physical and Mental Sides

The Physical Side
Mary visited me when she was 39 years old. One year before she had been diagnosed as having advanced breast cancer. Her oncologist prescribed the standard routine treatments for cancer – radiation and chemotherapy – but to no avail. Several weeks later she was submitted for surgery to amputate her right breast. The operation took place shortly before for her monthly period. Her doctors informed her that they "got all the cancer" and the situation was now under control. Little they knew at the time that, according to the latest findings of *chronobiology,* there is a four times higher risk for reoccurrence of cancer in women who undergo surgery for breast cancer one week before or during menstruation. This is the time when a woman's immunity and iron levels are measurably low and her body is not able to destroy all the cancer cells that are left over from surgery. Hence the high risk for metastasis.

One year after the mastectomy, Mary complained of severe pain in the lower spine and in left knee. Ten years earlier she had been diagnosed as having *cervical spondylosis* in her lower spine, caused by abnormal outgrowth and ossified cartilage around the margins of joints of the vertebral column. This time, however, the examinations revealed that she had developed bone cancer in her lower spine and left knee. The breast surgery had, as so often is the case, caused the dispersion of millions of cancer cells which deposited themselves in other parts of the body, especially in her lower spine where the resistance to cancer formation was particularly low.

Mary had also been suffering from severe menstrual problems as long as she remembered. In addition, she was diagnosed as having anaemia. But despite taking iron tablets regularly for years, which caused her frequent nausea, she remained anaemic. She stated that her digestive system, too, "never worked properly," and constipation often lasted for as many as three to five days in a row. My examinations revealed that her liver was clogged with thousands of gallstones.

The Mental Side
Mary experienced a very sad childhood because her parents had serious problems in relating with each other. She couldn't remember an instant when there had not been tension between them. Being a very sensitive person at heart, she took everything more seriously than her brother and consequently felt very insecure, frightened, and depressed. With a painful smile on her face she said that she felt torn between her two parents and could not make a choice over which one to

favour. Eating with the parents was particularly difficult for her. She was forced to sit and eat with them even while the atmosphere was very tense. Up to this very day she has a strong aversion to food and gobbles it down very quickly, while standing.

Mary also faces great difficulties at work. Being a schoolteacher, she feels that the students are allowed to take out their own frustrations on her but she has to keep it all inside. When she returns home though she shouts at her own children, which creates much guilt in her. Mary never wanted to be a schoolteacher, she always dreamt of becoming a gymnastics teacher.

The frustration that arises from not being able to fulfil one's desires has been a major cause for Mary's cancer. Right from the beginning of her life she was taught to "conform with the system" which meant that she always had to do what she was told to do. Deep inside herself she had dreams that she could never fulfil because she didn't want to stir up tension, or make other people think badly of her.

To keep the peace she went along with what her parents demanded of her but inside herself she was boiling with rage. When Mary walked into my office that morning, she gave me a beautiful smile, which did not reveal the pain she was feeling inside. But it wasn't the physical pain that hurt, it was all the bottled-up frustration, fear, and insecurity that threatened the sensitive feelings in her heart. The physical pains only reminded her of her real heartache. All the years of suppressing or hiding her true inner feelings while she was a child were still a vivid part of her.

Torn between her parents for many years and trying to please both of them, Mary was never bold enough to make a choice that would please her and her only. This division within her mind sapped all her natural energy and happiness. The cancer started in her divided mind and in all the unexpressed grief and frustration that filled her early life.

Whatever happens in our mind occurs in the body as well. The real cancer is a trapped and isolated emotion, a feeling of "having no choice." Through the mind/body connection, repressed feelings of wanting harmony, peace, stability, and simple joy in life are translated into the appropriate physical responses in the body. This effectively deprives the body cells of all these qualities as well. The mental suffocation caused so much anger and frustration in Mary, that for fear of not being loved or liked by others, she targeted these negative emotions at her own body. The toxic mind became a toxic body and threatened its very survival.

The constant tension, which Mary experienced during dinnertime at her parental home, had greatly impaired her digestive functions. To eat while being emotionally upset suppresses the secretion of balanced amounts of digestive juices. The bile flora parrticularly is altered when feeling angry and unhappy. Consequently gallstones begin obstructing the bile ducts, which lowers AGNI, the digestive fire. Mary is still associating eating with the tension she experienced while at the parental dinner table. Since she is programmed by her unconscious attempt to avoid everything that has to do with food and eating, her body does the same. Food eaten in a hurry and while standing cannot be properly utilised by the body, hence the accumulation of large quantities of toxic waste in the small and large intestines. Chronic constipation and the subsequent low rate of absorption of nutrients, including calcium, zinc, and magnesium, had increasingly depleted and weakened her bone tissue, bone marrow, and reproductive functions.

When the reproductive tissue, which maintains the genetic blueprint (DNA) of the cells, is starved of oxygen and nutrients, it is only a matter of time before normal and healthy cells begin to mutate their genes in order survive the "famine." Normally, pancreatic enzymes or vitamins break down tumour cells. Most of the digestive enzymes are "used up" quickly when the diet is rich in animal protein such as pork, fish, and cheese, all foods that Mary ate plenty of. This means that there were practically not enough pancreatic enzymes left to break down the cancer cells. Most cancers occur when digestive functions are continually disrupted.

The *spondylosis* of Mary's lower spine signifies weakening of her internal and external support system; it manifested in direct response to the lack of support and encouragement by her parents. Mary's body slumps forward while she sits, looking half its size. She appears as if she is trying to protect her heart from being hurt again. Also her breathing is shallow and insufficient, as if she does not want to be noticed or criticised by her parents. The knees serve as a support system for the entire body. A lifetime of "giving in" and "not standing on her own feet" manifested as the knee problems she developed over the years.

Mary's Personal Remedy

Japanese research has shown that all cancer patients, who had spontaneous remissions of their tumours, experienced a profound transformation in their attitude towards themselves before the sudden cure occurred. Mary needed to make several major changes in her life; one of it was to change her job, even if it meant fewer earnings. While still being highly susceptible to stressful situations and chaotic noise the tense atmosphere present at her school was hardly conducive to the healing process. She also needed to spend more time in nature, walk in the sun and on the beach, paint her impressions, listen to her favourite music, and devote some time in quietness and meditation every day.

Apart from following the Ayurvedic daily routine and diet, Mary began to use a number of cleansing procedures to rid her colon of old faecal matter and to purify the blood, liver, and connective tissue from accumulated toxins.

The most important thing for Mary was to become more conscious about everything in her life. This included, eating, emotional releases, listening to the body's signals of thirst, hunger, tiredness, etc. She needed to become aware of her needs and desires and begin to implement them even if it took time. The most important realisation she had to make was that she didn't need to do anything that didn't please her. Her friends and family also needed to understand that Mary was at a very crucial stage of recovery where every positive thoughts and feeling towards her could serve as a tremendous support system, one that she never had when she was young. Mary started to improve steadily six months after she adopted about 60% percent of the recommended advice. Today she feels that the disease has brought her a deeper understanding of life and led to an inner awakening she had never experienced before.

Cancer -- a Form of Rejection

Jeromy has *Hodgkin's* disease, which is the most common *lymphoma*. *Lymphomas* are malignant neoplasms of lymphoid tissue that vary in growth rate, also known as lymph cancer. Contemporary medicine has no explanation as to what causes the disease. *Hodgkin's* disease usually begins in adolescence or between 50 and 70 years of age.

When Jeromy was 22 years old he noticed two enlarged lymph nodes in the neck. A few days later he was diagnosed as having Hodgkin's disease. In some people the disease leads to death within a few months but others have few signs of it for many years, Jeromy being one of them. Being a *Kapha* type, he has a very athletic and strongly built body and is naturally endowed with a lot of stamina and physical endurance. His *Kapha*'s slow metabolic rate can be considered to be responsible for the slow progress of the disease.

He received his first chemotherapy in 1979 soon after diagnosis of the disease, but to no avail. Multiple radiation was added to the regular chemotherapy in 1982, which produced severe side effects, including loss of all body hair and his sense of taste. Yet despite the traumatic experiences caused by the various treatment programmes over the following fourteen years he was not willing to give into depression and desperation. His strong fighting spirit permitted him to continue his work as a general manager of a successful business enterprise.

The Ayurvedic Pulse Diagnosis and Eye Interpretation revealed that when he was about four years old his digestive functions and lymph drainage began to decline very rapidly. His liver contained a large number of gallstones. As it turned out, Jeromy went through a very traumatic experience at that time, although at first he had difficulties remembering. For Jeromy, the most traumatic event was at age 21 when his long-term girl friend suddenly left him for another man. Exactly one year before that he discovered the lymph swellings in his neck. The rejection by his girl friend was one of the most heart-breaking experiences of his life. Yet this experience triggered the memory of an even more traumatic rejection.

The Ghost of Memory

Jeromy was born in a developing country with an unstable political situation. When he reached the age of four, his parents sent him to a boarding school in another developing country, for his own safety. Unable to understand the reasons behind this move, he felt that they stopped loving him and no longer wanted him. All he remembers is the feeling of being cut off from what he considered his life line, the closeness to his parents. Although his parents believed that sending him away was in Jeromy's best interest, he had lost the love of the most important people in his life at an age when he needed it most. His little world had collapsed on this first "black" day in his life, and his body's main functions began to decline, too.

Jeromy dedicated the major part of his life to proving to his parents that he was worthy of their love. He was not aware, however, of his incessant drive to succeed in life. He proudly told me that he never gives up in life and that would not allow anything to get him down. One part of him never acknowledged that he was gravely ill. His physical appearance, except for being bald, would not reveal the battle his body was fighting. He spent all his energy and time in his work and he was very good at it.

To heal himself, Jeromy needed to become aware of the "rejected" child within him which he had "buried" in his subconscious when he was 4 years old and a second time when he was 21 years old. The deep hurt caused by what he considered to be a rejection by his parents had been amplified by the second rejection. The brain stores our experiences in "filing cabinets." All the anger we have experienced in life goes into one file, all sad events into another, and all rejections are filed in a third one, etc. All these experiences feed "the ghost of memory." The impressions are not stored according to linear time but compiled in terms of similarity. Once a file is "full up" then even a small event can trigger a devastating eruption.

The first "rejection" which Jeromy experienced as a four-year-old was right there in his awareness when his girl friend left him. By ignoring or denying the fact that this "rejection" ever took place, he unconsciously "instructed" his body to create the identical response, which was a cancer in the very system that is responsible for neutralising and removing toxic waste in the body, the lymphatic system. Unable to get rid of the ghost of memory, which was past, deep-seated anger from feeling rejected, Jeromy was also no longer able to get rid of toxins. Both his liver and gallbladder had accumulated thousands of gallstones, which nearly suffocated him. His body had no other choice but to give physical expression to the cancer that had occupied his mind for so many years.

Giving up the Need to Fight

All events in life that appear to be negative are in fact unique opportunities to learn and to move forward in life. Whenever we need to give ourselves more love, time, and appreciation but fail to fulfil these essential needs, there will be someone or something in our life that pushes us in that direction. Feeling rejected by or being disappointed and angry with another person highlights a lack in taking responsibility for the negative things that happen to us. Blaming someone else or oneself for an unfortunate situation can eventually manifest as disease, and if we cannot understand its accompanying message we may even have to face death to appreciate life or living.

Jeromy needed to give himself the love and appreciation he didn't feel he was getting from his parents. He also needed to make room for enjoyment and pleasure, and to take time for himself, for mediation, for self-reflection. Giving up the need to fight in life reprograms the DNA of the body, from a course of self-destruction to healthy reproduction. And this gives the cancer cells a chance to be accepted again to the family of all the other cells. Cancer cells are normal cells that have been "rejected" by what they "considered" home, i.e., and the body. They are deprived of proper nourishment and support. In their desperation to survive, they grab everything they can find to live on, even toxins or other metabolic waste. This practically makes them "outcasts."

But just as *we* want to be loved, cancer cells also need to know that they are loved. Cutting them out of the body through surgery, or destroying them with poisonous drugs or radiation may add even more violence to the body. We need to be friends with all the various aspects of the body, especially with cancer cells. Jeromy's cause of cancer was a lack of self-appreciation, a feeling of not being wanted, or not being worthy. By waiting for his parents to show him their love, he effectively denied this love to himself. Jeromy realised that his disease was in fact a great blessing in disguise that could help him find himself and love himself, for the very first time.

It is not Cancer that Kills

Cancer, like any other disease, is not a clearly definable disorder that suddenly and randomly appears in parts of the body like mushrooms emerge from the soil. It is rather the result of many crises of toxicity that have as their common cause an energy-depleting influence. Stimulants, emotional trauma, repressed emotions, irregular lifestyle, dehydration, nutritional deficiency, overeating, stress reactions, lack of sleep, etc., all hinder the body in its effort to remove metabolic toxins. When they accumulate in a certain part of the body they cause irritation, swelling, hardening, inflammation, ulceration, and finally a tumour. Like every other disease, cancer is a crisis of toxicity, a final attempt by the body to rid itself of septic poisons caused by the retention of toxins in the body.

Cancer cannot be its own cause. Treating it as if it were its own cause is like cleaning a dirty pot with filthy water, it never gets clean. Despite the huge effort and expenditure on behalf of the medical establishment, mortality rates from cancer remain unchanged. Although X-rays, chemotherapy drugs, or surgery can certainly help neutralise or eliminate a lot of the septic poison and in some cases improve the condition they nevertheless fail to remove the cause(s) of cancer. A cancer patient may return home after a "successful" treatment, relieved and obviously "cured," but continue depleting his body's energy and gathering toxins as he did before. The immune system, already battered by one traumatic intervention, may not make it through a second one. If the patient dies, it is not the cancer that killed him but it's untreated cause(s).

Tumour cells are cells that "panic" due to lack of food, water, oxygen, and space. Survival is their basic genetic instinct, just as it is ours. To survive in such a non-supportive environment the defective cells are forced to mutate and begin devouring everything they can get hold of. They pull more nutrients such as glucose, magnesium, calcium from the connective tissue etc. than they would need to if they were normally growing cells. Their neighbouring cells, however, begin to gradually waste away in the process, and eventually an entire organ becomes dysfunctional due to exhaustion, malnutrition, or wasting.

It seems so obvious that the cancer cells must be responsible for the death of a person –the main reason why almost the entire medical approach is geared towards destroying them. But cancer cells may not be the culprits after all. In fact, they help the body to survive a little longer than it would without them. The immune system knows that, for which reason it notoriously ignores cancer cells that cluster together as tumours. Cancer cells are like the type of mushrooms in the forest that attract and absorb poisons from the soil and air in order to allow for healthy growth of the forest and its inhabitants. That cancer cells become more "poisonous" or malignant in the process is unavoidable, but it is not their choice.

To continue doing their increasingly difficult job, cancer cells need to grow, even if it is at the expense of other healthy cells. Some of the cancer cells may even leave a tumour site and enter lymph fluid, which carries them to other parts of the body. This is known as *metastasis*. Yet cancer cells are programmed to settle only where there is a "fertile" ground of high toxicity (acidity), where they can survive and continue their rescue mission. They have mutated to be able to live in a toxic, non-oxygenated environment and to help neutralise at least some of the toxic waste, such as lactic acid (see below). Given the circumstances, it would be a fatal mistake by the immune system to destroy these types of "estranged" cells as they are doing part of the immune system's work; large amounts of septic poison would seep into the blood and kill the host within several days. Cancer cells are still the body's cells and one "call" from the DNA would stop them from behaving like "lunatics," if need be.

The body has to exert a lot more effort in maintaining a tumour than eliminating it, and if it wasn't forced to use cancer growth as one of its last survival tactics, it would never opt for this final form of self-destruction. We ought to give the most developed and complex system in the universe – the human body – a little more credit and trust that it knows perfectly well how to conduct its affairs even under the most grim circumstances.

Cancer is *"Not Loving Oneself"*

Many cancer patients have devoted their entire lives to helping others, which in itself is a noble quality. But at the same time they have been sacrificing and neglecting their own well being to avoid facing the more painful aspects of themselves. They are "selflessly" devoted to please others so that they may be loved and appreciated for their contributions, which is an unconscious acknowledgement of *not loving oneself*. This may lock up unresolved issues and feelings of unworthiness in the organs and tissues of the body.

"Love your neighbour as you love yourself" is one of the most a basic requirements for curing cancer. This phrase means that we can only love others as much as we are able to love and appreciate ourselves, no less and no more. The degree we are able to care about the well being of our body, mind, and spirit determines the degree we are able to care about other people, too.

The body always follows the commands given by the mind. All thoughts, emotions, feelings, desires, drives, likes, dislikes, etc., are the key instructions that the cells receive via the mind/body connection and they have no other choice but to obey these orders. You can change the instructions in any way you want to, provided you are truly self-aware. Once you know who you really are you cannot help but loving yourself. The bonding effect of love unites differences and keeps everything together, including the cells of the body. When love, which should not be confused with attachment, is no longer a conscious experience, the body deteriorates fast.

It is the expansion of love that is the main purpose of our existence here on earth. Those who love themselves also love others and those who love others also love themselves. The two aspects of love always go hand in hand. Such people have no real fear of death; they die peacefully without any resentment in their heart. Whenever this love declines, the body declines too. It is known that widows and people, who are socially isolated or have nobody to share their deepest feelings with, are the most prone to developing cancer.

Our cells are our most intimate "neighbours" and they require the love frequency to know that they belong to us and that they are part of our life. Giving yourself an oil massage, going to sleep on time, eating nutritious foods, etc., etc., are messages of love that motivate the cells to function in harmony with each other. They are also messages that keep elimination of toxins flawless and efficient. There is nothing unscientific about this. You can go around a number of hospitals and ask all the patients whether they felt good about their own and their partner's life prior to falling ill. The overwhelming response would be "no." Without being a medical researcher, you would have conducted one of the most important research studies anyone could ever do. You would have stumbled over the commonest cause of ill health, which is "not loving oneself," or, to use a different expression, "not being happy with one's life." Not being happy or satisfied in life is probably the most severe form of emotional stress and therefore a major risk factor for many diseases.

A recently published study suggests that severe emotional stress can triple the risk of breast cancer. One hundred women who had a breast lump were interviewed before they knew that they had breast cancer. One in two who had the disease had suffered an adverse life event, such as bereavement, within the previous five years. The effects of emotional stress or unhappiness can severely impair digestion, elimination, and immunity, thus leading to a dangerously high level of toxicity in the body.

Is Cancer just the Body's Final Attempt to Survive?

Nobody wants to be attacked by anyone in life; this also applies to the cells of the body. Cells only go into a defensive mode and turn malignant if they need to ensure both the body's and their own survival, at least for as long they possibly can. A spontaneous remission occurs when cells no longer need to defend themselves. Like every other disease, cancer is a toxicity crisis, which when allowed to come to its natural conclusion will relinquish its symptoms.

Out of the 30 billion cells that our body turns over each day at least one percent are cancer cells, but this does not mean we all will get cancer. These cancer cells are products of "programmed mutation" that keep our immune system alert, active, and stimulated. If due to constant energy depleting influences the body can no longer remove all the worn out, damaged, or cancerous cells they begin to disintegrate and leave behind a mass of toxic protein particles. To clean up this mess, the body begins to deposit some of these proteins in the connective tissue and in the basement membranes of the blood vessels, leading to blood and lymph congestion. The normal metabolic processes become disrupted and isolated groups of cells begin to "malfunction" and become malignant. The result is a toxicity crisis, which is the body's method of breaking down harmful toxic substances.

With the correct approach, a cancer tumour as big as an egg can spontaneously regress and disappear, regardless of whether it is in the brain, in the stomach, or in an ovary. The cure begins when the toxicity crisis stops. A toxicity crisis ends when we cease to deplete the body's energy (see chapters 3&4) and when we remove existing toxins from the blood, bile ducts, lymph ducts, and cell tissues. Unless the body has been seriously damaged, it is perfectly capable of taking care of the rest. Medical intervention, on the other hand, reduces the possibility of a spontaneous remission to almost zero because it has a suppressive and weakening effect.

Cancer may occur when we make the mistake of ignoring its warning signs: The headaches that we stop with pain killers; the tiredness that we keep subduing by having a cup of coffee, tea, or coke; the nervousness we want to control through smoking; the cold which we don't have time to let pass on its own; the time we never have for ourselves; the conflicts we always try to avoid; the pretence that we are always fine. All these are signs that we are at risk of developing cancer or another illness.

There are no principle physiological differences between a simple cold and the occurrence of a cancer. Both are attempts by the body to rid itself of toxins, but with varied degrees of intensity. To stop a cold through drugs before the body even has the chance to eliminate the accumulated toxins has a suffocating effect on the cells of the body. This coerces the body to keep large amounts of cellular waste products and toxic chemicals from drugs in the extracellular fluid (connective tissue) surrounding the cells. Consequently, the cells are effectively cut off their supply routes of oxygen and nutrients. This alters their basic metabolism and eventually affects the DNA molecule itself.

Located in the nucleus of every cell the DNA makes use of its six billion genes to mastermind and control every single aspect of the body. Without the adequate supply of vital nutrients the DNA is left with no other choice than to alter its genetic programmes in order to guarantee the cell's survival, even if it is in an environment of toxic waste. Soon ancer cells begin to draw nutrients from other surrounding cells. This forces more and more cells into genetic mutation, which leads to the spreading or enlargement of the cancer. This also destroys cancerous growths, which are anaerobic, i.e. develop without the use of oxygen.

Nobel Prize winner Dr. Otto Warburg was one of the first scientists to demonstrate the principal difference between a normal cell and a cancer cell. Both derive energy from glucose but the normal cell utilises oxygen to combine with the glucose, whereas the cancer cell breaks down glucose without oxygen, yielding only 1/15 the energy per glucose molecule that the normal cell produces. It is very obvious that cancer cells opt for this relatively inefficient and unproductive method of obtaining energy because they have no access to oxygen anymore. Either, the capillaries supplying oxygen to a group of cells, or the connective tissues surrounding them, (usually both) are severely congested with toxic material, excessive proteins, or dead cell debris.

For this reason (blocked nutrient supply) cancer cells have such an insatiable appetite for sugar. This may also explain why people with constant cravings for sugary foods have a higher risk for developing cancer cells, or why cancer patients often want to eat large amounts of sweets. The main waste product resulting from the anaerobic breakdown of glucose by cancer cells is lactic acid, which may explain why the body of cancer patients becomes so acidic versus the body of healthy person being naturally alkaline. To deal with the dangerously high levels of lactic acid (and to find another source of energy) the liver converts some of it back into glucose. In doing so the liver uses 1/5 the energy per glucose molecule than a normal cell can derive from it, but that's three times the energy a cancer cell will get from it. This basically means that the more the damaged cancer cells multiply, the less energy is available to the normal cells. In a toxic environment the levels of both oxygen and energy tend to be low. This is the environment where cancer spreads most easily. Unless the toxins and the cancer's food source are eliminated and oxygen levels are sharply increased the wasteful metabolism associated with cancer becomes self-sustaining and the cancer spreads further. If death occurs it is not caused by the cancer itself due to wasting of body tissues and final acidosis (over-acidification).

Genetic mutation is believed to be the main **cause** of cancer, yet in truth it is only an **effect** of "cellular famine" and nothing more or less than the body's desperate but often unsuccessful attempt to survive. Something similar occurs in a person's body when he uses antibiotics to fight an infection. Most of the infection-causing bacteria that are attacked by the antibiotics will be killed, but some of them will survive and reprogram their genes to become antibiotic-resistant. Nobody really wants to die, and this includes bacteria. The same law of nature applies to our body cells. *Cancer is the final attempt of the body to live, and not, as most people assume, to die.* Without gene mutation, the cells in the body that live in a toxic (anaerobic) environment would simply suffocate and die. Similar to the case of bacteria that are combated with antibiotics, many cells in fact do succumb and die, but some manage to adjust to the abnormal changes of their natural environment. The cells know that they will eventually die, too, once their final survival tactics fail to keep the body alive.

To truly understand cancer, we may have to radically alter our currently held views about it and ask what its purpose is in the body and why the immune system fails to stop it from spreading. It is not good enough to say that cancer is a disease that is out to kill the body when in truth cancer may be the body's final attempt to live.

By removing toxins from the connective tissues, blood and lymph vessels, bile ducts, etc., many of the cancer cells may be forced to mutate once more, but this time the mutations would gear them towards becoming normal healthy cells once again. Those cells that cannot make the adjustment to live in a clean oxygenated environment may simply die off. By thoroughly cleansing the liver and gallbladder from gallstones and other toxins, AGNI, the digestive power improves drastically, thus increasing the amount of digestive enzymes. Digestive enzymes have a very powerful anti-tumour action; permanently damaged cells or tumour particles are easily neutralised and removed.

Many people in the world have cured cancer in this way. Some are aware of it because they were diagnosed as having cancer before a spontaneous remission occurred but most of them will never know that they even had it because they have never seen a doctor. After passing through a bout of flu, a week's cough, or a couple of days of very high fever many people eliminate massive amounts of toxins and with them tumour tissue. Recent cancer research on gravely ill patients at M.D. Anderson Cancer Center, Houston, Texas, USA, revealed a promising treatment to kill cancer cells by giving them a cold, that is injecting tumours with a cold virus. It may still take a while, though, before researchers will discover that catching a few colds can do the same job. This way, without interfering with the body's self-repair mechanisms, a person may experience a spontaneous remission of cancer, easily and only with very little discomfort.

Most Cancers Go by Themselves

There is indeed scientific evidence now to suggest that most cancers disappear by themselves if left alone. A 1992 Swedish study found that of 223 men who had early prostrate cancer but did not receive *any* kind of medical treatment, only 19 died within ten years of diagnosis. Considering that a third of men in the European Community have prostrate cancer but only 1 percent of them die (not necessarily from the cancer), it is very questionable to treat it at all. This is especially after research has revealed that treatment of the disease has not decreased mortality rates. On the contrary, survival rates are higher in groups of men whose "treatment" consists merely of watchful waiting, compared with groups undergoing prostate surgery. Moreover, more men who were screened with the PSA (prostate-specific-antigen) screening test died from prostate cancer compared with those who were not.

If men learnt how to avoid a build-up of toxins in the body, prostate cancer could perhaps be the least common and the most harmless of all cancers. Aggressive treatment of early prostrate cancer is now a controversial issue, but it should be controversial for every type of cancer, at whatever stage of development.

Without knowing it, the researchers may have tumbled over the solution to the cancer problem. Every toxicity crisis (disease) can be a healing crisis if it is supported and not interfered with by symptom-suppressive measures. But unfortunately, no researcher dares to pursue the matter. Rose Papac, MD, a professor of *oncology* at Yale University School of Medicine, in New Haven, Connecticut, USA once pointed out that there is little opportunity these days to see what happens to cancers if left untreated. "Everyone feels impelled to treat immediately when they see these diseases," says Papac who has studied cases of spontaneous remissions of cancer. Being stifled with fear and in some cases being paranoid about finding a quick-acting remedy for the dreaded illness, many people don't give their bodies the chance to cure themselves but instead run towards destroying what does not need to be destroyed. This may be one of the main reasons spontaneous remissions occur in so few cases today.

Yet numerous researchers have reported over the years that various conditions such as typhoid fever, coma, menopause, pneumonia, chickenpox, and even haemorrhage can spark spontaneous remissions of cancer. However, there are no official explanations available that can explain how the remissions relate to the disappearance of the cancer. Because they are unexplained phenomena (having no scientific basis), they cannot be used for further cancer research. Hence the chances of discovering the mechanism how the body cures cancer remain almost nil. The "miracle cures" seems to happen most frequently in certain types of malignancies: kidney cancer, melanoma (cancer of the skin), lymphomas (cancers of the lymph), and neuroblastoma (a nerve cell cancer that affects infants).

Considering that most of the body's organs have eliminative functions, it is obvious that liver, kidney, lymph, and skin cancers are more likely to disappear when these major organs and systems of elimination are no longer overloaded with toxins. A toxicity crisis like pneumonia or chickenpox removes massive amounts of toxins and helps the cells to "breathe" again. Fever, sweat, loss of blood, mucous discharge, etc., are additional outlets for toxins to leave the body. After breaking down and removing the toxins in an unhindered way, the immune system naturally receives a boost. A renewed immune stimulation based on reduced overall toxicity in the body can be sufficient to do away with a malignant tumour. The unwanted or undesirable chickenpox, pneumonia, fever, etc. may actually be "a gift of God" (to use another unscientific expression) that could save a person's life. Refusing to accept the gift could take his life.

The suppression of children's diseases through immunisation can put them into a higher risk level of eventually developing cancer. Chickenpox, measles, and other self-immunisation programmes (called "children's diseases") help increase the immune system's ability to counteract foreign disease-agents more efficiently and without a major toxicity crisis.

With 500,000 annual cancer deaths in the USA alone, the justification of mandatory immunisation programmes in this country is questionable. The standard approach of establishing immunity, which is unproved and unscientific (see chapter 10), may sabotage the body's own far superior programmes of self-immunisation. The body gains natural immunity through a healing crisis, which naturally eliminates cancer-producing toxins. Whether man-made immunisation directly causes cancer or indirectly is irrelevant. It is important to know, however, that conventional immunisation programmes can prevent the body from developing a potentially life-saving healing crisis.

Cancer -- *Who* Cures It?

Those who have gone into complete remission of cancer and remained free of it are the most likely candidates to reveal the mechanisms of causing and curing cancer.

Anne was forty-three when she was diagnosed with an incurable form of lymphoma and was given only a short time to live. She was strongly recommended to have radiation and chemotherapy treatments, which are the two most commonly used methods of combating cancer cells. Anne was aware that the treatments could greatly increase the risk of secondary cancer and have strong side effects. She refused the treatment, arguing that if the cancer was incurable anyway, why treat it and suffer painful side effects.

Having accepted that she had an incurable disease, which meant that she came to terms with death, Anne felt free to look for alternative ways to make the "transition" easier. Rather than passively accepting her fate, she decided to focus on feeling well and began taking an *active* role in improving her well being. She tried everything from acupuncture and herbal medicine to meditation and visualisation, which were all definite signals of *caring attention* sent to her body cells. Anne's cancer went into remission a few months later. Within a year all apparent signs of cancer had disappeared, much to the astonishment of her oncologist. Today, thirteen years later, she is not only without a trace of cancer but she also feels that she has never been healthier and more vital as she is now.

Linda was diagnosed with a malignant melanoma (the most aggressive form of skin cancer) when she was thirty-eight. After several unsuccessful operations she was informed that her cancer had progressed to the point that it was "terminal" and that she had only one year to live. She too refused treatment with chemotherapy and radiation and instead focused on the more positive approaches of healing including yoga, praying, meditation, and daily visualisations. Today, after twelve years of having "outlived " her death sentence, she is as healthy as she can be with no trace of even a skin irritation.

Both Anne and Linda have changed their entire attitude to life from being passive victims of an uncontrollable "invasive" disease, to being active participants in the creation of a healthy body and mind. Taking self-responsibility was their first step to remove the focus from cancer and direct it towards generation of health.

To call the remissions "miracle cures" is certainly not correct. Remarkable recoveries have been documented with every type of cancer and with nearly every other disorder, from diabetes to warts and even AIDS. The fact that a spontaneous remission of cancer can occur even in the final stages of the illness shows that the immune system has not only the potential to quickly and effectively clear the body from existing tumours but also to prevent new ones from being formed, provided their origins have been uprooted. A shift in attitude from "having" to attack and kill cancer cells to leaving them in peace and eliminating the energy-depleting influences in life, may be enough reason for the immune system to do the rest. Without its roots, cancer is as harmless as a simple cold.

People like Anne and Linda don't have to be the exception, they can be the rule. When Michalis, a Cypriot businessman came to me with kidney cancer he told me that he his doctors had given him only one month to live. They had already removed one of his kidneys and believed that his second one "would not make it much longer either." Yet one month was sufficient for Michalis to remove enough toxins from his body to stop the cancer from growing. The cleansing procedures described in chapters 6 and 7 turned out to be very effective for him. Formerly a heavy drinker, meat eater, and late nighter, he stopped depleting his energy from one day to the next. His next visit to a German cancer clinic three months later (much to the doctors' surprise, as they didn't expect to see him alive) revealed no trace of kidney cancer or any other disease, and after eight years he is as healthy and active as ever.

The body regards cancer as a toxic obstruction that can be overcome through a healing crisis and cleansing. Spontaneous remissions rarely occur by themselves, though. Active participation in the healing process and taking self-responsibility is an absolute necessity in the treatment of every type of disorder, including cancer. After having examined numerous cancer patients in my practice I discovered that all of them, regardless of the type of cancer, have large amounts of gallstones in the liver and gallbladder. If all stones are removed from the liver and gallbladder through a series of liver cleanses and the colon and kidneys are cleansed before and after each liver cleanse, any type of cancer can go into spontaneous remission.

If a healthy diet and lifestyle is maintained hence forward, the cure is likely to be permanent. There is plenty of evidence that fruits and vegetables have cancer-curing and cancer-preventive properties. Research carried out at Britain's Institute of Food Research has revealed that brassica vegetables such as broccoli contain anticarcinogenic compounds, stimulating cancer cells to commit suicide. The vegetables have strong purifying effects on tissues and blood. This greatly reduces overall toxicity and eliminates the need for cancer cells.

Can UV-Radiation Prevent and Cure Cancer?

A major concern of our scientists today is the dramatic increase of skin cancers around the world. Ultraviolet light (UV) is considered to be the major cause of skin cancer. The theory that UV radiation causes skin cancer is based on the assumption that our thinning ozone layer permits too much of the germicidal UV to penetrate to the surface of the earth and cause destruction of all kinds, including damage to our skin and eye cells. Yet the theory has major flaws, and no scientific backing.

The germicidal frequency of UV destroys or is filtered out by the ozone layer in the Earth's stratosphere and only small amounts – necessary to purify the air we breathe and the water we drink – actually reach the surface of the earth. Actual measurements, taken in the United States since 1974, show that the amount of UV radiation reaching the surface of the earth is decreasing and continues decreasing slightly each year. The research was conducted to detect the frequency of UV radiation that causes sunburn. UV radiation had dropped on average 0.7% per year over the period from 1974 to 1985 and continued to do so afterwards.

The fact that skin cancers in the United States had doubled within this period of 11 years contradicts the theory that UV light causes skin cancer. The number of malignant skin cancers (melanomas) discovered in 1980 in the United States was 8,000, and eight years later it had increased by 250% to 28,000. In 1930 the expectancy of developing melanoma was as low as 1 in 1,300 people. By the end of the century more than 1 in 100 can expect to have it. However, melanomas, which account for 75 percent of all skin cancer deaths, make up only 5 percent of all reported skin cancers. This would make one in five Americans contract skin cancer of one kind by the end of the century. Since UV radiation is decreasing every year, what else could be held responsible for causing skin cancer?

The More UV, the Less Cancer

Even if UV penetration did increase by, for example, 1% percent each year (which is not the case), such slight increases would in fact still be hundreds if not thousands of times less than the normal variations which people experience because of differences in geography. Let's assume you move from an area near either one of the Polar Regions, e.g. Iceland, or Finland, towards the equator, e.g. Kenya or Uganda in East Africa. By the time you reach the equator, you will have increased your body's exposure to UV light by 5,000 percent! If you live in England and decide to move to Northern Australia you will increase your exposure by 600 percent! Calculations show that for every six miles you are moving closer to the equator you will increase your exposure to UV light by 1 percent.

Today, millions of people around the world travel from low exposure places to areas of high exposure near the equator. Many thousands of tourists travel to areas that are located at much higher altitudes than where they normally live. For every 100 feet of elevation there is a significant increase in UV radiation. But this does not prevent people from climbing mountains or living in countries like Switzerland or at the high altitudes of the Himalayan Mountains. According to the UV/Cancer theory, most Kenyan's, Tibetans, or Swiss people should be having skin cancer today. Yet this is not the case at all. *Those living at high altitudes or at the equator where UV radiation is the most concentrated are virtually free of all cancers!* The human body has a unique ability to become accustomed to all these kinds of variations. This shows that UV radiation does only not cause cancer but can even prevent it.

Our body is equipped with perfect self-regulating mechanisms that protect it against damage from the natural elements. Overexposure to swimming in the sea or a lake can lead to extensive skin swelling, shivering, and circulatory problems. Our body will let us know when it is time to get out of the water. Getting to close to a fire will heat us up and urge us to move away from it. Rainwater is natural but standing in the rain for too long can drain our immune system and make us susceptible to catching a cold. Eating sustains our lives but overeating can lead to obesity, heart disease, and cancer. Sleeping recharges our "batteries" and revitalises our body and mind, yet too much of it makes us sluggish, depressed, and ill. Likewise, sunlight has healing properties unless we use it to burn holes into our skin. Why should any of these natural elements or processes cause us harm unless we abuse them?

Preference over unnatural things like junk foods, stimulants, alcohol, drugs, medical intervention (unless it is for an emergency), as well as pollution, irregular lifestyle, stress, excessive greed for money and power, and the lack of contact with nature, etc., are much more likely to cause such diseases as skin cancer and cataract than natural phenomena that have kept life on the planet balanced throughout the ages.

It is encouraging to see that treatments using light are increasingly seen as breakthrough methods for cancer and many other diseases. The U.S. Food and Drug Administration recently approved "light therapy" to fight advanced oesophageal cancer and early lung cancer - with fewer risks than surgery and chemotherapy. Although it has been known for over 100 years that light can kill diseased cells, it is only since a number of convincing research studies have been conducted that there has been a sudden resurgence of interest in light therapy. There is promising success in bladder cancer, infertility-causing endometriosis, advanced lung and Oesophagus cancers, skin cancer, diseases leading to blindness, psoriasis, and autoimmune disorders. In one study, light therapy eliminated 79 percent of early lung cancer. Regular exposure to sunlight still seems to be one of the best measures one can take to prevent cancer, including that of the skin.

Skin Cancer From Sun Protection

The sun is completely harmless unless we expose our bodies to it for unduly long periods of time, especially between 10am and 3pm (during the summer). Overexposure to sunlight makes most people feel very hot and bothered and burns their skin. To avoid being burnt and to find relief, our body's natural instinct urges us to look for a shady place or to take a cold shower. Sunscreens, however, interfere with our natural response to sunlight.

A British medical report, released in July 1996 and published as the lead article in the prestigious British Medical Journal, showed that the use of sunscreens might encourage skin cancer because they prompt people to stay in the sun far too long. Their use can postpone the onset of sunburn by many hours. Most people think that this is advantageous whereas in fact it puts their lives at risk. The doctors who edited the report cited studies conducted in 1995 in Western Europe and Scandinavia, which showed that frequent users of sunscreen lotion actually suffered disproportionately higher rates of skin cancer. The report says: "Sunscreens containing only ultraviolet B blocks protect against sunburn and therefore enable greater exposure to ultraviolet A (UVA) than would otherwise be possible to obtain." In other words, many sunbathers expose themselves to much more UVA than they would if they didn't use screens. *Sunburn* in fact is the body's natural defence response against more serious damage such as skin cancer.

Without sunscreen your skin would begin to itch uncomfortably if it was exposed to too much sunlight. However, by using a sunscreen, you would not notice when your body has had enough of it because your first line of defence -- sunburn -- has been crippled. This would lead to overexposure of UVA that together with other internal toxins might cause skin cancer. Under normal conditions (without sunscreen) you would never get too much UVA even if you were lying in the sun for five hours. Instead, you would burn your skin heavily through overexposure to UVB.

Although sunburn can impair immune functions and damage the skin, there is no proof that it can cause skin cancer. The above report stated that medical experts know "little about the precise relation between sunburn and skin cancer." This includes the fatal type of skin cancer, the malignant melanoma. Despite the enormous amount of research done on skin cancers, there has been no indication that malignant melanoma has any links with UV exposure. But what is known for sure is that sunscreen does not only fail to prevent skin cancer but on the contrary encourages it by amplifying UVA exposure. This makes sunscreens more dangerous than UV light could ever be.

The question remains whether sunscreens that are made to block out both the UVA and UVB radiation could solve the problem? Research has shown that they don't prevent skin cancer either. There are more people suffering from skin cancer today who have no or only very little exposure to sunlight. Those who live mostly outdoors, at high altitudes, or near the equator, have the lowest incidence of skin cancers. But those who work under artificial lighting are the most susceptible.

The average American, for example, spends twenty-two hours a day indoors beneath and around artificial light. During the winter season most of the working population in the cities never even get to see the daylight, except through windows that reflect UV light. Incandescent light has a narrow band compared to sunlight and is known to weaken natural immunity (a Russian study showed that workers who are exposed to UV light during working hours suffer 50% fewer colds than those who are deprived do). A weak immune system cannot properly defend itself against disease, and that includes skin cancer!

Researcher Dr. Helen Shaw and her research team conducted a melanoma study at the London School of Hygiene and Tropical Medicine, and Sydney Melanoma Clinic, Sydney Hospital, and found that office workers had twice the incidence of the deadly cancer as people who work outdoors. The results of the study were published in 1982 by the British medical journal *Lancet*. Dr. Shaw proved that those who spend most of their time sunbathing have the lowest risk of developing skin cancer. By contrast, office workers who were exposed to fluorescent light during most of their working days had the highest risk of developing melanomas. She also discovered that fluorescent lights cause mutations in cultures of animal cells.

Dr. Shaw's research lead to the conclusion that both in Australia and Great Britain, melanoma rates were high among professional and office workers, and low in people working outdoors. In other words, the Australians and British would be better off spending more time outside where there is plenty of UV light! Similar controlled studies were conducted at the New York University School of Medicine, which confirmed and substantiated Dr. Shaw's research results.

Pittas -Watch Out!

Australians who are not Aboriginals usually have a fair and often freckled skin, reddish-blond hair, and light-coloured eyes. Most Australians are *Pitta* types, which means that UV light penetrates deeper into their skin than into those who have a darker skin or are *Vata* or *Kapha* types. In addition, many Australians are fond of drinking beer, which has a strong diuretic effect and draws water from the skin, leaving it unprotected against heat rays. Both are risk factors for damaging skin cells.

Our skin has *melanocyte* cells that release *melanin* when exposed to sunlight. *Melanin* is the skin's protective darkening pigment whose presence we refer to as a tan. *Pitta* types are very sensitive to heat and their bodies will quickly tell them if the amount of *melanin* produced is not sufficient to protect them against burning. *Pitta* types should therefore *not* use sunscreens. Blocking out UVB may turn out to be disastrous for their skin. Blocking out both UVB and UVA altogether can turn out to be even more harmful for them.

If *Pittas* expose themselves to the direct sun (avoid the 10.00-15.00 sun) for just a few minutes a day to begin with, they will soon be able to increase their body's exposure to a maximum of twenty minutes a day, without having any signs of reddening. Their skins will improve and *melanin* production increase. This will give them enough UV light to remain healthy, provided they do *not* use devices and solutions that alter or filter out light, including sunscreens or sunglasses. Exposing their skin to the sun under the influence of alcohol or other diuretics such as coffee, tea, soft drinks, etc. greatly increases the chances of damaging the skin.

The Danger of Suntan Lotions

Most suntan lotions contain *para-aminobenzoic acid* (PABA) which filters out sunburn-causing rays but still allows some tanning rays to pass. This does not only block out the therapeutic and healing effects of sunlight, but may also cause genetic damage to the skin. A recent report issued by the U.S. Food and Drug Administration included evidence that fourteen out of seventeen suntan lotions containing PABAs may be carcinogenic, i.e. cause cancer. Further research has shown that PABA causes increased genetic damage to the DNA in skin cells during exposure to sunlight. The damage done to the genes and chromosomes impairs the cell's ability to properly reproduce itself. UV light induces damage to the DNA in the presence of PABAs but to implicate UV light for this effect is tantamount to saying oxygen is dangerous because when it reacts with carbon atoms it can be become harmful for us.

Contrary to general belief, skin cancer is not caused by the sun but by the lack of it. A balanced diet of sunlight, which includes all the various frequency bands of ultraviolet light reaching the earth, as well as good nutrition and a natural lifestyle are still the best protection against all types of diseases. Solar research from all over the world has shown that exposure to ultraviolet light is probably the most comprehensive and impressive healing method there is. The following are a few examples of what ultraviolet light can do for you.

Ultraviolet light
- improves electrocardiogram
- lowers blood pressure and resting heart rate
- improves cardiac output
- reduces cholesterol if required
- increases glycogen stores in liver
- balances blood sugar
- enhances energy, endurance, and muscular strength improves the body's resistance to infections (increase of lymphocytes and phagocytic index)
- enhances oxygen carrying capacity of the blood
- increases sex hormones
- improves tans and resistance of skin to infections
- raises one's tolerance to stress and reduces depression

Possible Consequences of Lacking Exposure to UV Light

Sunlight does not only purify seawater to a depth of 12 feet, but also disinfects the skin from harmful germs. The longer the ultraviolet wavelength, the deeper it penetrates the skin. At 290nm, about 50% of the ultraviolet light penetrate a little deeper than to the superficial layers of the skin, whereas at 400nm, 50% reaches the deeper layers. The deeper reaching rays can even penetrate the brain. The human body was designed to absorb UV light for very good reasons, otherwise we would have been born with a natural sunscreen for UV light on our skin and eyes! One of them is that UV radiation is necessary for normal cell division. A lack of it disturbs normal cell growth, which can lead to cancer as confirmed by Dr. Shaw's research. The use of sunglasses, including regular UV reflecting spectacles and eye lenses, are responsible for certain degenerative eye diseases, such as macular degeneration. Most people who use them report continuously weakening eyesight.

Our typical indoor lifestyle, coupled with excessive overstimulation through highly acid-forming foods and drinks, the cholesterol increasing and dehydrating effects of television, and various other stress factors are cause enough to damage body cells, including those that make up the eyes. By shutting out the much-needed UV light, the eyes are unable to properly repair themselves and replace worn out eye cells. The increased incidence of blindness and eye disease in the industrialised world may result, to a large extent, from the misinformation that the sun is dangerous.

The reason so many people are attracted to being in the sun is imbibed in the natural instinct of the body to expose itself to the healing and cleansing properties of sunlight. Without being tricked into overexposure by "protective" sunscreens, the body will naturally know how much sunlight is good for its balanced growth. And even if circumstances lead to sunburn, the human body is perfectly equipped to handle it.

Chemical interference in this process of self-protection, however, can have serious consequences. By regularly using any of the following drugs or chemicals internally or externally, both skin and eyes become oversensitive to sunlight and the skin may badly burn even after a few minutes of exposure. Among them are antibacterial agents such as Sulfa, PABAs; hypoglycaemic agents used to treat diabetics; diuretics for high blood pressure; tranquillisers for nervous condition; broad-spectrum antibiotics; antiarrhytmic Quinidine used to suppress abnormal heart rhythms; halogenated antiseptic compounds used in cosmetics; many types of soaps and other consumer products; antihistamines used for colds and allergies; etc. In addition, gallstones in the liver prevent the liver from detoxifying drugs, alcohol, and other toxins, which overtaxes the skin as an eliminative organ and makes its vulnerable to the natural elements, including sunlight. Skin cancer (and cataracts) can only occur if the liver is congested.

It is much easier to treat the cause of a physical problem than to suppress its symptoms. If you are taking any of the above drugs and wish to treat the cause rather than the effect of an illness, consult your doctor about how to phase them out gradually, and at the same time begin exposing your body to the sun starting with 1-2 minutes and building up to a few more minutes each day. Make sure, though, your skin doesn't get burnt. Also expose your eyes to natural light as long as it is comfortable until you no longer require sunglasses. To avoid dehydration of the skin, drink fresh water before and after exposure to the sun.

CHAPTER 9

Rethinking AIDS

Could the AIDS Theory be Flawed?

It was over fifteen years ago when the first AIDS cases were diagnosed but despite the most colossal efforts by scientists and policy makers AIDS has remained a mystery disease. Commonly believed to be caused by the HIV or *Human Immune Deficiency Virus*, scientists still haven't found an antidote for the disease. There is no medical knowledge as to *how* the pathogen HIV is supposed to cause AIDS. The current AIDS theory also falls short in predicting the kind of AIDS disease an infected person may be manifesting and there is no safe system to determine how long it will take for the disease to develop. The theory contains no information that can help identify those who are at risk of developing AIDS.

With regard to "treating" AIDS, until recently patients were able to choose between a small number of drugs that were originally developed as cancer chemotherapies but had to bear the extreme side effects such as loss of hair, anaemia, muscle deterioration, nausea, and other immune suppressing effects. A recently introduced cocktail of three drugs (protease inhibitors), which are less toxic than the originally used drugs, seemed promising at first in being able to suppress HIV. Yet the cumulative failure rate of the new drugs has now reached 50 per cent and continues to increase as strains of HIV develop resistance to them. Already between 20 and 30 per cent of patients are now infected with viruses resistant to protease inhibitors and the situation is worsening day by day. Although the drugs have given many AIDS patients a "new lease of life" (not necessarily because the drugs suppress HIV but because they also subdue most other disease-causing agents, at least for a while), the initial euphoria about the new AIDS treatment has died down and so has the hope of finding a cure, at least within the medical field.

The fact that there is no reliable latency period -- the length of time from being infected with HIV and developing AIDS symptoms -- makes it virtually impossible to predict the beginning of the disease. The first AIDS victims were told that they could expect to die within one year after infection but today the grace period ranges from 12 to15 years, which makes immediate treatment after HIV infection dubious. This is certainly not the last revision since the majority of HIV infected people continue to be AIDS-free and only a fraction of them develop AIDS symptoms such as pneumonia, cancer of the blood, or dementia.

To add more confusion to the situation, health officials are unable to predict how many people will be afflicted with AIDS in the future as only a small percentage of the one million HIV-infected Americans, for example, will get the disease. As it has been since the beginning of the epidemic, 95% of the AIDS cases are among the major health risk groups – highly active homosexuals, heroin addicts, or, in a few cases, haemophiliacs.

With the officially proclaimed mortality rate of 50-100 percent among HIV infected people we should have had many more deaths in Africa where the number of infected is as large as six to eight million and also in Haiti where over six percent of the population test HIV-positive. Yet within the last decade the African continent had only 250.000 AIDS cases and Haiti almost none. This leads to the simple but most important and almost forsaken question regarding AIDS: *'What causes it?'*

So far, there is no scientific evidence that AIDS is a contagious disease, although it seems to be that way to most people. What *is* known from recently published research, however, is that HIV rarely spreads heterosexually and can therefore not be responsible for an epidemic that involves millions of AIDS victims around the world. There is also no proof to show that HIV causes AIDS. On the other hand, it is an established fact that the retrovirus HIV, which is composed of human gene fragments, is incapable of destroying human cells – yet cell destruction is the main characteristic of every AIDS disease. Even the principal discoverer of HIV, Luc Montagnier, no longer believes that HIV is solely responsible for causing AIDS. There is also increasing evidence that AIDS may be a toxicity syndrome or metabolic disorder that is caused by immunity risk factors, including heroin, sex drugs, antibiotics, commonly prescribed AIDS drugs, rectal intercourse, malnutrition and dehydration. Dozens of prominent scientists working at the forefront of the AIDS research are now openly questioning the virus hypothesis of AIDS.

Is HIV Harmless after all?

If a germ or virus has infected a person, the disease-causing microbe is present in high concentrations within the patient's body. In the case of AIDS, there should be *large* amounts of virus material in the affected tissues. Small amounts would not be sufficient to cause such extensive destruction as seen in the body of an AIDS victim. Therefore, active virus material should profusely be present in the white cells of the immune system, particularly in the T-helper cells, as well as in lesions of *Kaposi's sarcoma* and in the brain neurones of those afflicted with dementia. Yet this is not the case at all. The HIV retrovirus cannot be found in *any* of the diseased tissues of AIDS patients.

If HIV were capable of infecting T-cells or other parts of the immune system, then, as is the case with every other type of viral infections, the cell-free virus particles or *virions* would easily be detected in the blood stream. However, in the majority of AIDS patients there are no viruses found anywhere and in the remaining few there are not even enough present in the blood to cause as much as a simple cold. This makes AIDS patients de facto HIV-negative.

Like other viruses, HIV becomes quickly inactivated by rapid antibody production of the host's immune system. When it first infects the body, HIV can achieve high levels of virus and for a brief period cause mild flu-like symptoms if any at all. The immune system then quickly neutralises the retrovirus and puts it into a dormant state. Since AIDS patients who test HIV positive have been infected many years before they die, their HIV retrovirus remains inactive.

An HIV test can *only* detect either the dormant, inactive virus or antibodies that the immune system produces to remain immune to the virus in the future. Therefore, the HIV-test itself proves the harmlessness of HIV. Although it is rarely mentioned in the medical literature, HIV has never been found in the lymph nodes, macrophage cells, dendritic cells, and elsewhere in the body of an AIDS victim; there has never been even a sign of a hidden virus infection.

Faulty HIV Tests

HIV can only be detected in the human body after the immune system has already killed the virus through its arsenal of antibodies. The presence of HIV antibodies proves that the virus has been rendered harmless with no further role to play. The very HIV-testing procedure is therefore a means to tell infected people that *the virus has been successfully destroyed.*

The most frequently HIV test used today is ELISA and, in theory, it seems to be very accurate. A sample of the patient's blood is added to a mixture of HIV proteins. If the blood contains HIV antibodies, they react to the proteins. This is supposed to proof that the patient has been infected with HIV. Another test called Western Blot is often used as a confirmation. Besides being unable to detect actual virus in the blood of a patient, these tests are so unreliable that they are not only useless but also dangerous. In Russia, in 1990, after 20,000 "patients" had tested positive with the ELISA test only 112 were confirmed using the Western Blot (the French government has recently withdrawn 9 HIV tests because they were so unreliable). If the "success" rates of these testing procedures, which are rather extreme failure rates, were applied to the overall figure of the HIV infected population in the world (21 million according to the WHO) we would have a mere total of 118.000 people infected with HIV. Nobody could call this an epidemic.

The above figure may in fact be much lower. Both HIV tests react to proteins that are shared by all other retroviruses that have been found to live in the human body and do no harm. P24 is one of them. If a patient has produced antibodies to p24, which is generally accepted to be proof of the existence of HIV, the chances that he is infected with HIV are in fact very slim, considering the large number of retroviruses existing in the body.

In one study, 41 percent of patients with multiple sclerosis (MS) showed presence of antibodies to p24 in their blood. This didn't mean, however, that they were infected with HIV, although the ELISA test would have implied exactly that. As the co-discoverer of HIV and leading virologist Dr Robert Gallo has repeatedly pointed out, P24 is not unique to HIV. If the ELISA test is applied to people who have been or are infected with the viruses that cause malaria, hepatitis B and C, tuberculosis, glandular fever, papilloma virus warts, syphilis, leprosy, and many other conditions, the chances they are declared AIDS victims are extremely high. In Africa and other developing countries the HIV test is usually given to people who feel unwell or are already diagnosed with one of these diseases. Given the large number of people affected by them (hundreds of millions), the number of false-positive results could well exceed 10 to 15 million. Dr Max Essex, a highly respected and leading AIDS expert from Harvard University School of Public Health found that some 85 percent of Africans, who tested HIV positive with the Western Blot test, were later found negative.

Another source of false-positive results from HIV tests is the large variety of antibodies which people produce after undergoing blood transfusions or when exposed to foreign semen and virus material during homosexual activity, and after taking drugs. Drug users and homosexuals are known to make many more antibodies than the average person does. The chances that they become victims of a false AIDS test are therefore most likely.

What all this basically means is that there is no reliable way of telling how many people are infected with the HIV virus. Nor could anything be said about how many of the so-called AIDS diseases are in reality HIV-related, if they are at all.
Nobel laureate Kary Mullis, who invented the first HIV test, has openly questioned the validity of the "AIDS virus." According to Mullis, his highly sensitive detection technique known as PCR can only be used to find *dormant, inactive HIV*, incapable of harming anyone. Mullis says: "I can't find a single virologist who will give me references which show that HIV is the probable cause of AIDS..." *PCR proves that AIDS cannot be caused by a virus.* This also means that AIDS can occur without the presence of virus.

HIV Cannot Cause as much as the Flu

Contrary to the original HIV-AIDS hypothesis, which says there is a 50-100 per cent probability of death from infection, there are only few HIV infected people who actually die, at least not more than in any other category of disease. When blood from AIDS patients was injected into chimpanzees in 1983, all of them tested HIV positive but when tested 10 years later, none of them had developed any signs of sickness. In another experiment, over 150 chimpanzees received injections of purified (highly concentrated) HIV in 1984 but developed no symptoms of disease to this very day. However, what the experiments did show was that their immune systems had produced antibodies against the virus within a month, just as in humans. The presence of antibodies ensures that immunity against the microbes has been secured on a permanent basis. Just as animals cannot get AIDS from HIV so do human beings not get AIDS from HIV either.

Among other human viruses such as those causing polio, flu, hepatitis, etc., HIV may be one of the most harmless ones; it is quickly and easily neutralised by our immune system. The incubation period for every known virus does not exceed more than a maximum of 6 weeks, as is the case with the human hepatitis virus. It is a well-established biological law that any germ that does not cause symptoms before it is cleared by the immune system cannot be considered a cause of disease. No virus is capable of surviving 10-15 years in a normal healthy body with an active immune system. And even if it were possible in theory that a few virus particles would survive so long, they still would have to overcome the immune system, and they would certainly not be enough in number to impair immunity.

The AIDS theory suggests that HIV destroys the immune system's T4 cells, thereby leaving the body susceptible to all kinds of infections and diseases. It had already been discovered in the mid-eighties that the number of HIV infected T4 cells is far too small to cause widespread destruction and the human body is perfectly capable of replacing T4 cells faster than HIV could destroy them.

Since the beginning of AIDS, many thousands of people, including medical workers, and haemophiliacs were accidentally infected with HIV, but only few of them developed AIDS, not more than any other group in society. Among the health workers who developed AIDS, 90 percent belonged to the risk group of AIDS cases – highly active homosexuals and intravenous drug users. Among haemophiliacs, who are "naturally" immune-deficient, there are just as many HIV-negatives dying as there are HIV-positives dying. In other words, whether a haemophiliac is infected or not, his chances of developing an AIDS-type disease are the same. Up till now there has not been even one human or animal that has developed AIDS after being infected only with HIV. This fact may be reason enough to reconsider the role of HIV as being *the* sole responsible agent for causing dozens of different kinds of (AIDS) diseases. Luc Montagnier, co-discoverer of the HIV virus, has already pointed out that, without another co-factor, HIV cannot cause AIDS.

HIV Behaves like Every Other Virus

Man lived with the HIV virus long before it was discovered and before large numbers of people have had AIDS tests. The same applies to other types of viruses. For example, the *herpes* virus is present in 2 out of 3 Americans, another two thirds carry the herpes class *cytomegalovirus*. Four out of five Americans walk around with the *Eppstein-Barr virus,* which in few of them causes mononucleosis or "kissing disease." Even more people are host to the *papilloma virus*, which is known to cause warts. There is hardly anyone living on this planet who does not carry at least a dozen or so viruses in his body, each one related to a specific infectious disease. Yet no scientist in the world would use these facts to announce a mass outbreak of viral epidemics; every virologist knows that all these viruses are dormant, i.e., have been neutralised by the immune system. He also knows that this makes the infected people immune against re-infection, *unless* of course the immune system is damaged or suppressed through other factors.

If HIV, herpes, and all the other types of viruses that are latent in humans and animals living on the planet, were capable of killing people, there would hardly be anyone left to treat the billions of sufferers. HIV, being a human retrovirus (produced by the body itself), is totally benign to its host cells and it is therefore unable to destroy any cell it has infected. This applies especially to the cells of the immune system, which are equipped with highly sophisticated defence mechanisms. For HIV to have any destructive value, it would have to literally flood the body with active viral particles. Yet HIV can barely be detected even in late stage AIDS patients, despite using the most sensitive of tests. The traces of HIV virus found in some AIDS patients is inactive, which means, it is harmless, and therefore not responsible for the destruction of the body. If HIV *did* cause AIDS it would have to do this during the two phases of HIV infection where blood levels of HIV are significant:

1. Soon after infection when the immune system produces antibodies.
2. At the very end stage of AIDS when the levels of *all* viral activity increase *because the immune system has collapsed* (due other reasons than HIV infection).

There is enough scientific data to show that HIV, being and remaining inactive even in AIDS patients, *does not kill T-cells* and therefore *cannot cause AIDS*!

Research under Scrutiny

There are numerous studies which all seem to prove that only HIV-infected persons develop AIDS in comparison with those not infected. This correlation, although it is not a cause and effect relation, has become the most powerful and persuasive argument to convince both scientists and the general population to believe that HIV causes AIDS. Yet by analysing any of these studies one will find that the HIV-infected groups consisted *only* of members who were in the AIDS risk category, e.g., very active homosexuals, heroin addicts, and those having long histories of diseases. By contrast, the non-infected control groups consisted of healthy heterosexuals. In other words, AIDS seems to develop only in people whose immune system is already impaired due to other causes than HIV.

Official statistics reveal that 90 percent of all AIDS victims are men and 95 percent of all AIDS victims living in wealthy nations belong to one or more of the above risk categories. But there exists no such distinction in the above studies. The only common factor between the two groups is age. Yet it is very obvious that a 25-year old immune deficient heroin addict is more likely to suffer an immune disease than a 25-year old healthy medical student, regardless of whether he has one or several inactive viruses in his body or not.

In the last 10 years, several scientists have proposed conducting a case-controlled study that would compare a large number of HIV-infected people with a similar number of a uninfected people, all of whom would have *exactly the same health risks*. Yet there hasn't been much interest in conducting such a study as the main focus is still on destroying a virus rather than on immune suppressive influences.

HIV + Pneumonia = AIDS?

In the meanwhile, more and more studies are being published to show that the AIDS syndrome, which cannot be classified as a disease because every case displays a different combination of symptoms, occurs *only* in people who test HIV-positive. Before HIV was discovered, pneumonia, dementia, herpes-infections, weight loss, tuberculosis, *Kaposi's sarcoma*, chronic diarrhoea, several lymphomas, yeast infection, and other opportunistic infections were considered separate diseases. Depending on whether a patient had already a deficient immune system or belonged to a certain health risk group, the symptoms of these diseases exactly matched those which are now considered AIDS diseases.

Before the HIV-AIDS hypothesis, a patient who died from pneumonia, tuberculosis, or a lymphoma died from the respective causes of these diseases. Today, however, a patient who dies from pneumonia *and* has HIV antibodies in his blood, is listed as an AIDS victim. People with a low T-cell count in their blood are considered immune deficient, but if they have the same problem after testing HIV-positive, they are automatically "sentenced" to AIDS, with or without clinical symptoms.

There are already over 30 such diseases now that have been renamed AIDS in this way. One of the latest ones is cervical cancer, which has become the first AIDS disease that can only affect the female gender. This may give the impression that AIDS is now penetrating the heterosexual community as well. The inclusion of cervical cancer as an AIDS disease has "increased" the number of AIDS victims among women quite dramatically, yet at the same time it has "decreased" the number of ordinary cervical cancers among women. Overall, the mortality rate of these diseases has not changed at all.

The renaming of old diseases further supports the hypothesis that the AIDS syndrome is never found in anyone and in any nation apart from HIV infection. By definition, there is no AIDS without HIV, regardless how many non-HIV people may die from the same symptoms. Anything that even remotely resembles immune deficiency now counts as an AIDS disease despite the fact that AIDS patients with *Kaposi's sarcoma* have been reported to have normal immune systems. It has been argued that wherever there is HIV, AIDS will appear, too. This, however, isn't correct either. AIDS-like indigenous diseases existed long before the testing of antibodies for HIV was introduced. What is different today is that the old diseases are renamed and become AIDS diseases once HIV is found to be present as well. In real terms, though, there are not more AIDS cases in the world than there would be without HIV.

Statistical Errors

In the United States alone the estimated number of 1 million HIV-infected people has remained constant ever since the HIV test has been made available in 1985 (given the fact that HIV tests produce more false positives than correct positives there may only be very few HIV infected Americans). Of these (regardless of whether they were true positives or not), less than 1/3 had been diagnosed with AIDS by the year 1993 and 121,000 of them were still alive. Over two thirds of the HIV infected Americans have not developed any AIDS symptoms since 1985, and the already huge gap is widening each year. The number of new AIDS cases has actually been levelling off for several years and has dropped dramatically in 1996 despite the fact that the new yearly AIDS cases are always added to the totals of all AIDS victims so far. During the same period, although the new AIDS treatments were only made available in 1996, the number of AIDS deaths across the United States has dropped considerably, with a decrease of 44 percent during the first half of 1997.

An artificially contrived AIDS explosion took place at midnight, January 1, 1993. On New Year's Eve 1992, the Los Angeles Times reported: "As many as 40,000 Americans who are HIV-positive will wake up on New Year's Day with a diagnosis of AIDS." As forecast, the number of new AIDS cases climbed by 204 percent within the first three months of 1993 compared to the same period of the previous year. This statistical "error" and similar ones occurred because much milder forms of diseases had been included in the official list of AIDS diseases.

The same manipulation of data has also influenced world AIDS figures. More and more indigenous types of disease occurring in developing countries are integrated into the AIDS defined disease groups, thus giving the false impression that there is an AIDS explosion in the Third World. Statistics released by the WHO show that in 1995 AIDS soared by 25 percent, reaching a total of 1.3 million.

In those areas of the world, where there are more HIV infected people than in America, the actual number of AIDS cases is significantly less. For example, only 250,000 of the six to eight million Africans who were reportedly infected with HIV since the mid-1980s have contracted AIDS or whatever one may want to call the diseases formerly known as tuberculosis, glandular fever, diarrhoea and slim disease (unlike our wasting syndrome). All these old diseases have all been renamed AIDS diseases. Even if we oversee this statistical "error," the number of AIDS cases still only reaches a total of 250.000. This AIDS figure is lower than that of the United States, where there are one million HIV positives. Given the large number of people dying from tuberculosis alone (millions each year) and the high failure rate of AIDS tests in Africa (up to 85 percent), it may well be that the number of *real* AIDS cases there is less than 50,000.

Zaire alone with its 3 million HIV-infected people has only a few hundred AIDS cases, that is less than 0,02%. No scientific study would remotely consider AIDS to be caused by HIV when the number is so minute. Her neighbouring country Uganda with its one million HIV-infected people had only generated 8,000 AIDS cases. Out of the 360,000 HIV-infected Haitians, only a few hundred have AIDS. The Haitian AIDS patients, most of them undernourished, suffer from *toxoplasmosis,* which has *always* been a common cause of death. These figures may still be very conservative, as the old HIV tests, which were far less accurate and produced even more false positives than the new ELISA and Western Blot tests, were applied to millions of people worldwide.

Developing countries may have such low AIDS rates because they do not have such extraordinary health risks as the ones found among very active homosexuals, intravenous drug addicts, and haemophiliacs. Those who have long histories of various opportunistic infections or used "poppers" regularly in the past, had anal sex, received blood transfusions and took poisonous addictive drugs, belong to the risk group for AIDS. Because all these factors severely damage the immune system, the individuals being in this risk group are the most likely candidates to "acquire" the Human Immune Deficiency Syndrome.

The health risks specific for each group are responsible for the specific types of diseases. Heroin addicts are the most likely to develop tuberculosis, herpes infection, and weight loss and haemophiliacs produce pneumonia, with or without HIV. This makes HIV a harmless passenger virus. There are as many cases of pneumonia and tuberculosis today *without* HIV as there are *with* HIV. *Kaposi's sarcoma* also is no longer an exclusive "AIDS disease." "Slim disease" is as common among Africans who test positive for HIV as it is for their HIV-negative counterparts. The lack of HIV test equipment in most parts of Africa compels doctors to diagnose prospective AIDS patients merely by symptoms, a very unreliable and unscientific practice. Yet the numbers of these cases are added to the overall statistical "evidence" that AIDS is still with us, hence the "soaring" of AIDS in Africa.

HIV is not a New Virus

Most of the statistical errors have occurred because of faulty testing procedures and the wrong assumption that HIV is a new virus. Everyone who tests HIV positive is believed to have acquired the virus from someone else. The HIV testing procedure reveals nothing about how long the virus has been in a person's body. So, in the assumption that HIV must be a new virus (because nobody has discovered it or tested for it before 1983), we have never even considered the possibility that HIV, like so many other human retroviruses, could have been around for decades or even centuries. If HIV is an old virus - there is ample evidence now to support this claim - we should be able to find its traces (antibodies for HIV) in large numbers of people, especially in developing countries.

HIV turns out to be a virus that has certainly existed long before 1980. In 1998, research conducted at the Aaron Diamond AIDS Research Center at Rockefeller University, USA proved through blood tests gathered in Africa between 1959 and 1982 that the HIV virus already existed in 1959. Based on this and other related research it is now estimated that the virus first got into people sometime in the 1940s or early '50s.

Since the HIV test was introduced to the Western Hemisphere in 1985, the number of HIV-infections has remained constant world-wide. But once the screening campaigns of HIV were extended to new countries in Africa and now also in Asia the number of infected people "rose dramatically." There is no information available on how long these people carried the HIV virus or even whether they had received it from their parents.

By definition, HIV infected people will automatically contract AIDS within several years, and subsequently die. This, however, is not correct, although it may apply to a small number of HIV infected persons whose immune system has been destroyed through major health risks, which are discussed below. Since major health risks exist almost everywhere in the world, a "rise" in the number HIV infected people in areas where no one had been tested before is more than likely, especially since HIV has been around since the 1940s. In its "New World Health Report 1996", the World Health Organisation (WHO) states that there are now more than 21 million people infected with HIV. The report omits the fact that this "rise" in numbers stems mostly from the extension of the (highly inaccurate) HIV-test to previously uncovered populations in the world. In actuality, HIV has stopped spreading long ago.

New Evidence: HIV is Rarely Spreads Heterosexually
At least in the developing world the virus has existed for a long time because HIV is rarely spread heterosexually. As was discovered by testing the wives of infected haemophiliacs, an HIV-positive person requires over 1,000 unprotected sexual contacts with an HIV-negative person from the opposite sex to pass along the virus just once. In a more recent study, published in the Lancet, 1997, 349:851-2, French doctors at the Cochin-Port Royal hospital in Paris made a similar discovery after working with couples wanting a baby where the man was HIV-positive. Their findings are in line with infection rates of 1 per 1000 acts of unprotected sex among stable heterosexual couples. For the average person with a sexual activity of 2-3 times a week it would therefore take about *seven years* to infect another person with HIV. This effectively means that it would take 1 million couples, of whom the male partner is HIV infected, 2.739 *years* of *daily* unprotected sex to be able to infect all their female partners! In the developing world, unprotected sex among heterosexuals can therefore not be responsible for the high number of people who tested HIV positive (using the most inaccurate of tests).

However, the situation is different with regard to infected pregnant women. A baby is directly and constantly exposed to the mother's blood for a period of 9 months. During this period the virus has a 50% chance of being passed on to the baby. Retroviruses survive when they reach a new host prenatally (passed from mother to child). This way of passing on a virus is at least 500 times more efficient than through sexual transmission. (Blood transfusion is another obvious way of contracting the virus.)

In contrast to the situation in wealthy nations, HIV in Third World countries is equally distributed among both sexes, which means it must have been passed on from mother to child for many centuries. Had HIV been a deadly killer virus, then the babies of infected mothers would have been born deformed, miscarried, or dead because newly born babies have not developed adequate immunity to defend themselves against a killer virus. Even if they somehow managed to survive, they could only last for a maximum of two years -- the latency period given to infected babies before developing AIDS. The spreading of the virus would have been ended automatically through the destruction of all new babies that were infected by their mothers.

Due to the low rates of homosexuality in developing countries, the prenatal route of transmission has been their only efficient way (50 percent chance) to pass on HIV to the new generations. The female children, once grown enough to become mothers, would again have a 50 percent chance of passing the virus to their children. Therefore, in Africa alone, HIV must have been around for many generations before it was able to infect as many as 6-8 million people. The latest argument that the increased condom use in Africa helped to slow the rate of infection is hardly convincing since the main route of HIV infection in Africa is from mother to child.

Who Gets AIDS?

The situation is much different in the industrialised world where HIV can be transmitted through different routes. The most likely to be infected are very active homosexuals, needle sharing heroin addicts, and haemophiliacs who receive transfusions. They represent the main routes through which any disease-causing microbes can easily be passed on to others who share one common thing: immune deficiency. In other words, the groups in society where HIV is commonly present amongst their members, are also the groups with the biggest health risks and therefore more likely to produce AIDS symptoms. Still, HIV's most concentrated occurrence among health risk groups cannot be blamed for causing AIDS diseases just as elevated *cholesterol* levels cannot be held responsible for causing heart disease. These are mere correlations. The other problem is that gay men, drug users, and haemophiliacs who are exposed to semen, drugs, blood transfusions, hepatitis, the Epstein Barr virus, and many other diseases or factors known to cause biological false positives in HIV tests, represent the most unreliable groups in society to demonstrate real presence of HIV.

AIDS has not invaded the heterosexual community as prophesied 13 years ago. Although cervical cancer and other female diseases have now been renamed AIDS diseases, AIDS has not significantly affected the female population either. As it was ten years ago, nine out of ten AIDS patients are male. Anything and everything that strongly abuses the body and depletes the immune system must be held responsible for causing illness, regardless of whether it is a stroke, cancer, or an AIDS disease. Emotional stress, insufficient nutrition, dehydration, sleep deprivation, alcohol, cigarettes, antibiotics, hard drugs, excessive sexual activity, etc., can all damage the immune system. A dormant piece of viral material such as HIV, on the other hand, can do no harm in a healthy body.

Whoever continuously exposes himself to immune risk factors is also more susceptible to developing the *Acquired Human Immune Deficiency Syndrome*. Someone may argue: "What about an innocent baby who became infected with HIV by its parents and dies from pneumonia? Is that not AIDS?" The fact is that at least as many children die from pneumonia with or without HIV and it doesn't significantly influence the outcome of the disease whether they had a previous encounter with HIV or not. What *can* make a big difference, however, is *how* the pneumonia is treated.

What Causes AIDS?

Over thirty diseases have now been renamed AIDS diseases, all supposedly caused by one single (inactive) virus. What has been considered normal pneumonia until a few years ago, if linked with HIV, is now an AIDS disease. The same applies to *Candida* infection, tuberculosis, *Kaposi's sarcoma,* and cervical cancer. If an African suffers from "slim disease" and has HIV antibodies in his blood, he is said to have AIDS. If he dies from the disease, he obviously must have died from AIDS. This simple logic may sound persuasive to a lay person.

On the other hand, if an African is diagnosed with having "slim disease" without previous HIV infection and subsequently dies, AIDS is not considered the cause of death. It is worthy to note that there are at least as many cases of slim disease without HIV as there are with HIV and that the retrovirus HIV has proven to be incapable of causing cell destruction, which is the main characteristic accompanying "slim disease". If the HIV virus cannot be held responsible for causing AIDS diseases, then what *is* the cause of AIDS?

1. Narcotic Drugs

Roughly ten years before the discovery of AIDS, the industrial world experienced a dramatic increase in the use of non-prescribed drugs ranging from hashish, marijuana, and psychedelics to LDS, MDA, PCP, heroin, cocaine, amyl and butyl nitrites, amphetamines, barbiturates, ethyl chloride, opium, mushrooms and other "tailor-made" drugs. By 1974 five million Americans had used the drug cocaine, and only eleven years later, the figure had jumped to over 22 million. In 1990, the American Drug Enforcement Administration had confiscated 100,000 kilograms of cocaine, compared to a mere 500 kilograms in 1980. Within a decade the cocaine overdose victims had increased from 3,000 in 1981 to 80,000 in 1990, that is an increase by 2,400 percent! Amphetamine use also jumped dramatically. In 1989 the Drug Enforcement Administration had seized 97 million doses, up from 2 million doses in 1981. Also aphrodisiacs became extremely popular during the 1970s. By 1980 five million Americans had become regular users of akyl nitrites or "poppers."

The AIDS epidemic followed a huge jump in drug abuse. Every practising physician who has seen the severe destruction of body and mind in drug-using patients, can have no doubt in his mind that drugs are capable of doing even more harm than just kill. Drugs are known for their powerful effect of systematically destroying a person's vital functions, including the immune system. The figures given above can in no way represent the total use of drugs within the population, but they certainly indicate that drug abuse could be playing a major role if not the biggest in causing AIDS.

Drug use is concentrated mostly among young men aged 25-44. AIDS too is most common among this age group. Nine out of every ten AIDS cases is male and 90 percent of all people arrested for possession of hard drugs are male, too. Seventy five percent of these are aged 25-44 and 72 percent of all AIDS cases among men occur within exactly the same age group. Could this be pure coincidence?

Between 1983 and 1987, the death rate among young men of this age group increased by an average of 10,000 per year and so did the number of AIDS deaths within the same period. During the 1980s, deaths from overdose drug intakes doubled in men of this age group, while deaths from blood poisoning -- an indirect result of the injection of drugs into the blood - quadrupled. The same happened to the AIDS sufferers of the same age group during the same period of time.

Three quarters of all heterosexual AIDS cases and two thirds of all female AIDS cases are injection drug users. Two thirds of all babies born with AIDS have mothers who inject drugs. These figures do *not* include the use of drugs taken orally or in inhaled form.

The major percentage of AIDS cases, however, is found among the highly active homosexual men aged 25-44. This group not only abuses large quantities of narcotic drugs but also antibiotics, antifungals, antivirals (AZT, ddI, ddC, d4T, acyclovir, gancyclovir), etc. A large number of American studies confirmed that over 95 percent of male homosexual AIDS patients typically admitted to popper inhalation and regular use of hard drugs.

AIDS patients suffer from a pre-existing immune damage, which in many cases is caused by years of drug abuse. Without an already damaged immune system, AIDS diseases are extremely unlikely to develop. If any of the above risk groups take an AIDS test they are highly likely to test positive, due to the large number of antibodies their bodies have produced to counteract diseases caused by drugs, semen, blood, viruses, etc.

When Babies get AIDS

Also babies are affected by the drug intake of their mothers. Two thirds of all babies with AIDS symptoms, regardless of whether they test HIV-positive or not, have mothers who inject drugs; some large percentage of the rest have mothers who use non-injected drugs. Heroin is one of the most commonly injected drugs. Persistent drug users show symptoms of loss of white blood cells, the main upholder of immunity, as well as lymph node swelling, fever, rapid weight loss, brain dysfunction and dementia, and a marked susceptibility to infections. Heroin addicts often die from pneumonia, tuberculosis, and other opportunistic infections, as well as from wasting syndromes. In all these diseases, the protein p24, generally accepted to be proof of the existence of HIV, is amply present. Although p24 is not unique to HIV but shared with most infectious diseases, they have nevertheless been classified as AIDS diseases.

What is very saddening is that babies are defenceless against drug poisoning. Recent research has shown that pregnant women who smoke cigarettes pass cancer-forming chemicals to their babies. It is difficult to imagine what must be taking place in the developing brain of an embryo when it is exposed to heroin injected directly into his mother's blood, which is also his blood.

Babies born to cocaine-using mothers are born with severe mental retardation and are vulnerable to tuberculosis and lung diseases. The major experimental drugs are so poisonous that regular use can result in dementia, serious bacterial infections, and total destruction of the immune system. The drugs certainly possess a much higher probability of impairing immune functions so typical to AIDS than a simple, inactive virus.

2. Antibiotics

Most of the patients suffering from AIDS also have a long history of taking antibiotics. Antibiotics may be a major co-factor in developing AIDS among the very active homosexual men who depend on them in order to ward off the many venereal diseases and parasites arising from unhygienic sexual practices. Many gays have received open prescriptions for antibiotics from their doctors who advised them to swallow the drugs before their sexual encounters. Some of them had been on such toxic drugs as Tetracycline for as many as 18 years before their immune system succumbed to the side effects. The drug causes extreme sensitivity against sunlight, which can burn one's skin beyond repair. Those affected often suffer from Seasonal Affective Disorder (SAD), a form of depression that arises from lack of exposure to sunlight. The drug is also known to disturb the body's basic metabolic functions, which may result in virtually any type of disease. It also works as a strong immune suppressant and perhaps one of its worst side effects is the destruction of the body's friendly bacteria in the gut. The destruction of the useful bacteria makes room for yeast and other infection-causing bacteria to spread throughout the body and cause an entire range of symptoms and diseases.

Other commonly used drugs include flagyl and diiodohydroxquin. Both are used to combat amoeba-caused diarrhoea. The drugs can produce hallucination and depression.

Corticosteroids, sulfa drugs, and septra are prescribed for various other conditions, all with serious side effects. They cause severe digestive disturbances, and if worsened by a lack of good, healthy nutrients so common among active homosexuals, they systematically destroy their bodies' defences against disease-causing bacteria, viruses, and parasites. The formerly strong and healthy young men increasingly suffer from opportunistic infections which speed up ageing indicators similar to those found only in old and fragile people.

3. Blood Transfusion

All the above mentioned risk factors cause 94 percent of all AIDS cases in the United States, a typical representative for other industrialised nations. But the rest of 6 percent do not seem to fall into any of the risk categories. Over half of this small percentage "contracted" AIDS through blood transfusions, which to the general population would appear to be a definite indication for HIV to be the cause of AIDS.

However, a closer analysis of the AIDS survival statistics reveals that over half of all blood transfusion recipients die within the first year after transfusion. Exactly the same applies to patients who are not HIV-infected. The risk groups for failing blood transfusions are found among the very young and the very old, and those who are severely injured.

Under normal circumstances, healthy people never get a blood transfusion. They are given only to people who have already suffered from long-standing illnesses or after traumatic medical intervention, such as surgery. Anaesthesia alone serves as an immune- suppressant and so do antibiotics administered after surgery to ward off infectious microbes. If a patient undergoes an organ transplant, he will receive steroids and other drugs that prevent his immune system from rejecting the new organ. Many people have to take these drugs for the rest of their lives but since all other immune responses are subdued too, they often die from "unrelated" problems within a very short time. If these problems, however, occur in HIV-positive patients, the cause of death is considered to be AIDS. The victims become part of the "statistical evidence" that AIDS can be transmitted through blood transfusion.

In the United States, out of the 20,000 haemophiliacs, who rely on regular blood transfusions, only few are diagnosed with AIDS despite the fact that over three-quarters were infected with HIV through blood supply. Mortality rates for haemophiliacs in fact have never been as low as they are today.

It has been proved that also blood transfusions can bring up false-positive HIV test results. In a study published in the *Lancet* patients showed the presence of large quantities of HIV antibodies in their blood immediately after blood transfusion, decreasing thereafter. One healthy volunteer who received six consecutive blood injections at four-day intervals tested HIV-negative after the first injection, but with each subsequent transfusion the HIV-positive antibody response increased. The argument that HIV can be transmitted through blood transfusions may therefore only be partially true. As the above experiment shows, blood transfusion can actually produce human retrovirus material that may be identical or similar to HIV. This doesn't necessarily mean that an AIDS disease will automatically develop as a result of blood transfusion (most haemophiliacs don't develop AIDS). But if the immune system is already severely damaged or low due to other factors such as drug abuse or surgery then certainly blood transfusions can greatly increase the risk of developing a life-threatening immune deficiency disease or AIDS (see also "Business with Our Blood" in the following chapter).

4. AIDS – A Metabolic Disorder, not an Infectious Disease

For several years it has been known that AIDS sufferers develop a drastic imbalance of very important amino acids *before* they actually deteriorate. A balanced protein metabolism is the main prerequisite for a healthy immune system. If the concentration of some of the amino acids in the body is too high or too low the immune system can no longer fight acute infections. This is particularly true for AIDS diseases.

The physiological imbalances of basic protein metabolism in AIDS patients can be caused by any of the above factors, which all have highly stressful effects on the body. To combat such severe stress, the body triggers stress hormones such as *cortisone* that are designed to break down muscle proteins into basic amino acids needed for emergency reuse. This effectively means that the body is feeding off itself. If the stress persists, the amino acid balance can no longer be maintained which eventually causes the collapse of the immune system so typical of an AIDS disease.

During the process of destroying its own cells to obtain essential amino acids, the body has to deal with a large amount of cell debris, including the fragments from destroyed cell nucleus. It seems that some of these DNA or RNA fragments are labelled as the retrovirus HIV. Since there are various types of such fragments, there are also several types of HIV, i.e., HIV1, HIV2, etc. as well. This may explain why there are so many people now who are HIV-positive but have never been infected by HIV contaminated blood or been in contact with HIV-infected people. Research by Dr. Hulda Clark, Canada, showed that babies can test HIV-positive despite the fact that their parents are HIV-negative.

HIV is much more common than most people think. Many people, who go through periods of extreme stress, may have a strong presence of HIV in their blood for which their immune systems produce antibodies. Since they are unlikely to test for AIDS, they may never find out that they have encountered this virus. Even if they have an AIDS test, they may not test positive for HIV1 but they might for HIV3 or another of its variations. For many years and in most countries testing facilities could only detect one of the many HIV types. Today a person's blood may be screened for two types of HIV, which is still not enough to determine whether he is HIV positive or not (considering the high false-positive rates of HIV tests).

Unless the stress reaction continues he may lead a perfectly healthy life. But if stress-caused cellular destruction becomes a long-term issue the amino acid balance becomes increasingly disturbed. This in turn drains the immune system to such an extent that it can no longer defend the body against even the low level infection-causing agents that permanently linger in everyone's body. When the host's immune system fails to neutralise the germs, a simple bacterium can cause a life-threatening infection, as seen among many AIDS patients.

Drug addicts, very active homosexuals, babies born to mothers with an unbalanced amino acid pool, people who are in need of a blood transfusion, and those who are undernourished or starve, all are suffering from an unbalanced amino acid pool and are therefore possible candidates of HIV particle generation. Intense stress responses cause the breaking down of cell nucleus, which results in an increased presence of DNA or RNA fragments. The first and natural response by the body is to produce antibodies to these fragments. However, if immunity is subdued through constant stress, a flood of disease-causing agents begins to invade the body. Wherever they find easy access first that is where the AIDS disease will begin.

How Narcotic Drugs and Rectal Intercourse can cause AIDS

Use of intravenous morphine and heroin alters the basic metabolism of the body. The body's own natural morphine compounds, called *endorphins*, are not only capable of reducing pain and producing euphoria, but they also suppress hunger sensation. People who use heroin or morphine lose their appetite and subsequently stop eating and drinking properly. The body, while detecting a famine and dehydration, starts off the cortisone release mechanisms to attempt surviving the food and water shortage. When this mechanism reaches a certain level, it will cause an imbalance of the amino acid pool in the blood and lead to an increased breakdown of cell nucleus. The DNA assembly line (double-stranded helix) collapses into its segments of proteins which the body in turn uses to restore the balance of amino acid to whatever extent possible. These fragments are what tests reveal to be HIV particles.

HIV is produced by a strong imbalance of essential amino acids in the body, in this case caused by drug abuse. This understanding of HIV matches the basic characteristic of HIV, that is, being a retrovirus, which due to its natural design is not able to kill cells. HIV by itself has no capability of entering a living cell and breaking up the DNA or RNA assembly line, but the body's own *cortisone* can if stress is severe and prolonged.

Intravenous drug users who share HIV contaminated needles may test HIV-positive as a result of exposure to the foreign DNA fragments (HIV) but if they die from an AIDS disease it is because of an imbalance in their own amino acid pool. The continued depletion of certain amino acids such as *cystine, cysteine,* or *tryptophan* leads to a suspension of antibody production and a total collapse of the immune system. This is called AIDS. All intravenous dug users are at risk of eventually producing HIV particles and developing AIDS diseases.

The same applies to people who have regular rectal intercourse, not because they can infect each other with HIV but because this unnatural form of sexual practice causes constantly occurring intestinal injury, thus depleting the body's amino acid reserves. A massive number of cells need to be dismembered, cleared, and replaced continually, which produces a long-term run on the body's protein reserves. When one or more amino acids get depleted, DNA or RNA molecules break apart, leaving behind their protein fragments labelled HIV. Therefore HIV is the *effect* of immune deficiency and *not* its cause.

The cells of AIDS patients are consistently short of the amino acid *cysteine* and its precursor *cystine*, which may result from one or several of the causes shown before. as Laboratory research has demonstrated that when such cells are given the missing amino acids their HIV production stops because their DNA and RNA molecules are able to sustain their assembly line.

In addition, regular discharge of human semen into the rectum, which has no natural defence lines against the immune repressive properties of the semen that bathes the sperm, eventually leads to a shut down of normal repair work and cell replacement. This causes chronic toxicity, which in itself is a constant blow to an already weakened immune system.

How Malnutrition, Dehydration, and Starvation can cause AIDS

As in drug-caused malnutrition, lack of proper nourishment activates the body's stress responses to the point that it starts feeding on itself. This is necessary to keep the amino acid pool balanced. But when too many muscle cells are broken down to release the missing amino acids, large amounts of DNA or RNA fragments are generated which the body tries to neutralise by producing antibodies. The same stress response occurs in cellular dehydration. Such a person would therefore test HIV-positive.

In the developing world, particularly in Africa, malnutrition, dehydration, and even starvation have existed for centuries. During a famine, many people feed on their own bodies. The by-product of this emergency measure of the body is generation of HIV (DNA or RNA fragments). Consequently, the immune system produces antibodies to render the viral particles harmless. Although many of the people in Africa have received the inactive HIV from their parents who at some stage in their lives have gone through a famine, others have produced it themselves from their bodies' natural response to malnutrition.

Wherever the AIDS test is introduced in developing countries large numbers of the population test HIV positive either because of false-positive HIV tests or because they or their parents had to endure a famine. *Their* HIV is mainly caused by malnutrition, which is clearly demonstrated in the case of the 360,000 HIV-infected and undernourished Haitians. By contrast, the HIV of developed countries results mostly from the above mentioned causes. HIV and AIDS, although being two completely separate issues, are more likely to occur *together* in developed nations than in Third World countries where homosexual intercourse, intravenous drug abuse, and blood transfusions, etc., are far less common. AIDS diseases in poor nations are more linked to wasting disorders such as "slims disease," tuberculosis, and malaria.

Summary: HIV, which consists of human DNA or RNA fragments, cannot be considered to be the cause of AIDS because it is the result of a metabolic disorder that is caused by one or more major risk factors. If a *healthy* person acquires HIV through an external source, i.e., through contact with HIV-infected blood or through the mother, it is rendered harmless and inactive by the host's immune system. Such a person has produced antibodies for HIV in his blood as he has for any other previously encountered viral particles. He is in no greater danger of developing an AIDS disease than any other person without HIV does, as can be seen, for example, in the vast majority of HIV-infected Africans or Asians.

The occurrence of DNA or RNA fragments (HIV) in the blood of a person who produces abnormal cell destruction, however, indicates a serious immune deficiency. Malnutrition, starvation, dehydration, injury, or cell suffocation from internal congestion results in an imbalance of the body's amino acid pool. To correct the imbalance the body begins to break down its own cell nuclei to obtain the missing amino acids. If there is a shortage of even one amino acid in the body, the percentage composition of all the other amino acids becomes unbalanced too. This can have a simultaneous catastrophic effect on all the cells and their nucleus throughout the body. The destruction of cell nucleus results in DNA or RNA fragments; the fragments consist of human proteins called retrovirus. HIV is one the many retroviruses that can be generated in this way. Thus, HIV, which is generated within the body through destruction of cell nucleus, cannot be considered to be the cause of AIDS; it is an unavoidable by-product of the body's fight for survival. This fight may eventually lead to the destruction of the immune system which is called AIDS.

AIDS as a Process of Awakening

Mankind is rapidly awakening to a new level of understanding, which will discriminate between false and correct information. We are living in a time where scandals can no longer be concealed from the public eye. Whatever may be the truth about any subject it will eventually dominate in collective consciousness. People will simply know from within themselves what is right and what is wrong. AIDS is one of today's great challenges that can urge someone to search for the solutions to his problems within. Andrew, who was my first AIDS patient, made this realisation almost instantly.

When I met Andrew 5 years ago he was a young homosexual with fully developed AIDS symptoms. He was emotionally unbalanced, depressed and extremely sensitive. He was living in Athens where, in his opinion, nightlife was the only thing "worth living for." First of all I motivated him to become a "day person" again. The Ayurvedic routine, cleansing procedures, improved nutrition, daily meditation, etc., soon improved the multiple lesions on his skin, steadily increased his T-cell counts, and what he felt was most remarkable, improved his appetite and digestion. With all that, his joy of living returned but the new kind of joy was quite different to what he experienced ever before. It was the joy of waking up, of appreciating the sun, nature, and day-life rather than clubs, drugs, and nightlife.

When I met Andrew a few years later, he had no sign of AIDS anymore. He was used to the idea that he was still HIV positive but he knew that he had overcome AIDS, which was most important to his self-esteem and his happiness. The stigma of HIV was no longer a matter of disgrace to him. Andrew had changed from being a victim of some sort to a person worthy of love, appreciation, and recognition. This is what AIDS can do. It can awaken a person to living his life with greater love, dignity, and purpose.

CHAPTER 10

Global Misinformation

1. Antibiotics; Bugs and how We Attract them

Are Antibiotics Really Necessary?

Antibiotics have dominated the field of health for nearly fifty years. Known as "magic bullet" treatment or "miracle drugs," antibiotics, meaning "against life", can speedily destroy hordes of disease-causing bacteria. They are the most popular choice of the medical profession when it comes to stopping infections, relieving pain, or curing numerous types of diseases. For every illness there is a man-made drug which promises quick relief. At least one of six prescriptions written each year is for an antibiotic drug.

Having grown up in a generation where antibiotics are readily prescribed for a stubborn case of cystitis, a sore throat, or the common cold, we may accept without hesitation that the "magic bullet" we are given is the best option there is to deal with an infection that is caused by bacteria. Although every medical student knows that viral infections, (including those that cause cold and flue), do not at all respond to antibiotics, millions of people who are afflicted with these ills still receive antibiotic prescriptions from their GPs. In 1983 more than 32 million Americans visited a doctor for treatment of the common cold and 95 percent of them went home with a prescription drug. More than half of them were unnecessarily given a prescription for an antibiotic.

Patients are rarely informed that even one dose of broad spectrum antibiotics can severely damage the natural flora of the intestinal tract and the blood forming red bone marrow for as many as four to five years. What is most disturbing about this is that many doctors themselves don't know that penicillin, for example, won't cure a cold or flu. In the majority of cases, patients do not even read the list of side effects written on the instruction sheet that accompanies the drug. Because of their very design, antibiotics impair the immune system and hence may sow the seeds for more serious problems than a simple cold. Besides, a cold is not an illness but the body's first best emergency measure to rid itself of toxins; the virus serves as a trigger for this response.

Since most people prefer a quick-fix "cure" to a time-consuming one, antibiotics have become one of the most preferable forms of treatment today. However, it may take at least 24 hours before infection-causing bacteria can be identified. So the doctor, being pressed for time, tends to use a broad-spectrum drug that can wipe out every microorganism it meets, including those that help us to *fight* disease. This may be justified in the rare event of a life-threatening infection, but certainly not for the vast majority of relatively mild infections. In a large number of cases, specific antibiotics are administered to patients with symptoms of infection even before the lab sample has been analysed. The chances that they have received the wrong drug, or taken it for no reason, are at least fifty-fifty.

If a patient leaves the doctor's office empty-handed and only receives advice on how to deal with his illness in a more natural way, he may think that the doctor hasn't done his job. The physician too, facing a viral infection, often prefers the comparatively "safe" option of an antibiotic to being blamed for not doing enough for the patient, particularly when the patient is a child. Otherwise he may even risk a lawsuit against him. Even though the probability that a child really requires antibiotics is as low as 1 in 100,000, nearly 95 percent of all children taken to the doctor are given such drugs. In most these cases, antibiotics are being abused to act as placebos "to please" overly worried mothers.

Antibiotics Damage the Immune System

Antibiotics are routinely prescribed for infections, including benign ones. An infection, however, is not a disease, it rather is the body's natural response of neutralising and removing toxic substances that have been caused by such simple things as overeating, dehydration, consumption of junk foods, and previous exposure to antibiotics. The body has to pay a high price for being forced to deal with antibiotics. The poison of the drug destroys not only infection-causing microbes but also friendly bacteria that help us digest food, remove toxins, and produce important micro-nutrients such as B-vitamins. As these essential bacteria become increasingly depleted the population of harmful bacteria begin to increase in number and finally dominate in the intestinal tract (see section on *Candida*), turning even nutritious foods into pure poison.

The immune system, of which 80 percent is located in the intestines, tries to neutralise the hostile bacteria and the poison by mobilising its defence forces. The result is inflammation, which may occur anywhere in the body. Swelling of the lymph nodes, fever, skin eruptions, etc., are indications that the immune system is responding and still active and intact. This fight can take from 2-6 days or longer, depending on the extent a previous course of antibiotics has suppressed the immune system and damaged the natural intestinal flora. Antibiotic treatment only succeeds in masking the symptom while giving the impression that we have conquered the illness whereas in truth we have made it worse: we have prepared the ground for chronic disease. The toxins are still in the body; this time, however, they are no longer circulating but are deposited in the more hidden structures of the body, i.e., the tissues and organs. Much of the antibiotics remain in the liver, which changes bile flora and causes gallstones to be formed there.

Each further course of antibiotics impairs immune system and intestinal flora as well as bile flora even more, making room for disease-causing microbes to spread throughout the body. With regular intake of antibiotics, the immune system becomes so weak and passive that it is no longer able to defend the body against real life-threatening diseases like cancer, MS, and AIDS. This applies to people everywhere, in the developed and the underdeveloped world.

For decades, the large groups of the East African population have been exposed to antibiotics for "experimental purposes." Many drugs that have been banned in industrialised nations because of life endangering side effects can now be found in the drug stores of developing countries. Their powerful immune-suppressive effects may explain the appearance of many new types of diseases that have never occurred in such countries before. In the event, they might have triggered the recurrence of old infectious diseases.

Biological Warfare

The antibiotic approach of treatment is costing human society more than anyone could have anticipated. The bugs that were "successfully" subdued for decades with antibiotics are now taking revenge, producing what is known as "antibiotic resistant organisms," i.e., germs that defy antibiotic treatment.

Antibiotics stop the symptoms of disease by destroying harmful bacteria. Since the drugs cannot discriminate between good and bad bacteria, they also damage the intestinal flora as well as the bile flora. Because antibiotics are products of microbes that have been derived, for example, from carcasses, they are deadly for living bacteria.

It is a law of nature that every living organism wants to live and survive as long as it possibly can. Bacteria that are exposed to regular supplies of the toxic anti-biotic substances will therefore try to become immune to the poisons. To survive such assaults they have their own sophisticated defence strategies, which are in a way similar to ours when we need to defend ourselves against invasive bacteria or viruses. One possible way for bacteria to evade an antibiotic attack is to mutate their genes. As a result, the bacteria become resistant to the active ingredients of a drug, which renders the drug ineffective. You may have wondered why most types of antibiotics stay in the market only for relatively short periods of time. One of the reasons for this is that the bacteria have outsmarted the antibiotics and more powerful drugs need to be employed to kill the newly mutated strains of bacteria. [Another reason for being withdrawn from the market is the more frequent occurrence of serious side effects that arise from giving the drugs to large numbers of people.]

What is most disturbing is that the more you use the drugs, the more resistant the bacteria will become. Top researchers in this field already admit that they are fighting a losing battle. We have overused antibiotics to such an extent that every disease-causing bacterium has now mutated versions that resist at least one antibiotic. When an antibiotic attacks a colony of bacteria, *most* of them die. Yet some of the microbes know how to survive because they harbour mutant genes that resist their destruction. These mutant bacteria then pass on their resistant genes to other bacteria and within 24 hours each of them may have left an estimated 16,777,220 offspring, equally resistant to the antibiotic drug.

The nightmare doesn't stop there. The mutant bacteria begin to share their resistant genes with other unrelated microbes they come into contact with, making all sorts of micro-organisms resistant to treatment as well. The well-known microbiologist Stanley Falkow once said that bacteria are "clever little devils" that can become resistant to drugs they've never met and anticipate confrontations with other ones. In this way, bacteria become super-germs or super-bugs, capable of evading any attack through drugs. They lurk particularly in places where antibiotics are used more often than elsewhere, i.e. hospitals and nursing homes. According to recent findings, five to ten percent of all people checking into hospitals today are going to get infected as a result of antibiotic resistant bacteria lodging within these buildings.

Except for the sterile environment of surgery theatres, the super-bugs can be found riding on dust particles of the heating and air-conditioning systems, in bathrooms and toilets, and even in the food. They account for most of the deaths in hospitals today. The super-bugs "choose" those patients whose immune systems have already been impaired through sickness, surgery, and/or previous encounters with antibiotics. Under normal circumstances we can live with the bugs without ever getting infected and if we do get infected, our body can deal with them effectively and become immune to them at the same time. This natural resistance to the bugs decreases drastically though with the first course of antibiotics taken for a simple infection.

Because of the excessive use of antibiotics in and out of hospitals, antibiotic resistant organisms have now become the commonest cause of infection. To make matters worse, in many countries people can now acquire antibiotics over the counter. Since precise dosage depends on the individual and the potency of the infection, and since there is no set time limit to the number of courses a person may require, antibiotics can never be considered "safe." Interrupted intake or too low a drug dose can encourage the growth of resistant bacteria, which then can be passed on to other people as well. This may increase the risk of infection for those who are near a person who takes antibiotics and may explain why infection is higher in families where they have been used before.

Indiscriminate use of antibiotics seems to be doing more damage than we can even begin to understand. Antibiotics are among the most powerful immune suppressants that exist. Most people who are ill and die don't actually die from their diseases. They die from opportunistic bacterial infections while their immune systems are low. This applies to cancer, AIDS, and most other killer diseases. Autopsies revealed that many of the patients who died from an "AIDS" disease had never actually been infected with HIV but were killed by *antibiotic resistant superbugs.* The bugs caused similar symptoms to the ones considered being AIDS-diseases.

Losing the Battle with Disease?

The world is not only experiencing a vast number of new man-made epidemics, but old ones, too, seem to be making a comeback. In 1978, the United Nations adopted a "Health for All, 2000" resolution, setting the goals for eradicating infectious disease by the century's end. But the germs didn't co-operate. Apart from at least 29 previously unknown diseases, 20 well known ones have re-emerged, including malaria, tuberculosis, pneumonia, cholera, yellow fever and dysentery. The germs causing the diseases are rapidly mutating to forms beyond the reach of today's antibiotics.

Drugs that once cured malaria are being foiled by the mosquito-borne-parasite. Its "changing coat" of mutations baffles scientists. The "super drugs" of yesterday have become today's weapons of self-destruction. A century of using quinine-based drugs as a prophylactic in people who did not even have malaria has fostered the evolution of new strains of quinine-resistant malaria that defy conventional treatment.

Haemorrhagic dengue, another mosquito fever, has struck in India, Africa, and parts of Latin America for the first time in at least a half-century. An Asian strain of cholera reached Latin America in 1991 and at least 1,3 million people have been stricken since. But not only the developing world is afflicted. The U.S. death rate from infectious diseases rose 58 percent between 1980 and 1992. In 1995 haemorrhagic dengue reached Texas. We seem to be in a battle we cannot win. What is most disconcerting is that those who have used the "magic bullet" approach to disease in the past have contributed greatly to the new wave of infectious diseases that are sweeping the globe. In a sense, man is now forced to become aware of his mistakes and to employ natural methods of healing instead of drugs that are designed to kill biological organisms. Tuberculosis (TB) is a typical example of this learning process.

Tuberculosis – Nature is Fighting Back

Once killer disease number one, TB has now developed multiple drug resistance and claims millions of lives each year. The World Health Organisation has declared TB a global emergency. In 1990 the disease earned itself the title of being the world's number one killer pathogen, responsible for the deaths of nearly three million people worldwide. Fifty years of using antibiotics in the treatment of diseases have made the TB bug so resistant to treatment that wherever it finds a fertile ground it causes death, especially in developing countries where hygiene is often very poor.

The Western Hemisphere, however, is no longer safe from TB either. The first modern epidemic broke out in New York in 1990 followed by others in several parts of America and Britain. The super-bugs can travel around the world in almost no time. AIDS patients and those regularly treated with antibiotics or living in poor and unhygienic environments, are particularly endangered. Out of the 40 variations of antibiotics available for the treatment of TB, only one or two still seem to have an effect. What is going to happen when the TB pathogens become resistant to them as well or when they are given to persons whose immune systems are already greatly impaired is hard to imagine. Nobody can foresee the consequences of our collective action that has made antibiotics to be the treatment of preference for infectious diseases. But you and I can make a difference when it comes to creating a healthy world, by choosing not to use antibiotics unless it is in an emergency.

Several years ago a major report on drug prescription revealed that 80 percent of all prescribed drugs are of only "marginal" use which means that it would not make a difference whether we took them or not, except for the side effects they produce. In addition, we are now reaping the consequences of this massive abuse of "medical" drugs. We have created an entire armoury consisting of highly sophisticated antibiotic resistant weapons, super-germs that defy treatment.

TB took 1,000 million lives within the previous two centuries, but then the deadly disease was nearly eradicated from the surface of the earth through a combination of public hygiene measures and antibiotics. One may argue that without the use of antibiotics the disease could never have been brought under control. However, the latest statistical reviews show that TB had decreased *dramatically* through the introduction of new hygiene measures *before* TB-antibiotics were introduced. This clearly demonstrates that antibiotics did not eradicate TB but improved hygiene measures did.

Today, the situation is not much different. TB strikes where hygiene is poor. Good hygiene, however, does not only include having clean fresh, water, nutritious food, and proper sanitary conditions, it is a measure of how clean we are inside our body. Dirt is a major source of spreading infectious diseases. Modern lifestyle and eating habits have turned our intestines into ideal breeding places for microbes.

TB and other infectious diseases that defy modern treatment compel man to make major changes in his life. In fact, to live comfortably and without mass epidemics we will have to change nearly everything, from improving our diet, balancing our lifestyle, drastically reducing environmental pollution, to increasing psychological health. These are the factors that make all the difference when it comes to building natural resistance to disease-causing germs of any kind, including TB.

Antibiotic resistant organisms cannot be eradicated from the surface of the earth, and this may not even be necessary. Although genetically mutated, they are still microbes that require an unclean environment to live and to survive; their population is naturally reduced in size when their food supply becomes limited. Our body's "ecosystem" is not exempted from this law of nature. The belief that man is powerful enough to bypass the laws of nature and use antibiotic drugs for minor infectious diseases is crushed by a few evasive microbes which we cannot even see with our bare eyes. The more people stop "feeding and fighting" them, the less dangerous they will become for us humans. This is a major lesson for survival on the planet.

Candida – Microbes Versus Microbes
One of the commonest side effects of using antibiotics against infection is overgrowth of *Candida* albicans, a natural and even necessary yeast inhabitant of our gut. *Candida* bacteria help to break down toxins. Under normal circumstances, *Candida*, which lives in most mucous membranes, is kept in check by our friendly bacteria known as *lactobacillus acidophilus* and the *bifido* bacteria. We have more friendly bacteria in our body than we have cells and one third of our eliminated faecal matter consists of these tiny helpers; without them we could not live.

Antibiotics, which target the specific microbes linked to infection, also kill off the friendly bacteria and subsequently *Candida* production goes into overdrive and spreads like mould throughout the intestinal tract. This interferes with the activity of enzymes that break down food, resulting in poor digestion and bloating. If the *Candida* continues to grow, it develops tentacles that penetrate the bowel walls allowing toxins to enter other parts of the body, including the brain. This can cause an entire range of physical and emotional symptoms. They include sinusitis, ear infections, gastrointestinal dysfunction, weight gain, water retention, hormonal imbalance, mental confusion, depression, insomnia, anxiety, chronic fatigue, vaginitis, increased pre-menstrual tension, urinary tract infection (cystitis), oral thrush, skin and nail infection, conjunctivitis, constipation, kidney problems, gallstones, and food cravings, particularly for sugar and sweets.

Besides antibiotics, other drugs, including the contraceptive pill and Hormone Replacement Therapy (HRT) have been shown to cause *Candida*. The latter two increase vaginal glucose by up to 80 percent, which means more food for the *Candida* bacteria. The typical junk food diet of modern life high in fat and sugar contributes to a further spread of *Candida*. Like most other diseases, *Candida* too is a toxicity crisis, which is a natural response of the body to rid itself of accumulated toxins. *Candida* spreads wherever there are toxins that need to be "digested." Any weakening influence that robs the body of its energy reserves leads to a build-up of toxins and helps to spread *Candida* further.

Dealing with Candida Infection

A survey of 3.000 patients who had been treated for *Candida*-related problems revealed that 90 percent of them had reported excessive and prolonged use of broad-spectrum antibiotics before being infected. *Antibiotics cannot eradicate candida bacteria*. The more you try to get rid of them with drugs the more resistant they become and the faster they repopulate.

If you are infected with *Candida* you can starve them by depriving them of the toxins and foods that cause them to multiply. As long as there are gallstones in the liver, re-infection is almost guaranteed. A series of liver cleanses and three days of fasting with only taking water is one of the fastest ways to deal with them, although the latter may be difficult for many people. The yeast bacteria will soon begin to withdraw to their original sites and shrink in numbers. Consequently, a diet consisting of foods they dislike can take care of the rest. Eat fresh vegetables, Basmati rice, beans, lentils, poultry (only if unavoidable), freshly prepared vegetable soups, wholemeal pasta (unless you are a Pitta type or have a wheat allergy), rice crackers, porridge, bananas. Avoid meat, fish, or their products. Drink plenty of fresh water and herbal teas that have a bitter taste, *chaparral* being one of the most effective ones. Also 2-4 cups of *Lapacho* tea a day can quickly clear *Candida*.

Apply the muscle test to all the foods and drinks you normally consume. It is most likely that the following food items will make your arm muscle weak and further the growth of *Candida*: Sugar, yeast or yeast containing foods such as bread; cakes, biscuits, chocolate, other sweets; tomato ketchup, fruit (except banana), alcohol, marmite, mushrooms, hard and blue cheeses, fermented products such as vinegar; coffee, tea, soft drinks, cigarettes or any other stimulants. It will also be necessary that you go off the Pill and HRT, if applicable. After a month you may be able to reintroduce some of these foods to your diet but if you find you get bloated again they are most likely not part of your natural body-type requirements. *Candida* can be a way to lead you towards a healthier and more fulfilling lifestyle (refer to chapters 6 and 7 for details).

Could Antibiotics be Responsible for the Narcotic Drugs Epidemic?

The overuse of antibiotics may have ruined not only individual lives but also entire families. American research showed that the use of narcotic drugs rose by 400 percent within a period of twenty years (1968-1988); the research linked 95 percent of the total increase to the frequent intake of prescribed medical drugs by the subjects prior to drug involvement. Only five percent of the total increase during this period was presumably caused by factors such as curiosity, pressure by social groups, drug cartels, etc.

Recent findings in the field of neuro-physiology offer some explanations as to how antibiotics may cause substance addiction. Once ingested, antibiotics, as well as painkillers, tranquillisers, and mind-altering drugs, occupy receptor sites on the surface of our cells which trigger the corresponding expected responses such a relief of pain, calmness, or lessening of depression. Occupied by these external chemical agents, the cells' receptor sites can no longer receive and respond to the body's own drugs. Naturally, the body begins to reduce production of its own drugs like *endorphins, interleukins, serotonin, dopamine,* etc. These drugs are related to the experience of satisfaction, happiness, and creativity, something a person naturally wishes to have.

Endorphins, for example, consist of very strong *morphine* compounds that are needed for a "happy" and harmonious functioning of the entire mind/body system. We are naturally addicted to them. When they are no longer secreted in sufficient quantities, we begin to look for alternatives. Constant strong cravings for chocolate, alcohol, sugar, tobacco, etc., may already indicate a reduced secretion of these brain drugs. When someone begins to have the feeling that he desperately "needs" a coke, a coffee, or a drink, he is already addicted and has interfered with the production of the body's own pleasure drugs. Further interference may even urge him to look for much stronger *morphine*-type or *morphine*-producing substances which promise to give him the relief or pleasure that his body is no longer able to supply.

The regular use of antibiotics and other medical drugs by young people is certainly not the only cause of interfering with the production of the body's own pleasure drugs. Addiction to narcotic drugs is a complex problem that involves unresolved personal conflicts, family issues, social discrimination, and certain amount of karmic discrepancies which all interfere with happiness in life. Narcotic drugs are certainly not the main culprits that make the young people addicted. Their inner lack of happiness and pleasure hormone production makes them already "addicted" long before they get tempted to go on a "trip." Only dissatisfied and unhappy people, regardless of age, background, or social status feel the urge for external substitutes of happiness. They all belong to the risk group of substance addicts.

Regular courses of antibiotics given to babies and children may not only impair many of the vital functions in their body, including digestion and immunity, but also deprive them of the sense of internal happiness and satisfaction in life, and what's even worse, rob them of the basic right of development. A nine-month survey by the Development Delay Registry of 800 families in the US found that children who had taken more than 20 courses of antibiotics between the ages of one and 12 years were 50 percent more likely to suffer from development problems, from autism to speech difficulties. Most of the affected children had been developing normally before they were put on antibiotics.

During a medical conference, doctors reported observing children between the ages one and two regressing, losing their speech and developing signs of withdrawal and behavioural problems after being administered antibiotics. Children who have taken antibiotics often show signs of restlessness, anxiety, boredom, irritability, and outbursts of anger. Antibiotics may therefore indirectly contribute to substance abuse, whether it is tobacco, coffee, alcohol, or non-prescribed drugs.

Nature Knows Best
Nature has a cure for every ill. This feature is a built-in necessity to sustain life on the planet. If nature were not able to cure itself from disease, life on Earth would have vanished millions of years ago. All the forms of vegetation, including the trees, flowers, fruits and vegetables, as well as all the animals and insects down to the smallest amoeba and bacteria, are equipped with highly sophisticated defence mechanisms to maintain their own and the planet's existence.

Man's immune system is the most sophisticated among all species and can develop immunity to any invading organism. Our healing system, however, depends for its power on our thoughts, feeling, emotions, the food we eat, the kind of air we inhale, the water we drink, the environment we are in, and the things we choose to do, see, and hear. If all or most of these various influences make us feel good, our immune system remains efficient. Even one lingering depressing thought or fearful emotion is sufficient to suppress the immune system, which may make our body susceptible to invading microorganisms. Recent research found that *toxic* personalities have a much higher risk of becoming ill than *positive* personalities do.

To understand how such simple things as negative thoughts, emotions, or physical experiences can quickly disrupt the energy distribution to the body's muscles, organs, and immune system, apply the muscle test described in chapter 1. It will help you become more selective in what you think, do, see, hear, and eat. To support your immune system in its fight against disease or infections you can use natural remedies known in the traditional forms of medicine.

Ayurvedic Medicine, Chinese Medicine, and Homeopathy, for example, can offer excellent remedies for almost every ill. They do not interfere with the mechanism of healing in the body, as is the case with drugs. Instead, their cleansing procedures and immune-stimulating medicines make it easier for the body to rid itself of toxins or fight microbial infection. A major *side benefit* of these natural methods and substances is that they are much more likely to trigger a good placebo response in the body than drugs do.

If you suffer from an infection or any other illness, there is no reason to panic! Your attitude to the disease is the most powerful tool you have to overcome the problem. Fear interferes with your body's healing response. If you ask a friend to test your arm muscle while experiencing this fear you will find that your energy flow to your muscles is extremely low. Instead of succumbing to this weakening influence decide to take positive steps to support the body in its healing efforts. Trust that there cannot be a better doctor in the world than your own body because it is equipped with the best pharmacy that could ever exist. It is best to use natural cleansing remedies (that pass the Kinesiology muscle test) before considering taking antibiotics or other drugs. The latter are useful and necessary *only* in life threatening situations. And if they are taken, it is good to counterbalance the harmful side effects through a programme of cleansing.

For example, coffee enemas, and preferably the Liver Cleanse can help the liver to rid itself from accumulated antibiotic residues and a lot of other toxins as well. Both *chaparral tea* and *lapacho tea* can cleanse the liver and the blood from such remnants, too. A kidney cleanse ensures that the toxins which your body releases are actually removed and don't get stuck in the organs of elimination, such as the kidneys, the bladder, or the skin. The Ayurvedic hot water treatment (drinking ionised water) cleanses the tissues. Early bedtimes improve digestion and immune functions. In addition, a nourishing diet according to your body-type makes assimilation of food easier and more effective. Exercise serves as a means to bring more oxygen into your cells and helps with the removal of toxic waste from the body. Also don't underestimate the healing powers of sunlight. If properly used, sunlight alone can eliminate many of our ills. And drinking large amounts of fresh water ensures that the body remains hydrated and detoxification can take place smoothly and efficiently.

2. Business with Our Blood

Are Blood Transfusions Really Necessary?

Most of us grew up with the distinct impression that donating blood is a highly humanitarian act and helps to save many people's lives. Blood transfusions, however, which are part of the medical emergency procedure to rescue a patient who has suffered a life-threatening trauma with loss of blood or awaits major surgery, may not be as safe or necessary as commonly believed. An increasing number of medical experts regard blood transfusion to be an outmoded, unproved, and even dangerous procedure. Yet it is still routinely used as the main method of medical intervention in emergencies – in many cases without any medical justification for its use and no guidelines as to when it should be applied.

There are different parts of the blood that are used for the medical procedures, including blood albumin, plasma, and whole blood or red blood cells. In its 1989 publication entitled "Blood Technologies, Services and Issues," the Office of Technology Assessment Task Force in the U.S. examined the overuse of the various blood products and came to the conclusion that as much as 20-25 per cent of the red blood cells, 90 per cent of the albumin and 95 per cent of the fresh-frozen plasma transfused into patients are unnecessary.

A major Canadian study, which was published in 1998 in the Journal of the American Medical Association, revealed that fewer patients died when they were given a restricted amount of transfused blood. During the trial, 52 per cent fewer transfusions were given to the restrictive group, and transfusion was avoided altogether in one-third of those patients. The death rate in the control group, which received normal, liberal amounts of blood transfusions, was 24 per cent, compared with 18 per cent in the restrictive transfusion group. "The bottom line is less transfusion is better than more transfusion" said Paul Herbert, the trial's principle investigator. This policy could means that one life could be saved for every 17 patients transfused with the restrictive strategy.

The most common trigger for authorising a blood transfusion for hospital patients awaiting surgery is a low *haemoglobin* level (*haemoglobin* in red blood cells is used to transport oxygen to all the other cells in the body). Women naturally have a lower red blood cell count than men but medics use the same trigger levels for both men and women. "Iron deficiency anaemia continues to be among the leading reasons for transfusions, even though it rarely warrants [them]," said the USA Office of Technology report in its concluding statement.

The standard haemoglobin trigger level for justifying a transfusion lies at below ten gram (g) per 100 millilitres (ml) of blood. This figure emerged from a misreading by a haematologist during a study of haemoglobin levels in *dogs*! The results of the study, which showed no established links with human physiology, became the main referential guideline for all anaesthesiology students thereafter.

Dangers in the Blood

It is commonly known that diseases can be transmitted by way of blood transfusions. But apart from receiving viruses through foreign blood, patients may develop even more serious complications as a result of a transfusion. Numerous studies show that blood transfusions given to cancer patients can cause depression of their immune system leading to a high rate of recurrence and secondary cancers.

In a controlled study of patients with larynx cancer, the recurrence rate was 14 per cent among those who did not receive blood transfusions compared to 65 per cent among those who did. More specific research showed that half of a number of patients who suffered from colonic, rectal, cervical and prostrate cancers and received whole blood were reported to have a recurrence compared to a quarter among those who received only red blood cells.

Blood components are routinely irradiated supposedly to avert rejection of the foreign blood by the recipient's immune system. There are no studies to show that this practice is harmless for the blood cells, it is simply *assumed* that it has no negative consequences. But knowing what we know today about the dangers of radiation it can equally be assumed that irradiating blood cells could be hazardous to health, especially if it is given to babies and pregnant mothers.

What makes blood transfusion so risky is that there has never been a randomised, double-blind control study to demonstrate its effectiveness and safety. There is no scientific proof at all that could justify its use. Like an antibiotic drug, blood transfusion may have its place as a measure of last resort measure to save a person's life, but as a standard practice it does not only fail to achieve the desired results but it may be doing more harm than it does good.

A number of studies confirmed that receiving a transfusion during an operation increases the risk of infection fourfold. Considering the high sterility of objects and environment in operation rooms, having a blood transfusion takes a patient practically back to surgical conditions that existed over two hundred years ago, when precautions against infection didn't exist.

Genetic blood research has proven that blood, like our fingerprints, is uniquely individual, implying that it cannot be transferred to another person without risking complications. Each person's blood contains a multiplicity of antibodies, antigens, and infectious agents. Science has yet to identify most of them. This makes transfusions even more risky because the majority of infectious agents contained in blood has not even been identified and can therefore not be targeted with drugs. But even if a blood-borne infection *is* diagnosed, it is a little too late. In the United States there are 230,000 new cases of hepatitis a year that are purely the result of blood transfusions. Just as is the case with the AIDS test, the screening of blood for the hepatitis C virus, for example, has turned out to be an equally futile undertaking. Most of the newly developed tests, including Riba-2 and Murex ELISA, proved wrong three-quarters of the time.

Furthermore, a blood transfusion increases a patient's risk of acquiring human T-cell leukaemia by tenfold when compared with contracting HIV through blood. It may also trigger unforeseeable, life-threatening allergic reactions. In patients undergoing major abdominal surgery, blood transfusion is the most dominating contributing factor to organ system failure. It is more and more obvious that there is neither a safe blood transfusion nor "pure" or "safe" foreign blood.

The Alternatives

There is clear evidence that a person's red blood cell count is not as important as his total circulating volume of fluid. With a high volume your body can speed up the flow of even a low red blood cell count. It is much more problematic if a patient loses a large amount of fluid from the circulatory system, which would coerce the heart to make an enormous effort to send those red blood cells around all the vital organs. All alternative techniques to blood transfusion are based on first stopping the bleeding and second replacing the lost amount of circulating fluids. This can be achieved in a number of ways.

Autotransfusion is a very safe method to supply patients who have undergone major surgery, including coronary bypasses, congenital heart surgery, or surgical removal of cancer with their own blood donated ahead of time.

Haemodilution is a technique that maintains the amount of fluid circulating around the body through artificial volume expanders that could be either *colloids* (starches or gelatine) or *crystalloids* (sugar or saline solutions). A major study of over 10,000 surgery patients showed that adults can undergo rapid loss of 1,000 - 2,000 ml blood (about a third of their total volume) and will not go into irreversible shock if adequate haemodilution is maintained. Many other studies also demonstrate that adult patients can tolerate seven to ten times lower levels of *haemoglobin* during surgery than is normal and still survive. A very large study of 6,000 open heart surgery patients confirmed that by disregarding blood transfusions altogether and using only volume expanders, patients had improved outcomes, and had to pay less. In addition they had eliminated the risk contracting diseases from other people's blood.

There are also other methods in use to help lowering a patient's temperature and blood pressure to conserve blood loss and excessive bleeding as well as drugs that can increase red blood cell production. All of them have very little or no side effects. Whenever doctors have to conduct surgery on members of the Jehovah's Witnesses, they have no other choice but to use the blood-free procedures (with higher success rates than those obtained by ordinary transfusion). The success has motivated the doctors and some of their colleagues to adopt the procedures for all their patients.

Your Blood is Your Life

Blood carries much more importance than just being a vehicle for the distribution of nutrients and oxygen. Our blood is the most precious thing we have in the body. It carries all our thoughts, emotions, and memories and makes them available to every part of the body. Blood is the creator of life in our body and is different in every person. Each of us has a unique design of blood type, which is co-responsible for the uniqueness of our physical structure and personality. The categorisation of blood into a few groups ignores this fundamental uniqueness of every human being.

There is only one type of blood for one person in the world. Blood carries decoded DNA, which knows what nutrients need to be sent where. It knows of and responds to all our needs, discrepancies, strengths, and weaknesses. The blood is filled with patterns and geometric designs that reorganise themselves according to our state of consciousness. Every new desire, feeling, or intention reprograms the blood instantly and all the parts of the body it is in contact with. When you take on another person's blood you also take on his genetic information and part of his personality. The immune system can easily get depressed when foreign DNA (or several kinds of DNA if the blood comes from various donors) suddenly and unexpectedly enters a person's blood through a transfusion. In many cases, the immune system is not able to fight off the many viral particles and toxins that are present in the donor's blood.

The quality of our blood changes according to our thoughts, feelings, and emotions. Negative thoughts create toxic blood whereas happy thoughts make healthy blood. Fearful thoughts, for example fill your blood with *adrenaline*, loving thoughts flood it with *interleukins*. Both literally move your heart but with contrary effects. The *adrenaline*-shot causes panic to the heart, the *interleukin*-shot creates emotions of happiness in the heart and protects you against cancer.

Having a blood transfusion may create confusion and chaos within the body and mind. On the other hand, refusing a blood transfusion and not resorting to alternatives may put your life in danger. If you need a blood transfusion but prefer an alternative method contact the Blood Transfusion Society in your country. They may be able to put you in touch with a practitioner who is experienced in any of the above transfusion procedures. If you pretend to be a Jehovah's Witness the hospital will arrange for an alternative approach.

3. Risks of Ultrasound Scans

By the mid-eighties more than 100 million people throughout the world had ultrasound scans before they were born. Today, practically every pregnant woman in Europe and in North America will have at least one ultrasound scan during her pregnancy. Most expecting women receive their first prescription for a scan during their first ante-natal appointment; only few of them question whether it is necessary and even less know of its potential harm. Most women's magazines, newspapers, and pregnancy books tend to recommend ultrasound scans to ensure safety and healthy development of the foetus despite the fact that there is no study that proves that ultrasound scans have any more benefits than not having them. In an official statement the American College of Obstetrics and Gynecology (ACOG) admitted that *no well controlled study has yet proved that routine scanning of prenatal patients will improve the outcome of pregnancy.*

On the other hand, in New York researchers studied 15,000 pregnant women and concluded that scanning provided no benefits whatsoever in any of the categories such as premature babies, foetal death, multiple births, late-term-pregnancies, etc. In fact, up to this date ultrasound scans have not revealed any information that is of any clinical value. On the contrary, there is more evidence today than ever before that scans can be harmful for both the mother and the unborn child. There are cases of women recorded by the Association for Improvements in the Maternity Services (AIMS), England, who aborted their perfectly fit and healthy babies as a result of misinterpreted scans. It is almost impossible to estimate how many women went through similar ordeals since most of them are not reported.

In 1990 researchers conducted a large trial study with ultrasound in Finland; 250 women were diagnosed as having *praevia placenta* in early pregnancy, a condition where the placenta lies low which could prevent the baby being born vaginally. The mothers were informed that they should expect a *Caesarean* section. But when it came to giving birth, only four women had *praevia placenta*. In almost all cases the placenta moved out of the way when the womb began to grow. Ironically, the control group, which received no ultrasound scanning, also had four women with *praevia placenta*; all of them delivered their babies safely.

Human Guinea-pigs

Millions of women around the world, without being aware of the potential health hazards of ultrasounds, are participating in the largest medical experiment of all times. Their babies are the guinea pigs in this experiment. They become vulnerable to external and internal harmful influences when their delicate Electromagnetic fields are distorted, misaligned or damaged by highly concentrated doses of ultrasound; exposure to that is neither natural nor suitable for any human being. We cannot solely rely on machines for diagnostic purposes just because machines are considered less likely to make mistakes than a doctor is. All findings have to be interpreted properly before they can serve as a guide for treatment. As demonstrated in the above study, 98,4% of the initial complications during the women's pregnancy cleared on their own simply because the body knows how to handle such problems perfectly well without intervention. Machines don't know that the readings they produce may actually turn out to be a wrong diagnosis.

A false diagnosis is not the only disadvantage that may arise from using ultrasound indiscriminately. In 1993 Australian researchers studied 3,000 women and found that frequent ultrasound scanning between 18 and 38 weeks of pregnancy could produce babies up to a third smaller than normal. Similar studies revealed that babies who had received *Doppler* ultrasound (to scan the baby's blood supply) had a lower birth weight than babies that didn't receive a scan.

If the birth weight of a baby is reduced through ultrasound what about other functions which are even more important for a baby's growth? One professor in Calgary, Canada, discovered that children developed speech problems twice as often when exposed to ultrasound in the womb. Surgeon James Campbell from Canada found that even one prenatal scan may be sufficient to cause delayed speech. Norwegian studies suggested ultrasound scanning might even lead to mild brain damage in the developing foetus.

Ultrasound was approved as a medical tool of diagnosis that falls under a different category than the ones used to approve drugs. Science has not yet studied the effects of using these different powers of energy. As long as this is the case ultrasound examinations are under the umbrella of "legal protection." The complete lack of scientific research backing up the safety of ultrasound scans should caution both doctors and pregnant women.

Yet the scanning of pregnant woman has become so much of a routine practice and practicality today that not many women want to go without it. Scans give parents the opportunity to get to know their baby long before it is born, although women were able to be in touch with their babies before the invention of ultrasound. Today you can find out whether your baby is male or female, which leaves no room for surprises. You can also get the exact date of delivery. But provided there are no complications you can calculate the birth date of your child yourself. An ultrasound scan may reveal if a baby suffers from Down's syndrome but it doesn't tell you how serious the condition is. The added information that ultrasound can give you makes little or no difference because babies in general cannot be treated before or shortly after birth. After examining all the results from published trials using ultrasound scans, a team of doctors from Switzerland failed to come up with evidence suggesting that the use of ultrasound could improve the condition of the babies.

Furthermore, a large trial study in the United States concluded that there was no difference in prenatal mortality rates or in sick babies among groups with or without ultrasound. What is most disconcerting, however, is the latest ultrasound technology to be introduced into use, without trials. It consists of a vaginal probe that is covered by a condom and inserted directly into the woman's vagina. With the new technology, doctors will get an even better picture of the foetus but the baby will also get a much higher dose of ultrasound.

Even though there is an increasing number of health professionals who are very concerned about the wholesale use of scans, pregnant women are not informed about the possible harmful consequences that accompany their use. Scans are prescribed routinely but you have the right to refuse one. An Ultrasound scan should only be considered if a woman suffers localised pain or complications for which a doctor or midwife cannot find a plausible reason. Such cases though are rare. As for now, Ultrasound has been repeatedly shown to make no difference whatsoever to the outcome of a normal pregnancy.

4. Immunisation Programmes under Scrutiny

Poisonous Vaccines against Harmless Infections

For many decades leading scientists and doctors have vehemently promoted the idea that immunisation of children is necessary to protect them from contracting such diseases as diphtheria, polio, cholera, typhoid, or malaria. Yet there is mounting evidence that immunisation may not only be unnecessary but even harmful. Can we expect our rivers and oceans to remain healthy by dumping toxic waste into them? Pouring deadly chemicals into a lake doesn't make it immune to pollutants. Likewise, by injecting live poisons contained in vaccines into the bloodstream of children the future generations hardly stand a chance to lead truly healthy lives. American children can receive some 30 vaccinations within the first 6 years of their life and children in the UK can expect to be vaccinated about 25 times. Most of the vaccinations, which include a total of up to nine or more different antigens, are pumped into the immature immune systems of babies within the first 15 months of life.

Despite the colossal efforts and large sums of money spent on vaccine research, medicine has never been able to devise a cholera vaccine that works and the drugs for malaria aren't as effective as a single herb. Diphtheria is still combated with toxic immunisation programmes even though it has almost completely disappeared from the surface of the earth. When diphtheria broke out in Chicago in 1969, 11 of the 16 victims were either already immune or had been *immunised* against diphtheria. In another report, 14 out of 23 victims were completely immune. This shows that vaccination makes no difference when it comes to protection against diphtheria, on the contrary, it can even *increase* the chance of being infected.

Immunisation against mumps is also highly dubious. Even though it initially reduces the likelihood of becoming infected, the risk for mumps infection increases after immunity subsides. In 1995 a study conducted by UK's Public Health Laboratory Service and published in the *Lancet* showed that children given the measles/mumps/rubella jab were *three times* more likely to suffer from convulsions than those children who didn't receive it. The study also found that the MMR vaccine increased the number of children suffering a rare blood disorder by five times.

It is interesting to note that the mortality rate from measles declined by 95 per cent before the measles vaccine was introduced. In the United Kingdom, despite widespread vaccination among toddlers, cases of measles recently increased by nearly 25 per cent. The United States has been suffering from a steadily increasing epidemic of measles, although (or because) the measles vaccine has been in effect since 1957. After a few sudden drops and rises, the cases of measles are now suddenly dropping again. The Center of Disease Control (CDC) acknowledged that this could be related to an overall decrease in the occurrence of measles in the Western Hemisphere.

Besides all that, there are many studies that show the measles vaccine isn't effective. For example, as reported by the *New England Journal of Medicine* in 1987, in a 1986 outbreak of measles in Corpus Christi, Texas, 99 per cent of the victims had been vaccinated. In 1987, 60 per cent of the cases of measles occurred in children who had been properly vaccinated at the appropriate age. One year later, this figure rose to 80 per cent.

Apart from not protecting against measles and possibly even increasing the risk of contracting the disease, the MMR vaccine has been proved to produce numerous adverse effects. Among them are encephalitis, brain complications, convulsions, retardation of mental and physical growth, high fever, pneumonia, meningitis, aseptic meningitis, mumps, atypical measles, blood disorders such as thrombocytopenia, fatal shock, arthritis, SSPE, one-sided paralysis, and death. According to a study published in the *Lancet* in 1985, if children develop "mild measles" as a result of receiving the vaccine the accompanying *underdeveloped* rash may be responsible for causing degenerative diseases such as cancer later in life.

In reality, measles is not a dangerous childhood illness at all. The belief that measles can lead to blindness is a myth that finds it roots in an increased sensitivity to light during illness. The problem subsides when the room is dimmed and vanishes completely with recovery. Measles was for a long time believed to increase the risk of a brain infection (encephalitis) which is known to occur only among children who live in poverty and suffer from malnutrition. Among upper class children there is only 1 out of 100,000 who can become infected. Besides, less than half of children given a measles booster are protected against the disease.

In a report issued by German health authorities and published in 1989 in the *Lancet*, the mumps vaccine was revealed to have caused 27 neurological reactions, including meningitis, febrile convulsions, encephalitis, and epilepsy. A Yugoslavian study linked 1 per 1,000 cases of mumps encephalitis directly to the vaccine. The *Pediatric Infectious Disease Journal* in the US reported in 1989 that the rate varies from 1 in 405 to 1 in 7,000 shots.

Although mumps is mostly a mild illness and the vaccine's side effects are so severe, it is still included in the MMR vaccine. And so is the vaccine for rubella, although it is known to cause arthritis in up to 3 per cent of children and in up to 20 per cent of adult women who take it. In 1994 the Department of Health admitted to doctors that 11 per cent of first-time recipients of the rubella vaccine will get arthritis. Symptoms range from mild aches to severe crippling. Other studies show a 30 per cent chance of developing arthritis in direct response to the rubella vaccine.

Research confirms that the whooping cough vaccine is only effective in 36 per cent of children. A report by Professor Gordon Stewart, which was published in 1994 in *World Medicine*, demonstrated that the risks of the whooping cough vaccine outweighed the benefits. The whooping cough or pertussis vaccine is by far the most dangerous of all the vaccines. DTP, the whooping cough vaccine that was used in the US until 1992, contained the carcinogen formaldehyde, and the highly toxic metals aluminium and mercury. Both this vaccine and its "improved" version DTaP have never been tested for safety, only for efficacy.

The new vaccine has proved to be no better than the old one. Both versions cause death, near-death, seizures, development delay, and hospitalisation. DTaP is given to babies as young as six weeks old, although the vaccine has never been tested on this age group. Among 17 different health problems, the whooping cough vaccine is known to cause sudden infant death syndrome (SIDS). According to an estimate from the University of California at Los Angeles, there are 1,000 infants a year in the US who die as a direct result of receiving the vaccine.

Immunisation programmes against polio have no other than economic benefits for vaccine producers. The scientist who eliminated polio is now suspecting that the handful of polio cases, which have occurred in the USA since the seventies, are caused by the live viruses that were used as vaccines. In Finland and Sweden, where the use of live vaccines for polio is prohibited, there has not been a single case of polio in ten years. If life viruses used as a vaccine for polio can cause polio today when hygiene is generally high, it may well be that the polio epidemics 40 to 50 years ago were also caused by immunisation against polio while hygiene, sanitation, housing, and nutritional standards were still very low. In the United States, cases of polio increased by 50 per cent between 1957, and by 80 per cent from 1958 to 1959 *after* the introduction so mass immunisation. In some five states, cases of polio doubled after the polio vaccine was given to large numbers of the population. As soon as hygiene and sanitation improved, *despite* the immunisation programmes the viral disease quickly disappeared. Whatever may have been the reason for polio outbreaks in the past (see section on natural immunisation), it is highly questionable today to immunise an entire population against a disease that does not even exist anymore. It raises major questions about the motives behind polio vaccination.

The much-acclaimed benefits of the latest vaccine against Hib meningitis also seem to be unfounded. In a pro-vaccine study published in 1993 in the Journal of the American Medical Association, the children in the control group, which didn't receive the vaccine, also experienced a drastic reduction in the cases of Hib infection – from 99,3 to 68,5 per 100,000.

The latest problem arising from the use of vaccines is that they can cause the body to develop viral 'mutants' and even spread the newly created disease in the population at large. Since viral mutants are rarely detected in blood donor screening they can easily be transmitted through donated blood. This way, the original vaccines may be able to wipe out the strains of virus that are known to cause these various diseases but in the same stroke they cause other mutant strains of virus to thrive.

Research also showed that a single injection of any kind could increase the risk of paralysis fivefold. Polio for example is more common in developing countries where children receive more injections than in developed countries. A study published in 1995 by the New England Journal of Medicine showed that injection of the polio vaccine actually caused outbreaks of the disease.

A 1993 report, released by the American National Academy of Science Institute of Medicine, concluded that virtually all nine vaccines given to children have at some time been proved to cause damage, including such complications as shock, convulsions, or paralysis. The problem is that a child's body doesn't just have to cope with one type of poison contained in one vaccine, but with several different ones contained in as many as 9 vaccines, and that not only once. Many children have died or became permanently and severely brain damaged within days after immunisation. In many cases, however, the adverse effects from vaccination are less devastating but still serious enough to take a good look at the reasons why parents have been told or, as is the case in many countries, are forced by law to immunise their children.

Is the Need for Immunisation Based on Statistical Errors?

The idea to vaccinate our bodies in order to protect them against possible infectious diseases came from the famous Louis Pasteur (1822-1895) who was considered to be the pioneer of immunisation. In 1993 historian Gerald L. Geison handed over to the public all the 100 private diaries of Pasteur. His *diary entries* contained especially negative results of experiments with vaccines whereas the *publicised data* had been made to look revolutionary. The published results of his most spectacular immunisation experiments turned out to be a complete fraud. The authenticity of his research was never questioned until official statistical research revealed that immunisation programmes directly led to dramatic increases of those diseases they were supposed to eradicate.

Analysis of the official statistics from several countries and their historical development of smallpox, diphtheria, cholera, typhoid, poliomyelitis, tuberculosis, bronchitis, tetanus, etc. revealed astounding findings. For example, diphtheria in France increased to an all-time high with the onset of compulsory immunisation and immediately dropped again after the vaccine was withdrawn. The situation was not much different in Germany when compulsory immunisation for diphtheria was introduced on a mass scale from 1925 to 1944. During this period the number of diphtheria victims increased from 40,000 to 240,000, with the incidence of infection being higher in immunised patients. In 1945 at the end of World War II vaccines were no longer available in Germany and within a few years the number of diseased dropped to below 50,000.

Statistical data shows that most of these diseases were in rapid and continuous decline well before the introduction of immunisation programmes. The big epidemics began occurring when people from the rural areas moved into the big cities. The streets were used as garbage dumps, contaminating air and water and becoming the source of infectious diseases. Only major cleanup of the congested cities and improved sanitation, hygiene, and housing were able to halt the epidemics and lead to drastic improvements in individual and collective health. Vaccination programmes had nothing to do with it.

How to Acquire Natural Immunisation

It seems that we humans tend to go from one extreme to the other. Now, the natural balance between immunity and viral presence is once again upset. But this time the cause may be "exaggerated hygiene" which can inhibit the natural development of immunity to disease-causing agents. The causative agent of poliomyelitis, for instance, is very common among the natural populations in the world; yet to them the virus is completely harmless. They immunise themselves by staying in close contact with the soil, nature, and also dirt. They rarely wash their hands before taking a meal and whatever else gets into their mouth with the food helps to build their natural resistance to harmful micro-organisms.

In the Western Hemisphere, poliomyelitis became a frightening disease only at the beginning of this century, with the onset of the high standard of hygienic living conditions. On the other hand, these measures were necessary in the densely populated areas of big cities where there was little ventilation of air and inadequate sanitation.

Indigenous populations didn't have such needs. If need be, they boosted their immune systems by injuring each other during rituals or by scarring their skin. They allowed their wounds to suppurate, which from what we know today is a very efficient way to strengthen one's immunity. For them, blood letting was a necessary act of survival during times of continuous meat consumption when other types of food were not available; this helped them to keep their blood thin and reduce their body's protein stores, which otherwise could have led to life-endangering diseases (see also chapter 8 on heart disease).

Very often children "accidentally" injure themselves or even eat dirt because their immune systems are run down and need a major boost to cope with more serious issues of defence. So when you intentionally cut yourself, try to see it from a holistic perspective. You may have excessive protein in your blood or blood vessels and the bleeding may just be the thing to cause thinning of the blood and to prevent heart problems. This self-regulating mechanism is very powerful and keeps you healthier than any immunisation programme or mega doses of vitamin and mineral supplements. This unspecified form of immunisation may be necessary from time to time in order to maintain a strong and healthy intestinal flora (two thirds of our immune system are located in the intestinal tract). To remain healthy and immune we *need* the daily fight with the bacteria and viruses.

A recent study conducted at the Institute of Child Health at Bristol University, UK, observed every aspect of 14,000 children's lives over a period of 7 years and found that too much hygiene could be damaging children's health, weakening their immune systems and making them prone to illnesses such as asthma. A few decades ago such diseases as asthma, eczema, and hayfever were almost unheard of. Today, as many as one third of the population suffer from allergies. Scientists now say that our obsession with the latest anti-germ potions and over-reliance on soap and water may explain why the Western world has been hit by a spate of viruses, immune-related diseases, and allergies.

The principle "what we don't use becomes useless" also applies to our immune system; it needs the regular exposure and adaptation to everyday bugs and germs in order to exercise its ability to recognise what's truly harmful. Rigorous hygiene drastically reduces the number of bacteria and other infectious agents that a developing immune system needs to meet to become stronger and more efficient. Allergies occur when the immune system mistakes for harmful invaders those harmless particles (house dust, pollen, etc.) it has rarely been exposed to before. To fight them off, the body covers them with poison, which in turn results in inflammation, itching, swelling, and such symptoms as a runny nose. The Bristol study found, for example, that those children who washed their face and hands three or four times a day and bathed once a day suffered a significantly higher incidence of asthma than did the children who used soap and water much less frequently.

Children from larger families are also less likely to suffer from asthma or hayfever. With many children living under one roof, minor infections are constantly brought into the household, which means that the immune system is kept busy and alert almost all the time. If an infection occurs as a result of the body's natural reaction to invading bacteria, the immune system produces 'fighter cells' called antibodies. But if this normal response, that is, an infection, is undermined or prevented by artificial disinfectants or antibiotics, antibodies are no longer made and the immune system is weakened and begins to malfunction. By contrast, letting the infection take its full course strengthens the immune system, making it much more resilient to disease-causing germs afterwards.

Exaggerated cleanliness and fear of infection usually go hand in hand. Many people who fail to employ the natural ways of strengthening the immune system are paranoid about becoming infected; for them, also antibiotics and vaccines remain ineffective.

Vaccination -- Attack on Body, Brain and Spirit

Vaccines are composed of protein, bacterial and viral material, as well as preservatives, neutralisers, and carrying agents. The vaccine against bacterial meningitis is made from the brains and heart of cows among other highly toxic components. Alarmed by the outbreak of *mad cows disease*, the Italian authorities have ordered the seizure of the vaccine in January 1997 for fear it could cause the human version of the disease. By injecting such cocktails of foreign and destructive substances directly into the blood stream, the human body stands little or no chance of neutralising the poisons.

Under normal circumstances, all ingested foods, drinks, etc. have to pass through the mucous membranes, the intestinal walls, or the liver before they are permitted into such important areas as the blood, the heart, or the brain. The sudden appearance of the poison in the blood stream is often (depending on whether a young person's immune system has matured enough) met by a counterattack of the immune system which uses an entire arsenal of antibodies to prevent death from poisoning (allergic reaction). This allergic response can lead to a sudden, sometimes fatal, collapse known as anaphylactic shock response. Amongst the causes of anaphylactic shock are immunisations for diphtheria, tetanus, hepatitis B, and whooping cough.

Not less dangerous is the Guillain-Barre {*note for the editor: please put an ' over the e*} syndrome which leads to paralysis and is caused by immunisations for measles, diphtheria, influenza, tetanus, and the oral polio vaccine. This is hardly surprising when one considers the high toxicity of the vaccines. It is well known that children, whose immune systems are already weak, experience more serious complications than those do whose constitution and immune system are much stronger. Still, inoculations are being given indiscriminately regardless of the children's health status. Many children at infancy are never even given a chance to become healthy later in life because they are regularly pumped full with these poisons. At this stage of development a child has not yet acquired full natural immunity and has little chance to defend itself against the assault.

There is also increasing evidence that chronic diseases, such as rheumatoid arthritis, encephalitis, multiple sclerosis, leukaemia, other forms of cancer and even AIDS diseases, are linked to vaccinations administered in the early stages of life. Rheumatoid arthritis is an inflammatory disease of the joints, which has been thought to afflict only the elderly. More recently though, the crippling disease has spread among the young generation and measles and rubella inoculations have been identified as the cause.

Researchers from the American Food and Drug Administration discovered that vaccinations, particularly the hepatitis B shot, could cause hair loss. They estimate that 50,000 Americans suffer hair loss (alopecia) after immunisation every year. The report was published by the Journal of the American Medical Association in 1997.

It is nearly impossible to estimate the damage and suffering that has been created and is going to occur in the future as a result of inadequate information about the dangers of modern immunisation programmes. Parents want to do what is best for their children and they carry a heavy burden of responsibility to keep them healthy and safe. Misinformation can create a strong conflict in parents because they don't want to neglect their children's health or cause them any harm.

Statistical research on medical history in the United States covering the years between 1940 and 1970 showed that autistic children were most common among wealthy families. After the year 1970 autism was equally distributed amongst all income groups. At the end of the sixties certain immunisation programmes that until then were affordable only by the well-off parts of society, were extended to the poor as well. The same trends were observed in other industrialised nations. Although this is only a statistical correlation, there may be a possible link.

Clearly caused by vaccinations, however, are small-scale brain damage, growth inhibition, hyperactivity, learning difficulties, etc. Previously belittled as simple problems of growing up, medical researchers now recognise them as forms of encephalitis (inflammatory disease of the brain). More than 20% of the American children -- one out of five -- suffer from these or related problems.

The documented evidence against the value of immunisation is so comprehensive that in 1986 the American Congress passed federal legislation to compensate children for damages arising from vaccination. According to the law, the government is no longer liable for damages, but instead doctors and vaccine producers have to pay millions of dollars for compensation. In the interest of everyone involved it would be useful to re-examine and re-evaluate the basic theory of Louis Pasteur that immunisation is useful or necessary. Could nature have made such a crucial mistake to make us depended on injecting foreign, toxic material into our blood when we have an immune system so complex and highly developed that millions of sophisticated computers could not imitate its performance? This is rather unlikely.

How To Stay Naturally Immune

The damage that has been caused so far is considerable and surpasses many times the problems that could possibly arise from having no immunisation programme whatsoever. There are many natural ways to acquire immunity. All the procedures and natural remedies described in this book can assist you and your family to maintain natural immunity against disease throughout life. "The best vaccine against common infectious diseases," according to the World Health Organisation, is "an adequate diet." Unprocessed, unrefined foods, including plenty of fresh fruits and vegetables, help a child to build up natural immunity and the adult to maintain it.

The most powerful and all-protective immunisation programme a newborn baby can receive is breastfeeding. This way, the infant gets all the necessary antibodies to build up a sound system of immunity to effectively deal with any type of infectious agent in the future. Should an illness arise nevertheless, the body will deal with it rapidly and without suffering harm, in fact it can greatly benefit from it.

The normal inflammatory response to an infectious disorder such as a rash, a fever, or a cough demonstrates that the body's defensive abilities to remove the accumulated toxins and infectious agent from the system are active and intact. The encounter will naturally and profoundly stimulate the immune system, so that when the child or adult recovers from the illness he is equipped with enough immunity to respond to other forms of infection without delay or falling ill again.

For a healthy immune system to mature fully and properly in our less than perfect environment, it is necessary for a child once in a while to contract an infectious disease such as the measles, chickenpox, and mumps. We all have to learn to trust nature and our body more than man-made theories and practices. The human DNA managed to survive millions of years on the planet and it certainly knows how to deal with a few harmless infectious diseases, particularly when they help to make our immune system stronger than before.

Natural Methods of Nursing

If your child is diagnosed as having chickenpox, mumps, or measles, it may indicate that it requires an immunity boost. Most children who have gone through these common childhood illnesses have greatly benefited from them; they are stronger afterwards and even have a growth spur, either physically or emotionally, or both. Most natural health practitioners see the normal childhood illness as a good opportunity to develop immunity. By nursing a child with natural methods, you can help him to become healthier and more resistant to disease in the long run.

When children become ill with any of these illnesses, the main advice is to encourage their own healing powers. This is first accomplished by letting them get as much rest as possible. Take them out of school, the nursery, etc., and nurse them at home. Drugs such as liquid paracetamol only suppress the body's healing response and lead to many more "unrelated" physical and emotional problems in the future.

For a child, the period of illness is often a way to receive more caring attention from his parents than normal. He may get many extra cuddles, meals in bed, stories at bedtime, etc. Of course, there may be parents who feel that their child's illness is very inconvenient and they let them feel their frustration by being harsh and abrupt with them. Sick children need and deserve special treatment and reassurance, especially when they are frightened or anxious.

A sick child should not be excited or stimulated by exposing it to too much radio, television, or even visitors. Quiet activities such as reading to them, drawing, and board games help them to avoid dwelling on their illness too much. Make sure that they get extra sleep with early nights. Encourage daytime naps if they feel tired.

Sick children need to drink plenty of liquid to help remove toxins from the system. Warm water is the best drink for them and should be the first option; herb teas and freshly pressed, diluted fruit juices (except citrus fruit juices if your child has mumps) can be taken additionally. Avoid giving your child anything cold, such as cold drinks, ice creams, sugar, or sugar containing foods; milk, yoghurt or other dairy products; meat, chicken, fish or any other form of protein food. As the child's digestive power is impaired during the illness, such foods will only putrefy and acidify the digestive system and further irritate the mucous lining. Sick children, like sick animals, generally do not want or need food. Fasting, with taking only water, is the best way to encourage the body's healing response. When your child feels hungry, give him freshly cooked vegetable purees, soups, hot cereals like porridge with a little maple syrup, or with good quality honey (which should only be added after the food has cooled down to less than 45 degrees).

Children need to know what is happening to them during an illness and that it is going to pass soon. They also want reassurance that you are going to be there for them all the way. If you child develops a fever, it is a sign of a healthy immune response. A raised temperature shows that the body has taken active charge of the situation and is fighting off an infection. A child that has a high temperature may look and feel ill, but the fever only shows that the immune system is dealing with the illness fast and effectively. Parents should remember that a high temperature does not necessarily mean that their child is very ill. As has been discovered recently, even a temperature of 41 degrees Celsius and slightly above is still not considered dangerous.

In 1983, when I lay ill with malaria in India, I refused to take fever-reducing tablets for a temperature of 41,5 degrees Celsius and after the fever broke at the end of the third attack, I recovered very quickly and had no relapse or weakness ever since. The only important thing to remember is that children and babies aged less than six months, who are afflicted with fever, need to drink plenty of water, as they tend to dehydrate quickly. Sponging them down with tepid water helps to keep the body more comfortable during this phase of healing. Expose and sponge one part of the body at a time until it feels cool, then turn to the next one. Sponging the child's face and forehead also brings relieve.

Another basic rule is to keep a chilly, feverish child warm and covered. This will make him sweat, particularly at night, and help to break the fever, which indicates that the body's "fight" is nearly over. Hot, feverish children should be kept cool and occasionally be immersed in a bath of tepid water. If your child has accompanying symptoms such as itchy rashes, painful swollen glands, and a cough or sore, sticky eyes, he is most likely to recover without any complications. In case he has any unusual symptoms, you may consult a natural practitioner of Ayurveda, Homeopathy, Chinese Medicine, etc., for home treatment remedies. It is better not to give *aspirin* to children during or after an illness as this can interfere with the body's own healing response. If your doctor insists on giving antibiotics to your child when he has one of the above illnesses or symptoms, try to find another doctor to give you a second opinion. In most cases, there is no need for drugs. In one large study published in 1987 in the *British Medical Journal* 18,000 children received a homeopathic remedy against meningitis. None of the children got infected and there was not a single adverse effect from the treatment.

As a general precaution, don't take your child to day-care centres or nursery too early. This can protect him from many childhood diseases. Day-care facilities increase the risk of Hib meningitis, for example, by 24 times. Many of the commercially run centres are frequently "visited" by all sorts of bugs. The safest environment for a child in the first years of his life is his home.

5. Protection against the Flu

The vaccine industry insists that their vaccines against the flu serve as the key to a healthy winter. Although there has not been a serious flu epidemic for 38 years, their vaccines are prescribed to millions of people each year. You may wonder why perfectly healthy people are injected with a normally harmless bug whose strains mutate from year to year? Although flu vaccines can never be accurate, encouraged by their employers, millions of employees submit to a flu jab each year trying to avoid the loss of working days.

Influenza always starts in the Far East, and then spreads to the West in early winter, reaching its peak during February and March. It may come in either of three types, A, B, or C. During the last several years, type A has been the dominating version. What makes vaccination against the flu so unsuccessful is that the strains of the flu virus are different every year and the so-called protection lasts for only six months. So each autumn you require a new vaccination for a different virus. The trouble is, drug companies have no way of knowing in summer which new strain of the flu virus is going to hit the Western Hemisphere during the winter months.

The vaccine producers grow the vaccines, consisting of live viruses, in hen's eggs, which when injected into the body can cause side effects such as redness and soreness at the injection site and a mild form of flu. Very serious complications arise in people who are taking immune-suppressing drugs or who have a heart condition. If you are allergic to eggs, you may also endanger your health.

For the average healthy person, coming down with the flu is not serious at all. On the contrary, it can build up natural immunity even against future encounters with new strains of the flu virus. The very reason why nature creates these new forms of virus every year and spreads them with accurate timing is to ensure continued ecological balance and strong immunity in plants, animals, and humans alike. Anyone, who is prone to repeated infections, is likely to have a toxic liver with many hundreds of stones accumulated in his liver and gallbladder. Gallstones, which harbour many types of infectious bacteria and viruses, are a constant source of immune suppression. Cleansing the liver of all gallstones is about the best preventive against any type of infection. People who have cleansed their liver in this way have reported that they never catch a cold or the flu anymore.

Flu Jabs may Cause Flu and More...

Flu jabs lower natural immunity by injecting alien and toxic substances directly into the blood stream. No other animal in the world takes recourse to such unnatural, superficial and crude means to defend itself against invading viruses. The normal route of contact with a viral particle is via the lungs. The vast majority of the population has a normal, healthy immune system and is perfectly capable of dealing with the invaders without getting sick. But if the body's infection fighters have temporarily gone "on strike" for reasons other than the lack of a vaccine, the flu virus can gain unrestricted access into the body and cause an infection.

Regular vaccination (of any kind) is one of the major causes of depleted immunity. The yearly-administered flu jabs burden the immune system and cells of the body with foreign toxic material without giving them a chance to remove them again. The toxic viral particles can remain latent in the cells and gallstones for as long as 20 years; when they emerge they can cause serious cell damage. With each new vaccination the immune system becomes more and more restricted in its effort to neutralise the live virus that suddenly appears in the blood. It may produce antibodies for the virus (although in many cases the immune system fails to do even that), which is finally subdued, but this encounter leaves the host's immune system unnecessarily tired and weak.

Besides immune damage, vaccines of all kinds produce alterations in genetic material and thereby cause a whole range of malfunctions in the body. Vaccines may even be the cause of the increasing incidence of malignant diseases in children. Mass immunisation programmes have created such weak immune systems that they are even susceptible to such harmless viruses as the one causing the flu. We may have gone as far as to replace mumps and measles with cancer, leukaemia, and ME.

Flu vaccinations are mainly targeted at the older generation. In the United Kingdom about 10,000 people, most of them are of very advanced age, die from flu-related illnesses. It may therefore sound reasonable to vaccinate the older people to protect them against the flu virus. But there is no total protection even among those vaccinated. Around 20 percent of the elderly people who get the vaccine still get bad flu. The same is true for the people in the same age group who haven't been immunised. The weak and elderly people are more likely to be the ones who die, *regardless* whether they have been immunised or not. The bottom line is that there is no real advantage in having a flu jab.

Instead of giving them vaccines, thinking that this will take care of them, we could help them much more by improving their general resistance to disease through good diet and exercise programmes. Many old people don't have adequate nutrition and suffer from depression; both these factors work as powerful immune suppressants. Others don't have a warm home or they live alone. Research has shown that these are the major risk factors for illness and death in the older generation. A series of liver cleanses alone can strengthen natural immunity, improve digestion, retard the ageing process, restore health, and foremost of all, enhance mental functions.

In developing countries, where the elderly play an important role in society, general illness is low, provided there is enough food available. In these countries it is more likely that old people die from malnutrition than they do from a strain of virus.

There is an increasing number of reports that indicate a worsening of high blood pressure, diabetes, gout, and Parkinson's disease as well as an increase in all kinds of allergic complaints in adults who regularly receive flu jabs. In 1976 an extensive flu vaccination programme in America led to a massive outbreak of Guillain-Barre syndrome, a disease affecting the nervous system. The outbreak, known as the "Great Swine Flue Fiasco," paralysed 656 people and 30 elderly persons were found dead within hours after they were vaccinated. Compensation claims were enormous, which helped slowing down the programme, but only for a while.

In the Name of Prevention

The pharmaceutical companies producing the vaccines seem to have a more powerful effect on the population than the scientists have who invented them. As early as 1980, Dr Albert Sabin, one of the world's leading virologists and pioneer of the polio vaccine, spoke vehemently against the use of the flu vaccine, claiming that it was unnecessary for over 90 percent of the population. This, however, has not discouraged the vaccination industry to endorse vaccination for *all* in the name of health and protection against disease.

What makes matters worse is that there has never been a properly controlled clinical trial with the flu vaccine. Because we don't know anything about it's long-term effects, we may be unknowingly producing generations of people with debilitated immune systems and chronic diseases. Flu vaccination is an unproved and unscientific practice and there is nothing in the scientific literature that can certify or guarantee its safety. The most effective way to fight infections, including the flu, is to prevent it. There is no substitute for a health-increasing regimen. Vaccination, on the other hand, offers no real protection. Injecting the body with foreign and poisonous viral material is counterproductive to improving our well being. Dr. John Seal from the American National Institute for Allergies and Infectious Diseases warned that we have to assume that every flu vaccination can cause the Guillain-Barre Syndrome. In this sense, prevention is *not* better than cure.

6. Alcohol - Man's Legal Drug

There is much controversy around alcohol. Some people say that alcohol can liven you up, reduce tension and inhibitions, and bring more fun into your life. Getting drunk is often seen as a means to "escape" the burden of personal and interpersonal problems, at least for a while. Alcohol may make you feel euphoric and relaxed but it also has unwanted side effects. You lose control over your mind, your senses, and your body's co-ordination skills. A hangover demonstrates the powerful toxic effects that alcohol has on the normal functioning of the mind, body, and spirit.

But why do people drink alcoholic beverages? Getting drunk can hardly be considered fun because loss of self-control does not really make a person happy. However, despite the accompanying side effects, many people are drawn repeatedly to having "another drink." And why does alcohol make us get drunk in the first place?

The answer to both these questions may lie in the brain hormone *serotonin*, which is the main chemical equivalent to pleasure and happiness. With the increasing darkness of the night *serotonin* gets broken down into the hormone melatonin. Alcohol, however, slows down this process and thereby maintains a "good mood." However, if *serotonin* is not broken down on time it to react with the toxic substance *acetaldehyde* which the body produces from the ingested alcohol.

The chemical reaction generates an entire group of chemicals that have hallucinating effects; they are known as t*etrahydro-ss-carboline.' Salsolinol,* a substance synthesised in the presence of the brain chemical *dopamine,* blocks the breakdown of *serotonin. Dopamine* then begins to form into a new chemical called *norlaudanosolin,* a precursor of morphine and 2.000 other types of *alkaloids*. In other words, if you think you may are addicted to alcohol you are wrong. In reality you are addicted to morphine.

However, alcohol consumption does not necessarily turn into an addiction. Genetic predisposition makes some people produce more morphine or opiate from *acetaldehyde* than others do. Under normal conditions, the side effects that arise from drunkenness prevent most people from further drinking. So the body rarely gets the chance to make sufficient amounts of such hallucinogenic drugs and to cause an addiction. Yet regular consumption of alcohol can eventually increase this chance.

There are people who cannot afford to drink alcohol at all. Asians in general and Chinese and Koreans in particular lack the enzyme that breaks down the toxic *acetaldehyde* and even small amounts of alcohol lead to a fast pulse, abdominal pain, and a red face. For this reason, alcoholism is rarely existent in Asia. Also alcoholics who pass out after the first (and only drink), have no natural defences against *acetaldehyde*.

Beer -- Hypnotism and a Big Tummy

If you ever had the chance to smell a hop plant then you know it has hypnotic effects. Harvesting any of the plants of the hemp family can make you quite sleepy. Cannabis, which is used to produce Hashish and Marihuana, is a close relative of hops. The relaxing effect that beer has on the consumer, comes, besides other substances, from the hops ingredient *hopein*. Hopein is a form of morphine.

Except in Muslim countries, beer consumption is legal, yet taking morphine, marihuana, or other hallucinogenic drugs is treated as a criminal act. If a person regularly gets drunk by drinking large quantities of beer, he is not less "out of himself" or physically and mentally incompetent than he would be under drug-induced hallucination. It would not make a difference whether a hallucinating drug user runs over an innocent pedestrian or a drunk who has had a few bottles of morphine-containing beer. If a person is caught driving while drunk he will receive punishment by law. If he gets drunk and is not driving, the law cannot touch him. If someone becomes violent under the influence of beer, it is due to similar reasons that a drug user becomes violent under the influence of hallucinogenic drugs.

Apart from their mind-altering effects, hops are known to work as an anti-aphrodisiac, suppressing sexual drive and performance in men. Hops contain the female sex hormones *daidzein* and *genistein,* which are generally used to fatten calf, sheep, and chickens. Contrary to general belief, the body cannot utilise any of the many calories contained in whisky or other alcoholic beverages for producing energy or increasing fat reserves. Beer contains another female hormone, an oestrogen, which is also formed in a woman's ovaries. The typical beer belly and breast growth of a beer drinker is caused by these female hormones and has nothing to do with beer calories.

Besides the above mind-altering chemicals of beer, the malt in beer also has a substance in it that influences the psyche; it is called *hordenin*. Hordenin results from the germination of barley and is related to the well-known stimulants *ephedrine* and *mescaline*. It also has a strong diuretic effect, which causes frequent urination, especially during the night. To process one glass of beer, the body's cells have to supply at least three glasses of water. Hence beer can cause severe dehydration so typically found among heavy beer drinkers. When the beer drinker's body signals dehydration he may be tempted to drink even more beer, which increases dehydration further.

All these factors may result in weight gain, tissue acidification, retention of toxins, and swelling of the body. The use of extremely "hard" water, rich in inorganic (metallic) calcium, in beer production may be responsible for the high incidence of kidney stones and kidney problems among beer drinkers. In addition, regular consumption of all alcoholic drinks causes gallstones in the liver and gallbladder. Alcohol is extremely acidic which alters the pH of the alkaline bile to the point of thickening, leading to blockage of bile ducts. In this respect, alcohol consumption can become a cause for any illness in the body.

Solving the Red Wine Mystery

Despite of what we know today about the destructive effects that alcoholic beverages can have on liver and brain cells apart from dehydrating the body, you may have been advised to drink a glass of red wine or two on a daily basis because this could benefit your arteries. This advice, however, is misleading. It makes you believe that drinking alcohol is not so bad for you after all, whereas in truth it is not the alcohol in the wine that is beneficial for the heart. A study led by Dr. John Folts of the University of Wisconsin Medical School found that 8 or 10 ounces a day of the purple variety of grape juice has a potent effect on the blood cells called platelets, making them less likely to form clots that can lead to heart attacks.

A group of natural substances found in many kinds of foods, called *flavonoids*, seem to have powerful anti-clotting properties. They are amply present in purple grape juice and to a lesser extent also in red wine. Purple grape juice might even be more potent than aspirin, which is widely recommended as a way of warding off heart attacks. The study found that both aspirin and red wine slow the activity of blood platelets by about 45 percent, while purple grape juice dampens them by 75 percent. It is not clear, however, whether the thinning of blood after drinking red wine is caused by flavonoids or by the diuretic effects of the alcohol contained in the wine.

If you turn the purple grape juice into wine it loses some of its flavonoids. To have the benefits advocated for red wine and more, it is better to drink the fresh juice of purple grapes. Plant foods contain about 4,000 flavonoids. Eating a diet rich in fruits and vegetables is one of the best ways to maintain a healthy circulatory system, alcohol isn't. Although the flavonoids contained in red wine may have some beneficial effects on the blood, the alcohol that goes with it, after initially thinning the blood due the alcohol's diuretic effects, makes it thicker than it was before. If you need proof, ask a friend to apply the muscle test of chapter 1 on you, while you hold a bottle of red wine (or any other alcoholic beverage) in your hand. If your arm muscle tests weak it shows that any benefit that may be been left in the red wine from the grape juice has been voided. The alcohol in the wine causes the blocked flow of energy to the muscles.

CHAPTER 11

What's Supposed to be Good for Us

1. Vitamin Euphoria – A Shot in the Dark

Vitamins seem to be good for everything. The newly born needs them to grow properly; women take them to be happy; men use them to maintain or increase potency; athletes ingest them to stay fit; and old people take them to become younger or to avoid the flu. Even foods are categorised into bad or good, depending on how few or many vitamins they contain. Ever since vitamins were produced synthetically they were made available in every drugstore or health shop around the world. Now you don't have to eat all that vitamin-rich food anymore to stay healthy, all you need is to pop in a couple of vitamin pills a day, so the advertising goes. But if you don't pay heed to this advice, you are told that you may eventually be suffering the consequences of vitamin deficiency, which can greatly endanger your health.

If you feel tired or suffer from lack of concentration (which could be caused by lack of sleep or overeating), you may be prescribed vitamin B pills. Then there is vitamin C if you catch too many colds (which could result from stress, working too hard or eating too much junk food). Vitamin E, you are told, helps to prevent a heart attack (so you may no longer need to watch out for the real risk factors of heart disease). This way we spend billions of dollars on vitamin pills each year to fight off every kind of ill from the common cold to cancer.

Today vitamins are added to almost all processed foods, not because they are so good for our health but because those that are "enriched" sell better. Cereals, bread, milk, yoghurt, boiled sweets, even dog food with added vitamins leave the supermarket shelves faster than do those without them. Smokers, meat eaters, sugar addicts, or people who drink too much alcohol can now continue with their habits without having to fear the dreaded vitamin deficiency, thanks to the food industry. The magic food supplements have become an insurance policy against poor diet and nobody has to feel guilty anymore over eating junk food. And on top of that, scientific research suggests that taking large doses of supplements may protect you against disease, even though there is no real evidence that it does. As seen in the sales figures, the public believes that the more vitamins you take, the healthier you get.

But are vitamins really so good for your health? Despite the massive amounts of vitamins consumed in western societies, general health is declining everywhere. Could the mass consumption of vitamins be even co-responsible for this trend?

Sodium and water are essential to maintain sodium levels and hydrate the body, but too much of either can seriously upset the body's equilibrium. Overconsumption of vitamin A, for example, can cause loss of hair, double vision, headaches, and vomiting in women, all indications of vitamin poisoning. If a woman is pregnant, the supplement can even harm her unborn baby. As we will see, vitamins can even endanger a person's life.

Vitamin Deficiency -- Is There Such a Thing?
In the beginning of the 17th century, Japan was afflicted with a disease, called *beriberi*, which killed many people. By the year 1860, over 1/3 of Japan's marines had fallen ill with symptoms of weight loss, frequent heart complaints, loss of appetite, irritability, burning sensations in the feet, lack of concentration, and depression. The symptoms quickly disappeared whenever rice, Japan's most important staple food, was replaced with other foods.

Thirty years later the Dutch physician Christiaan Eijkman conducted an experiment feeding chicken with white rice. The chicken developed symptoms such as loss of weight, weakness, and signs of nerve infection, which Eijkman interpreted as *beriberi*. The symptoms disappeared again when the chickens were fed with brown rice. Soon later Eijkman discovered a few, previously unknown, substances within the bran of the whole rice; one of them was named B1. The era of vitamins had begun.

But beriberi wasn't caused by vitamin B1 deficiency. People no longer suffered from beriberi once they discontinued eating rice altogether. It should have been noticed that, with "no rice -- no vitamin B1 -- no beriberi," the disease must have had other causes than vitamin deficiency. Japanese marine soldiers died within three days after consuming white rice, yet it takes much longer than that to get a B1 deficiency. The origin of this mysterious disease was revealed when in 1891 a Japanese researcher discovered that beriberi is caused by the poison *citreoviridine*. Citreoviridine is produced by mould in white rice stored in filthy and humid environments.

Yet until today, the vitamin B1-beriberi-hypothesis is still maintained in medical text books around the world. Although it has never been proved that a B1 deficiency causes such symptoms as fatigue, loss of appetite, exhaustion, depression, irritability, and nerve damage, many patients having these symptoms are told that they have a vitamin-B deficiency. During vitamin B1 trial studies, all the participants complained about the highly monotonous diet they were given; they suffered fatigue and loss of appetite, regardless of whether they received B1 in their diet or not. As soon as they returned to their normal diet, even without B1, the symptoms spontaneously disappeared.

Another one of the B-vitamin group is *nicotinic acid* or also known as *niacin*. It has become very popular and is added to many foods. Niacin is supposed to safeguard us against diarrhoea, dementia, and the skin disease *pellagra*. Pellagra is more widespread among people who eat maize, though not everyone who eats maize gets pellagra. Pellagra was found to be caused by food poisoning through spoiled maize. The poison involved has been identified as *T2-toxine* and is known to disturb niacin metabolism, thus producing pellagra. Besides the great importance given to taking extra *niacin* today this substance is not a vitamin after all as it can be produced by the body itself.

Nobody Knows How Much of Them You Really Need

Governments and international organisations such as the WHO frequently release figures that propose a *Daily Ratio of Allowance* (DRA) for every vitamin that is supposed to be good for you. The nutritional experts in different countries however, have different opinions about how many of them we really need. An American, for example, is supposed to take 60mg of vitamin C, whereas a British citizen is considered better off taking only 30mg. A Frenchman can only remain healthy if he consumes 80mg of this vitamin whereas Italians are told they need 45mg. These figures are "adjusted" every few years, although our bodies' basic nutritional requirements have not changed over the past thousands of years.

Nobody really knows how many vitamins are good for us because the requirements, constitutions, and absorption rates for vitamins differ from person to person. Vitamins need to be digested before they can be made available to the cells and tissues. If AGNI, the digestive power, is low, then also vitamins cannot be digested properly.

When scientists calculate our vitamin requirements, they usually add a 50 percent "safety factor" to the original figures to make certain that we eat enough of them. Since vitamin extraction from food is much less than 100 percent, the figures are increased one more time. The official methods of analysing the amount of vitamins we require are inadequate because we *do not know* how much of each vitamin the human physiology needs. A Vata type, for example, may have a greater need for vitamin B 6 whereas a Kapha type can never really run out of it.

It is also not known how much of each vitamin is contained in a banana, in an apple or a cauliflower. Vitamin contents fluctuate greatly with the size of the fruits, their maturity, the condition of the soil, country of origin, and the use of pesticides. How many of the vitamins contained in these foods actually end up in the body depends on the digestive capacity and body-type. All this makes official nutritional figures highly unreliable and speculative.

The vitamin theories originate in the assumption that the human physiology has stores for vitamins that always must be full up to saturate the tissues of the body. This assumption, however, has never been proven by scientific research. While calculating human vitamin requirements, nutritional science assumes that the body's metabolic processes take place at a top speed, which would require plenty of vitamins. Our bodies, however, are not machines that are being at top capacity day and night. Most of us are *not* marathon runners, and even *they* don't run for 24 hour's day after day, month after month and year after year.

It is very questionable whether the saturation of our body tissues with vitamins is even desirable. We need a certain amount of fatty tissue in our body but this does not mean we should all be excessively filled with fat. Oxygen too is considered being vital for all our body's functioning but if its concentration in the air is consistently too high it can actually cause us bodily harm. Why should vitamins be an exception?

Vitamin Deficiency is not Caused by Lack of Vitamins

In the majority of cases, a vitamin deficiency does not occur because of insufficient vitamin intake in the diet. A vitamin deficiency is rather caused by a congested capillary network that is unable to diffuse sufficient amounts of the vitamins to the connective tissues surrounding the cells. This can have a number of reasons, overeating protein foods being one of the major ones.

A diet rich in protein foods such as meat, fish, pork, cheese, etc. eventually blocks the basement membrane (BM) of the small and large blood vessels in the body (see chapter 8 on heart disease). Stress, overstimulation, and dehydration can have a similar effect. The subsequent thickening of the BM and connective tissues makes it increasingly difficult for the basic nutrients, including vitamins, to reach the cells. This greatly increases the amount of metabolic waste and toxins in the body, overtaxes the liver, and causes the growth of gallstones (see chapter 3). The gallstones inhibit the flow of bile, which subdues AGNI, the digestive power and hinder the assimilation of nutrients even further. When fats are no longer properly digested the fat-soluble vitamins A, D, E, K, which are normally stored in the liver, become deficient. This problems is further amplified by eating low fat foods (see section 6, this chapter).

If vitamin A becomes deficient, for example, the *epithelial* cells, which are an essential part of all the organs, blood vessels, lymph vessels, etc. in the body, become damaged. This can literally cause any kind of disease. Vitamin A is also necessary to maintain the cornea of the eye, eyesight in dim light, and reduce the severity of microbial infection. Vitamin A is only absorbed from the small intestines satisfactorily if fat absorption is normal. Fat absorption cannot be normal as long as gallstones obstruct the bile flow in the liver and gallbladder. It is therefore only sensible to remove the gallstones and cleanse the digestive system so that the vitamins contained in food can actually reach the cells.

Taking extra vitamins can be harmful if the body is unable to make use of them and is given the additional burden of breaking them down or trying to eliminate them from the system. Because vitamins are strong acids, an overload can lead to vitamin poisoning (vitaminosis) and cause the same symptoms that accompany a vitamin deficiency. It is much more important to cleanse the body from toxins, including the stored protein in the blood vessels and the gallstones from the liver, than to ingest large doses of vitamins. Although taking mega doses of vitamins may temporarily increase the pressure of diffusion of these nutrients for a short time and quickly relieve symptoms, the "benefits" are often short-lived. If digestive functions are impaired, taking extra vitamins may be harmful.

The Hidden Perils of Vitamin Pills

Vitamins D and A

The following are some of the most important vitamins. ***Calciferol***, known as **vitamin D**, is not really a vitamin since the body is capable of producing it itself. With the help of UV light from the sun, the body synthesises it from *cholesterol* (7-dehydrocholesterol) in the human skin. Vitamin D, which acts more like a hormone, facilitates the absorption and utilisation of calcium and phosphorus, necessary for maintaining strong bones and teeth. Although vitamin D levels cannot be influenced through diet, the official nutritional textbooks speak of 2.5 µg daily requirement for adults. Babies and breast milk are supposed to have the biggest deficiencies in vitamin D, implying that nature made a crucial mistake when it invented breast milk. Mothers are warned that, without taking extra amounts of this important vitamin, their babies could risk rickets or bone deformation.

Yet mothers are rarely informed about the risks they take when they overuse vitamin D. Vitamin D poisoning leads to something very similar to rickets. Professor Dr Ernst Lindner from the University of Giessen in Germany has warned that if large amounts of vitamin D are given to a person, calcium is removed from the bones; this can cause bone deformation. He also states that it is very risky to add vitamin D to food.

Bone deformation is more likely to occur in babies who are *not* breast-fed. Until the expensive vitamin D pill came on the market, rickets was effectively treated with breast milk, for thousands of years.

Nature's deems it necessary to supply breast milk with only very little vitamin D. As studies have shown the vitamin D content of breast milk does not increase when the mother takes vitamin D supplements. This proves that a mother's body filters out vitamin D to protect the baby from being poisoned (by the vitamin). A baby's body easily synthesises vitamin D from sunlight once it is exposed to it. It is therefore unnecessary to have this vitamin present in the mother's milk. Hence the major cause of vitamin D deficiency among babies is being in dark rooms with little or no natural light. But even then the baby is still capable of absorbing sufficient amounts of calcium from the blood and building healthy bones. While being breast-fed, it receives plenty of milk sugar and phospho-caseins, both excellent transporting agents for calcium. If there is anything that could cause rickets in babies, it is lack of breast milk and exposure to natural light.

Adults are not so well protected against this vitamin as babies are. One report issued by the University of Tromso in Norway showed that the long-term intake of vitamin D at the dosage of just slightly above the 400 IU recommended amount (many people take as much as 4,000 to 5,000 IU per day!) may trigger a heart attack and cause degenerative joint disease and arthritis. Another finding emerged from the New York University Goldwater Memorial Hospital, which suggests that large doses of vitamin D can cause magnesium deficiency in the heart tissue and cause heart attacks.

Pregnant women are particularly at risk. Dietary intake of vitamin D has led to kidney calcification and severe mental retardation in their offspring. Children born to mothers, who take extra vitamin D in their diet, may develop a certain type of congenital heart disease called *supravalvular aortic stenosis* and show extreme deformations of facial bones.

Taking vitamin D supplements can also contribute to arteriosclerosis and even be fatal. In 1991, several Americans died from drinking milk. The vitamin D, which was added during the production process, had not been churned properly. In addition, milk can enhance the potency of vitamin D by ten times, a fact that is rarely known among milk producers. Milk that has been enriched by 90 units of vitamin D is poisonous and can kill. If you feel you need more vitamin D, then it is best to sunbathe regularly. But avoid using sunscreens.

It is also a well known fact that too much vitamin A causes deformity in unborn children. For this reason, there is a law preventing the use of this vitamin in food. Yet this law does not apply to animal feeds even though it is well known that vitamin A is accumulating in the liver of farm animals. Pregnant women are warned not to consume liver to avoid damaging their babies. If taking extra vitamin A is considered poisonous for pregnant women or unborn babies, it cannot be considered save for the rest of the population either.

B-vitamins

But what about the so-called essential B-vitamins? *Pyridoxine* or **vitamin B6** is a combination of six substances. Since most of this vitamin occurs in bound form, analytic methods fail to determine how much of it is contained in food. It is also not possible to make any statements about how much of it we require. Still the nutritional textbooks suggest a 1-2 µg daily intake. What *is* known, though, are its side effects.

Vitamin B6 is often used as a drug. Its use is indicated for depression, pre-menstrual tension, schizophrenia, and child asthma. It was considered safe until 1983 when scientists discovered a syndrome accompanied by strong circulatory problems in the hands and feet of a number of patients who were given large doses of vitamin B6. The patients developed symptoms similar to the ones caused by the drug *thalidomide* (which recently has been reintroduced for specific disorders). Mothers who had taken large amounts of B6 during their pregnancy also reported deformities in their children's bodies. It took a long time before the nerve damage was linked to vitamin poisoning. As it turned out, many patients, who had been diagnosed with *Multiple Sclerosis*, were poisoned by vitamin B6. There are many unsuspecting people taking vitamin B6 today without the faintest idea that they are gradually poisoning themselves.

The statement that *Cobalamins* or **B12 vitamins** can only be found in animal foods such as meat, fish, eggs, cheese, etc. is incorrect. B12 has been detected in fermented plant foods and algae. A deficiency of this vitamin is thought to cause pernicious anaemia and degeneration of nerve fibres of the spinal cord. The argument that people who don't consume any animal foods have a B12 deficiency and endanger their health is unscientific, unfounded, and misleading. Apart from producing vitamins K, B1 and B2, as well as energy-providing short-chain fatty acids, the friendly bacteria located in the large intestine produce plenty of B12. In addition, the liver can store B12 for many years and knows how to recycle this vitamin. This may explain why *vegans* (those who don't eat any type of animal product) almost never suffer from B12 deficiencies. And if the body for any reason required more of the vitamin, it would instinctively look for foods that can meet the increased demand. However, if the liver and large intestines are congested, a B12 deficiency may eventually develop, *regardless* of whether a person is a meat-eater, a vegetarian, or vegan.

Niacin, the now very popular B-vitamin found in many foods, including breakfast cereals, might also have serious side effects. After large doses of niacin (3g) had been given to patients suffering from psychiatric diseases, they developed hepatitis and other liver problems. Among other symptoms of niacin-poisoning were hot flushes, itching skin, arrhythmia, and nervousness. Illegal use of niacin in minced meat and hamburgers has often led to similar symptoms. The main reason for adding niacin to meat is to colour it red and give it the appearance of being fresh. If you turn bright red, like a tomato, and get an itch right after eating meat, then you are likely to have been poisoned with niacin.

The **B-vitamin** *Folic acid* is also used commonly in foods and potentially one of the most harmful ones. After researchers first discovered that people in malaria regions suffered from folic acid deficiency, they gave them this B vitamin in the belief that it would make their immune systems more resistant to the malaria bug. The children who were given this vitamin felt worse after the treatment and were found to have much higher concentrations of malaria-causing agents in their blood than before.

The explanation for this phenomenon lies in the understanding that the malaria bugs themselves require large amounts of folic acid to spread. People who have a deficiency in this vitamin are naturally protected from malaria infection. A British doctor in Kenya discovered that children who took folic acid developed malaria. He gave folic acid to one group of monkeys and compared them with another group monkeys who were folic acid deficient. All the monkeys with "normal" levels of this vitamin were infected with malaria whereas the ones with "abnormally low" levels stayed healthy.

Over 40 percent of the world's population are threatened by malaria today and it is no longer restricted to developing countries. Malaria is rapidly becoming the leading cause of death in the world. It is impossible to imagine the disastrous consequences that may have arisen from giving millions of healthy people vitamins to help their assumed vitamin deficiency. What is considered to be a vitamin deficiency for one person may be a life-saving response for another person. It is painful to know that many people have to pay with their lives because we so crudely interfere in the self-regulating mechanisms of nature and human physiology that protect us against disease.

Vitamin C

The most popular of all vitamins is ***Ascorbic acid*** or **vitamin C,** a deficiency of which is believed to cause multiple haemorrhages, slow wound healing, anaemia, and scurvy. It is in fact very easy to cure scurvy with red peppers and citrus fruits, both containing high concentrations of this vitamin. Since the Hungarian scientist Szent Gyoerkyi identified vitamin C as an effective substance, it became common knowledge that vitamin C and orange juice have the same effect. But scurvy cannot be cured by vitamin C alone, however high the dosage may be; the blood vessels remain damaged. By contrast, eating a few oranges or red peppers cures scurvy quickly, without a trace of damage left.

The fruits contain another ingredient, which is known as vitamin C2. Scurvy can only be cured if vitamin C and vitamin C2 are taken together. When Gyoerkyi studied vitamin C, he included both compounds of vitamin C. But as the years passed, the scientific literature began to omit C2 and today nobody talks about it anymore.

When vitamins became popular in the United States, there was a sudden jump in the number of newly born babies developing scurvy. It was thought that scurvy was a disease eradicated a long time ago. As the mysterious development was investigated, it was discovered that the mothers of the affected babies had taken extra vitamin C preparations (without C2) in the belief that it was good for their babies. Dosed with the vitamin, the mothers' bodies began to eliminate much of it. When the babies were born they too continued to remove whatever vitamin C they had received from the mother, because that is what they had learnt to do whilst in the womb. Since their baby food did not consist of large amounts of vitamin C, they soon developed the dangerous baby scurvy.

The body of an adult, who consumes vitamin C regularly, may eventually produce a similar response. He may even develop scurvy because the body becomes programmed to eliminate vitamin C faster and in larger quantities than it is absorbed. Adults can develop further symptoms, too when they suddenly stop taking vitamin C. It is known that large doses of vitamin C can destroy another vitamin, that is, vitamin B12. There is too little research to tell what further damage large amounts of vitamins can do to us but experimenting with these powerful substances on the human body is similar to handling an explosive device.

A friend of mine developed a dangerous swelling of his kidneys after taking 2g of Vitamin C a day for several weeks. By taking him off the vitamins and giving him lapacho tea to help remove the excessive vitamins from the kidneys was sufficient to restore them to their normal size and functions. Added to the current uncertainty and confusion about taking vitamins, there is no conclusive proof until this very day, that vitamin C protects you from infection, one of the main reasons why people use it.

Even if vitamin C could stop an infection, it would make its use even more dangerous. To prevent a cold from developing fully upsets the body's cleansing reactions and can be the first stage in a series of major illnesses. If the body is "toxic" because of an unhealthy lifestyle, diet, and stress, its most important primary response will be a toxicity crisis whereby the body can cleanse itself. A cold is not a disease, and it should not be treated as one. It is very ill advised to stop the body from eliminating toxins and purifying itself.

Handing out vitamin C as a preventive measure against colds is a practice that may also be counterproductive. In small doses vitamin C may help to start off a cleansing response in the body but it can only be hoped that the intake of large amounts of vitamin C is not effective enough to interfere with the cleansing process. The often-cited argument that all water-soluble vitamins, like vitamin C and B, are harmless because the body can easily eliminate excessive amounts without a problem is unscientific and misleading, and without any proof. *Cyanide* is also water-soluble but it can kill a person.

Conclusion: The vitamin euphoria has hit the world's population at a time when there are no reliable methods to determine when and if a person suffers from a vitamin deficiency. Reviewing the harmful effects caused by vitamin intake, it is likely that a deficiency, if it really exists, is either caused by an overtaxed digestive system and subsequent congestion of the capillary network or by overdosing the body with vitamins. Blood congestion as described in chapter 7 hinders vitamins from reaching the tissue cells and organs. Taking extra vitamins in such a situation can trigger an emergency response that empties the body's vitamin reserves.

It is not known how much of each vitamin each particular body-type requires to be vital and healthy, and it also not possible to find out how much of each vitamin the body extracts from the food it ingests. It is further incorrect to assume that by taking extra vitamins the body will automatically make use of them. We don't know how much of the vitamins will actually leave the stomach unharmed, in what amounts they are digested and how much of these are absorbed by the blood and the body cells. There cannot be two people with exactly the same vitamin requirements and absorption rates. What may be normal for one person may not be normal for another, which makes the "standardised vitamin requirements for all" unsuitable if not potentially harmful.

The argument that our foods today are so depleted of vitamins that we need to take additional helpings of synthetically derived vitamins is only partially correct. *Most* of the foods consumed by *most* people in advanced countries are highly acid forming, which means that they congest blood vessels and connective tissues and deplete the body's vitamins and minerals. The foods include most dairy products, meat and its products, tinned or frozen foods, white bread, white sugar, alcoholic beverages, diet drinks, soft drinks, packaged fruit juices, preserved foods, processed breakfast cereals, chocolates, ready-made cakes, crisps, and other junk foods. The exaggerated daily ratio of daily-required vitamins may apply only to the severely undernourished person. Fresh fruits, vegetables, pulses, and grain foods are still filled with more than enough vitamins to supply the body many times over.

Taking vitamin pills, which don't contain much *Prana* or *Life Energy,* does not substitute regular intake of healthy, fresh food. Vitamins that have been removed from their natural environment, i.e., fruits, vegetables, etc. can in fact upset both AGNI and the delicate balance of minerals and vitamins in the body. This especially applies to multivitamin preparations. Although there are conditions when taking extra vitamins can be beneficial, for example, before and after removing amalgam fillings from the teeth, they ought not to be taken in large doses and for more than 10-14 days at a time. This is best done under supervision of a health practitioner who is aware of the side effects they can have.

What about Taking Extra Minerals?

Unlike vitamins, minerals cannot be synthesised by plants. Plants take up mineral salts (inorganic compounds) from the soil and convert them into colloidal minerals (organic compounds). The inorganic minerals, also called metallic minerals, are very difficult to be absorbed by a healthy digestive system, and even more so if the small intestine is impacted with toxic waste material. In the case of a healthy adult, the absorption rate for metallic minerals is 3-5%; the rest merely passes through the body system without benefit. Although these minerals now come in chelated form, i.e., amino acids or protein are wrapped around them to improve assimilation, they are still inorganic and of very little use to the cells of the body. Colloidal minerals, on the other hand, have an absorption rate of 98%, which indicates that only minerals in colloidal form are meant to be used by the human physiology.

If the soil is not replenished with minerals after harvesting, it becomes increasingly mineral deficient. Modern methods of agriculture don't include putting minerals back into the soil. Before the era of continuous soil depletion, the topsoil consisted of as many as 90-100 different minerals. The great rivers such as the Nile in Egypt and the Ganges in India caused extensive flooding every year, bringing new minerals from the glaciers and mountains to the land, automatically fertilising it. The people living in these areas were generally in perfect health and lived on average 120-140 years. The situation changed with the erosion of forests and building of dams. Today, there are merely 12-20 minerals found in plant foods.

Whatever is contained in modern chemical fertilisers (nitrogen, phosphorus, and potassium) may be sufficient to raise normal looking crops; yet the healthy-looking plant foods are short of minerals, which is reflected in their poor taste. This may cause some mineral deficiencies in the body. We are consistently missing out on the majority of minerals. And if the digestive system does not function efficiently, a health crisis may arise. Almost every disease today is linked or coincides with a deficiency of one or several minerals or trace minerals.

Taking supplements consisting of metallic minerals is not only inefficient because of their relatively low absorption rate but also because of their non-physiological value. Large quantities of metallic minerals can even be toxic to the body, as seen in people who, for example, take iron tablets. The iron may make them feel sick, a natural response by the stomach against the toxic metal. Iron oxide is nothing other than "rust." Taking calcium tablets may weaken the bones by causing zinc deficiency. High dosed mineral supplements consisting of metallic minerals can block the absorption of other bio-usable minerals, which can upset the body's entire biochemical balance. Most of the metallic minerals are derived from oyster shell, limestone, soil, clay, calcium carbonate, and sea salts. In fact, taking metallic minerals can lead to serious mineral deficiencies.

It maybe beneficial, on the other hand, to take extra colloidal minerals. Plant derived minerals are water-soluble and enzymatically active which makes it very easy for the body to digest and utilise them. The iron, contained in lapacho tea, for example, is of colloidal form and has an immediate positive effect.

Plant-derived minerals have no negative side effects, even if you overdose on them. If you feel that you need extra minerals, try your local health food store. If they don't have a good preparation of colloidal minerals, you may contact "The Family Health News" in Florida, USA or the Nutri Centre in London (see Useful Addresses); they have 2 or 3 excellent products that contain up to sixty colloidal minerals in their naturally existing balanced combination. But as is the case with vitamins, most serious mineral deficiencies occur because of inadequate nutrition, too many acid-forming foods and drinks, overstimulation, dehydration, stress, etc. There is not much point in taking extra minerals when they are straight away removed or destroyed by one or more of these factors. So before spending a lot of money on mineral of vitamin supplements, try to eliminate the causes of the deficiency first.

2. Breakfast Cereals - Poison for the Children

"Super Food" of the Century

Breakfast cereals have never been more popular than they are today. Packed with vitamins and minerals, they promise power, health, and vitality, especially to the young generation. There is hardly a commercial breakfast cereal in the world that does not seem to contain everything a child needs to receive the "perfectly balanced" dietary nutrition. However, despite this "valuable" contribution to family health, a frightening number of children show signs of ill health and lacking immunity. The vitamins that are added to the cereals are supposed to protect the child against the vitamin-destroying sugar but it seems that this guarantee is no longer guaranteed.

Besides cornflakes, which still top the list of American and European breakfast cereals, the sales of new "tasty and healthy" breakfast foods soar as never before. The main marketing targets for these "healthy" breakfast foods are children. Research suggests that as many as 79% of all households use ready-made breakfast cereals to start the day. Children are usually very keen to try the latest cereal model, which contains essentially the same ingredients as all the other types but comes in a different shape and colour. The well designed packaging depicting a healthy-looking family or natural scenery promises the parents that the contents are of pure and natural origin, often organically grown, and good for the entire family. The kids love the happy friendly figures on the cardboard. "If Mickey Mouse, Donald Duck, Bugs Bunny, or the strong Dinosaurs like the cereal then it must be good for me, too", some children may argue.

A mother, who is naturally wants to secure the best possible nutrition for her child, finds her mind put at ease when she learns about the high nutritional value of the product in the food table. It convincingly states that the cereal has the balanced amounts of carbohydrates, protein, and fats, and is most importantly enriched with all the essential dietary supplements. If the right amount of milk (mostly pasteurised and homogenised) is added to the super food, the child would have the best possible start of the day that nature could provide, or so she may think.

Shocking News

Yet the reality of the matter is quite the opposite. An American team of researchers decided to prove to the world once and for all that breakfast cereals are truly man's super-food. So they fed the common breakfast cereals enriched with the most important vitamins and minerals to young, healthy laboratory rats. They divided a total of 240 rats into two groups; one group received cereal and water and the other one normal food and water. The experiment lasted for 45 days. The result was totally unexpected and devastating. The rats that were fed with cereals, which according to common nutritional sense and advertising should have turned them into strong and vital grown-up rats, were close to death. They suffered from fatty livers, anaemia, and high blood pressure. In a separate experiment rats were fed with cornflakes which consist of *useless* corn starch and white sugar. In this group some of the animals died.

The researchers had expected that the animals would grow faster with cereals, yet they did not grow at all, and some of them even lost weight. Especially the rats who received cereals with high sugar content (sugar is thought to be fattening), had the least growth rates. This is a summary of the results:

➢ The products that contained the least amounts of fat significantly increased the *cholesterol* levels of the rats. Some products were able to lower the rats' *cholesterol* levels but instead caused fatty livers.

➢ Those rats that were fed with cereals containing only small amounts of salt increased their blood pressure whereas the ones that received cereals with higher salt contents lowered their blood pressure.

> Some of the products were enriched with iron, which should have raised *haemoglobin* concentrations in the blood of the animals. However, the results took the researchers by surprise: **1)** There was no connection between higher intake of iron and *haemoglobin* levels. The rats stayed anaemic despite ingesting large amounts of iron. **2)** Those rats that had little iron in their blood deposited excessively large amounts of iron in their liver, which led to worsening of anaemia (for a similar reason it is very questionable to give extra iron to people who suffer from anaemia).

Poison that Tastes and Looks like Food

The main conclusion a person can draw from this experiment is that the purely theoretical approach to diet and nutrition (using food tables and daily nutritional recommendations) has not only been insufficient to raise the standard of health in the population but has in fact caused more harm and confusion than is currently assessable. Sanctified by theories of nutrition, which in actuality contradict the body's natural responses to food, the food industry has been given the green light to produce anything that fulfils the official nutritional requirements, even if the "foods" have a poisoning effect and create havoc in the body. There is no legislation to test man-made foods on animals before giving them to millions of human beings. The average consumer takes it for granted that the food produced by a reputable company must be safe for human consumption, even if it contains plastic.

The food industry is entitled to use a large variety of solvents and chemicals to improve the taste, colour, and texture of its products. The common practice of producing food *synthetically* and making it "healthier" by adding *synthetically* derived vitamins and minerals is at the root of many health problems afflicting both children and adults in the developed world.

To determine whether a cereal is healthy or harmful for you and for your family, use the simple muscle test described in chapter 1. Take your children to the supermarket and let them test out different products. This will teach them to trust their body and its responses and reactions and make them aware that not everything that *looks* healthy *is* healthy. Synthetically derived "nutrients" are foreign matter to both animals and humans alike. Making laboratory foods palatable and attractive does not mean they are harmless. The muscle test is one the most reliable tools you may have to protect yourself and your family from the harm caused by such non-foods.

Hot breakfast cereals, which were in common use before the era of cold, ready-made cereals, include cream of wheat, steel cut oats, the old fashioned porridge oats, rye flakes, millet, corn meal, cream of rice, etc. Although they take more time to prepare than the ready-made cereals, at least you know what's in it. Also check with your body-type food list.

Note: Most muesli mixtures or cereals with nuts and fruits in them contain the fruit preservative sulphur dioxide (E220), which can spark asthmatic attacks and is blacklisted by the Hyperactive Children Support Group in England. The cracked nuts react with oxygen and turn rancid, a common source of allergies. The dried fruits in cereals develop moulds, which can interfere with vitamin and mineral absorption and suppress immunity. Crunchy or roasted oats contain much sugar and inferior oils (see chapter 7, section 16 on sunlight and cancer).

The High Fibre Trap

Official health reports advise us to pack large amounts of whole grain and bran-enriched cereals into our diet. Studies have shown that those who follow this advice have a significantly lower fat intake compared with those who don't. They also want to eat fewer calories at lunchtime, which seems desirable. A high fibre cereal for breakfast subdues AGNI, the digestive fire for many hours, which might tempt you to even skip lunch (for lack of proper appetite). But by the evening, the body, sensing a "famine", wants to eat twice as much to make up for the lack of nutrient supplies during the day. By then AGNI is too low to handle large quantities of food, which results in the accumulation of toxic faecal matter in the intestines. Consequently you *put* on weight, *despite* your good "health habits."

The commonly held belief that indigestible fibre cannot be digested and leaves our body unaltered applies *only* to the small intestine. But once it reaches the large intestine the fibre is attacked and broken down by large numbers of residential bacteria. This causes fermentation and the common flatulence, headaches, heart pressure, irritability, tiredness, sleeping problems, etc.

Doctors at the South Manchester University Hospital, England, studying Irritable Bowel Syndrome (IBS) have discovered that after eating bran -- the one time cure-all food for IBS -- more than half of their patients felt much worse. Today over 20 percent of the British population suffers from IBS. High fibre cereals cause loose stools, a major reason why people with constipation choose bran or bran-enriched foods as a method of producing regular bowel movements. Added bran, however, pulls out minerals from the colon cells, weakens peristalsis, and causes chronic colon problems. If intake is discontinued, constipation results.

Many health-conscious people follow a low fat diet -- so highly recommended by nutritional experts. Yet if cereals don't contain enough fat or "fuel," which is required to properly digest and absorb carbohydrates, they pass through the small intestine too quickly. The colon bacteria then act on the undigested food, producing many unpleasant side effects, including flatulence, bad-smelling gases, diarrhoea, and even weight gain.

The high fibre theory definitely has its good sides, though. Another major factor of intestinal obstruction is small faeces. A diet rich in natural fibre produces larger faeces that retain a lot more water than a diet consisting of refined and processed foods. The average British meal takes about 83 hours to pass through the intestinal tract with an average stool weight of only 104g. By contrast, British vegetarians take about 41 hours and produce 208g of stools – whereas the average meal of a Ugandan villager, consisting of low protein high-fibre diet, takes only 36 hours and generates 470g of stools a day. Ugandans rarely suffer from constipation, and they *don't* add bran to their foods.

It is much better for the body to obtain fibre from fresh fruit, salads, cooked grains, beans and vegetables. Cooked vegetables in particular contain plenty of fibre which helps the digestive process but does not overwhelm the colon in the same way as added bran does. Also the high water content of cooked foods and fruits generally make the passage through the intestinal tract much easier. This brings us to the next subject: Is eating raw and unprepared food better than eating cooked and prepared food?

3. Raw Whole Foods

Pro and Contra

The arguments in favour of a raw food diet sound very convincing: Food should be left whole and unprepared, only then can we benefit from its natural goodness and vitality. With the plenty of vitamins, minerals, and trace elements contained in raw food you will never suffer any deficiencies. We should live like all the other animals in nature; they don't prepare their food, cook their vegetables, or bake bread – the reason why they are so healthy and strong. On the other hand, we destroy most of the essential and health- promoting nutrients through methods of cooking, preparing, and baking, causing all the vitamin and mineral deficiencies prevalent today.

The promoters of raw food diets propose that if the general population ate more of the untreated whole foods, many diseases could be prevented. This could save billions of dollars in treatment costs. Many chronically ill patients have found sudden relief and improvement, thanks to raw vegetables and soaked grains.

The initial benefits of a raw whole food diet can be so promising that a person may decide to continue eating this food, although he may not like the taste of it. But could it be possible that raw and whole foods, except fruits, which are already "cooked" or ripened by the sun, are not so beneficial for us after all if eaten on a continual basis? And why do 98 percent of the world's population favour prepared and warm foods to raw and cold foods? Have we all forsaken our natural instincts?

Karl Pirlet, Professor of Medicine at the University of Frankfurt, Germany, claims that he has a nearly endless collection of cases whose health was restored after they stopped eating a raw whole food diet. He found that most of these patients suffered a physical breakdown after several years (in some cases after 10-20 years) of eating raw whole foods. The effects were varied but were all marked by the occurrence of sudden ageing as seen in a deterioration of joints and arteries. Most patients looked fragile, felt low in energy, and had excessively bloated stomachs. Their bodies could no longer cope with breaking down hard grains and raw vegetables; they were literally starving themselves to death.

So does this mean that raw foods are not good for us? This depends on each person's constitution and condition. Young Pitta types with a strong AGNI and plenty of exercise can cope with such a diet for many years without harmful side effects. But eventually even their digestive systems too may become exhausted from trying to breakdown raw whole grains and raw vegetables.

Most people who start on a raw whole food diet have already suffered from health problems and a weak AGNI. Unable to break down the high fibre foods, the intestinal bacteria start doing this job instead. This results in fermentation and putrefaction of the foods. The poison produced by the bacteria leads to a massive stimulation of the immune system, which attempts to neutralise and eliminate them. This cleansing reaction helps clear the intestines from impacted faecal matter, stops constipation, and through the intense immune activity releases plenty of energy. The relief from congestion and constipation and the increase in energy are very noticeable to the person and strike him as very "positive" signs. This response can even lead to a spontaneous remission of cancer or the relief of arthritic pains. But eventually the intestines begin to bloat up like a balloon, unable to deal with the toxic gases and poisonous compounds.

Many nutritionists and dieticians may then give the advice to eat even more fibre because only fibre can absorb such toxic substances as ammonia and protect the intestinal walls from damage. But it is highly unlikely that that a fermenting and putrefying mass of undigested fibre, which produces ammonia, *reabsorbs* it in the same "breath". Nutritional science assumes that the nutritional ingredients of food alone determine whether they have physiological value for us or not. Such an approach, however, is incomplete and misleading unless we include the common-sense-understanding that we need a well functioning digestive system to digest, absorb, and metabolise these nutrient components in order to benefit from them. A weak digestive system can even make poison out of nectar. The saying "You are what you eat" is therefore only partially correct. You rather are the food you are able to digest and metabolise. In other words, a long-term raw food diet is only good for you as long as you are able to digest it properly.

What Makes Plants Poisonous

Every microbe, insect, plant, animal, and human being on this planet wants to survive. But there are potential dangers out there that can lead to their destruction. For this reason, every living thing, including plants, have developed a sophisticated defence apparatus to ward off anyone who wants to eat or harm them.

It is only natural for the species of any life form to create difficulties for the invading or devouring enemies; otherwise ecological balance could not be possible. Despite innumerable numbers of lice, pests, beetles, and locusts, plants have managed to survive and keep the planet green and oxygenated. This is due to their own highly advanced "healthcare system." Similar to our body, plants have an immune system to ensure their own survival and health. They use prickly thorns, poison as in the case of the deadly nightshades, or they envelop themselves in a wax-covering that is impenetrable for microbes. If microbes do somehow manage to enter the plant's interior, inborn defence mechanisms begin to destroy the invaders, not dissimilar to our own defence responses.

Most microbes that are present in the air, food, and water never reach the inside of our body. They are promptly neutralised by enzymes located in our nose, lungs, saliva, and stomach juices. The rest of them are taken care of by our immune system with its sophisticated antigens and immune cells, including the macrophages and T-cells.

Plants, however, have to do more to protect themselves since locusts and animals such as cows, mice, or man can eat them altogether. For this reason, they produce antibodies of which 20,000 kinds are known to date, still only a fraction of what they are capable of producing. These antibodies, when ingested by animals or humans can make them sick, which stops them from eating the plants. It is for this reason why all ancient civilisations traditionally prepared their foods.

Why Prepare Foods?

The populations of the High Andes were the first ones to introduce the potato to their cultures. But the potatoes had to undergo vigorous cleansing procedures before they were considered eatable. First, they were spread on the ground to freeze them overnight. This ensured that the cells burst open. Then the men and women trampled on the potatoes to destroy their skins. Still frozen, the potatoes were then placed into a well base for several weeks to surround them with water. This removed 97% of the *alkaloids* and turned the green pulps into a snow-white colour. After pressing the potatoes, they exposed them to the hot sun. You may ask: "But what about the so-important vitamins and minerals?" The Andes populations with their high standards of health and stamina obviously preferred taste to nutritional values. They knew that most bitter substances are poisonous and they trusted their taste buds more than any theories of nutrition.

Ayurveda, the most ancient health science in the world, categorises foods only according to their tastes and after effects. It emphasises that if the body receives all the six tastes, i.e., sweet, sour, salty, pungent, astringent, and bitter, it will be stimulated to produce many of the important nutrients itself and thus remain balanced. The sense of taste is our body's supreme judge to know whether certain foods are right for us or not. Situated in the taste buds of the tongue and in co-ordination with the constantly changing requirements of the body, the sense of taste controls our natural instinct and desire for healthy food.

The taste buds for bitter taste are very developed and can detect even the slightest trace of bitter-tasting substances. We have this facility because bitter foods may contain alkaloids and can be poisonous. If toxins build up in the blood the body requires a bitter- tasting antidote or medicine that purifies it and restores its balance. Blood-cleansing herbs or teas generally taste very bitter. The human body accepts chocolate, coffee, tea, and beer, which are of predominantly bitter taste, only after our persuasive mind or added sugar manage to override the taste barrier. Such foods or drinks become desirable quite quickly because they contain morphine-type compounds. This may lead to a substance addiction. There are many types of foods that have a slightly bitter taste to them, including lettuce, broccoli, and leafy green vegetables. Yet the bitterness of these foods is well balanced by the their natural sweet taste, caused by the sugar-composed carbohydrates. Hence these foods have a cleansing effect but do not poison you.

The natural Indian populations of South America eat potatoes only if there is as scarcity of food. But when they eat them they mix them with clay from the Earth which is known to absorb any toxins that may be left in the potatoes and remove them from the system. This practice also removes vitamins and minerals, which seems to make no difference to their health. Clay is used by many forms of folk medicine around the world to absorb the toxins generated by bacteria during diarrhoea.

The Aboriginals who live in the wilderness prepare their food similar to our cooking procedures. Each plant, seed, or root requires a separate process of preparation to make it edible. Certain roots, for instance, are peeled, soaked for half a day, and then baked for thirty minutes. The sometimes-elaborate preparation of their food serves a very important purpose, that is, the removal of natural food poisons or antibodies.

Even animals "prepare" their food. Cows, for example, bring up their food and chew it again after it has been "cooked" in the stomach. In fact they have 12 stomachs to make certain that the blood does not absorb the ingredients of flowers, grains or grass before they are thoroughly detoxified. Birds are equipped with goitres to soak (ferment) the grains before their muscle stomachs "chew" them up. Rabbits have their own way of dealing with the potentially dangerous food; they eat part of their own faeces, which is an alternative to chewing the same food twice.

Low Nutrient Foods – A Key to Survival

The time-tested methods of food preparation may weaken the theory that we are supposed to eat our food in the state nature has given it to us, with all the nutrients retained. But how could the original inhabitants of our planet have survived for so many thousands of years without having sufficient vitamins and minerals in their diet? They made certain that only very few toxins could enter their digestive systems. With so little toxicity to deal with, the small amounts of nutrients contained in their foods were almost sufficient to keep up the healthy functioning of their physiology. Their bodies produced the rest.

It is known, for example, that the human body has eight different ways to make calcium, using bicarbonate of soda (a product of our digestive system), other minerals and certain enzymes. The body is its own factory. It can make many minerals and even vitamins. Whatever it cannot produce itself, the trillions of friendly bacteria residing in our guts produce for us. Whatever the body requires in terms of nutrient complexes it is capable of producing them from even the simplest of foods. This may explain why certain North Mexican tribes can live on eating only corn (mainly starch) and some beans and be more healthy and fit than the healthiest and fittest individuals in the "well-fed" world. Out of necessity, their digestive systems are so sophisticated and efficient that they can produce everything their body needs from corn (and beans). In comparison, ours are so inefficient that they have even "forgotten" how to make essential vitamins and amino acids.

Raw whole foods supply us with plenty of vitamins and if the soil is naturally fertile also with many minerals. But this doesn't necessarily mean that we need them all and that we can use them in such large quantities. The initial boost in energy and vitality after going on a raw food diet is not due to the vitamins; it is rather caused by the sudden mobilisation of the immune system which tries to counteract the massive influx of enzyme inhibitors and antibodies contained in the food. In time, the digestive system becomes increasingly dependent on large supplies of vitamins and minerals. And when suddenly there is not enough of them in the food we eat, the body begins to suffer from what is generally called a vitamin or mineral deficiency, which is just another word for weak digestion. Our time is characterised by lazy digestive systems. We have cultivated our own dependency on large quantities of external supplies of these basic nutrients.

We can easily afford to eat a fresh salad with our meal today because we have "cultivated away" the natural antibodies of the plants and vegetables. This makes them less "poisonous" for us but at the same time also more vulnerable to all kinds of attacks by insects, lice, bugs, beetles, locusts, fungus, and harsh climatic conditions. To make them resistant against the bewildering number of possible enemies we give the plants synthetically derived poisons (insecticides, pesticides, and other fertilisers) to make up for the missing antibodies. We have effectively impaired the plants' immune systems, and without our chemical assistance, most cultured plant foods would never reach the ripening stage.

By contrast, the wild-growing herbs have retained their immunity and know very well how to survive. They contain potent medicinal substances, which are nothing other than the plants' antibodies. If they are cultivated, too, away from their natural environment and climatic conditions, their medicinal properties become less potent, which makes them less useful as a medicine. Many of them no longer have medicinal values and they are now merely used in cooking to flavour the food.

The Grain Food Mystery

If you give pigs too much grain feeds, their growth rate is retarded. By contrast, the same grains fed to cattle, ferment in their stomachs without a problem. Grains contain several substances that can reduce our ability and that of other animals to absorb minerals, trace elements, and even vitamin B1. They also can block our digestive enzymes and render proteins indigestible. Wheat in particular contains material components that interfere with the digestion of fats by blocking such enzymes as the *lipase* of the pancreas. Our ancestors have traditionally used plenty of lard or oil when preparing dishes made from grain, often at the ratio of 1:1. This may explain why people who eat too little fat with their bread and other wheat products often develop excessive weight; they suffer from a disturbed fat metabolism.

Each type of grain has specific antibodies and enzyme inhibitors that can inhibit growth and disrupt digestion. They are naturally found in the most "precious" parts of the grain, the wheat germ, and in the the layer directly under the husk. The husk itself is wooden, enhanced by stored silicate, and contains *tannins* which bond with proteins. The putrefaction of these proteins produces bad-smelling gases, ammonia, and toxins. If eaten as raw grain muesli it can virtually "burst" one's intestines.

But even wholemeal bread has become difficult to digest for most people since the old baking procedures have been "modernised", saving time and money. For thousands of years, man has imitated the fermentation process that grains undergo in the cow's stomach system. The dough used to be left alone for as long as twenty hours. This helped to pre-digest the grains and break down some of the most notorious antibodies or *alkaloids*, freeing the otherwise useless nutrients. The initial stages of baking also increased the process of fermentation, which got rid of the rest of the poisons.

Today's time-saving baking methods use a mixture of chemicals that reduce the need for long fermentation but fail to break down the toxic contents of the grain. The use of yeast completely inhibits their destruction. The result is that the bread, though tasting delicious is difficult to digest and causes bloating. However, it may work very well as a laxative. Most people who either eat uncooked whole grains, commercial whole wheat bread or even just added wheat bran find that their bowel movements begins to be "normalised". To be relieved from constipation is certainly a great advantage over being all blocked up. Still, the main reason for the sudden "improvement" is the body's desperate attempt to remove the toxic antibodies in the wheat products as quickly as it can. This should not be confused with a voluntary healthy bowel movement; it simply is a normal immune response. But if the situation continues, the constant irritation can lead to Irritable Bowel Syndrome, diarrhoea, Crohn's disease, or cancer of the colon.

Another immediate advantage of properly fermenting bread dough is the production of various types of natural antibiotics, which help to ward off mould-producing microbes. This protects the intestinal lining against possible irritation. Commercial wholemeal bread and wheat flakes in breakfast cereals have therefore no natural defences against mould attack, which makes them "risky" foods. Allergies are a common result.

That in most cultures of the world white bread has been the dominating wheat product for thousands of years shows that the older generations knew more about the potential dangers of whole wheat than we do. The Ancient Egyptians sifted the flower again after milling. Even Hippokrates declared 2,500 years ago that white bread was more nourishing and the ancient Romans favoured white flour too. Too much of it, however, is constipating. French baking is known to have avoided wheat bran for hundreds of years. Rye, on the other hand, has never been refined which gives rye bread its darker colour. Barley is usually eaten in roasted form. Oats are normally heat-treated; otherwise they would taste bitter. Cooked as porridge, they are good for an irritated stomach. Rice obviously is edible only in cooked form.

Conclusion:

Nutrients are not the only components of our food. Natural food also contains toxic antibodies, a fact that should be considered by all those who live on unaltered whole foods. Ayurveda knew of these dangers even 6,000 years ago and recommends that we prepare and cook a considerable portion of our foods. Mankind has used fire for food preparation for over one million years to make food digestible and to remove any toxic components. A mixed diet, consisting of raw and possibly organically grown salad foods, fruit, cooked vegetables, cooked staple foods such as rice, wheat, and other grain foods, as well as legumes offer a large selection of natural foods that can accommodate every body-type.

Balanced *Pitta*s, with their naturally strong AGNI or digestive fire, can eat relatively more raw foods than the other two major body-types, particularly in the summer season. *Vata* and *Kapha* types benefit more from eating mostly warm and cooked foods, as their bodies tend to be cool by nature. A *Kapha*'s AGNI may easily get "subdued" by a lot of raw food, and a *Vata*, whose AGNI is "changeable" can become constipated, nervous, and depressed if he eats too much of it. But whatever body-type you are start trusting your intuition and listening to the signals from your body each and every moment of the day. One day you may have eaten a particular food such as a bar of chocolate and the next day you suffer a headache. If you ate a salad or fruit for supper, you may feel sluggish and irritable the next morning, because it has fermented in your intestines during the night. Nobody knows your body better than you do.

If you feel inclined to only eating raw, unprepared foods, it means that your body may require cleansing. Still, keep listening to your body's signals of comfort and discomfort. If one day you get an aversion to these foods, return to a mixed diet immediately because your body is telling you that it has had enough and can no longer cope with so many toxic and irritating antibodies. A cleanse consisting of raw vegetables or their juices has saved many people's lives by triggering a strong immune response. This helped remove toxic waste that may have lingered in the intestinal tract for many years. The body usually sends a clear message of discomfort when the antibodies begin to damage the intestines, which is the time to stop the cleansing.

Your physical needs, emotional state, behaviour, digestive ability, environmental factors, geographic conditions, and many other influences determine what kind of food, of what quality and how much of it your body requires each new day. You are not a machine that runs with one specific fuel oil; you are a living organism that is changing every moment according to uncountable influences. By increasingly relying on the body's wisdom and natural instinct regarding the choice of food we can break out of the man-made, restrictive rules of nutrition and discover what we really need to nourish ourselves.

4. The Milk Controversy

Is Cow's Milk Suitable for Human Consumption?

Dairy milk has become a major target of criticism over the past few years due to its long lists of negative side effects. More and more health practitioners report that patients are allergic to dairy products or suffer from food intolerance to milk-containing foods. Eczema, asthma, migraine, constipation, hay fever, arthritis, stomach trouble, heart disease, and testicular cancer are all linked with high consumption of dairy products.

One such case was Tim who just turned 11 years old when his parents brought him to see me. He had developed asthma when he was 5 months old. The former treatment consisted of three different types of drugs, including *cortisone* and an inhaler. The boy's condition worsened steadily and he developed herpes and other symptoms of toxicity. Six months before his visit to me, Tim had caught a cold, which was treated with antibiotics. Since then his lungs showed strong signs of congestion. He complained about being tired all the time and unable to run or play with his friends. Muscle testing revealed that Tim was highly allergic to milk or milk products. His parents confirmed that by the age of 5 months he was no longer breast-fed but was instead given milk formulae.

Tim's asthma was caused by his body's inability to break down the protein of cow's milk. The fragments of undigested protein caused a strong immune response aggravating the entire mucous lining from the anus to the lungs. His condition was chronic because he consumed large quantities of animal protein, including milk and dairy products throughout his young life. After two weeks of abstinence from these foods, his asthma and herpes subsided and have never recurred since then.

Could it be that cows milk is meant only for calves just as cats milk is meant only for kittens? Would we consider feeding our babies with, for example, dog's milk instead of human breast milk? The ratio of nutrients contained in dog's milk does not suit human requirements. Yet the same applies to cows milk. Cows milk contains three times as much protein and almost four times as much calcium as human breast milk. These amounts are unsuitable for the human physiology at any age.

Cows milk is designed to contain the exact amount of calcium and protein necessary to feed a calf that will end up being at least 3-4 times larger than the human body is. If we gave human breast milk to a calf, it would not grow strong enough even to survive. By contrast, human babies require more carbohydrates in the beginning stages of their lives than calves do. For this reason, cows milk contains only 50 per cent carbohydrates compared to human milk. Calves on the other hand require more salt than human babies do, so salt content in cow's milk is three times higher as in human milk. It is therefore not surprising that most of the original populations living in Asia, Africa, and Australia, and South America don't regard cows milk as a food fit for human consumption.

Once weaned, mammals no longer look for milk to satisfy their hunger or thirst. If human babies, who have been breast-fed for 11-12 months, were given the option of choosing from various types of natural and suitable foods, two out of three would no longer want breast milk as a food. Babies who are fed with cow's milk tend to look puffy, bloated, and fat. It is not uncommon for 1-year olds to have gallstones in the liver as a result of drinking, and not digesting, cows milk. Many of them suffer from colic and gas which makes them cry and develop sleeping problems.

Milk-caused Osteoporosis

Since milk intolerance is becoming increasingly common among all age groups in the Western world, nutritionists and doctors are starting to suspect that cows milk may not be such a natural food for humans after all.

Milk is a highly mucus-forming food that can cause irritation and congestion throughout the gastrointestinal tract. If regularly consumed, milk can leave an increasingly hardening and almost impermeable coating on the inside of the intestinal membranes. This restricts absorption of nutrients, including the calcium, magnesium and zinc needed to form bones. It is virtually impossible to treat people with natural medicines as long as they continue to clog up their digestive systems with milk or dairy foods; the medicines are not able to penetrate the hardened layer of mucous in the intestines.

Most people wouldn't drink milk if they weren't so influenced by the myth that milk is essential for the bones. If you are prone to Osteoporosis, or Osteoarthritis, then consider the following facts:

- Cows milk may be very rich in calcium but its high calcium to magnesium ratio can make it difficult to absorb. In certain people or body-types, the calcium may be deposited in places where it is not required, hence the development of calcification of bones and other parts of the body.

- Most of the calcium contained in cows milk is bound by the milk chemical *casein*, which makes it far too crude for proper absorption by the human intestinal membranes. Cows milk contains 300 times more *casein* than human milk. You can get more absorbable calcium out of 6-8 almonds or a teaspoon of molasses than you can get from one litre of cow's milk.

- There is quantitatively more phosphorus in cow's milk than there is calcium. To metabolise that much phosphorus, the body requires extra amounts of calcium, which it extracts from the bones, teeth, and muscles. This leads to a calcium deficiency in these parts of the body. To compensate the sudden loss of calcium, the body tries to mobilise more of it. As mentioned before, it has several methods to manufacture the much-needed mineral. If the body depended totally on external supplies of calcium, 80% of today's population would have lost at least one third of their bone mass by the age of 30. Because of this self-regulating mechanism, we are able to survive even extremely one-sided diets with very little calcium intake. We can even fast on distilled water for long periods of time without developing a calcium deficiency. Yet if the consumption of dairy foods continues for a long time, the calcium reserves get depleted faster than they can be replenished, leading to damage of the bone tissue.

- Milk proteins contain about three times as many sulphur containing amino acids as proteins from vegetable origin do. Through regular consumption of milk and dairy products the blood would become too acid if the body didn't mobilise large amounts of minerals to save the body from acid death. Yet, in the long term, this emergency measure leads to demineralisation of the tissues and organs and subsequent acidosis.

- Storage of excessive amounts of milk protein in the connective tissues and basement membranes of the capillaries reduces the diffusion of essential minerals and vitamins to the tissues of the body. This causes a depletion of nutrients in the tissues, especially of those that form the bones and joints.

Cows maintain strong and hardy bones and teeth throughout their lives and get most of their calcium from the greens they eat. Gorillas, elephants, and other strong animals too do not suffer from osteoporosis. Occasionally they lick on limestone but this is certainly not enough to supply the large quantities of calcium they require to build and rebuild their heavy skeletons. If milk were the most useful and important source of calcium for grown animals then nature would certainly have designed ways of supplying them with milk throughout their lives. But as it turns out, they have access to milk only at the beginning stages of their lives.

To digest whole milk the human body requires large amounts of bile. Drinking whole milk regularly can eventually exhaust the liver's bile-producing capacity. Drinking low fat milk makes matters even worse. Low fat milk requires less bile to digest the fat contained in the milk, yet milk protein cannot be digested without the natural amounts of milk fat. Added to that, without sufficient bile, calcium cannot be properly digested or absorbed either. The large amounts of undigested milk protein increase acidity in the body and the unused crude milk calcium can cause calcification of joints, arteries, or kidneys. This can make protein foods with lowered fat-content hazardous to health.

Leafy green vegetables contain four times more calcium than whole milk. There is also plenty of calcium in almonds, black molasses, sesame seeds, broccoli, brazil nuts, millet, oats, and citrus fruits. The difference with this type of calcium is that it is readily absorbed by the human digestive system, provided it functions well. Osteoporosis or Osteoarthritis are basically metabolic disorders that are caused by severe congestion unbalanced diet and almost never by insufficient calcium intake. Osteoporosis is virtually unknown in places such as Africa where people eat far fewer proteins than those living in developed countries do.

Milk Consumption Linked to Diabetes and Allergies

Initial studies on diabetes revealed that the frequency of *insulin dependent diabetes* is linked to breast-feeding. The longer children were breast-fed by their mothers, the less was their risk of developing diabetes later in life. The interpretation of this finding was revised, however, after it was found that children who are fed with cows milk formulae rather than with breast milk were the most likely candidates for diabetes. More precise studies revealed that diabetics have a striking number of antibodies against a particular protein in their blood. Diabetes is an "autoimmune disease" which means that the body directs its defences against itself. The particular protein that the body tries to combat here comes from the whey of cow's milk.

Ever since cows milk has been used to make cheese, whey, which is a waste product of cheese production, has been fed to pigs. This practice continued even after scientists attributed great nutritional value to whey. Since nobody really liked drinking this "precious" ingredient of milk it was mixed in with foods. This "coincided" with a dramatic increase in allergies in the developed world. Scientists have discovered that the *beta-casein* (a particular protein) in cow's milk can trigger an immune response that may, in turn, cross-react with an antigen to cause an allergic reaction. An allergy is the body's response to fight a substance that it considers dangerous to its health and survival.

Today, millions of people in the Western Hemisphere are suffering from allergies caused by milk or products that contain milk powder or whey. Maybe it is for this reason that most populations in the world avoid drinking cows milk. The current "allergy epidemic" in developed countries may have well been caused by the "miracle food" whey which is added to so many food products, including children's foods, fresh cheese, ready-made soups, diet foods, etc. We are literally bombarded with this milk protein unless we live off purely natural foods.

Watch out for the Milk Hormone

Bovine somatotrophin (BST) is a hormone which when fed to cows can increase their milk yield by 20-30 percent. In the United States BST has been licensed by the American Food and Drug Administration (FDA) in 1994. This effectively gave farmers the legal permission to treat their herds with the controversial hormone. The licence was accompanied with a new labelling policy, previously unheard of in the United States. Traditional dairy farmers are prohibited from labelling their milk as "hormone free" -- while those using the hormone are not required to say that they use BST. Because uncontrolled hormone intake is linked to a number of serious health problems there has been great concern among milk hormone using farmers that people would prefer the natural milk to the hormone treated one. Their pressure ensured the above legislation.

The granting of a licence to increase milk production through hormones comes at a time when milk production is already much higher than is milk consumption. Most industrialised nations destroy enormous quantities of milk and butter to manipulate the prices with no regard to the cows' health. Cows are naturally made to produce a certain amount of milk according to the demand from their offspring. The hormone-induced artificial increase of milk yield causes a number of cow's diseases that are met by administering large quantities of antibiotics. The drug's poisons seep into the milk and its products. How much a cow must be suffering when its udder is being extended to beyond it natural capacity is not considered an issue.

Is Milk Bad for Everyone?

If milk causes allergies or other diseases why does not everyone who consumes milk regularly suffer from the same problems? One reason may be that they don't remove the fat from the milk. Left unaltered, cows milk is completely balanced regarding its natural ingredients. By removing one essential part of the milk, i.e., fat, the milk protein can no longer be digested completely, hence there will be a "leftover" of undigested, and irritating proteins against which the body's immune system begins to take up a fight.

In my practice I have found that persons who are of *Vata* constitution seem to digest and metabolise milk much better than *Kapha* types, provided it is fresh, whole fat, and boiled before consumption. *Vata* types suffer from dryness, lightness, and coldness. The mucous- producing effect of milk may help actually lubricate their intestinal lining, which has the tendency to be dry. The milk's heavy and warming qualities may pacify *Vata* and thereby outweigh any possible negative effects that milk may have for other body-types. *Vata* types and to some extent also *Pitta* types seem to produce enough of the specific digestive enzymes which are used to break down milk proteins.

In *Kapha* types, however, milk protein remains undigested and can trigger allergic reactions with intense mucous irritation and sinus congestion. The Kapha's blood vessel walls tend to clog up quickly with excessive proteins as a result of overeating dairy foods or meat. This may explain why this particular body-type is more prone to obesity and congestive heart failure than the Vata type is.

Once milk is pasteurised, i.e., ultra heat-treated, its natural enzyme population is destroyed. Yet the enzymes are needed to make the milk nutrients available to the body cells. Newly born calves die within 6 months if they are fed with pasteurised cows milk. One can imagine the turmoil that must be going on in the tiny intestinal tract of a baby who is fed with pasteurised milk or sterilised milk formulae. Babies usually develop colic, become bloated and chubby, discharge mucus, catch colds frequently, are restless, and cry a lot. The best advise is breast feed as long as is possible, avoid dairy-based formulae altogether, use alternatives such as organic soya formulae, and give freshly mashed fruits, vegetables and rice when the baby is ready to eat solids.

Boiling fresh, unpasteurised milk before consumption seems to have a beneficial effect. Milk protein begins to break down into amino acids during boiling, which makes it easier to digest and absorb. Many of the milk's enzymes survive. This may be one of the reasons why Indians always boil their milk before use. They also know that milk has adverse effects when its fat is removed. To preserve milk and to kill any existing germs they simply put a silver coin in the milk. Silver is strongly anti-bacterial. And to avoid mucous congestion, they put 2-3 pinches of either turmeric or dry ginger into the milk before boiling it. Pasteurised milk seems to upset all the three *doshas* but boiling the milk helps to reduce its irritating effect.

Cold milk on the other hand is very difficult to digest. As the cold milk touches the warm stomach lining, the nerve endings of the stomach become "numb" or insensitive and its cells contract. This inhibits the secretion of gastric juices, which is required to digest protein. The cold condition of the milk may even be responsible for leaving those proteins undigested that are known to cause allergic reactions. Enzymes require a certain temperature to act upon the food; if it is too low the proteins won't be broken down properly, hence an intense irritation of the mucous lining may develop. *Vata* types who are very sensitive to cold are rarely attracted to taking milk cold (from the refrigerator). *Pitta*s often have an excessively high temperature in their stomach, which gets lowered only slightly by cold milk. Consequently *Pitta*s are still able to secret the necessary amount of gastric juices to digest the milk proteins. But if they take milk cold on a regular basis, their AGNI or digestive power also begins to get affected.

If you have access to fresh, full-fat, and non-pasteurised milk and if you are a *Vata* or *Pitta* type with no *Kapha* imbalance (signs of excessive mucous in chest, nose, or sinuses), you may use milk by applying the above procedures of preparation. If milk still causes you mucous, then it is simply a "no-food" for you.

There are now various brands of non-pasteurised milk available in many countries such as the "Vorzugsmilch" in Germany, which literally means the "milk of preference." Again, if you are not sure about its health benefits for you apply the muscle test and your body will give you the correct answer. As with everything, generalised clear cut answers rarely exist. Your individual response makes all the difference when it comes to creating health or treating ill health.

5. Artificial Sweeteners – A Major Health Risk

Aspartame and *saccharin* are the two most commonly used artificial sweeteners that have gained huge popularity among people who are concerned about their weight. In the belief that they are doing something good for themselves, they are thrilled to have found the "ideal" sweetener that satisfies their sweet tooth yet doesn't make them fat. However, there is mounting evidence that artificial sweeteners are a major health risk and can cause brain damage and other problems of the nervous system.

The use of artificial sweeteners in Britain alone has rocketed from a total of 615,000 tons in 1988 to 1,801,000 tons in 1993, an increase of 370 per cent for *aspartame* and 250 per cent for *saccharin* in five years. The sharp increase in the use of artificial sweeteners is very significant in relation to their sweetening potency. *Saccharin* is more than 400 times as sweet as regular sugar and *aspartame* 200 times as much.

Considered non-toxic and safe by the British government, both *saccharin* and *aspartame* have found their way into the food chain. Both sweeteners are not only found in drinks but also in children's jellies, lollies, puddings, crops, beans, and even tinned pasta. *Aspartame*, which is sold under the names NutraSweet, Hermesetas, Gold Choice, and Canderel, has been included in some 9000 foods in America and hundreds of products in Great Britain and other European countries. The products include fruit drinks, diet soda, frozen lollies, as a sugar substitute for tea or coffee, instant breakfasts, chewing gum, cocoa and other instant drinks, drugs, supplements and even yoghurt.

The British government has issued a call for clear warning labels (why warning people if it is safe?), but only few manufacturers have complied, claiming that it would "clutter up" their labels and confuse consumers. Yet it is more confusing to the consumer not to know whether a food product contains *aspartame* or *saccharin* than to know it.

A survey conducted by BBC2's *Money Programme* revealed that up to 40 per cent of the public do not expect to find artificial sweeteners in their fruit drinks, not to mention in their foods. But there is hardly any drink on the market that does not contain an artificial sweetener, even if the drink is labelled "sugar free." The most popular brands are sold to the public, giving the impression that these products are totally natural whereas in truth they contain synthetically derived sweeteners. The European Union has urged producers to label these drinks "With sweetener" but surveys have shown that up to 50 per cent of consumers would no longer buy these products.

Seven European countries discontinued the use of sweeteners for a good reason. Tests on animals have revealed that *saccharin* can cause cancer of the bladder. The European Food Commission is particularly concerned about the overconsumption of sweeteners by children. Seven years ago, the British government announced that 2,5 mg/kg was the acceptable (safe) daily intake (ADI) of *saccharin*. It is important to know, however, that this figure is not based on control studies but on mere estimates. Through repeated intake of the sweeteners, many children and adults "expect" that a variety of foods and drinks taste very sweet, a characteristic most of them never have in their natural form. The masking of the natural taste of these products has consequences and there is a price to be paid for falling into the "sweet" trap.

They are Fattening, too

A major American controlled study on 80,000 women showed that those who regularly use artificial sweeteners put on more weight per year than those who do not use them. What is even more surprising is the finding that with the widespread use of sweeteners the consumption of ordinary sugar and sugary foods has increased, too. The following explanation resolves this mystery.

The body has a self-regulating mechanism, a kind of thermostat that measures the amount of energy (or calories) it can obtain from a particular meal. When your body has received enough energy from the food you have eaten, then your mouth, stomach, intestines, and liver send messages to the brain that all energy requirements have been met. Subsequently, your nervous system secretes hormones that stop your desire for more food. This point of saturation is essential for your well being, without it you would continuously want to eat and never feel satisfied. If, for instance, during one particular meal you eat foods that contain only very little energy or at least not enough to fulfil your energy requirements, then your body will tempt you to eat more during the next meal. This way, the body makes up for the loss of energy during the previous meal. The same happens when your AGNI or digestive power is low and you are not deriving sufficient energy from the food you eat.

On the other hand, when during one particular meal you eat food that has a higher content of calories than your body really requires at this moment, it will signal for less energy during the next meal. If there is only very little energy in the food you are eating during a meal, the more you need to eat from it in order to reach your individual "set point" or body weight that can keep your energy distribution as balanced and normal as possible. Whenever you deprive yourself of eating enough and are unable to meet the energy needs of your body, you will look for more food the next day, the day after, and so on. This leads to chronic overeating which packs plenty of low-energy food into your intestinal tract. Incapable of digesting and absorbing low-energy food properly, your body turns it into fat and waste and clogs up your lymphatic, digestive, and circulatory systems.

This is the time when your body signals "famine." You start craving foods, particularly refined carbohydrates such as ordinary sugar, chocolate, sweet drinks, coffee, etc., which all give you an instant boost of energy. But they also contain only "empty" energy and just raise your sugar level in the blood for a short time. After a little while the sugar levels drops below normal, which may cause depression, moodiness, and exhaustion.

If you are overweight and believe that you can reduce weight by restricting your daily intake of calories, you will be very disappointed. Within a few days, your body will run out of energy and wants to eat, hence the increased appetite or craving. If you still don't eat enough, you will fall into a depression, which may cause you bingeing food ravenously. Your body thinks there are regular famines going on and tries to convert some of the food into fat to deposit it for the next one. After each "voluntary famine" or "weight reducing" diet, your body will put on weight much faster than it did before. This is known as the yo-yo effect.

Under normal circumstances, the body converts calories into heat, which then simply evaporates. Well-circulated brown fat tissue, which is located near the large arteries and in the underarms, is the main source of this energy. There is new research that suggests that in some obese people this mechanism may be disturbed and that the best dietary rules would be of no avail. Abusing the body's digestive system through frequent strict dieting may be the main cause of this problem.

Because artificial sweeteners are low-energy foods and non-physiological, the body deals with them in the same way as described above. It recognises their complete absence of potential energy and signals "lack of energy supply". As a result it increases its appetite to stimulate the desire for more food. This principle is a well-known and commonly applied practice, both in the food industry and in animal feeding. Animal feeds contain highly concentrated *saccharin* to stimulate the animal's appetite so that they eat more frequently and grow fat faster. The same mechanism applies to the human body.

Deceiving the Body

For both humans and animals, *aspartame* and *saccharin* belong to the category of "sweet" food. The sweetness of natural foods is caused by sugar. Because sugar can move straight through the stomach walls, it will appear in the blood stream within 3-5 minutes. However, the body has to keep the blood sugar level in check since too little or too much of it can be dangerous. The body regulates sugar levels automatically through simple reflex mechanisms. When sugar touches the taste buds for sweet taste on the tongue, the pancreas is given the instruction to secrete *insulin,* which is required to make it (the sugar) available to the cells.

If you eat artificial sweeteners, the body naturally responds to their sweet taste by secreting *insulin*. Expecting the sugar to enter the blood, it, however, receives only a combination of protein compounds. Doing its normal job, the pancreas has already prepared a portion of *insulin* that now floats about in the blood stream searching for the expected sugar. Since it can't find it there, the insulin removes some of the blood sugar instead. This effectively lowers your sugar levels. However, since this situation can be life endangering, your body quickly signals "hunger" which becomes a sudden, strong "craving." Since foods with artificial sweeteners are not able to meet the demand for an increase in blood sugar, you begin to look for sugary foods

Instead of saving the calories that are contained in ordinary sugar, you have artificially increased your need and appetite for more sweet food. If you try to satisfy this desire by eating more foods that have been sweetened with artificial sweeteners (without calories), the urge to eat will become even stronger than before and you will start *overeating*. Researchers have found that the urge to eat more food after ingesting artificial sweeteners in a drink can last up to 90 minutes, even when all blood tests show normal values.

A more serious situation arises when the body is given artificial sweeteners on an ongoing basis. Since the sweeteners repeatedly stimulate the taste buds responsible for detecting sugar, the brain maintains an almost continuous urge to eat. At the same time, the liver is instructed by the brain to store sugar supplies rather than to release them, which causes chronic fatigue. The pancreas, which had wrongly assumed that real sugar was entering the blood stream, eventually realises that it has been cheated. Hence it reduces its secretion of *insulin*. One might think that this solves the problem but the body reacts with depression.

Sweeteners may Cause Obesity, Depression, and Brain Damage

Sugar is known to "improve" moods for relatively short periods of time. With the help of *insulin*, sugar increases the secretion of *serotonin* in the brain. *Serotonin* is the neurotransmitter of happiness. If *insulin* secretion fails to occur, happiness remains low. The only way to get out of this situation, it seems, is to eat sugar so that the body can secrete *insulin* again.

You may believe that the fewer calories you eat the more weight you will lose. But food manufactures know that the more artificially sweetened foods and drinks you consume the more you will want their normal sugar containing foods and drinks as well. Diet foods and diet drinks have not only contributed to a massive increase of sugar consumption and obesity but also led to an epidemic of depression. I have seen numerous depressed people over the years, a large percentage of whom regularly use artificial sweeteners. By cutting out diet foods and light products, they have returned to their normal self, *and* they have lost the excessive weight, too.

Apart from causing obesity and depression, sweeteners have been linked to insomnia, headaches, giddiness, loss of memory, nausea, pre-menstrual syndrome, panic attacks, epileptic fits, and even overstimulation of breast glands leading to breast cancer. *Aspartame* in particular may cause extensive damage to the central nervous system. Once it has entered the intestinal tract, *aspartame* is converted into two highly excitatory neurotransmitter amino acids, *aspartic acid* and *phenylalinine*, as well as into *methyl alcohol* (wood-grain alcohol) and *formaldehyde (embalming fluid)*.

Wood alcohol is one of the most dangerous substances that result from eating artificial sweeteners. It may directly enter the blood stream and move through the brain barrier into the central nervous system where it can influence the neurotransmitters, alter brain function, and cause brain damage. Wood alcohol can cause blindness and formaldehyde can cause cancer. In some cases *aspartame* may suppress appetite and "kill" AGNI, the digestive fire, altogether. Both can lead to quick, excessive weigh gain. According to Consumer Reports, aspartame has only a shelf life of between two and three months. After that it begins to break down and pose an increasing danger to the consumer. The same occurs when aspartame or an aspartame-containing food is heated.

Aspartame accounts for more than 75 per cent of the total of adverse reactions to food reported to the US Federal Drug Administration. Hundreds of pilots have reported symptoms of memory loss and confusion, headaches, seizures, visual disturbances and gastrointestinal reactions as a result of consuming sweeteners. If pregnant women consume large quantities of diet sodas to avoid weight gain, their placenta may accumulate methyl alcohol, causing mental retardation in the foetus. They also risk maternal malnutrition because of the gastrointestinal problems and diarrhoea associated with sweeteners.

Other sweeteners than aspartame have similar effects. Added to soft drinks, they are now even linked with damage of the testicles and other key areas of the body. Stimulating the brain of a child with these "pleasure-enhancing" chemicals in beverages will, in some cases, program their senses to look for and use stronger addictive substances such as hard drugs or large amounts of alcohol later in life. The latest sweetener, *acesulfame K*, may be even carcinogenic, i.e. cause cancer, according a report published in the British Medical Journal in 1996. To avoid serious health problems, it is best to stick to foods and drinks that come from purely natural sources.

6. Light-Foods Increase Weight

"Foolproof" Slimming Diets

Most dietary approaches in the past were based on the simple mathematical concept that, because 1 kg of body fat contains 7,000 calories, by taking in 1,000 calories less each day a person would lose 1 kg of body fat a week. Since this equation sounded so logical and convincing many people tried to shed the undesirable weight by controlling their daily intake of calories. However, this theory collapsed like a card house. The more these people reduced their calorie intake the faster they put on weight.

When you analyse the results of all the prominent slimming techniques and dietary plans, you face the following facts. Most people, who go on a diet, give up before completing it, and of those who continue only few lose weight, and of those who lose weight most put it back on again. The biggest craze on the slimming market concerns the consumption of "light" food. As the name suggests, the new products promise to make you lighter. You can eat as much as you like and will not put on weight because the products contain only little fat or no fattening substances at all. Now you don't have to restrict yourself or curb your appetite any longer and at the same time you become slim.

For these or similar reasons light-food has become extremely popular in industrialised nations. At last, food manufacturers have complied with the demands made by nutritional scientists and dieticians to produce foods with fewer calories. Consumers feel relieved that the new food is fat-free and without sugar and instead contains fat substitutes, water and artificial sweeteners. This saves massive amounts of calories. And by adding artificial flavours to the food and using other forms of chemical manipulation, the taste buds believe that it is the real thing. Man seems to have finally succeeded in creating the ideal food for man; at least this is what the majority of consumers have started to believe.

"Light Fats" and their "Amazing" Effects

Take for instance "light-butter" or half-fat butter, which has been heralded as one of the greatest "achievements" of food technology so far. In this high-tech product, at least half of the fat content of butter is replaced with water. It tastes like butter, it spreads like butter and it melts like butter in the mouth, but in reality it is mostly water. To turn water into butter you have to mix it with a thickening agent like gelatine, an emulsifier that permits mixing fat with water, and artificial colouring, aromas, and preservatives. It is difficult, though, for a layperson to detect from the labels whether a product has been manipulated in this way. Still there is one way to find out. Place the light butter or light margarine in your frying pan and see what happens. The artificial fats quickly disintegrate and turn into what they really are, that is, mostly water.

However, not all food imitations can be enriched with water. Fat-free salad dressings contain modified starch as a fat substitute. Principally being very dry by nature, starch (mostly cornstarch) is treated with hydrochloric acid and enzymes derived from mould. The end product leaves you with the feeling of cream in the mouth. The same can be achieved by using cheap protein and other carbohydrates. The products have such fancy names as "Trailblazer," and Nutrifat PC and have already been on the US-market for several years.

"*Olestra*" is the name for pseudo-fat that has recently been approved for sale on the US market to fill the gap for zero-cholesterol fat. Fat-free chips, diet-friendly crisps, and cholesterol lowering tortillas can now be staples of the otherwise fatty American diet. Is seems wonderful to be able to have all these "naughty" foods and not become fat or risk heart disease. The only problem with this non-physiological food is its side effects.

The pseudo-fat can actually cause substantial anal leakage and diarrhoea. It is as indigestible as plastic, which means it comes out completely unaltered. To prevent the product from becoming unpopular, the manufacturers have now added an "anti-anal leakage agent," a mixture that slows the elimination of the oil from the large intestine. The pseudo-fat mimics the properties of ordinary fats, with a similar "mouth-feel" and taste.

One of the more serious side effects of such products is that they are capable of removing the fat-solvable vitamins A, D, E, and K from the body as they pass through the intestinal tract. For this reason, US food manufacturers are required to fortify their olestra-containing products with all these vitamins, which gives the wrong impression that these foods are now safe for human consumption. But uncontrolled intake of vitamin K can endanger the lives of haemophiliacs; and a pregnant mother may risk her baby's life by taking too much vitamin A. Apart from removing vitamins from the body (and thoroughly confusing the body), olestra also reduces the absorption of *carotenoids* that help us to prevent cancer, heart disease, and strokes.

Pseudo-fats cannot fool even animals. When the fat replacement olestra was fed to dogs for 20 months, their weight had not decreased but increased.

Olestra is the first food additive with negative nutritional value. It is hard to conceive how much damage the plastic food will do if it remains in our food chain for several decades and, what makes things worse, it will be extremely difficult to trace the damage to the use of olestra. It is very unlikely that there will be any further research done on the side effects of olestra or similar foods. Hence it is up to each one of us to take more responsibility for our health and that of our families. If we desist from buying such synthetic foods they will disappear from the market as fast as they appeared.

Low Energy Foods Deplete Energy

Many people wonder why they have put on so much weight since consuming light-foods. Or, they may ask, why don't light-foods seem to contribute to slimming? The answer to this question is quite simple. After eating light-foods a couple of times, your body begins to realise that it is deprived of energy. Consequently, it sends you urgent messages of wanting energy-containing foods but you will eat more of them than you normally would. This natural response occurs in everyone, even in children.

Children are generally more in touch with their natural instincts and have not yet been influenced by theories about diets, calories, and light-foods. When researchers tested the eating habits of children, they wanted to find out whether children extract less calories from their food and lose weight if they consume light-products. The scientists were surpised to discover that those children whose diet included light-foods (low calorie) had actually *increased* their appetites and started eating more to balance the loss of energy caused by the light-foods.

The body is constantly aware of how much energy is required to conduct all its activities and subsequently sends the appropriate signals of how much we should eat in order to satisfy its needs. The requirements of course change as the day goes on. A theoretical system of how much you should eat at each meal and how many calories you can use up without becoming fat is therefore useless, if not harmful. It strongly interferes with the body's natural and uniquely programmed weight control mechanisms. The accompanied anxiety of eating too much or eating the wrong type of food may even shut down the digestive functions, which means you are converting much of the ingested food into undigested toxic waste. This clogs up the system even more and adds extra weight to the body.

The body always knows when it has reached a point of satiety. This was shown in another experiment during which a group of children were given the permission to eat as much as they wanted and whatever they wanted for six consecutive days. They were even allowed sweets, cakes, and other kinds of "unhealthy" foods. Parents were not permitted to influence their children in any way.

The researchers carefully recorded what and how much of each food a child ate during each meal, throughout the six 24-hour periods. Some children ate only minute amounts during some meals but then greatly increased the amounts at other meal(s). The children's calorie intake fluctuated substantially from meal to meal; yet, when calculated for an entire day, calorie consumption remained the same.

Gaining "Waste-weight"

There are many studies that show that light-foods encourage appetite and overeating and do **not** reduce weight. The more of enzymatic energy is contained in food, the faster we feel satisfied. But not only light-foods are energy depleted and dissatisfying. Refined, processed, chemically treated foods contain no *Prana* or life energy, which is the type of energy the body needs to help digest food.

There may be plenty of calories in the highly refined white flour products but the body is not able use this form of "dead" energy. Our digestive system is naturally programmed to extract energy from *life foods* or complex staple foods, which contain plenty of *Prana*. The body regards such lifeless foods as meat, cornflakes or light-foods to be indigestible and tries to "dump" them as quickly as possible. All they do is to congest the intestines where they ferment and putrefy. This is the first location in the body where waste, meaning extra weight, starts to accumulate and when the intestinal "container" is full up it begins distributing the waste to other areas of the body as well.

This increase of waste-weight may tempt you to go on a restrictive diet for a while. But the more often you go on a diet, the less successful it becomes. Each new diet requires a different way of metabolism. The continual abuse of your natural weight regulation reduces AGNI, the digestive fire, to a point when almost no foods, even fresh and healthy foods, can be tolerated and be utilised by the body. At such a stage, obese people complain that they are putting on weight although they are hardly eating anything.

The producers of light-foods know all that. Since light-foods have become available in the supermarkets, the sales of normal foods have increased too. If light-food had the effect of curbing appetites and reducing the consumption of ordinary foods, you can take it for granted that light-products would have never made it into the food market. These man-made foods have certainly not been made available to create a healthier population.

The Calorie-plan Dilemma

What is most discouraging in the confusion around food today is that our generation is perhaps the first one in the entire history of mankind that has lost its natural instinct to know which foods are good for us and which ones are not. We have left it to experts or nutritional scientists to make certain that we are being nourished in the best possible way. Food is no longer considered to be God's gift to man but a mere collection of chemical components, including calories, Joule, vitamins, fats, proteins and their various amino acid components, carbohydrates, trace elements, etc. If the figures of nutritional daily requirements were correct, no one in the world could ever be healthy because everyone would miss out on one vitamin, mineral, trace element, or the other. For example, we would have to eat massive amounts of liver and herring, to avoid vitamin D deficiency. Yet those who never ate fish or liver in their entire lives have no less vitamin D in their body than those who do.

The official figures for nutritional requirements are unreliable and misleading. In a major study at the University Hospital in Vienna, researchers first calculated the nutritional values of the patients' diet according to the official nutritional figures and then analysed the same food items in the laboratory for their true nutritional contents. The experiment lasted for 38 days and the results were astounding. The calculated figures for calories were 1/3 higher than were actually found through chemical analysis. The difference with regard to carbohydrates was 44 percent, with regard to protein 50 percent, and with regard to fats 60 percent! The conclusion of the study was that there is no reliable way to figure out what really is contained in the food. Besides, foods such as tomatoes, potatoes, fruits, and vegetables change their nutritional contents according to seasons, preparation, and storage and are different in different countries due to varied climatic, soil, and geographical conditions.

In addition, the information that indigestible fibre contained in whole foods doesn't release calories is incorrect. It is true that *our body* has no enzymes to digest fibre but we have plenty of *bacteria* in our intestinal tract that can do this job even better than enzymes do. All fibre reaches the colon in undigested form. Just as easily as the bacteria in nature break down food fibre, so easily do the bacteria of the intestinal flora digest the fibre that passes through the intestines. This may result in undesirable gases caused by fermentation and release various fatty acids that are absorbed by the large intestines and serve as a source of energy, which means they provide calories. Pectin, for example, is a fibre found in apples and can provide 283 calories per 100g, as much as in a 100g ice cream!

The dilemma that arises from eating according to a calorie plan is that nobody can tell you for sure how many calories are locked in a particular food, nor is it known how many calories are being utilised by each individual. A *Kapha* type, for instance, has a slow metabolic rate and uses up less energy than a *Vata* type who has a very fast metabolic rate. *Vata*s may eat three times as many calories and still put on no extra weight whereas *Kapha*s may just "look" at food and put on weight. If a healthy *Pitta* type eats excess amounts of calories, let's assume 2,000 instead of the recommended 1,000, he simply converts the unused calories into heat and becomes slightly more "energetic" than before. His body weight will remain unchanged, unless he overeats regularly. Research has documented that the average overweight person does not consume more calories than a slim person does.

If excessive consumption of calories always led to weight gain, then most people in the world would be obese by now. According to the calorie theory, a person who eats two pieces of chocolate a day (50 calories) too much should put on 25kg of body fat within a period of ten years. Imagine how this person would look if he ate that much chocolate for sixty years, according to the theory.

Fortunately, the body is not a machine that counts calories. A strong digestive fire (AGNI) can make use of more calories than a weak one. If AGNI is weak, then most of them are not used which means that there is be plenty of unused and undigested food leftover. Consequently, the energy requirements of the body are no longer met. This lowers the metabolic rate and general circulation, and the resulting accumulation of toxic waste congests vital areas of tissues and organs in the body. The lymphatic system becomes severely blocked and retains large amounts of lymph, hence the swelling that accompanies weight gain.

Weight Regulation is Natural

Weight loss occurs spontaneously when the natural weight regulation mechanisms are restored. Excessive body weight is a symptom of disturbed digestion and metabolism and a sign of chronic toxicity in the body and should not be treated on its own level. Trying to remove the symptom (excessive weight) can turn out to be very harmful and disappointing when the toxins are not removed first.

The body has a natural resistance to losing excessive weight quickly because sudden weight loss could release a flood of trapped toxins into the circulation and even have fatal side effects (collapse of liver functions, kidney failure, heart attack). The body never behaves in an irrational way. Weight regulation has to begin by removing the root causes of the metabolic problems that accompany weight gain.

People who put on extra weight may have been weakened by the following factors: Overstimulation; overworking; exhaustion; lack of *before-midnight* sleep, irregular eating habits; heavy meals at night time; overeating due to intake of non-nutritious and low energy foods; stimulants such as coffee, tea, and cigarettes; soft drinks; lack of water intake; negative responses to stress; alcohol consumption; unresolved conflicts (impairing digestion); fear and other emotional upsets; any other weakening influence that prevents the body from removing toxins.

The body needs to be cleansed of toxins before natural weight regulation can be restored. Cleaning it also ensures that weight takes place smoothly and without causing adverse effects. The most powerful and influential of all cleansing procedures described in this book is the *Liver Cleanse*. Its most important effect is to restore AGNI. When AGNI is stronger, food is digested more efficiently and less waste is deposited in the intestines. This, however, can happen only if you also clean out your colon through colonic irrigation. A kidney cleanse makes sure that the toxins released by the body don't get stuck in the kidneys. The main principle here is that for weight loss to take place naturally the eliminative organs must be cleared of any waste deposits first.

All this will effectively restore the body's health and natural weight. One liver cleanse, however, will not be sufficient to restore AGNI on a permanent basis. You need as many such cleanses as it takes to remove all the gallstones. After each cleanse, there will be a sudden increase in energy, the abdomen will feel tighter, and you may lose several pounds. Yet within less than a week, some of the old sluggishness may return and food cravings re-emerge. This shows that gallstones from the far "corners" of the liver have moved forward and clogged up major bile ducts, thereby affecting AGNI once again. By the time your liver is completely clean your body weight will be ideal and your energy boundless.

A Healthy Body – Normal Weight

Only a healthy body can be of normal weight. Theories of how much each person should weigh (calculated according to gender, height, etc.) ignore each person's unique constitutional requirements. Healthy body weight varies according to individual body-types. A healthy *Vata* type will always be very slim, and a healthy *Kapha* type will always be corpulent and muscular. The bones of *Vatas* are light, thin built, whereas *Kaphas* have very heavy, dense, and compact bones. Both body-types have very different if not completely opposite requirements regarding, food, exercise, and living conditions. *Pitta* types, which have more heat in their body, have entirely different energy requirements than the other body-types.

Weight loss for the right reasons, i.e., to improve your health, is easy. Trying to shed weight without removing the accumulated toxins first goes against the body's principles of survival and is therefore difficult to achieve. All you need to do is to restore your health. Once you have learnt the lessons of creating health from the current shape of your body, you are ready to change it into a better one. Your newly created body will serve you as an apt vehicle to fulfil your desires and lead a life filled with happiness, vitality, abundance, and wisdom.

CHAPTER 12

What's Useful to Know…

1. Potential Dangers of Medical Diagnosis

The categorisation of disease begins with its diagnosis. Depending on the particular symptom of discomfort or pain a person may be complaining about, a visit to the doctor will most likely result in the diagnosis of a disease, which the physician knows by its name and description. However, before you are given the certainty of diagnosis, you may have to undergo a series of routine examinations. There is the stethoscope, which has become a symbol of the healing profession; a measuring device to take the blood pressure; counting of the heart beat through feeling of the pulse; blood and urine tests; maybe x-rays, EEG, EKG, and more… In total, there are over 1,400 test procedures available that the modern doctor can use today to monitor and measure virtually every bit of your body.

Although in some cases, the use of these methods of diagnosis is justified and can save a person's life, in the vast majority of cases it is unjustified, misleading, and potentially harmful. Although in theory high tech diagnostic tools seem to be impartial and yield correct results, in reality they are grossly unreliable and can be as dangerous to health as some of the most risky drugs and surgical procedures. It is therefore important that they are not applied routinely, but much more selectively and if possible only during emergency situations. The following are some of the most commonly used methods of diagnosis and their discrepancies.

ECG and EEG – Machines *can* Lie
One of the instruments most frequently used to monitor heart activities is the *Electrocardiogram* or ECG. Repeatedly conducted tests have shown that at least 20 percent of diagnoses made by ECG experts were false. In addition, 20 percent of all ECG readings turned out to be different when the same person was tested a second time. When ECG measurements were taken of people who had suffered a heart attack, the machine could detect an abnormal heart function in only one quarter of the patients, no sign of a heart attack in the second quarter, and indecisive results in one half of all patients. A sudden "abnormal" curve in the ECG reading, caused by a jet flying over the hospital, can put a person into the "risk" of suffering a possible heart attack.

One 1992 report published in the *New England Journal of Medicine* proved that ECGs couldn't be trusted. When ECGs were taken on a group of perfectly healthy people over 50 percent of them showed an extremely abnormal heart condition. In other words, if a healthy child or an adult goes through a highly recommended health check-up and is diagnosed by an ECG expert as having an abnormally behaving heart that requires urgent treatment, the chances of the diagnosis being false-positive are fifty/fifty. To avoid being treated unnecessarily with potentially harmful drugs it is necessary that additional methods of diagnosis be employed to verify the correctness of the ECG readings. It is also highly recommended to have a second or third ECG reading at another hospital, just to be on the safe side.

The *Electroencephalogram* (EEG), which is used to measure brain activity and detect brain tumours and epilepsy, often gives highly unreliable diagnostic results, too. Twenty percent of people who suffer from epileptic fits produce normal readings. What is even worse, 15-20 percent of healthy people produce an abnormal EEG. To show how unreliable the EEG machine can be, when once connected to the head of a doll it showed that the doll was *alive*. In order to avoid costly and potentially risky treatment programmes, one should not solely rely on the diagnosis produced by the EEG.

X-rays -- Handle with Care!

One of the most risky of all diagnostic tools is the x-ray machine. Most people who have visit a doctor will experience at least one exposure to the high-frequency waves of ionizing radiation (x-rays). These are the facts that have *so far* been discovered about the adverse effects of x-rays:

- If children are exposed to x-rays while in the mother's womb (in utero) their risk of all cancers is increased by 40 per cent, of tumours of the nervous system by 50 per cent, and of leukaemias by 70 per cent.
- Today there are thousands of people with damaged thyroid glands, many of them with cancer, who had been radiated with x-rays on head, neck, shoulder, or upper chest 20-30 years ago.
- Ten x-ray shots at the dentist are sufficient to produce cancer of the thyroid.
- Multiple x-rays have been linked with multiple myeloma – a form of bone cancer.
- Scientists have told the American Congress that x-radiation of the lower abdominal region puts a person into the risk of developing genetic damage that can be passed on to the next generation. They also linked the "typical diseases of ageing" such as diabetes, high blood pressure, coronary heart disease, strokes, and cataracts with previous exposure to x-rays.
- It is estimated that at least 4,000 Americans die each year from x-ray related illnesses.
- In the UK, one fifth to one half of all x-rays given to patients are without real necessity. In the US, the FDA reckons that a third of all radiation is unnecessary.
- In the UK, x-rays ordered by doctors, account for over 90 per cent of the total radiation exposure of the population (Cambridge University Press, 1993).
- In Canada, almost everyone gets an annual x-ray of one sort.
- Old x-ray equipment still used in many hospitals, gives off 20 to 30 times higher doses of radiation than is necessary for diagnostic purposes.

Unless it is for an emergency situation, x-rays should be avoided because their harmful side effects may pose a greater health risk than does the original problem itself. As a patient you have the right to refuse x-ray diagnosis. By discussing your specific health problem with your physician you can find out whether taking x-rays is really necessary or not. Many physicians today share this concern with their patients and try to find other ways to determine their exact condition.

Mammography – Yes or No?

A recent study showed that mammography -- a diagnostic tool using x-rays to detect breast cancer in women -- is highly inaccurate. Only between 1 and 10 out of 100 "positive" mammography tests are truly positive, which means that there is a 90% - 99% chance that a woman is diagnosed with breast cancer but doesn't have it. Since these tests are not only taken once in a lifetime, the chances of becoming a victim of false diagnosis for breast cancer are very high.

In Great Britain, there are about 100,000 women a year who receive a false diagnosis for breast cancer. The women undergo many unnecessary biopsies and an unknown number of mastectomies (breast amputations). Many of the women suffer unnecessarily from depression, desperation, and fear of dying as a result of the diagnosis. In the United States mastectomies have rocketed since mammography became the most popular "preventive" method for diagnosing breast cancer.

To see mammography as a diagnostic tool for detecting pre-symptomatic stages of cancer is dubious. In most cases of breast cancer, it is irrelevant whether breast cancer is detected at an early or late stage. It is rather the type of cancer and whether it tends to metastasise (spread to other parts of the body) at an early stage or not, that determines the outcome of the disease. Also with many mammograms performed, a woman may put herself into the risk of developing the very disease mammography is supposed to prevent.

A 1997 report by the American National Cancer Institute stated that *mammograms* showed no mortality benefit unless women in their 40s had been followed for 10 years. Despite the fact that over 90 per cent of the abnormalities discovered by *mammography* are known to be benign (not cancerous), still 63 per cent of U.S. women in their 40s have had a mammogram in the last two years.

Prevention of breast cancer does not begin with having a *mammography*; it starts with taking active responsibility for one's body and mind. It can be said that all things that occur naturally have a cancer preventive effect and this includes food. Commenting on a recently released study on prevention of cancer, John Pezzuto, leader of a food research group at the University of Illinois at Chicago, USA, said: "...the study does show that a diet loaded with fruits and vegetables is a good defence against cancer." Research has identified a substance in grapes called *resveratol* that has proven to help cells from turning cancerous and inhibit the spread of cells that are malignant already. Most other natural foods contain similar or even more powerful substances.

Women don't need to rely on the *mammography* test to feel safeguarded against breast cancer, especially since it is highly unreliable as a diagnostic tool. A series of two liver, kidney and colon cleanses are often enough to prevent, stop and regress any type of cancer.

Hair dyes (highlights are OK), make-up, chemical deodorants, chemical toothpaste, commercial synthetic shampoos, etc., all release large amounts of chemical toxins into the lymph ducts of the breasts, causing lymphatic congestion and high levels of toxicity there. Wearing bras regularly also impairs proper lymph flow and may greatly increase the chance of breast cancer. If you are concerned about getting breast cancer, it is best to avoid anything that is as unnatural as the above factors. A women can actively contribute to a carefree future by taking care of their bodies' daily needs and requirements (also see "Cancer –Who Makes It, Chapter 8).

Medical Laboratories are Unreliable
Some of the weakest points in the field of medical diagnosis concern the bacteriological tests conducted in medical laboratories. In 1975, the Center for Disease Control (CDC) in the United States released the findings of an investigation of medical laboratories throughout the country and published the following results:
- 10-15 percent of the bacteriological tests were insufficient.
- 30-35 percent of the simplest clinical tests turned out to be outright false.
- 12-18 percent of tests determining the correct blood groups and blood types, and   20-30 percent of tests determining the blood serum and haemoglobin levels, were   sloppy.
- Over one quarter of all tests showed faulty results.
- 31 percent of the laboratories were not even capable of detecting a simple form of anaemia.
- Other laboratories falsely found infectious mononucleosis (glandular fever) in one out of every three tested persons. Between 10 and 20 percent of the laboratories detected Leukaemia (blood cancer) in samples that were free of it.

Another countrywide American study showed that over 50 percent of the laboratories with "high standards" and permission to conduct all the different types of medical work did not fulfil national requirements. The worst results surfaced during a study when 197 out of 200 tested persons with abnormal test results turned out to be completely healthy after they were tested a second time! It may be added that the CDC is observing only the best laboratories, which make up less than ten percent of the total number of medical labs in the whole of the United States.

In 1989, an editorial in the Lancet bluntly announced that many routine laboratory diagnostic tests are a waste of time and money. One study showed that the diseases of only six out of 630 patients were diagnosed from routine blood and urine tests. In another major study involving 1,000 patients only 1 per cent benefited from routine blood and urine tests.

Hypertension can be Produced in the Doctor's Office

If your visit to the doctor is accompanied by the fear of anticipating a serious physical problem, your anxiety may trigger a stress response and raise your blood pressure. This phenomenon is known as "white-coat hypertension." While the doctor is measuring your blood pressure (using the old system of measurement), the pressure of the inflating cuff against your blood vessels and accompanying nerves raises it even more. By the time the pressure in the cuff is lowered to read the pulsation level, you inevitably have an artificially raised blood pressure. Both factors, the anxiety and the taking of the blood pressure, may be sufficient to "make" a person hypertensive.

A healthy blood pressure can vary tremendously – as much as 30 mm Hg – over the cause of any day. To be really certain that you are hypertensive, the doctor would either have to take several readings each day over a period of six months (as recommended by the WHO) or give you a portable electronic device to do the same. Another problem arises because the systolic blood pressure may vary between each arm by as much as 8 mm Hg. In some cases the difference can be up to 20 mm Hg. With regard to testing the blood pressure in pregnant women, there is no consensus as yet on which of the several available tests are truly reliable.

High blood pressure often is a temporary stress-related phenomenon and returns to normal after things calm down. In the case of white-coat hypertension, your blood pressure may drop to normal levels soon after you leave the doctor's surgery. But whether your blood pressure is chronically elevated or not, you may be asked to take anti-hypertensive drugs that have little or no effect on your real condition but may produce severe side effects including headaches, lethargy, nausea, sleepiness, and impotence. Anti-hypertensive drugs are so popular today because patients believe that by swallowing a pill a day they can prevent a possible heart attack. Research published in 1997 by the Journal of the American Medical Association found that drugs for high blood pressure may be over-prescribed, especially if blood pressure measurements are taken by the doctor instead of by the portable device used for ambulatory monitoring.

While research has established that mortality rates remain uninfluenced by the drugs, their side effects are often severe and include collapse of the lungs and heart attacks. By contrast, there are many controlled studies, which show that relaxation therapies, and a change of diet and lifestyle can lower a person's blood pressure faster and more consistently than medication. Going on a balanced vegetarian diet alone can normalise blood pressure on a permanent basis. The *water therapy* described earlier on is also a natural and quick method to restore normal blood pressure. The daily full body oil massage and all the other cleansing methods described in this book can significantly improve blood pressure, too. In most cases a few liver cleanses and a kidney cleanse one are sufficient to eliminate hypertension altogether.

Conclusion: I have used the examples of several diagnostic techniques to highlight the potential disadvantages and dangers of *just having a test*. There are many other tests that are equally risky as the ones mentioned above, including angiography, bone scans, Cat scans, MRI scans, oscopy, AFP, and of course smear tests. The high percentage of false positive readings with these "objective" methods of diagnosis show that diagnosis of disease is not as clear cut and obvious as it may seem to a layperson.

Today's methods of clinical diagnosis for chronic problems are mostly symptom-oriented and therefore leave the causes of the symptoms concealed and untreated. The cause-oriented diagnostic skills of an experienced practitioner of natural medicine, on the other hand, may be able to reveal the true nature of imbalance prevalent in the body of a chronically ill patient. The health practitioner would incorporate in his treatment plan the elimination of the four major risk factors of disease as outlined in chapter 3.

However, in the case of an accident, an injury, burns, or other acute health problems, etc., there can hardly be any better option than to place one's life in the hands of an experienced practitioner of conventional medicine.

2. Medical Treatment Isn't Always Safe

In conventional medicine, the treatment of disease is a highly controversial issue. On the one hand, many lives are *saved* through the procedures and drugs used during medical intervention. On the other hand, harmful side effects arising from the treatment can *take* lives.

When you visit a doctor and receive a prescription for a drug or procedure aimed at a specific complaint you have, you (and your doctor) are most likely to presume that what he recommends has been proved by extensive testing and scientific reviews. Yet it is a well documented and published fact that 85-90% of all the medical treatments we believe to be "scientifically verified" and "proven effective," have been adopted and widely used without a single scientific study backing up their claims.

Drugs should be the Exception, not the Rule

The illusion that there is a successful treatment for every disease has led to the escalation of increasingly complex forms of illness and health care costs. Many patients who are released from hospitals leave with the conviction that they are healed from whatever was wrong with them. They believe that since the problem has been "fixed" they can *just get on with their lives again*. Particularly drugs can deceive in this way.

When penicillin came on the market it was considered a wonder drug that could bring dying patients back to life within a few days. In fact, penicillin did save many lives, although simple methods of cleansing and supporting the body in its effort to throw out poisonous substances could have achieved the same. Today penicillin causes the very same problems for which it is being prescribed. Side effects include skin eruptions, diarrhoea, fever, vomiting, mononucleosis, allergic shock, fainting, heart collapse, arrhythmia, and low blood pressure. What applies to penicillin also applies to most other drugs. Their side effects often outweigh their benefits and patients should be aware of the complications they may generate before they agree taking them. The side effects are always listed on the instruction list accompanying the drug.

Doctor-caused Diseases on the Rise

Iatrogenesis (illness caused by the doctor) is one of the most rapidly spreading epidemics of our time. Medical intervention used for some of the most benign conditions has created even life-threatening situations for many patients.

Antibiotics may have their place if someone is dying and could be saved by the drugs. But it is very risky, for instance, to give children who are infected with the flu virus H the antibiotic ***Chloramphenicol***. The drug is known to destroy bone marrow, which requires subsequent blood transfusions and many other therapies that cannot guarantee a recovery at all. Chloramphenicol preparations are still prescribed even for such small problems as a sore throat.

According to studies cited by the American magazine *Newsweek* seven out of ten Americans who seek treatment for the simple cold receive antibiotics – even though it is a fact that antibiotics are useless against viral infections such as the common cold or the flu. When these powerful yet ineffective drugs are administered to patients with such relatively mild illnesses, neither patient nor doctor seem to be aware of the "mess" the drugs can create in the body of an infected person. After killing most of the invading germs and substantial numbers of friendly bacteria in the host's intestines, the body's immune system is left with the nearly impossible task of removing their rotting carcasses. Since the good bacteria have been destroyed too, there is "nobody" left to clear up this toxic mess, consisting in most part of putrefying protein. Some of the protein though does end up in the connective tissues and is packed into the basement membranes of the capillaries and arteries. In time, the increased congestion in the circulatory system may lead to heart attacks, stroke, or congestive heart failure.

Nearly every day, drugs are removed from the market because they have shown to produce such strong side effects that their use is "no longer" justified. Yet all drugs are potentially dangerous because the poison they contain is "anti body" oriented, which means that they are also destroying parts of the body.

The heart drug ***nifedipine***, a **calcium-channel blocker** used to treat high blood pressure, has been linked with serious (sometimes-fatal) side effects, including heart attacks and other cardiac abnormalities. Although the Journal of the American Medical Association argues that because of its severe side effects the drug should be abandoned, it is still prescribed world-wide in certain hypertensive emergencies. Also, the US national Heart, Lung and Blood Institute has warned doctors to use nifedipine only with great caution, if at all. One study published in 1995 in the *Lancet* found that patients who received calcium-channel blockers were 60 per cent more likely to suffer a heart attack than those put on either diuretics or beta-blockers. Nifedipine turned out to be the most dangerous of all the calcium-channel blockers.

But beta-blockers are hazardous, too. In 1998 the Journal of the American Medical Association reported that apart from not being effective the elderly are more likely to suffer a sudden and fatal heart attack while taking the drugs. New analysis of 10 trials from a Medline search revealed that beta-blockers, which have been used for over 30 years to treat high blood pressure, are no more effective than a sugar pill.

The American drug ***reserpin***, which is also used to lower elevated blood pressure, has been shown to increase the risk of breast cancer by *300 percent* but is still given to patients with high blood pressure. Several other classes of drugs -- including **diuretics and antihypertensives** (for lowering blood pressure) – are suspected to cause cancer of the kidney. The beta-blocker ***atenol*** became a suspect, too after it was discovered that cancer was twice as common in hypertensive sufferers taking the therapy. Both British studies and US studies showed that only a fifth to a third of patients on drugs managed to reach blood pressure target set by their doctors. Even placebos are able to achieve that. These makes the so urgently-advised treatment of high blood pressure more than questionable.

Another major side effect of hypertensive drugs is *hypotension* – or a sudden drop in blood pressure when one stands up. The drugs are also the major cause of hip fractures among senior citizens. In 1994, the British Medical Journal published a study, showing that diuretics (drugs used to lower blood pressure) cause an 11-fold increase in diabetes. . As reported in the Journal of the American Medical Association in 1993, **ACE inhibitors** can cause potentially fatal kidney damage. They can cause death, if they are given to soon after a heart attack.

Even the highly praised "miracle" drug *insulin*, which is injected into diabetics, has now been proved to cause diabetic blindness. Another drug is the antimalarial drug *plaquenil,* which is also supposed to be useful against lupus, rheumatoid arthritis, and skin problems. Its sale is legal in the UK but prohibited in the United States. The UK authorities have no objections to recommending the drug to children provided the dose does not exceed 6,5 mg per kg of body weight a day. In the US, any doctor who prescribes plaquenil to a child faces a lawsuit because a number of fatalities have been reported among children who have taken doses as low as 0,75 g. But not only children risk their health and possibly their lives by using the drug. Those suffering eye problems, psoriasis, or liver problems, and also alcoholics and pregnant women could find their condition worsening. Side effects of the drug include irritability, nervousness, nightmares, convulsions, nerve deafness, blurred vision, oedema, bleaching of the hair, alopecia, aplastic anaemia, anorexia, and nausea.

The most favoured **antidepressant drug** to make people "happy" is *Prosac* (fluoxetine). In the US, it is now used by millions of people to cope with the stressful living conditions. But the first studies on *Prosac* show that the drug is not harmless after all. Researchers from the University of California made the discovery that women who take *Prosac* while pregnant are more than twice as likely to give birth to babies with defects. If the drug is still taken at the third trimester, the baby is nearly five times more likely to be born prematurely and twice as likely to need the help of special-care nurseries. The baby also faces nine times the risk of having breathing difficulties, cyanosis (lack of oxygen) on feeding, and jitteriness. Other published side effects of Prozac drug include: Anxiety, significant weight loss, cardiac arrhythmia, visual disturbances, tremors, nausea, diarrhoea, asthma, arthritis, osteoporosis, stomach bleeding, loss of sex drive and impotence.

Researchers from the University of Toronto recently published a study in the Lancet, showing that all classes of antidepressants are dangerous for the elderly (aged 66 and over) to take, and will greatly increase their risk for a fall and fracturing a hip.

In recent years, the herb Saint John's-wort or Hypericum perforatum has been recommended by numerous psychiatrists for their patients suffering depression; the herb, which is often taken in pill form, is at least as effective as Prosac and other antidepressants, and has little or no side effects.

A medical investigation in the United States has shown that more people die from legal prescription drugs than from narcotic drugs such as heroine and cocaine. The ratio is an astonishing 76 to 24 percent! This study does not account for the contra-indications of the drugs, which kill a further 20,000 to 30,000 a year. It is nearly impossible to know how many people are being hospitalised because of contra-indications from drugs but careful official estimates indicate that they make up about 5 per cent of all the patients lying in American and British hospitals today.

Steroids belong to another group of drugs that were formerly used only for extreme life-threatening conditions. Today, they are used for such minor problems as sunburn, skin eruptions, acne, and glandular fever. Patients are rarely aware of the dangers that may arise from taking these drugs. Side effects include: High blood pressure, stomach ulcers with possible opening of the stomach wall (this is how my father died), cramps and dizziness, inhibiting growth in children, irregular menstruation, weakening of muscle strength, slowed healing of wounds, problems of vision, skin atrophy, allergic shock, loss of libido, decrease in bone density, slow growth in children after six weeks, manic depression, and emergence of latent diabetes. Steroids are now handed out even to babies, at the first sign of inflammation of any sort. But the drugs cannot cure a single condition, all they do is stop the body responding to an abnormal condition. The new diseases caused by the drugs may require further treatment through even stronger drugs, adding more side effects to the ones that already occurred.

Read the List of Side Effects, it can Save your Life

The latest new "breakthrough" drugs for **arthritis** produce such strong side effects that it might be better to live with arthritis than risking one's life. The manufacturer of one popular brand known as ***Butazolidin alka*** was obliged to warn the consumer that this particular drug was very strong and had led to cases of leukaemia (cancer of the blood) even after short term use. Additionally, the drug can have 92 side effects including hepatitis, high blood pressure, dizziness and unconsciousness, as well as headaches. The manufacturer advises the treating doctor to enlighten their patients about the possible dangers that can arise from taken the drug, particularly if they are over 40 years old, and to use the smallest possible but still effective dose. The manufacturers admit that that the drug can cause serious and life threatening reactions while having no effect in improving the condition of the disease!

NSAID's, the common name for over a dozen or more **non-steroidal anti-inflammatory drugs**, are used to treat rheumatoid and osteoarthritis. But since a few years the drugs are given for such simple complaints as recurring headaches or inflammation. In return for the pain relief, however, the patient may die as result of gastric bleeding caused by the extreme toxicity of the drugs. A warning placed on each NSAID prescription says: "Serious gastrointestinal toxicity such as bleeding, ulceration, and perforation can occur at any time, with or without warning symptoms, in patients treated chronically with NSAID therapy." If this doesn't sound like *Russian Roulette* to you, the death toll from taken the drugs may convince you otherwise. In the UK, 4,000 people die each year from taking NSAIDS. In the US the fatality figure is up to five times as high as it is in the UK. Each year hundreds of thousands of people are hospitalised due to gastric bleeding in direct connection with taking these drugs. Other side effects include perforation of the colon, colitis, Crohn's disease, blurred vision, Parkinson's disease, liver and kidney damage, hepatitis, hypertension,

With the enormous variety of drugs available today many doctors no longer have the time to study the side effects of each drug they prescribe and most patients never read the list of side effects that accompanies the drug. Also only few patients read the small printed contraindications or ask their doctor about the possible dangers of the drugs. Most doctors don't seem to have the time to warn their patients about possible side effects. One report on a survey published in one 1996-issue of the British Medical Journal found that less than two-thirds of patients recalled receiving any advice from their doctor on potential side effect. Although the doctor has a moral and also legal obligation to inform the patient about the risks of treatment, in most cases this is omitted. The drug company is legally protected as long as the side effects and contra-indications are listed and it is up to the patient to decide whether to take a drug or not.

Dubious Business with Drugs

Naprosyn is another common drug of American origin used for treating arthritis. Even though the FDA had discovered that the drug company had forged the documents of its drug tests on animals with regard to tumour formation and mortality, it is not in the power of the government to prohibit the sale of the drug.

Similar scandals are occurring in the treatment of hyperactive or tense children. Over one million American children, whose behaviour is considered not according to the norm, receive ***psycho-pharmaceutical drugs*** although there is not a single diagnostic technique to date to determine whether a child suffers from one of the nearly two dozen symptoms related to tension. Yet the children are treated as "slightly brain damaged". The side effects of the drugs are often severe. The children show signs of retarded growth, develop high blood pressure, nervousness, and sleeplessness, and turn excessively passive and lethargic. They become depressed and apathetic as nearly everyone else would who took the drugs. Cutting out all the stimulating foods such as sugar, chocolates, and other unnatural sweets, crisps and the common breakfast cereals, and basically all junk food can help most of these children. Many children are highly allergic to artificial colourings and preservatives, soft drinks, packaged fruit juices, and foremost of all, to artificial sweeteners which may cause brain damage and are found in most unnatural, sweet tasting foods or drinks.

Most clinical tests on new drugs are financed by the pharmaceutical industry and nearly all information about the products' effects and benefits supplied to the doctors comes from the drug companies. An investigation conducted by respected scientists, including four Nobel Laureates, found that clinical tests on new drugs are highly scandalous. When the FDA made spot checks on these tests, it discovered that 20 percent of the involved researchers used highly irregular practices such as applying the wrong doses of drugs and forging of documents. In one third of the examined "clinical tests," there were no tests done at all and another third did not comply with the standard requirements for conducting such tests. The Journal of the American Medical Association reported on November 3, 1975 that the results of *only one third* of all checked clinical tests could be considered satisfactory.

So at a time when most drugs are entering the market without scientific backing and justification, both physicians and patients ought to be even more cautious in the use of drugs. Since there are no long term studies to prove that a certain drug a patient is using today will not cause him cancer, diabetes, or heart disease in 15-20 years from now, he can never be sure that they won't. As long as one's life is not in real danger it would be better to avoid drugs, especially if they are combined with other drugs (this amplifies the side effects by 2, 3, 4 and more times). If you want to know more about a drug, read the list of side effects accompanying the drug or consult the drug advisory board in your area (if available). Most medical doctors can give you only the information they receive from the drug manufacturers.

The whole drug-side-effect issue is complicated by the fact that drug reactions are only rarely reported by general practitioners. The British Journal of Clinical Pharmacology reported in 1997 that "most prescription drugs are more dangerous than they appear because doctors rarely report side effects to the appropriate authorities." This tragic situation was confirmed by the discovery by French researchers of massive underreporting of adverse reactions to prescription drugs. The French research revealed that only one out of 24,433 adverse reactions is reported to the various drug monitoring agencies. All drugs are poisonous; even if they happen to have a few beneficial side effects, in the majority of cases this doesn't warrant their use.

The Contraceptive Pill: New Risks...

In the United States alone, ten million pre-menopausal women are taking the contraceptive pill. The Pill seems to be the easiest method of preventing an unwanted pregnancy but also one of the most risky ones. Although natural methods of contraception have at least the same success rate and cost a fraction of the Pill or nothing at all, they are rarely publicised. Despite the warning by an increasing number of health officials about the strong side effects of the drug, it is still regarded as the "best and safest" method of contraception.

Women who continually use the contraceptive pill are more likely to develop circulatory problems, liver tumours, headaches, depression, and cancer than those who don't use them. The risk increases with age. Also women who take the Pill and are aged between 30 and 40 have a three times higher risk of dying from a heart attack than women of the same age group who are non-users. Women who are over forty and still use the contraceptive pill have a six times higher risk of developing high blood pressure, a four times higher risk of having strokes, and a five times higher risk of developing thrombosis and embolism, a condition where a blood clot may form in an artery and lodge in an artery close to the heart. The risk of suffering thrombosis is greatest among short-term users.

In August 1996 the papers were awash with the shocking news that the Pill has a "time bomb" effect in causing breast cancer. A four-year study on the Pill, carried out by the Imperial Cancer research Fund in Oxford, reanalysed epidemiological evidence on the Pill of more than 150,000 women. The results show that *all* users face a risk of breast cancer, even for up to 10 years after they stop taking it.

According to the study, which was published in 1996 in the *Lancet*, women on the Pill faced a 25 per cent increase in the risk of breast cancer and the risk is still 16 per cent up to five years after it is discontinued. Another large study conducted at the Netherlands Cancer Institute, also published in the *Lancet*, showed that girls who started taking the Pill before 20 were three and a half times more likely to get breast cancer. Among the women over 36, who took the Pill for less than 4 years, the risk of developing breast cancer increased by 40 per cent. What is very disturbing news is that 97 per cent of the women under 36 years of age who had contracted breast cancer had taken the Pill at some point in their lives, even for a short length of time. This raises a lot of questions, such as "is taking the pill by a large portion of the female population responsible for the continuous breast cancer epidemic?"

Klim McPherson, arguably the most experienced British epidemiologist on HRT and the Pill, estimates that up to one in four long-term Pill users who start on it early in life will wind up with breast cancer. More studies are surfacing almost every other month. Another major Pill study concluded in September 1996 has determined that women who have taken the Pill at any time have a 60 per cent increase in the risk of cervical cancer. The repeatedly used medical argument that the risk of developing breast cancer with the Pill is outweighed by its benefits of protecting women against endometrial and ovarian cancer, is no longer valid. In any event, risking one type of fatal cancer to prevent another type of fatal cancer is a very questionable conclusion. Because the Pill causes breast cancer and other diseases, it is outright dangerous and should not sold to unsuspecting women.

The *intrauterine device* (IUD), also known as coil or loop, is not a safe method of contraception either. The IUD has been associated with a number of debilitating side effects. A 1974 report by the *Lancet* showed that women who have an IUD fitted are 50% more likely to have a miscarriage as opposed to 17% for those using any other kind of contraceptive. Also pelvic inflammatory disease is common among users. Other problems include cramping, backache, risk of ectopic pregnancy, perforation of uterus, greater incidence of tubal infertility, skin rashes, and increased susceptibility to infection.

If you consider a potential pregnancy, which is not a dangerous illness, to be less a disadvantage than risking your life by developing breast cancer, cervical cancer, a stroke, or thrombosis, you are better off avoiding the Pill or any of the other highly invasive contraceptive methods such as *Inject-and-go contraception* and IUDs.

I personally recommend mental birth control, the most ancient method of conception choice, as the preferable method for avoiding an unwanted pregnancy. It is very effective, cost-free, and without any side effects. The method can be learned within a few minutes from the little book "Mental Birth Control" by Terry League and Milder Jackson (see Useful Addresses). My wife and I have been using this most natural of all methods for years, successfully I might add.

Other methods include "Fertility Testers" which can determine during which days of the month a woman is fertile; all that is required is a drop of her saliva. "Persona" is another new method of contraception. Through simple urine testing, a small, computerised device informs a woman of the days she is at risk of becoming pregnant. "Persona" is 93-95% reliable when used according to instructions, which makes it as reliable as the condom. It is readily available at all "Boots stores" in the UK. In any event, the condom is an option, too.

3. Risks of Hormone Replacement Therapy (HRT)

One of the most commonly treated "diseases" among women today is the appearance of menopausal symptoms – indications that a woman's body' may be going through major changes in her life. Doctors believe that these changes (and the symptoms) are caused by a falling off in the production of female hormones, oestrogens, and progestogens, which the body uses to conduct the monthly cycles, pregnancy, and birth, among other rhythms. To postpone the onset of the dreaded illness "menopause," which is often seen as a sign of rapid ageing, and to reduce or eliminate the accompanying symptoms, doctors prescribe a combination of hormones, known as *Hormone Replacement Therapy* (HRT). The drugs are also supposed to prevent major illnesses that have been linked with diminished hormone production, including osteoporosis, heart disease, stroke, and senile dementia.

Influenced by medical authorities and media reports, many menopausal women feel that they are suffering from a serious hormone deficiency, which may endanger their health, and that Hormone Replacement Therapy (HRT) can help them lead a more comfortable and carefree life during and after menopause.

Yet HRT turned out to be everything but preventive medicine and the risks involved are serious. Taking extra hormones can even endanger a woman's life. According to research conducted at the Boston University Medical Center, USA, the risks of suffering a thrombosis increases by 3,6 times with a "normal" dose of hormones and by nearly seven times if a woman is taking as much as 1,25 mg or more a day. Like with the contraceptive Pill, the researchers found the risk to be greatest during the first year of usage.

In the United States, five million menopausal women are at present using hormone replacements. Numerous studies show that the longer a woman takes HRT the greater is her risk of cancer. The breast cancer risk increases by three times and the risk of endometrial cancer by four times. An analysis of 16 studies on women who have been taking HRT for 15 years revealed that taking *oestrogen* alone increased the risk of womb cancer by 20 times and the combined HRT (oestrogen and progestogen) increased the risk by up to a third. A Swedish study, which looked at 23,000 women, showed that the addition of progestogen actually quadrupled the risk after four years. In this study, the risk increase of developing breast cancer in women using oestrogen-only was 80 percent. The most comprehensive combined analysis of studies (thirty-seven in number) of breast cancer risk found that long-term oestrogen use increases a woman's risk of breast cancer by 60 per cent. The results of the very large *Nurses' Health Study*, published in 1995 by the New England Journal of Medicine, found that for women over 60 the risk of breast cancer was 71 per cent. This is a severe blow to those doctors who recommend that women should take HRT for ever or at least from ten years after the menopause. In addition, one study by the American Cancer Society involving 200,000 menopausal women found that those who stay on HRT for more than 10 years show a 70 percent increase in ovarian cancer.

Apart from increasing the cancer risk, excessive oestrogen causes salt and fluid retention, increases body fat, impairs blood-sugar control, interferes with thyroid hormone, causes excessive hairiness and loss of scalp hair, increases blood clotting, causes depression and headaches, diminishes libido, reduces oxygen levels in all cells, causes decline of zinc and retention of copper and gives rise to a cystitis-like syndrome. Over 70 per cent of women on oestrogen or progestogen experience such strong side effects that half of them stop taking the drug after 6 months. In 1992 the British Medical Journal listed some of the side effects of HRT, which are very similar to the PMT-like symptoms these hormones are supposed to treat. They include: Monthly period-like withdrawal bleeding and eventual breakthrough bleeding, abdominal cramps, bloating, breast tenderness, irritability, depression, and anxiety.

Progestogens can also cause abnormally high calcium levels in the blood, alter its sugar and insulin concentrations, increase the severity of migraines, and lead to gallbladder disease, liver cancer, and urinary tract infections.

Yet many doctors still prescribe HRT routinely as a preventive to avoid discomfort during menopause, wrongly assuming that every woman who has menopause will also suffer from discomfort. Hormones are also sold as rejuvenation drugs and for circulatory problems. They are recommended to middle aged women who develop signs of depression, although depression can occur at any age and be caused by numerous other factors than lack of hormones.

In America, the doctors use a highly detailed manual called the *Physician's Desk Reference*. By law, the drug manufacturers are required to list all the risks of their drugs in the manual. The entry for Hormone Replacement Therapy includes: *womb cancer; breast tenderness/enlargement; undesirable weight gain/loss; elevated blood pressure; mental depression; reduced carbohydrate and glucose tolerance; hair loss; vaginal candidacies (thrush); jaundice; abdominal cramps; vomiting; cystitis-like syndrome.* Menopausal symptoms may be harmless when compared with any of these side effects.

HRT fails to Prevent Bone Loss

Many older women take HRT to prevent osteoporosis – a disease characterised by loss of minerals from bone tissue. A large number of them have been warned by their doctor that their bones would crumble if they didn't take it. The latest results from an ongoing study of 670 women in Framingham, Massachusetts (New England Journal of Medicine, October 1993) shows, however, that HRT fails to protect women from *osteoporosis* – therefore eliminating one of the main reasons for its use. Only those women being on HRT for longer than 7-10 years, which is far longer than most women stay on the drug, had higher bone mineral density. However, even those on HRT for 10 years were still not protected from osteoporosis. As soon as they stopped taking HRT, bone mineral density declined rapidly, so that by age 75 it was only 3,2 per cent higher than it was in women who had never taken the hormones.

Increased bone mineral density was always thought to be a positive effect of long-term use of oestrogen and progestogens as contained in HRT and the contraceptive pill. But researchers from the University of Pittsburgh, USA found that women whose bone mineral density increased as a result of taking extra hormones have a far higher chance of developing breast cancer. The indicator for breast cancer risk is therefore not, as previously assumed, bone mineral density but hormone supplementation.

Since most women have their menopause in their fifties and the greatest risk of fractures is when they are in their eighties, HRT offers no benefits, unless they take it for 30 years or longer. But in such case, the risk of developing cancer and other health problems is so high that taking the drug rarely warrants its use.

In 1992 the New England Journal of Medicine provided clear evidence that *lack of oestrogen does not cause osteoporosis*. In fact, there is some evidence that suggests that oestrogens actually contribute to osteoporosis. Women experience significant bone loss during the 10 to 15 years before menopause, despite an ample supply of oestrogen. During this time there is an almost total decline of *progesterone*, another female hormone. Synthetic progesterone, called *progestins*, is now given combined with oestrogen but has no less serious side effects than oestrogen. On the other hand, natural *progesterone*, as contained in wild yam, for example, has no negative side effects, but if applied topically in the form of a cream it can drastically reduce menopausal symptoms and rebuild bone. Natural progesterone affects the bone-building cells whereas oestrogen affects the cells in control of bone resorption. For this reason HRT can only temporarily reduce the rate of bone density loss but not stimulate the body's bone-building cells to produce more bone material.

There is an increasing number of health practitioners and woman who recognise that meat, milk, cheese, instant soups and puddings, soda such as colas, sugar and other stimulants such as caffeine and tobacco, alcohol chocolate can remove calcium and other minerals from the bones faster than can be absorbed or synthesised by the body, contributing to *osteoporosis* more than a decrease in hormones does (if at all). The rate of urinary calcium excretion, for example, is significantly increased after the consumption of a high protein meal, i.e. consisting of meat. According to a 1988 study of 1600 women, published in the *American Journal of Clinical Nutrition*, vegetarians have more bone density than age-matched meat eaters. Another safe way to increase bone mineral density is exercise. New research, published in 1996 in the *Lancet*, shows that exercise can substantially increase bone mineral density by between 14 and 37 per cent.

Calcium absorption is directly linked with the hormonal form of vitamin D, which is synthesised through sunlight. Lack of exposure to sunlight alone can lead to bone density loss. Also excessive exercise and activity deplete the body's calcium stores. One of the main reasons for decreased availability of calcium in the body is diminished bile secretion in the liver due to accumulation of gallstones in the bile ducts. Without enough bile, calcium cannot be absorbed properly. To meet all the calcium requirements of the bones the body has to rely on it's own abilities to produce this mineral. For example, the enzyme *alkaline phosphatase* works with magnesium to produce calcium-crystals in the bone. Women on HRT have the lowest levels of alkaline phosphatase and are therefore not able to produce enough bone tissue. (HRT only prevents the loss of old bone).

The body's original design does not include the premature destruction of its own skeleton. If it gets destroyed, it is due to other factors than hormone deficiency. Menopause is a natural phenomenon the body is well prepared for, provided its basic metabolic functions have not been interfered with.

But what about HRT Preventing Heart Disease?

Claims that HRT protects against coronary heart diseases are highly spurious. Why should we believe that while *oestrogen* in the contraceptive pill is known to increase the risk of cardiovascular disease, in HRT it prevents this condition? To clarify this confusion, a group of Dutch scientists analysed 18 major HRT studies and found that women on HRT are healthier than non-users, not because they were taking HRT, but because they represent a segment of society that can afford regular medical care and would likely have lower rates of all illnesses (British Medical Journal, May 1994).

Being in a low risk group for illness, however, is no guarantee for preventing the side effects of HRT. The extensive Nurse's Health Study, 1991, showed a 46 per cent increase in ischemic stroke risk among nurses using HRT, despite the fact that this group is comprised of women with less diabetes, less cigarette smoking, and less adiposity than those not using *oestrogen*. Six years earlier, the Framingham Massachusetts Study suggested that the risk of heart disease is actually increased with the use of HRT. Similar results were reported by the Journal of the American Medical Association in 1995; one of the first placebo-controlled trials into HRT and heart disease showed that there were more cases of heart disease in those taking HRT than those given a placebo.

Claims that HRT can prevent Alzheimer's disease are unfounded. There is not a shred of evidence that indicates HRT can keep the brain sharp. A 15-year study published in 1993 by the Journal of the American Medical Association has shown that oestrogen intake does not slow any reduction in cognitive functions among women.

4. The Purpose of Menopause

Menopausal symptoms are officially linked to a deficiency in the female hormones but this *cannot* be regarded as their cause. The observation that at a certain age a woman's body makes fewer hormones doesn't necessarily imply that she is hormone-deficient. To suffer from hormone deficiency and to have a decreased hormone production as a result of going through the menopause are two completely different things. It is therefore wrong to assume that a woman will "run out of hormones" and develop the disease "menopause" because she has reached a certain age.

In fact, there exists only a *correlation* but no *causal* relationship between low *oestrogen* and the frequent headaches, heavy bloating, hot flushes, and depression that some women experience as they enter the menopause. If a woman's body had been genetically programmed to develop a hormone deficiency and undermine all the vital functions during and after her mid-life, then every woman in the world reaching a certain age would suffer the same problems. Yet only a fraction of women world-wide encounter menopausal symptoms, most of them living in developing countries. Japanese women -- with their high Soya diet – have a much lower frequency of hot flushes and other menopausal symptoms than, for example, American women have. In 1991, the American Journal of Clinical Nutrition reported that Japanese women had phyto-oestrogens levels up to 1,000 times higher in their urine than their American counterparts had. Although phyto-oestrogens are not as strong as oestrogens themselves, their effects are comparable.

Women who view menopause negatively – as a sign of mental and physical decline – can experience adverse psychological consequences with the onset of menopause (Gannon 1985). By contrast, in countries where women achieve higher status in middle age, like Sweden, Finland, India and China, few if any signs of menopause are reported (Varpa 1970). These findings point out the importance of cultural attitudes. In other words, what women think or feel about the beginning of their mid-life period affects what they experience.

Menopause is one of the most important periods in a woman's life when major transformations take place on the physical, mental and spiritual levels. It is a time for re-evaluating life and entering a new phase of maturity, wisdom, and success. With a greater sense of maturity and wisdom a woman can more easily correct her habits, diet, and lifestyle and begin to focus on the deeper issues of life. Sometimes, changes in the marital relationship, children growing up, and leaving, ailing parents, etc. may coincide with hormonal changes and produce a crisis.

Because the transformation can use up a lot of her energy, immunity, and emotional strength, menopause may bring to light any hidden anxieties or physical imbalances that might have been left unnoticed for a long time. If a woman was able to live a detrimental lifestyle or have a poor diet without developing major health problems before menopause, she won't be able to afford doing the same during and after the transition. Her "new" purpose in life, whatever this may mean, requires a pure and well functioning physiology.

The ovaries of a woman entering the menopause *purposely* reduce their production of oestrogen. Menopause is not a sign of becoming old or the body becoming useless, it just prevents a woman from conceiving children so that she can devote the rest of her time and energy to the process of developing and maturing new and formerly unknown skills and capabilities. The role of producing enough of the hormones during mid-life and advanced age is taken over by the adrenal glands and fat cells. In a healthy woman, this is perfectly sufficient to keep her body vital and strong. All that has nothing to do with hormone deficiency. The story, however, is very different, if she hasn't been healthy before the onset of menopause.

It's not the Lack of Hormones...but...

Hormones are made from the food we eat. The ability of the body to produce the right amount of hormones is therefore subject to the quality of food, the digestive power, and the condition of the liver. Women who suffer menopausal symptoms do not suffer them because of a sudden lack of hormones but because a long-standing digestive weakness is suddenly becoming more apparent than before. At this stage of a woman's life, dietary mistakes and stress impacts may generate more chaos and confusion in the body and mind than they did before. As a direct result of this amplified interference in the balanced performance of mind and body, the woman's ovaries may receive fewer nutrients and thus lower hormone production. For similar reasons the adrenal glands and fat cells may also not be able to maintain their normal output of hormones.

Stress alone can greatly affect the endocrine system which controls blood sugar levels (mood swings), energy levels, calcium balance, weight and sex hormones. Stimulants have the same effect as stress. Regular consumption of alcohol, coffee, sugar, chocolate, soft drinks, or cigarettes strongly interferes with hormone production and is therefore sufficient to trigger strong menopausal symptoms. Cigarette smoking by itself accelerates the destruction of oestrogen. Since during menopause a woman's ovaries naturally cut down hormone production, any such stimulation, which triggers a stress response in the body, can cause sudden hormone deficiency. A middle-aged woman simply has no hormone reserves she can afford to waste. It is therefore incorrect to attribute the occurrence of menopausal symptoms to the natural decrease in ovarian hormones. If menopause is a "deficiency disease" it is certainly not caused by a lack of hormones.

A healthy Ayurvedic diet and lifestyle according to body-type, for example, can make a woman's transition into the next phase of her life much smoother and more comfortable. Both, liver cleansing and natural foods eaten at the right time keep *Pitta* in check. Hot flushes are not a sign of oestrogen deficiency, they show that the *Pitta* energies have moved upwards and the person is unable to digest food properly, causing food intolerance and food allergies. They also indicate excessive storage of protein in the blood and capillaries, which raises the blood protein values -- *haemocrit* and *haemoglobin* -- giving the appearance of redness in the face and chest (eating a high-protein diet also means that calcium is constantly leached from the bones, increasing the risk of osteoporosis). The thickening of the blood and connective tissues short-supply the cells, including the *oestrogen*-producing fat cells, with nutrients and thereby disturb hormonal balance. This may also result in a disturbance of *Kapha* (fluid retention) and a weakening of V*ata,* which causes nervous disorders, including headaches and depression.

By balancing *Vata*, *Pitta*, and *Kapha* and perhaps taking recourse to some energy boosting therapies such as Yoga, Shiatsu, Metamorphic, Reflexology, meditation and relaxation exercises, menopause can the most rewarding time in a woman's life. By contrast, although in some cases, hormone replacements can give almost instant relieve of symptoms they allow toxins to build up unnoticed to the point that a serious illness such as cancer or thrombosis may arise in the future. HRT does not correct metabolic imbalances in the body. Taking hormones, in fact, interferes with the body's own synthesis of hormones, generating harmful side effects and strong withdrawal symptoms once discontinued.

One of the most effective herbal compounds to regulate menstruation, ease menopausal symptoms and maintain proper hormone production by the pituitary gland are *Agnus Castus* and *False Unicorn Root*, best taken together. *Agnus Castus* safely removes fibroids, cysts, and endometriosis. If taking 25-35 drops of *Agnus Castus* tincture with water each day for three months, this herb normalises and stabilises female hormone production. It also helps with enlargement of the spleen. Another very effective natural alternative to HRT is Pfaffia (see "Guarana" chapter 6). Evening Primrose oil also helps ovaries maximise their output of oestrogen during the early stages of menopause. You can use Kinesiology muscles testing to determine which products are the most suitable ones for you.

Still, the best preventive for reducing or avoiding menopausal symptoms is a vegetarian, low- or no dairy, rich-in-natural-fibre diet, according to one's body type. It greatly reduces risk of: *bowel cancer; ovarian, uterine cancer; cardiovascular disease; osteoporosis; breast cysts and breast tenderness; polycystic ovary syndrome; endometriosis symptoms; heavy menstrual bleeding; fibroid symptoms; constipation; varicose veins; gallstones; and PMS.*

Menopausal problems can be an opportunity for a woman to put her life in order on all levels. As mentioned before, menopause brings to the surface what hasn't been dealt with properly for a long time. The mid-life period doesn't need to be a mid-life crisis. Instead, it can be a woman's greatest opportunity to deal with any unresolved issues in her life and to free herself from any limitations, physical, emotional, or spiritual.

5. Surgery is not Always Necessary

Several years ago a committee of the American Congress investigating procedures of surgery in the United States came to the conclusion that *2,4 million operations are performed unnecessarily each year*, costing 12,000 lives and 4 billion US dollars. The latest figures show that some six million unnecessary operations are performed each year.

Another study found that most people who were accepted for an operation did not actually need one and half of them did not even require medical treatment. Many of them were children suffering tonsil infection. Parents rarely object to the removal of their children's tonsils, especially since not many side effects are recorded for this type of surgery. The death rate from tonsil operations amounts to only 1 in 3,000 or even less.

Only few parents know that tonsils are an important part of the immune system and are needed to keep the head area free from toxins, bacteria, and viruses. It has been shown that many children become depressed, pessimistic, fearful, insecure, and shy after surgery, "character traits" that may stay with them for the rest of their lives. There are natural methods that can support the body in overcoming an infection of the tonsils without the need for surgery (see "Natural Methods of Nursing" in chapter 10). What applies to small operations, also applies to big operations. The need for surgical intervention is indicated only in certain extreme situations.

Most people believe removing an inflamed appendix is a necessity and diagnosing appendicitis is a reliable thing. But surgeons get it wrong up to 45 per cent of the time even when they perform a diagnostic *laparotomy*. False-negatives – claiming there isn't a problem when there is one -- also run high, at around 33 per cent. One in five patients with appendicitis leaves the hospital without a correct diagnosis ever being made, and one in five appendixes removed by surgery is found to be normal. In the US this amounts to 20,000 healthy appendixes mistakenly removed every year.

One of the most common operations today is coronary bypass surgery. A seven-year controlled study has demonstrated that except for very rare cases where the left aorta is affected, coronary by-pass surgery does nothing to improve heart condition. In addition, the mortality rate among patients with low risk heart disease undergoing a by-pass operation is higher than it is among those with a high risk. A 1998 study published by the New England Journal of Medicine showed that patients who suffer a mild heart attack and are given a bypass or balloon angioplasty are more likely to die as a result of the surgery. Another study that involved researchers from 14 major heart hospitals around the world found that up to one-third of all bypass operations were not only unnecessary but actually hastened the death of the patient.

Angioplasty, a relatively new procedure used to open arteries, offers an even lower survival rate than bypass surgery. Several research studies confirm that patients, who have undergone these types of surgery, are as likely to suffer a heart attack as the ones who haven't. The relief of chest pain (angina) that patients may experience after a bypass operation cannot be attributed to an actual improvement of the condition but rather to the cutting of nerve strands during the procedure, to the secretion of endorphins which are the body's natural painkillers, and/or to the placebo response.

In the case of a bypass operation, the newly inserted pieces of coronary arteries can block up easily again if the cause of arteriosclerosis is not removed. The US National Institutes of Health has estimated that 90 per cent of America's bypass surgery patients receive no benefits. Major lasting improvements are attributed to an improved diet and lifestyle, stress reduction, quitting smoking and regular exercise.

Fear-motivated Operations

In the States alone *over one million women a year* sacrifice their uterus to the scalpel. This means that more than half of all American women will have had a *hysterectomy* by the time they reach age 65. Many of these women will suffer from post-operative syndromes such as depression, anxiety, and increased susceptibility to stress. I have seen in my own practice that most women who had a hysterectomy developed ovary problems, breast lumps, digestive disorders, or breast cancer within 1-5 years after the operation.

An investigation carried out in six New York hospitals found *that 43 percent of all uterus operations were unjustified.* Other research shows that only 10% of hysterectomies are properly justified. There are thousands of women every year who have a *full* hysterectomy (including the removal of the ovaries) but have not given their consent prior to the surgery. Only few of them make use of the law to seek compensation, but money cannot return the status symbol of a woman, which is her womb.

Having a hysterectomy is not without a risk. The mortality rate is 1 in 1,000 procedures and serious complications occur 15 times more frequently than that. Side effects can occur in more than 40 per cent of operations; they include urinary retention or incontinence, significant reduction in sexual response, early ovarian failure, risk of a fatal blood clot, and bowel problems.

Pregnant women are generally treated with respect and special care, but the methods of delivery used today can have an adverse effect on mother and baby alike. Before the era of hospital deliveries the responsibility to handle deliveries was given to competent women. Home was considered the best place for all involved. This had been a common practice around the world for thousands of years. Provided that the appropriate hygienic measures were taken, there were very few birth complications. Today, however, with most deliveries being handled by male doctors and taking place in the sterile environment of a hospital room, we have the highest rates of complications at birth. Research from Britain, Switzerland, and Holland, published by the British Medical Journal in 1996, found that planned home births were the safest of all options, including hospital deliveries.

Induction, Cutting and Caesarean Section

In hospitals, delivering mothers are watched over by a number of electronic instruments and machines that monitor every possible change and that signal the need for an operation just in case something goes wrong. One of the most common types of surgery during delivery is known as "cutting." The procedure helps widening the vagina so that the baby's head and shoulders come out more easily. This routine operation is supposed to prevent tearing of the vagina. Yet if the mother wouldn't be induced and made numb by the drugs and were properly prepared for the delivery, she would know perfectly well how and when to press and when not, to release the child from the womb at the right time. The pain would tell her exactly what to do during the birth process. This would naturally prevent tearing of the vagina. And even if it did tear, the injury would heal much faster than a cut caused by a surgical knife. Because it cuts important nerves the operation also lowers the mother's sexual sensitivity, something that doesn't happen with "natural" tearing.

The second most unnecessary but most commonly applied operation during delivery is the *Caesarean Section*. If the monitoring electronic instruments indicate a sign of irregularity in the heartbeat of the baby, the mother is cut open and the baby is pulled out of the womb. It is well known that the baby's heart beat can react to a sudden loud noise made in the proximity of the mother, something that is more likely to occur in a hospital or operation room than it would at home. An unborn child may increase his heart beat because of irritating lights shone on the mother's stomach or strong electromagnetic fields caused by nearby electric appliances such as monitors. Controlled birth studies have shown that a Caesarean Section is performed 3-4 times more frequently if electronic devices were used to monitor the birth rather than a simple stethoscope.

Mothers during delivery often consent to a Caesarean Section when they see intensified signals of their baby's heart flashing on the monitor in front of them. It is quite likely that a baby's heart activity produces erratic changes when cold electrodes are attached to its head while it is squeezed through the narrow tube of the mother's womb. The procedure of connecting electrodes to the head of the baby before it is born is itself an invasion that may have serious consequences. A controlled study revealed that 65 percent of all children whose birth has been controlled electronically are at risk of developing growth and behavioural problems later in their lives.

The very set-up of a delivery room in the hospital, looking more like an operation theatre, can induce a fear and stress response in a sensitive mother. The sudden release of anxiety-provoking stress hormones of the mother may also affect the foetus and make him fearful. The mother's worries become his worries, and her fears become his fears. Recent studies have shown that within a fraction of a second after fear has caused racing of a mother's heart, a foetus's heart begins pounding at double its normal rate. Fear can paralyse many important functions in the body, including those needed for delivering a baby.

It is often also no longer in the hands of the mother to "decide" the time of delivering her baby. Unlike a wild animal, the human mother may be forced to give birth when the doctor tells her it is the "correct" time, even though, as it has been shown, his calculations can be wrong by several days or even weeks. Artificially induced delivery is considered more practical than natural delivery and is also more convenient to fit the doctor's schedule. But induced birth causes nearly three times as much pain to the mother than natural birth does. To deal with the pain she is given strong painkillers, all with side strong effects. It is a lesser-known fact that many of these mothers and newly born babies end up in intensive care units.

Over half of all Caesarean operations have serious complications. The mortality rate for mothers who have a Caesarean is *twenty six* times higher than among mothers who give birth naturally. Since 75-80 percent of them is performed unnecessarily due to excessive use of the new electronic monitoring devices, a change of policy could drastically reduce mortality rates among Caesarean mothers.

In addition to the harm done to mothers, babies who are delivered by Caesarean Section are exposed to the danger of developing serious lung damage which causes a shortage of breath previously only found in prematurely born babies. In naturally born babies, the uterus contractions press out all the accumulated secretions in the baby's chest and lungs and eliminate them through its mouth. Caesarean deliveries account for more than 25 per cent of all births today, of which only few are justified. They are indicated when there is a *real* emergency. The doctor normally knows well in advance when a Caesarean delivery is necessary.

Fewer Surgeons and Medical Interventions-- Fewer Deaths

The *American College of Surgeons* conceded that the US population would require only about 50 percent of the current number of surgeons to secure America's needs for surgery in the next fifty years. In 1976, the Los Angeles County registered a sudden reduction of its death rate by *eighteen* percent when the medical doctors went on strike against the increase of health insurance premiums for malpractice. In a study by Dr. Milton Roemer from the University of California Los Angeles, 17 of the largest hospitals in the County showed a total of *60 percent* fewer operations during the period of the strike. When the doctors resumed work and medical activities were back to normal, death rates also returned to pre-strike levels.

A similar event took place in Israel in 1973, when for one month the doctors reduced their daily number of patients from 65,000 to 7,000. For the entire month, death rates in Israel were down *fifty* percent. This seems to happen whenever doctors go on strike. In Bogota, Columbia, the death rate decreased by *thirty five* percent when no doctors were available for 52 days, except for emergencies.

6. Hospitals – A Major Health Threat

Unless you require an emergency treatment it is better to avoid hospitals altogether. Many hospitals today may pose a major risk to your health for the following reasons:
- They are filled with infection causing bacteria that cannot be found anywhere else. Hospitals, which house often very large numbers of sick people, are the ideal breeding environment for the sometimes-deadly bugs. Hospital patients generally have a lower level of immunity and offer only little or no resistance them. Many of the microbes are passed on to the patients through the cooling towers in hospitals, the air-conditioning, and heating systems. The hospital staff, who due to constant exposure to the bugs are fairly immune to them, may also pass them on to the patients by touching them or their food and cloths, etc.
- Contrary to general belief, hospitals are among the most contaminated places in the world. In fact it is virtually impossible to keep hospitals spotlessly clean and it does not take much dirt to become a breeding place for billions of deadly infectious bacteria.

- Doctors can be the worst transmitters of disease in hospitals. Most doctors do not wash their hands except before an operation, when they wear sterilised gloves and gowns anyway. They may sometimes touch many dozens of patients within several hours, one after the other, without washing their hands even once. Even the doctor's white gown is not as clean as it looks. It is only clean if it is washed every single day, which rarely happens. And when it is washed, it comes into in contact with the dirty laundry from the operation room, bed covers, pillowcases, etc. Many extremely harmful bugs survive the washing machine.
- Bed sheets may be clean but mattresses and pillows are not. The chance of being infected by bugs living in them is 1 in 20.
- Fifty percent of all infections in hospitals occur because of the patient's contact with non-sterile medical instruments such as catheters and intravenous infusion installations. Before they were in common use, such infections occurred only very rarely.
- In the United States, over 15,000 people a year die from hospital acquired infections. This figure does not account for those who are considered to be dying, or are already weakened by an operation. Yet they too are killed by a hospital acquired infection.
- A 1,500-page report of a 3-year study on the causes of death in American hospitals revealed that a further "300,000 Americans die each year in hospitals as a result of medical negligence."
- The most endangered places in a hospital are the maternity wards because infants have not gained immunity against any disease-causing agents. The most vulnerable babies are the ones who are deprived of the antibodies contained in breast milk.
- A hospital patient may receive up to 12 different kinds of medication, all of which produce side effects that can lead to serious complications and even death.
- Many studies have shown that between 25% to 50% of the patients staying in US and UK hospitals are suffering from malnutrition due to poor hospital diet. Malnutrition was found to be the major cause of death among old people in hospitals. An undernourished body is hardly able to defend itself against any type of illness. Add the toxic side effects of the drugs, the presence of deadly bugs, as well as the stress and anxiety that accompany an illness and the stay in a hospital, an poorly nourished elderly person has very little chance of surviving.
- A spot check of 105 US-hospitals conducted by the American government showed that 69 of them had violated basic laws and rules. The commission in charge of granting licenses to hospitals (JCAH), however, refused to close them down.

Most deliveries today take place in the operation theatres of hospitals, which when compared with home deliveries increases the infant's risk
- of injury during delivery by six times,
- of getting stuck in the mother's birth canal by eight times,
- of requiring revival techniques by four times,
- of becoming infected by four times
- of developing chronic physical problems by thirty times

In addition, a mother is three times as likely to haemorrhage if she is giving birth in a hospital.

Given these and other major health risks linked with a stay in a hospital, it can be said that hospitals are among the most dangerous places in the world. I therefore advise you do everything necessary to prevent illness from arising in the first place so that you can avoid them altogether, unless of course it is for an emergency, as in an accident.

Conclusion

This book may be challenging some of our most ardently held beliefs about the nature of disease manifestation, and the practices and theories of modern medicine and nutritional science. Our currently held worldviews seem no longer sufficient to provide for a prospering and healthy future, they may even superimpose on us the frightening premonition that the future of life on Earth is at stake. Yet the (new) world is just beginning. The abolishment of outdated principles of living that have kept mankind limited and fearful for centuries, leaves behind a mess of scattered pieces of knowledge that no longer make any sense. The views, which I have presented in these last few chapters, are certainly not the final answer to the puzzle of health and illness. As a matter of fact, any viewpoint is a limitation whereas our true potential is unlimited.

It is not correct to say that the drug AZT used to treat AIDS, or the chemotherapy drugs, radiation, or surgery applied to a malignant tumour etc., are all useless or harmful just as it is not right to claim that all natural treatments are useful or harmless. Considering the power that the placebo effect can have in any one person it becomes clear that even poison like AZT may turn into nectar if a patient is convinced that it will cure his AIDS. Both disease and medicine are illusory projections of ourselves that can turn into "reality" when we begin to identify with them or "energise" them in one way or another. It may well be that a hopeful person receiving radiation therapy for cancer experiences no negative side effects at all and has a spontaneous remission. On the other hand, a depressed person who swallows a placebo pill to combat a headache may suffer a stroke. There are instances where people become so enraged with anger that they suddenly suffer a fatal heart attack even though their blood vessels are perfectly clean. By contrast, a person with 100%-blocked arteries may create his own bypass and suffer no physical problems at all.

The deep conviction that a particular medicine can help you overcome a illness may just be as powerful as the pessimistic view that a certain illness like cancer can terminate your life. Deep trust, however, is rarely present in a person who has AIDS, MS, or cancer, diseases that are mainly caused by low self-worth and repressed emotions. As a recent study has found, distrust, anger, and doubt are more common among people who are ill. Happy, "non-toxic" personalities rarely fall ill.

Health and disease are accurate projections of ourselves, they mirror back to us everything we are or who we are. If a person wants to "uproot" his cancer, which may be a manifestation of repressed anger and frustration, through X-rays, chemotherapy, or radical surgery instead of learning to use the same energy to regain his piece of mind, the projection of his anger will sabotage any long-term benefits a given therapy may have. The basic message here is that *we can change the projection by changing ourselves*. This book suggests that you take responsibility for everything that happens to you. With it comes the power to make the appropriate changes that will unerringly lead you to the discovery that YOU ARE THE KEY TO HEALTH AND REJUVENATION.

Useful Addresses

- *British Biomagnetic Association*, The Williams Clinic, 31 St Marychurch Road, Torquay, Devon TQ1 3JF, UK Tel: 01803 293346.
- *The Nutri Centre*, 7 Park Crescent, London, W1N 3HE, Tel: 0171-436 5122, Fax: 0171-4365171; e-mail: nutricen@aol.com
- *The Family Health News*, 9845 N.E. 2nd Avenue, Miami Shores, Florida, 33138, USA; Tel: 305-759-9500, 800-284-6263; Fax: 305-759-8689, 800-284-6261.
- *The Metamorphic Association,* 67 Ritherdon Road, Tooting, London SW17 8QE, UK, Tel: 081-672 5951.
- *Thai Deodorant Stone,* Tel. London 071-589 5958.
- Resonance, 2 Lakeside View, Waterloo, Liverpool, L22 5QN, UK; Tel +44 151 920 5306; Fax +44 151 920 5307.

Other Books and Products by the Author

1. "It's Time to Wake Up" (*see note below)*

In this book the author brings to light a person's deep inner need for spiritual wisdom in life and helps the reader develop a new sense of reality that is based on love, power and compassion. He describes in detail our relationship with the natural world and how we can harness its tremendous powers for our personal and mankind's benefit. "It's Time to Wake Up" challenges some of our most commonly held beliefs and offers a way out of the restrictions and limitations we have created in our lives.

Topics include: What shapes our Destiny; Using the power of intention; Secrets of defying the ageing process; Doubting -- the cause of failure; Opening the heart; Material wealth and spiritual wealth; Fatigue – the major cause of stress; Methods of emotional transformation; Techniques of primordial healing; How to increase health and vitality of the 5 senses; Developing spiritual wisdom; The major causes of today's Earth changes; Entry into the new world; Twelve gateways to heaven on earth; and many more.

2. "The Amazing Liver Cleanse" (*see note below)*

This book addresses the most common but rarely recognised cause of illness -- a liver congested with gallstones. Twenty million adult Americans suffer from attacks of gallstones every year. In many cases, treatment consists of removing the gallbladder, at the cost of $5 billion a year. Yet many more Americans, including most people suffering a chronic illness such as heart disease, arthritis, MS or cancer, have hundreds if not thousands of gallstones blocking the bile ducts of their liver.

The book provides a thorough understanding of what causes gallstones in the liver and gall bladder. It shows how they can be recognised and gives the necessary instructions on how to remove them painlessly and in the comfort of one's home. It also shows the reader how to prevent new stones from being formed - a must in any programme of health care.

*Note: Both these books are available in printed and bound form and as electronic books on the Internet. They electronic versions may be downloaded into a computer from the publisher's website, www1stbooks.com .

The book "The Key to Health and Rejuvenation" used to run under the title "The Key to Perfect Health."

3. "Ener-Chi Art"

In collaboration with Dr. Lillian Maresch, Andreas Moritz has developed a new system of healing and rejuvenation that is designed to restore the basic life energy (Chi) of an organ or a system in the body, within a matter of minutes. Simultaneously, it also helps balance the emotional causes of illness.

Eastern approaches to healing, such as Acupuncture and Shiatsu, are intended to enhance well-being by stimulating and balancing the flow of Chi to the various organs and systems of the body. In a similar manner, the energetics of Ener-Chi Art are designed to restore a balanced flow of Chi throughout the body.

According to most ancient systems of health and healing, the balanced flow of Chi is the key determinant for a healthy body and mind. When Chi flows through the body unhindered, health and vitality are maintained. By contrast, if the flow of Chi is disrupted or reduced, health and vitality tend to decline.

A person can determine the degree to which the flow of Chi is balanced in the body's organs and systems by using a simple muscle testing procedure. To reveal the effectiveness of Ener-Chi Art, it is important to apply this test both before and after viewing each Ener-Chi Art picture.

To allow for easy application of this system, Andreas has created a number of healing paintings that have been "activated" through a unique procedure that imbues each work of art with specific colour rays. To receive the full benefit of an Ener-Chi Art picture all that is necessary is to look at it for about two minutes. During this time, the flow of Chi within the organ or system becomes fully restored. When applied to all the organs and systems of the body, Ener-Chi Art sets the precondition for the whole body to self-heal and rejuvenate in their its own time.

To order individual prints or complete sets of these pictures contact the address below.

For further information contact:

Ener-Chi Resources, Inc.
P.O. Box 52
Excelsior, Minnesota 55331
USA

Fax: +1-612-470- 9889
E-mail: EnerChiArt@aol.com

About the Author

Andreas Moritz is a health consultant and practitioner of Ayurvedic Medicine. Born in Southwest Germany in 1954, Andreas had to deal with several severe illnesses from an early age, which compelled him to study diet, nutrition, and various methods of natural healing while still a child.

By the age of 20 he had completed his training in iridology - the diagnostic science of eye interpretation - and dietetics. A year later he qualified as a teacher of meditation. In 1981 he began studying Ayurvedic Medicine in India and completed his training as a qualified practitioner of Ayurveda in New Zealand in 1991. Andreas has had particular success with cases of terminal disease where conventional methods of healing were futile. Since 1988, he has been practising the Japanese healing art of Shiatsu, which has given him profound insights into the energy system of the body. In addition, he devoted eight years of active research into consciousness and its important role in the field of mind/body medicine.

Andreas Moritz is also the author of "The Amazing Liver Cleanse" and "It's Time to Wake Up." During his extensive travels throughout the world he has consulted with heads of state and members of governments in Europe, Asia, and Africa, and has lectured widely on the subject of health and mind/body medicine. He is currently involved in developing a new system of healing and rejuvenation - ***Ener-Chi Art*** - that can help restore the vital energy flow of organs and systems in the body.